BY EXECUTIVE ORDER

By Executive Order

BUREAUCRATIC MANAGEMENT AND
THE LIMITS OF PRESIDENTIAL POWER

ANDREW RUDALEVIGE

PRINCETON UNIVERSITY PRESS

PRINCETON & OXFORD

Published by Princeton University Press
41 William Street, Princeton, New Jersey 08540
6 Oxford Street, Woodstock, Oxfordshire OX20 1TR

press.princeton.edu

All Rights Reserved

Library of Congress Control Number: 2021930515
ISBN 978-0-691-19435-6
ISBN (pbk.) 978-0-691-19436-3
ISBN (e-book) 978-0-691-20371-3

British Library Cataloging-in-Publication Data is available

Editorial: Bridget Flannery-McCoy and Alena Chekanov
Production Editorial: Jill Harris
Cover Design: Pamela L. Schnitter
Production: Brigid Ackerman
Publicity: Kate Hensley and Kathryn Stevens

Cover images: Shutterstock

This book has been composed in Arno

Printed on acid-free paper. ∞

Printed in the United States of America

10 9 8 7 6 5 4 3 2 1

For Christine, Eliza, and Owen

'Tis the gift to come down where we ought to be

CONTENTS

PREFACE AND ACKNOWLEDGMENTS

BACK IN 1904, Edward Stanwood introduced his *History of the Presidency* by saying he refused "to include an account of the development of the presidential office." After all, he argued, "there has been no such development to record, since the office is now what it was in the time of Washington—neither of greater nor of less weight in the government than it was then."[1]

Even if Stanwood was right then (and while I hate to impugn a distinguished alumnus of my present employer, he was not), it would be hard to arrive at the same conclusion now. The growth of the presidency during the twentieth century tracked the immense growth of the American administrative state, combining affirmative statutory delegation and de facto legislative lassitude to structure what Arthur M. Schlesinger Jr. enduringly dubbed the "imperial presidency."[2] In recent years students of the American presidency have returned to the study of formal authority and unilateral possibility, even before real-life events—especially the terrorist attacks of September 11, 2001—ramped up the stakes for presidential leadership and the legitimacy of enhanced unilateralism.

The scholarship on presidential directives has expanded concurrently, exploring the empirics and (albeit slightly later) theories of unilateral action. Forty-five years ago a leading textbook on the presidency might omit the term "executive orders" even from its index; these days it would be more likely to carve out a full chapter devoted to the topic.[3] The first wave of research focused on tallying executive orders and identifying political contexts (such as divided government or presidential approval levels) associated with their issuance. Later work has added both analytical breadth and theoretical nuance, examining executive orders' substance and divergent significance, reaching past executive orders to other presidential directives, and uncovering other actors with an effect on the decision making behind unilateral action.

This book centers on that last point. It adds back into the president's political environment a player at once critical and, to date, largely ignored: the executive branch itself. Most of our research starts when an order is issued, having sprung into being—if not from thin air, exactly, then at least without much reference to any formulation process. That process is irrelevant if presidents are in ultimate control of a branch of government that faces no collective action problems and thus no managerial transaction costs in producing executive orders that align with presidential preferences. But is that the case? In these pages I will argue (and, I hope, demonstrate) that even in initiatives achieved "by executive order," bureaucratic politics are crucial to how policy is made—that even in what we term "unilateralism," there is pluralism. That is, presidents need to manage the executive branch to produce executive actions. Tracking how that management works, both in theory and in practice, is the theme of much of what follows.

Doing so highlights the importance of bureaucratic influence in presidential policymaking. That influence can be negative, even stifling, and of course all presidents on occasion see the bureaucracy as an obstacle to be overcome rather than a resource. But agencies' sway ultimately flows from their substantive knowledge, the result of long public investment in neutral expertise. Politics and administration are hardly distinct in the way Woodrow Wilson once seemed to hope; but administrative expertise can be managed by smart presidents in a way that benefits both politics and polity. Both governance and political standing, that is, can spring from better—more coherent, more competent—policy. Such a claim, written during the Trump administration, must acknowledge that presidents do not always recognize those benefits and may even be hostile to this premise. Yet that very example shows why undermining bureaucratic capacity broadly runs counter even to a president's short-term interests: surely President Trump would have received an electoral boost from an informed response to the coronavirus crisis. I hope this book will help future chief executives understand that while a well-managed executive branch may complicate the meaning of unilateralism, it can simplify the overwhelming job of serving as president.

The book itself originated from discovering archival files detailing the fate of executive orders in the course of a different research project, an institutional history of the Office of Management and Budget. If I ever thought spinning off a "small" research topic from a ridiculously large one guaranteed rapid completion, I have learned my lesson. But this book's long gestation did allow me the privilege of accumulating the scholarly debts that make the academic life worthwhile. It is a pleasure to acknowledge some of them now.

For instance, it seems possible that some version of this research has been inflicted on every member of the Presidents and Executive Politics section of the American Political Science Association (or even of APSA itself): various iterations were presented at annual meetings of APSA, the Midwest Political Science Association, and the American Politics Group (part of the UK's Political Studies Association); at Bowdoin College, Clemson University, Hofstra University, and Vanderbilt University; and at research symposia on executive power hosted successively by Princeton University, the University of Michigan, Washington University in St. Louis, and the University of Houston.

I am grateful to all those who organized or took part in any of those or related conversations; I appreciate immensely both their interest and their constructive feedback, as well as the data and relevant work in progress so many shared. Thanks to all, including Eddie Ashbee, Matt Beckmann, Michelle Belco, Tony Bertelli, Boris Bershteyn, Meena Bose, Fang-Yi Chiou, Barry Clendenin, Jeff Cohen, Robert Cooper, Matt Dickinson, Mike Franz, Clodagh Harrington, Tom Hitter, Gary Hollibaugh, Will Howell, Karen Hult, Jeff Jenkins, George Krause, Doug Kriner, Dave Lewis, Kenneth Lowande, Cal Mackenzie, John Maltese, Bernie Martin, Ken Mayer, Nolan McCarty, Sid Milkis, Terry Moe, Yu Ouyang, Joe Pika, Rachel Potter, Andrew Reeves, Jon Rogowski, Brandon Rottinghaus, Wayne Steger, Sharece Thrower, Matt Vaeth, Justin Vaughn, Alex Waddan, Adam Warber, Geovette Washington, Jeffrey Weinberg, and Andy Wroe. The book is far stronger for their expertise and their probing what-ifs that drove me toward better questions and new evidence. (And also for the beer that accompanied many of these discussions.) I need to single out several of the individuals just named for their hugely helpful feedback over many years and just as importantly for their friendship. For substantive, methodological, career, Red Sox, Premier League, fish sandwich, child-rearing, and more than their share of executive order–related advice, all of it jumbled together—Matt Dickinson, Will Howell, George Krause, and especially Dave Lewis, thank you.

Further gratitude is owed to Princeton University Press's anonymous reviewers, who provided extensive, incisive comments, as did Doug Kriner. The revisions that resulted clarified my thoughts and improved the manuscript. Thanks go to others at PUP as well, notably Eric Crahan and Bridget Flannery-McCoy for their immediate interest in, and patient shepherding of, this project, as it moved from APSA barstool conversation to completed text. Key in the production process and thereafter were Brigid Ackerman, Jenn

Backer (whose sharp eye and copyediting pen spared me many blushes), Alena Chekanov, Dayna Hagewood, Jill Harris, Kate Hensley, Pamela Schnitter, Kathryn Stevens, and Pamela Weidman.

All of those mentioned are, of course, exempted from blame for the many improvements I no doubt failed to make. Whatever remains unclear is not their fault.

The same is true for those who helped me work with the encyclopedic government records that form the backbone of the research here. Special thanks go to Falisa Peoples-Tittle and the records staff supporting OMB, who eased my entry into the weird world of the Washington National Records Center and helped me locate many seemingly displaced files. More generally the hours lurking in reading rooms were made both productive and downright pleasant by all those who staff the archival facilities this project draws upon. From the National Archives proper to the presidential library system to private collections from Princeton to Palo Alto—thank you. I am truly grateful as well to the current and former executive branch staff members who fleshed out my understanding of archival documents and of central clearance in practice, whether or not they are identified in what follows.

Belated thanks to Dickinson College (especially Dean Neil Weissman and the members of the Political Science Department) for support at the genesis of this project. Bowdoin College helped me pick up the baton after my move there: thanks to Deans Cristle Collins Judd, Liz McCormack, and Jen Scanlon, along with all my Government Department colleagues and department co-ordinator extraordinaire Lynne Atkinson, for their unstinting support overall. With special regard to this project I want to make sure to thank former associate dean Jim Higginbotham; Cindi Smith (who oversaw my search for sufficient space to spread my archival piles); the staff and denizens of Bowdoin's libraries (notably Barbara Levergood, Sue O'Dell, and Jeff Cosgrove-Cook); and the Faculty Development Committee for grant support. Also: to whoever put the large-scale model of the USS *Constitution* in the basement of Hatch Library, well, I appreciate it.

Thanks also go to the American Philosophical Society for early financial support of this research. Some of it was first published in different form in "Executive Orders and Presidential Unilateralism," *Presidential Studies Quarterly* 42 (March 2012): 138–60, and "Executive Branch Management and Presidential Unilateralism: Centralization and the Issuance of Executive Orders," *Congress & the Presidency* 42, no. 3 (2015): 342–65. Thanks to the good people at Wiley and at Taylor & Francis, respectively, for permission to use that work here.

And finally, a last veer to the personal, with my appreciation to the friends and colleagues over the years who have provided safe haven, camaraderie, and just the right amount of mockery. For this project a special shout-out must go to the missed layups of the noontime basketball association, the denizens of Todd's Tavern (where it is always 10:10), and of course the membership of the FFC (which runs instead on Siff Time). It is harder, indeed impossible, to extend adequate thanks to my family for their role in this book and beyond it. You made this work possible—whether in actually reading the rough draft (thanks, Dad!), insulting political science at every opportunity (thanks, kids!), or simply putting the whole project in needed perspective. Ultimately it could not have been completed without the love and support of my wife, Christine, who hates the fact of this book by now—I hope not the final product—but (mostly) managed to turn a blind eye to its writing in the "spare time" left after the 2016 election and its aftermath devoured my actual sabbatical. I only regret that this pen "had not skill enough your worth to sing."

Brunswick, Maine
October 2020

ABBREVIATIONS

AEC   Atomic Energy Commission

AID   Agency for International Development

ARA   Area Redevelopment Administration

BOB   Bureau of the Budget (created 1921, reorganized as OMB in 1970)

CAB   Civil Aeronautics Board

CBP   U.S. Customs and Border Protection (part of DHS)

CEA   Council of Economic Advisers (within EOP)

CEQ   Council on Environmental Quality (within EOP)

CIA   Central Intelligence Agency

CSC   Civil Service Commission

DHS   U.S. Department of Homeland Security

DOC   U.S. Department of Commerce

DOD   U.S. Department of Defense

DOJ   U.S. Department of Justice

DPC   Domestic Policy Council (within EOP, Reagan-present)

EO   Executive Order (used interchangeably with "order")

EOP   Executive Office of the President

EPA   Environmental Protection Agency

EPC   Economic Policy Council (within Reagan EOP)

FAA   Federal Aviation Administration

FBI   Federal Bureau of Investigation

FDA   Food and Drug Administration

FDIC   Federal Deposit Insurance Corporation

FEMA   Federal Emergency Management Agency

FSLIC   Federal Savings and Loan Insurance Corporation

GAO   General Accounting Office (Government Accountability Office, 2004–)

GSA   General Services Administration

HEW   U.S. Department of Health, Education, and Welfare (after 1979 see HHS)

HHFA   Housing and Home Finance Agency (after 1965 see HUD)

HHS   U.S. Department of Health and Human Services

HUAC   U.S. House of Representatives Un-American Activities Committee

HUD   U.S. Department of Housing and Urban Development

IG   Inspector General

NARA   National Archives and Records Administration

NEC   National Economic Council (within EOP, Clinton-present)

NMB   National Mediation Board

NSA   National Security Agency

NSC   National Security Council (within EOP)

OEM   Office of Emergency Management (within EOP)

OEP   Office of Emergency Preparedness (within EOP)

OIRA   Office of Information and Regulatory Affairs (part of OMB)

OLC   Office of Legal Counsel (part of DOJ)

OMB   Office of Management and Budget, succeeds BoB

OPA   Office of Price Administration

OPIC   Overseas Private Investment Corporation

OPM   Office of Personnel Management

OSHA   Occupational Safety and Health Administration (part of DOL)

OSTP   Office of Science and Technology Policy (within EOP)

P.L.   Public Law

RMO   Resource Management Office (within OMB)

SBA   Small Business Administration (part of DOC)

USDA   U.S. Department of Agriculture

USTR   Office of the United States Trade Representative

WHO   White House Office (within EOP)

BY EXECUTIVE ORDER

1

"On My Own"?

EXECUTIVE ORDERS AND THE EXECUTIVE BRANCH

THE NEWS BROKE just before five o'clock on Friday afternoon, a week and a few hours after President Donald J. Trump had taken the oath of office. It was January 27, 2017, and the new president had just signed Executive Order (EO) 13769, grandly titled "Protecting the Nation from Foreign Terrorist Entry into the United States."

The order was the intended implementation of Trump's campaign pledge to enact a "total and complete shutdown of Muslims entering the United States" until vetting procedures had been enhanced. (Or at least, as Trump put it in December 2015, "until our country's representatives can figure out what the hell is going on.")[1] Citing the Immigration and Nationality Act and the "authority vested in me as President by the Constitution," EO 13769 prevented various populations "of particular concern" from entering the United States, effective immediately: anyone arriving from seven nations in the Middle East and North Africa for at least 90 days, and all refugees, regardless of their country of origin, for at least 120 days. Syrian refugees fleeing the civil war there were barred indefinitely. Case-by-case exceptions were allowed for refugees claiming religious-based persecution, giving priority to Christian applicants from Muslim-majority countries, but the maximum number of refugees that could be admitted to the United States in 2017 was more than cut in half. The stated goal was to "protect [American] citizens from foreign nationals who intend to commit terrorist attacks in the United States; and to prevent the admission of foreign nationals who intend to exploit United States immigration laws for malevolent purposes."[2] The president soon took to Twitter to tout his "Homeland Security travel ban" and told reporters that Americans "want to see people that can love our country come in, not people that are looking to destroy our country."[3]

That, of course, was only the start of the story. As word of the EO's release spread, so did public anger: thousands of protesters flooded more than a dozen airports from Los Angeles to New York, from Portland, Oregon, to Portland, Maine—as well as city squares, university quadrangles, and even the street in front of the Trump International Hotel in Washington, D.C.[4]

There they met "chaos, confusion, and bureaucratic heartburn," as CBS White House correspondent Major Garrett put it.[5] White House staff and Department of Homeland Security (DHS) lawyers struggled to come to agreement over what the EO actually meant and thus how it should be implemented.[6] The directive had gone into effect with hundreds of affected travelers already in the air and thousands of others at departure gates—but federal Customs and Border Patrol personnel were given no notice of its issuance. Nor did they receive advance guidance regarding its demands, which might have clarified, for example, whether the ban affected U.S. permanent residents holding green cards or travelers already issued valid visas. Iraq's government, working with the United States to battle the Islamic State terrorist group, howled in protest at being included in the measure; by contrast Saudi Arabia, home of most of the 9/11 terrorists cited in the EO as a rationale for its issuance, was *not* included. In short, it seemed the new administration itself had failed to figure out "what the hell is going on."

It became clear that the order had been formulated by "a handful of Trump political appointees" working in the White House with little expertise in the complications the policy invoked.[7] Sen. Lindsey Graham reportedly told the president that it appeared that "some third grader wrote it on the back of an envelope."[8] An array of relevant government agencies were purposefully cut out of the drafting process;[9] the DHS inspector general concluded that the department "and its components had no opportunity to provide expert input in drafting the EO. Answers to critical questions necessary for implementation were undefined when the EO issued."[10] In December 2018, former DHS secretary John Kelly acknowledged that "I had very little opportunity to look at" the drafts of the order.[11] (Blain Rethmeier, who worked on the DHS transition team, put it more colorfully: "[Kelly] got handed a shit sandwich the first week on the job.")[12]

Legal questions arose quickly as well: for instance, could an executive order actually bar permanent residents from reentry? Did the EO represent an impermissible religious test in operation? The acting attorney general (Trump's nominee to the post had not yet been confirmed) had not been consulted—and only learned of the EO's existence when her deputy read about its issuance on the *New York Times* website.[13] At first the Department of Justice (DOJ) denied all knowledge of the order; later it transpired that the acting head of DOJ's Office of Legal Counsel (OLC) had quickly reviewed it and issued a one-sentence statement saying the EO was "approved with regard to form and legality" (though in fact attorneys there had "strenuously objected that it needed further review").[14] The acting attorney general disagreed with OLC and decided the Justice Department would not defend the EO in court. She was immediately fired, and charged by the White House with "betrayal." But a series of judges soon took a similar view and blocked implementation of the order.[15]

As it struggled to deal with the aftermath, the administration issued reams of conflicting statements, then dropped EO 13769 altogether: on March 6, the president issued a second, revised executive order. Six months later, on September 24, a quite different version was promulgated, this time formatted as a proclamation. It was that third iteration of the "ban" that was ultimately upheld by a divided U.S. Supreme Court in late June 2018, eighteen months after the first version was issued.[16] By then, yet another EO had been issued allowing a trickle of refugees to enter the United States once more.[17]

The travel ban saga—the fact of the order, its substance, and the reaction to it—highlights two key elements of this book.

The first is simply that executive orders matter. President Trump's signature set in motion important and immediate alterations in U.S. government policy. More generally, EOs are a mechanism through which the president can exercise delegated statutory authority or constitutional powers, potentially producing consequential substantive change across a wide range of policy arenas. As increased partisan polarization makes legislative action ever harder to achieve, the importance of unilateral directives to presidential policymaking rises apace. And even though EOs are directly aimed at shaping the behavior of government employees, their impact on the public may be significant. It is no wonder presidents have long agreed with Clinton White House aide Paul Begala when it comes to unilateral action: "Stroke of the pen—law of the land. Kind of cool."[18]

Second, and far less intuitively: the executive *branch* matters to executive orders. Pundits often present such directives as literally unilateral, as do presidents: George W. Bush, for instance, told a group of supporters in 2004 that

"Congress wouldn't act, so I signed an executive order. That means I did it on my own."[19] But (as discussed in a moment) he did not. The "stroke of a pen" is cool—but it is also the culmination of the input, influence, and frequently even instigation of the wider bureaucracy. As a result, we can recast the issuance of executive orders as a function of presidential management.

The travel ban may seem an odd way to make this point: after all, President Trump really did act by himself, with the help of a White House aide or two. Yet given the chaos that ensued, from runways to courtrooms, the travel ban highlights the sway of executive branch engagement as an exception that proves the rule. As *Politico* reported later, the "nonpartisan experts had not been consulted before the orders were drafted. . . . Typically, an executive order of such immense impact would have undergone weeks, if not months, of . . . interagency review. Instead . . . former NSC staffers say they were asked to review the travel ban and about half a dozen other draft executive orders in less than a day."[20] The EO damaged the president, politically, because it was so poorly conceived and crafted, substantively. "If Trump really wanted to bar refugees or citizens from specific countries," the careerists said, "they would have helped him do it in a smarter way."[21] The version accepted by the Supreme Court more than a year later was much revised to reflect substantial bureaucratic input.

In the travel ban case, the influence of departments and agencies is visible as a photographic negative—that is, in the glaring legal and material errors its absence caused. As Sen. Lamar Alexander put it, "this vetting process needed more vetting."[22] But more generally, agency involvement is harnessed in order to drive positive changes to the substance of an EO. For the Bush "equal treatment" order just noted, staff located in the new Office of Faith-Based and Community Initiatives worked closely with White House lawyers and domestic policy advisors as well as a range of other experts across the bureaucracy invited to comment by the Office of Management and Budget in a comprehensive departmental review process. The Justice Department weighed in on constitutional issues of church and state; the Labor Department advised on matters relating to employment discrimination. Agency feedback and pushback were brought on board as the EO took final form. "Nobody was wanting to miss a loop," one Justice Department drafter noted later, given the importance of the order to Bush's domestic policy program.[23]

Agency influence may be even more extensive than this. Often a department serves as an order's originator—often to the president's benefit, as we will see, but not always to the president's pleasure. Even as criticism of EO

13769 grew, for instance, Trump repeatedly railed that DOJ's efforts to replace it were "bullshit," even tweeting angrily that "the Justice Dept. should have stayed with the original Travel Ban, not the watered down, politically correct version they submitted to [the Supreme Court]."[24] Yet it is Trump's signature on that "watered down" version. And if that variant of agency authority is uncommon, bureaucratic politics more broadly are not. Those politics, and the agency sway they reflect, mean that draft EOs are almost always amended, frequently delayed, and sometimes abandoned entirely.

Healthy Children and Logged Lobbyists

To make that point more concrete, let's consider a tale of two orders—or, more accurately, two tales that led to only one order.

Bill Clinton issued Executive Order 13045—"Protection of Children from Environmental Health Risks and Safety Risks"—on April 21, 1997.[25] The EO declared that children "may suffer disproportionately" from such risks, and thus, each federal agency was to "make it a high priority to identify and assess" them and to "ensure" they were addressed by "its policies, programs, activities, and standards." It created a task force (co-chaired by the Health and Human Services [HHS] secretary and by the administrator of the Environmental Protection Agency [EPA]) and also an "interagency forum" (convened by the Office of Management and Budget [OMB]) to track research regarding risks to children and produce an "annual compendium of the most important indicators" of their well-being.

Most critically, perhaps, the order added a new hook to the regulatory review function conducted by OMB's Office of Information and Regulatory Affairs (OIRA). Agencies still had to justify to OIRA why the benefits of a proposed regulation exceeded its costs, and then defend their "evaluation of the environmental health or safety effects of the planned regulation on children," and provide "an explanation of why the planned regulation is preferable to other potentially effective and reasonably feasible alternatives considered by the agency." As an aside, the new EO revoked a Reagan-era order requiring similar government-wide rulemaking attention to "family policymaking criteria," notably "the marital commitment."[26]

If surveyed solely from the point of issuance, EO 13045 has many attributes traditionally associated with unilateralism, suggesting a president imposing his will on the executive branch. The order created new, centralized processes to reflect presidential preferences and priorities. A predecessor's actions were set aside. Bureaucrats complained about its burdens. Outside critics grumbled—a front-page *Washington Times* story quoted riled representatives of the Heritage Foundation and the Family Research Council, while then senator Jeff Sessions introduced a bill to overturn Clinton's action—but could not gain much traction.[27] President one, agencies (and enemies) nil?

Yet if we pan out to include the formulation of the order in the analysis, the impact and influence of the wider executive branch quickly comes into view. That began at the beginning: in an August 12, 1996, memo to more than a dozen Cabinet and White House policy staff, EPA administrator Carol Browner noted that her agency would soon release a new *National Agenda to Protect Children's Health from Environmental Health Risks.*[28] Since "protecting children from environmental health threats has been one of EPA's highest priorities during the Clinton Administration," Browner told her colleagues, one "opportunit[y] for additional action" was a "potential executive order" that would tighten the standards set by government regulation to make rules "protective enough of the potentially heightened risks faced by children." By January 1997, the EPA—not a White House unit—had drafted such an order and sent it to OMB, which in turn sent it out for comment and review as part of its standard process of "central clearance." (This process is discussed in great detail in chapter 3.) Some seventeen executive agencies and EOP staff offices became involved, as the EPA sought to "generat[e] support within the White House" for its text.

While agencies uniformly said they supported the idea of protecting children from environmental hazards, concerns with the draft order surfaced immediately. Various staffs raised a number of objections—most colorfully, suggesting the order put a "kick-me sign" on their own backs. That is, since the EO would have required them not only to evaluate the effects of the planned regulation on children but to explain if their proposal *failed* to protect children fully—and to justify why it was issued anyway—it effectively directed opponents to the best grounds for a lawsuit. How, for instance, the Department of Health and Human Services asked, was it supposed to say why tobacco remained a legal product? Banning cigarettes would clearly be better for children's health.

A series of negotiations ensued over four months of meetings; "we have made significant drafting changes to accommodate concerns," Domestic Policy Council (DPC) staffer Diane Regas told her boss, Elena Kagan, in March. Those concerns came from within the Executive Office of the President (EOP) as well as the wider bureaucracy; indeed, a Kagan memo to Clinton chief of staff Erskine Bowles that same month noted that DPC, the National Economic Council (NEC), the Council on Environmental Quality (CEQ), and the Office of Science and Technology Policy (OSTP) were all involved. It was not until late March that Regas could note that "I think we have resolved all the kids e.o. issues *among W[hite] H[ouse] offices*."[29] And "serious last-minute objections" from the agencies remained, even as the EPA continued to press key Clinton aide Bruce Reed for support. Kagan's notes from an April 1 meeting transcribe EPA's somewhat exasperated objections to Treasury's "nervousness" and to others' continued queries: "we've redone [the order] to address concerns. Weakened already." Still, as it moved on, the draft order was amended repeatedly to be more and more tightly targeted. Agencies were to comply only "to the extent permitted by law and appropriate," and independent regulatory agencies were merely "encouraged" to participate in the order's implementation. The contentious section requiring agencies to identify better alternatives was tweaked to make the justification less defensive (and thus, not trivially, less work-intensive for bureaus).

In the end, then, it was something of an understatement to note (as the decision memo sent to the president did, on April 11, 1997) that "the proposed Executive Order . . . has been the subject of extensive discussion with affected agencies." Even then, several departments continued to press reservations, and Clinton listened: in approving the order, he requested still more conciliation to their objections. "Might want to ease burden a bit," the president scrawled in the margin, lessening the scope of the analysis of the alternative routes not taken. Yet another revision thus ensued before the order was formally issued.

At least that order *was* issued. Jimmy Carter, by contrast, had promised in 1976 to give America a "government as good as its people"; in the post-Watergate world that meant opening up his administration to new levels of accountability.[30] In February 1977 he asked his top domestic aide, "What can we do without legislation to maximize openness in government?"

Among the answers was to require all federal agencies to keep a public log of all their contacts with outside groups and individuals. Good government groups were strongly in favor of logging—"this is a chief item on the Common Cause agenda," White House domestic policy czar Stu Eizenstat told the president. Carter approved the idea in March and was promised it could be "implemented within one month."[31]

It was not. After White House lawyers worked with their counterparts at the Department of Justice to draft an executive order on the topic, Carter counsel Doug Huron passed the draft along to OMB for review. "This is a priority item," Huron emphasized, directing that it be ready for presidential signature in two weeks.[32] But four weeks later, an OMB attorney told Huron the order faced stiff opposition inside the administration. OMB had sent the draft out for comment to any executive branch entity with an interest in its substance, which given the order's topic meant more than sixty agencies and bureaus. Forty had responded to date—and the comments "were overwhelmingly opposed to the issuance of the proposed order."

Not surprisingly, as with the Clinton EO, agencies said they supported the president's aims. No one was willing to say they opposed transparency in government: "The goals of this proposed executive order are above reproach," EPA administrator Douglas Costle assured OMB. But it didn't take long for reproach to breach the surface. The Department of Transportation's response was typical: "While the Department believes that the proposed order attempts to accomplish worthy objectives, we find it so problematic that we oppose it strongly." Agencies said the order was administratively burdensome, unenforceable, and far too broad, trading immense record-keeping costs for speculative benefits; the prospect of love from good government liberals did not sway their calculations. "The sum total of the comments suggest that serious reevaluation of the basic concept of the proposed order is necessary," OMB summarized for the White House, warning that simply revising the text "may prove to be a costly error." Three pages of questions for the president followed, designed to prompt additional thought about the order's goals and worth.

The White House tried to salvage the order, and discussions continued for close to a year, into early 1978. But internal memos at OMB continued to report that "the latest prognosis is that this proposal has too much opposition." Ultimately the Carter domestic policy staff drafted a memo to the president. "After reviewing the agencies' comments," they wrote, "we recommend *against* issuing this Order."

White House aide Rick Neustadt let OMB know that Carter was being told to "bag the idea." The immediate reply was succinct. In its entirety: "We have the following comments: 1. Hooray!"[33]

OMB sent the order to the inactive file in June 1978, and a subsequent plea by Common Cause to reopen the question was unsuccessful.

Are these narratives typical? The empirical evidence presented in subsequent chapters suggests they are—that EOs, even those that originate in the White House, are subject to extensive review by and negotiation with the wider executive branch; that around six of every ten executive orders issued by the president are crafted preponderantly by departments and agencies instead of by centralized staff; and that a surprising number of proposed EOs, including some dear to the president, are never issued at all. The bureaucracy provides resources for unilateralism, and also shapes and bounds its use. OMB's caution to Carter is notable: that issuing a directive he desired might be so "costly" as to undermine him. We are perhaps used to that sort of warning coming from Congress or even the courts, to the point where wise presidents will calculate the anticipated reactions of the other branches of government to a potential order.[34] But we have rarely placed the executive branch in that category. This book argues that we should.

Doing so complicates what we mean by "unilateralism" in the first place, if policymaking is pluralistic. It has implications for presidential power: indeed, is it "power" if an agency carries out an order it had asked to be given in the first place? But most crucially, we need to think about executive orders as a question of presidential *management* rather than simply of command. This approach draws on another tradition of scholarship that considers presidential administration as a "two-way street," centered on the interaction and even negotiation between so-called principals and agents.[35] Executive orders provide an excellent if perhaps unexpected test of the reach of that thesis.

From the president's end of the metaphor, we need to consider the managerial costs of policy formulation. In a divided and diverse executive branch, these might vary by policy area, by agency expertise, or by other characteristics and contexts that shape the relative costs and benefits of formulating policy in the White House versus delegating that task to the wider bureaucracy. Either approach can be rational from the perspective of minimizing the transaction costs of producing presidential policy. This doesn't mean presidential preferences always or often lose, merely that additional information may amend those preferences or clarify where, within a range of options superior to the status quo, the net benefits of change are highest. Agencies, from their end of this byway, have divergent incentives and resources of their own. They seek to advise and may even initiate that policymaking process, shaping presidential options and providing substantive input—or may resist it.

This book traverses both the top-down and bottom-up frames these suggest. It defaults to the president's perspective, in considering how presidents develop institutions to protect themselves against both agency manipulation and White House staff ignorance, and when they will have to surmount enhanced hurdles of time and information as they construct their policy portfolio. But even from that vantage it recognizes that bargaining comple-ments command as a key dimension of executive orders—and, indeed, that bargaining with the bureaucracy may serve the president far better than does coercive command. Far from seeking to degrade executive expertise, presi-dents should invest in managerial strategies that take advantage of it.

To begin elaborating these claims, we turn first to consideration of what executive orders are, and how they have been studied so far, before previewing the argument to come.

Executive Orders as Presidential Administration

The fact that presidential unilateral directives—and in particular, executive orders—are important in their own right needs little justification at this point. Since the 1930s, the American national state has expanded dramatically in size and responsibility. The trajectory takes us through the New Deal, Great Soci-ety, and regulatory expansion of the 1970s, as well as World War II, Korea, the Cold War, the War on Terror, and the COVID-19 pandemic. The fiscal 2020 budget as adopted exceeded $4.5 trillion, funding more than a thousand dis-tinct programs administered by fifteen Cabinet departments containing close to two hundred subunits, along with dozens of stand-alone agencies of differ-ent types.[36] The coronavirus stimulus bills passed in the spring of 2020 then doubled that spending figure even while adding complex new programs and demanding their immediate implementation.

Meanwhile, the dramatic rise of partisan polarization in Congress across the postwar period, especially since the 1990s, made lawmaking—never easy—practically impossible. The last *six* years of the Obama administration barely managed the passage of as many public laws as the two years of the 80th Congress that Harry Truman denounced as "do-nothing." The number of recorded votes in the Senate—which include nominations and treaties, un-like the House—was lower in 2016 than in any year since 1957. Even the brief return of unified government in 2017–18 barely moved the needle of legislative productivity.[37]

These developments enhanced both presidents' motive and their opportu-nities to achieve their policy preferences through their control of bureaucratic behavior. They sought to achieve what in 2001 Elena Kagan (by now a law professor) called "presidential administration," while evading legislative grid-lock.[38] As Richard Nathan noted, "In a complex, technologically advanced society in which the role of government is pervasive, much of what we would define as policymaking is done through the execution of laws in the management process."[39] As far back as 1946, a Bureau of the Budget memo titled "The President's Management of Public Policy" stressed the White House's responsibility "not only for managing the administration of the Executive agencies, but their policy as well."[40]

Executive orders were one of many presidential tools for doing just that. The toolbox was large enough, in fact, that observers tracked an "imperial" presidency during the Vietnam and Watergate era and then a "new" imperial presidency after the September 11, 2001, terrorist attacks.[41] Such debates raged around George W. Bush's claims of presidential prerogative; again around Obama's aggressive interpretation of statutory discretion, most notably regarding immigration and environmental protection; and again when Trump took the same approach but to opposite ends, declaring a state of national emergency in early 2019 to unlock funding for his desired border wall and claiming "total authority" over pandemic response in 2020. Even before then the Trump White House had long touted executive action as a straightforward metric of presidential power. Its evidence that Trump had "accomplished more in his first 100 days than any other President since Franklin Roosevelt" was that the president had issued more executive orders during that time period than any newly elected president since 1933.[42]

None of these presidents were shy in praising executive action, often as a substitute for stalemated efforts to pass new legislation. "Since Congress can't get its act together on HealthCare," Trump tweeted, "I will be using the power of the pen to give great HealthCare to many people—FAST."[43] In 2014 Barack Obama pledged to use his own "pen to sign executive orders and take executive actions and administrative actions that move the ball forward," building on his declaration before the 2012 election that "we can't wait for an increasingly dysfunctional Congress to do its job. . . . [W]e're just going to go ahead and act on our own."[44] Bush's similar boast of acting "on my own" was noted above. Rahm Emanuel, then an aide to Bill Clinton, noted in 1998 that "sometimes we use [an executive order] in reaction to legislative delay or setbacks. . . . [Y]ou're willing to make whatever progress you can on an agenda item."[45]

Executive Orders

Executive orders "do not dwell amid the comfortable certainties of administrative law."[46] The Constitution does not mention a presidential power to issue unilateral directives. Yet every president—even William Henry Harrison, who died after barely a month in office—has done so.[47] As a way of implementing statute in ways that hew to presidential preference, executive orders have been utilized from the Washington administration forward as an implication of the constitutional "executive power" vested in the president.

In 1957, a House committee studying the matter defined executive orders as

> directives or actions by the President. When they are founded on the authority of the President derived from the Constitution or statute, they may have the force and effect of law. . . . Executive orders are generally directed to, and govern actions by, Government officials and agencies. They usually affect private individuals only indirectly.[48]

Phillip Cooper expanded this somewhat: "executive orders," he wrote, "are directives issued by the president to officers of the executive branch, requiring them to take an action, stop a certain type of activity, alter policy, change management practices, or accept a delegation of authority under which they will be responsible for the implementation of law."[49]

This covers a lot of potential ground. Executive orders are hardly uniformly consequential, as will be discussed in detail, but they have been used for everything from the internment of tens of thousands of American citizens of Japanese descent to the attempted nationalization of the steel industry to the reshaping of public sector employment. They often have spillover effects beyond the public sector. By changing how stringently cost-benefit analysis is applied to regulatory review, or what conditions are written into the half-trillion dollars' worth of contracts the federal government annually negotiates, presidents can shape a plethora of private decisions.[50] Thus, as Kenneth Mayer argued in his seminal 2001 book on the topic, "executive orders have played a critical role in the development and exercise of presidential power"; and compared to the many other kinds of presidential directives that exist, "executive orders combine the highest level of substance, discretion, and direct presidential involvement."[51]

Indeed, although the absolute number of EOs issued per year has diminished somewhat over time (see Figure A1.1 in the appendix to this chapter), studies find an upswing in the number of "significant" orders issued by presidents over time. Mayer's research, sampling more than one thousand orders from 1936 to 1999, found that about one in seven orders were significant overall. But as a proportion of the total, significant orders jumped to 22 percent in the 1970s and to 28 percent by the 1990s, up from between 9 and 16 percent in prior decades.[52] William Howell, measuring significance somewhat differently over a longer time frame (1900 to 1998), also found the annual number of significant orders trended upward as the century wore on.[53] By 1999, House Majority Leader Richard Armey (R-TX) was accusing Bill Clinton of "running roughshod over our Constitution. . . . With a stroke of his pen, he may have done irreparable harm to individual rights and liberties."[54] Barack Obama was attacked as "a dictator," and so was Donald Trump.[55] But if "complaints about dictatorship" is a meaningful metric, EOs have been consequential throughout the whole era of the modern presidency. A 1941 volume pondered the question of Franklin Roosevelt's purported "wicked enchantments" over the office in *Roosevelt: Dictator or Democrat?* (deciding upon the latter).[56] The Kennedy White House, for its part, received so many accusations of tyranny in connection with its efforts to plan for nuclear emergencies and civil defense ("these moves have all the earmarks of a dictator in action") that it was forced to develop a form letter defending the president ("these assertions are absolutely incorrect," one version read).[57] In 1975, a presidential staffer sent members of Congress a similar template they could use to answer letter-writers expressing "concern with the seemingly broad power exercised by the President through Executive orders. . . . Whatever the polemics of the time," the White House suggested telling constituents, "executive orders are the means whereby the President properly exercises the authority and responsibility vested in him by the Constitution and Congress."[58]

Executive Orders and Political Science

Contemporary political science caught up somewhat slowly to this empirical reality. To be sure, studies of "the ordinance-making powers of the president" appeared as early as the 1920s, tracking the newly activist administrations of Theodore Roosevelt and Woodrow Wilson.[59] By the late 1940s Edward Corwin's seminal textbook on the presidency observed that "executive interpretations of statutes flower. Nowadays they give rise to proclamations, orders, ordinances, rules, regulations, 'directives'—what have you?. . . . In a word, to *executive lawmaking.*"[60] But the behavioral revolution that swept political science after World War II centered on House roll calls and Gallup approval ratings; it had a harder time with presidential management of the executive branch. Richard Neustadt's hugely influential approach to *Presidential Power*, first published in 1960, took as his starting point the fact that presidents under the Constitution were not powerful but weak. As such, he wanted to explore

how they could prevail in influencing government outcomes. Though Neustadt agreed that formal powers were a key bargaining resource for presidents,
he warned that high-profile dictates could highlight failure as much as achieve
success; his focus was on the "skill and will" and public prestige divergent
"men in office" could deploy to persuade others in government to carry out
their wishes.[61] Others built on this new direction while neglecting its institutional foundation: one result was a research field often emphasizing what
Terry Moe would scathingly characterize as "the personal presidency," where
power was contingent on the attributes of individuals and their negotiating
acumen.[62]

Moe and others argued for a renewed focus on the institutional authorities
available to any president, regardless of their personality, and the incentives
and constraints for presidential behavior these implied. After all, he argued,
"institutionalization was and is at the core of the modern presidency."[63] As
study of the "institutional presidency" and variants of a "new institutionalism"
gained momentum, special emphasis fell on the role of executive action. A
flurry of literature ensued, notably in the late 1990s, with executive orders as
the key empirical element used as a proxy for presidential unilateralism.

The trajectory of this scholarship is discussed in the next section, but it is
worth noting that the theoretical underpinnings of unilateral action follow
from the same first principles identified by Neustadt: from the presidential
weakness tied up in the American constitutional system of intertwined
branches of government that grants each the standing to check their counterparts. Instead of focusing on bargaining as a way around this weakness, scholars such as Moe and Howell argued for another route. For presidents, they
pointed out, unilateralism promises a tractable way of transforming preferences directly into public policy, implementing change via decisive leadership
rather than through tedious parliamentary procedure.[64]

That approach echoes Alexander Hamilton's founding-era observations
about the president's place in the new Constitution. In *Federalist* #70, Hamilton argued that "unity"—having a single chief executive, rather than the plural
presidency some had pressed for—was "conducive to energy" in the executive
and thus a "leading character in the definition of good government." Unity
would empower "decision, activity, secrecy, and dispatch." Presidents would
be able to make quick, authoritative choices, discreetly if necessary—
something far more difficult for the multitudinous members spread across the
two chambers of the legislative branch. A few years later, serving as Treasury
secretary, Hamilton defended the Washington administration's decision to

stay neutral in the ongoing war between France and England. Congress was "free to perform its own duties according to its own sense of them," he said, should it be able to agree on a course of action. But in the meantime the president had leeway "to determine the condition of the Nation." In so doing, "the Executive in the exercise of its constitutional powers, may establish an antecedent state of things which ought to weigh in the legislative decisions."[65]

Better yet, such tactics are frequently successful in affecting that National condition. Research shows that executive orders are rarely overturned by Congress or by the courts, giving presidents latitude to shape policy outcomes in important ways. As a result, as Mayer argues, "in most cases, presidents retain a broad capacity to take significant action on their own, action that is meaningful both in substantive policy terms and in the sense of protecting and furthering the president's political and strategic interests."[66] In short—as Howell enduringly put it—presidents can assert "power without persuasion."[67]

Executive orders are hardly alone in their basic function. Despite the tendency of reporters, scholars, and even presidents to use "executive order" as a generic fill-in for any administrative edict—the Deferred Action for Childhood Arrivals (DACA) program, for the record, was established by departmental guidance memo—there is a wide range of tools with similar effect.[68] An incomplete 2008 listing compiled by the Congressional Research Service identified twenty-seven different types of presidential directive.[69] However, there is no reason the theoretical framework of this book could not be applied to these as well. And it is already clear, as noted, that in the aggregate executive orders are invaluable vehicles for carrying significant policy substance and indicating direct presidential involvement. Later chapters detail Office of Management and Budget exertions to ensure that only items appropriate to and worthy of issuance as executive orders take that form. As a Trump administration official told reporters on Air Force One in 2017, "The best thing that you can do in the realm of administrative action is an executive order. . . . [A]n executive order is a very muscular way of getting the agencies to begin [a policy] process." Indeed, he went on, "there is no higher statement of executive direction than the form of an executive order."[70]

The Chief Executive and the Executive Branch

Yet if researchers have verified that executive orders matter, they have paid far less attention to how the executive branch matters to those orders. To be sure, despite the singularity implied by the very word "unilateralism," no scholar would argue that the president literally acts alone in issuing directives. Studies of the presidency often stress the staffing resources presidents have amassed over time, to the point of creating a "presidential branch" of government.[71] Still, research in the field has not turned its attention to the complicated institutional reality of the executive branch itself as it applies to the use and formulation of executive orders.

Instead it has emphasized the importance of external actors, notably Congress and the judiciary. Indeed, while in 1997 Steven Shull and Brad Gomez could note that "few propositions and almost no general theories guide empirical research on presidential actions like executive orders," a wave of systematic research was already cresting to fill that void.[72] It centered first on tallying EOs, and then on teasing out the factors that might spur their issuance.[73] How many were issued, and under what circumstances? The answer was usually linked to a president's political environment on Capitol Hill and beyond. Did divided government, for instance, lead to more, or fewer, EOs? Did levels of presidential approval make a difference? How about the timing of an impending election? Some studies suggested increased presidential support in Congress led to more EOs, perhaps in recognition of the lower likelihood such directives would be overturned by statute. Others posited the opposite, arguing that EOs were not needed when legislation could be obtained instead; thus, it was divided government that prompted order issuance.[74]

While early research normally utilized a straightforward count of issued EOs, that assumed each order was an equivalent observation. Yet not all EOs are of equal substantive importance. Even as he issued orders limiting immigration and imposing economic sanctions, for instance, Donald Trump also approved a new seal for the National Credit Union Administration and changed the name of the President's Council on Physical Fitness and Sports to the President's Council on Sports, Fitness, and Nutrition.[75] Nor do all EOs serve the same purpose. Some promote routine administrative maintenance or shape advising structures. Some are aimed at substituting presidential preferences for legislators', stoking interbranch conflict—but others implement newly passed legislation, promoting interbranch cooperation. Recognizing these nuances, recent scholarship examines the text and subject matter of EOs by policy area,[76] by substantive significance,[77] by political objective,[78] and by their varied connections to the legislative process.[79] The role of public opinion in potentially constraining unilateral action has also received sustained attention.[80] Still other work has drawn on the wider range of presidential directives, at least tentatively considering when presidents might choose one such vehicle rather than another and when the conditions identified as relevant to EO issuance might hold for other directives.[81]

Another important advance was the addition of theory to fact: thinking through hypotheses that went beyond the multivariate measurement of orders and contexts to identify a core rationale for when presidents were more likely to issue orders and the scale of change those orders might rationally attempt. Building on the "pivotal politics" model developed by congressional scholars, Howell's breakthrough was to "clearly specify a set of joint conditions under which presidents will forgo the legislative route and exercise their unilateral powers instead."[82] Presidents should be able to anticipate the odds of their actions being overturned by those with the power to do so. Thus, the distance between the relative policy preferences of presidents and key legislators (that is, those at the "pivots" controlling Congress's ability to pass legislation or override a veto) and the dispersion of legislative preferences (since that affects Congress's ability to create the needed bipartisan coalition) predicted the likelihood of presidential action and the size of the policy space in which presidents could operate. That is: "the ability of presidents to act unilaterally depends on other institutions' abilities to stop them."[83]

Calculating those other institutions' abilities brings us back to the president's structural advantages vis-à-vis other branches of government, and thus to the key assumptions built into theories of unilateral action in the first place. There are two. Hamilton's observation regarding the president's ability to "establish an antecedent state of things" is here translated into the "first-mover advantage." Presidential action forces other political actors—Congress, the courts—to respond to a new state of play. But they, in turn, are burdened by difficult questions of collective action. The legislative branch is made up of more than five hundred individuals divided into separate chambers with myriad veto points. The courts cannot react to a presidential initiative unless a lawsuit is brought in a timely way by someone with standing to sue, a suit that must traverse several levels of judicial hierarchy before a final decision is reached. In either branch, many people must act for reality, rather than rhetoric, to change.

Hence the second key feature bolstering unilateral action: that "the president acts alone."[84] The presidency and the executive branch as a whole may be assumed to behave as a single, unitary actor, eliminating the transaction costs associated with the multilateral decision making fundamental to Congress. As Terry Moe argues, unlike legislators, "presidents are not hobbled by these collective action problems and, supreme within their institution, can simply make authoritative decisions about what is best."[85] As such, any issued order reflects presidential preferences, more or less purely enacted into action. Howell puts it this way: the theory "does not differentiate the president from the White House staff from members of the Executive Office of the President from civil servants in the executive branch, generally" and "attributes unilateral policy changes to the president alone."[86] In this telling EOs are born of an immaculate conception.

That is a reasonable assumption given the questions fundamental to the field so far. Indeed, it is worth stressing that the concept of a unitary executive detailed here *is* an assumption, extended for the purposes of gaining empirical traction. It is not meant as the ideological-verging-on-theological justification offered by some scholars and many more pundits and executive branch officials.[87] Nor is it intended as descriptive reality. Instead, it is stylized fact: a construct that provides theoretical and empirical leverage over presidential decision making, where its value lies in its predictive power.[88] It helps answer key questions about when (and how far) we should we expect presidents to take administrative action rather than seek legislative policy change. But it means that for studies centered on the political context of executive order issuance, on the external incentives for and constraints on presidential unilateral action, the backstory—the process inside the executive branch through which an order comes to be—is simply not the interaction of interest.

Yet that process is very much worth unpacking, substantively and theoretically. A long scholarly trail leads to a view of the executive branch as a "they," not an "it." The broader study of bureaucratic politics, still a strong presence in the public administration literature, approaches the executive branch as inherently pluralistic—as (in Hugh Heclo's framing) an "executive mélange."[89] In short, even presidents may have collective action problems.

In 1971, Graham Allison's pioneering *Essence of Decision* made clear how that mattered. His famous case study—or rather studies—of the Cuban Missile Crisis began by assuming the government was a unified rational actor. As such, the United States and Soviet Union were single entities with clear, hierarchical preferences assessing the costs and benefits of various options and making choices that maximized their net expected utility. But while many aspects of the Cuban Missile Crisis could be explained using that framework, Allison found that important developments and details remained baffling. "For some purposes," Allison noted, "governmental behavior can usefully be summarized as action chosen by a unitary, rational decision maker: centrally controlled, completely informed, and value maximizing." But a government is not an individual, he went on. Rather, it "consists of a conglomerate of semi-feudal, loosely allied organizations, each with a substantial life of its own."[90] A fuller understanding of what happened over the "thirteen days" required fleshing out the story by viewing it through additional lenses that brought into play the internal organizational dynamics of bureaucratic policymaking and the intra-governmental politicking in which political actors engaged.

These sequential complications serve as a useful template for this book's consideration of presidents and executive orders. In this telling the process of issuing a unilateral directive becomes less purely—or at least differently—unilateral as our lens widens. Scholars agree that "the boundaries of unilateral powers are fundamentally institutional in nature."[91] But thus far, the pivot points that define the range of policies the president might enact have been set by other branches of government. We need to take seriously the notion that presidential action can be bounded not just by legislators or judges but also by actors within the executive branch itself. The ultimate form of a given executive order may reflect agency needs, or the outcome of intrabranch negotiation, rather than pure ex ante presidential preferences. In some cases agencies might even seek to foist orders on the president, rather than vice versa. But of course allowing agencies to write an order may be a perfectly rational decision on the part of presidents who might not have strong preferences as to its specific form or who need to gather knowledge of what will work best to achieve their ends. They may desire to take action in a broad area, to change the status quo, but find it "cheaper" to opt for an alternative proffered by an agency or arrived at collaboratively.

The key point is that presidents do incur transaction costs as they engage the process of issuing directives that match their political, administrative, and substantive preferences. To minimize those costs, they will have to manage unilateral action and its complications—as it turns out, in ways that reflect the ways they manage interbranch relations. Indeed, managing the formulation of an executive order presents clear parallels to managing the formulation of a legislative proposal.[92]

As that suggests, this new approach complements and even compliments existing work. For instance, recent scholarship takes note of the relatively few significant executive actions actually taken, relative to the presidential advantages hypothesized in so doing: "the true puzzle," Dino Christenson and Douglas Kriner posit, "is the relative *paucity* of major unilateral actions, not their frequency." They argue that domestic public opinion is a key factor in suppressing the issuance of EOs.[93] But executive politics are a plausible additional constraint. Indeed, as in the Carter case presented above, presidents may find the costs of a given EO exceed its benefits and discard it—either because they discover information that sours them on its issuance or because bureaucratic friction makes it untenable. More broadly, as Howell presciently noted in *Power without Persuasion*, "directives regularly rise from below," and thus "future work should examine how administrative agencies can leverage their informational advantages to shape executive orders . . . to suit their individual interests. While the president has considerable discretion over whether or not to sign off on these directives, he does not always have complete control over their content."[94]

The handful of in-depth studies of individual EOs likewise indicate that the substance of orders often flows from coalition building, both outside the executive branch and within it.[95] Kenneth Mayer made clear in *With the Stroke of a Pen* that EOs may "percolate up from executive agencies" and that drafting frequently takes into account "comment and suggestions from affected agencies" in a process that can take years to navigate. His discussion of EO 12114, in which Jimmy Carter directed federal agencies to calculate the environmental impact of their actions abroad, tracks the long and often contentious negotiations between the White House and key bureaucratic actors over its issuance.[96] In a review of the broader literature Mayer therefore suggested that "we might make more progress looking at what happens before a president takes unilateral action, rather than after."[97]

Presidential Management and Presidential Power

This book does just that. It takes the origins and development of executive orders seriously and systematically. It considers the sorts of informational transaction costs that different combinations of agencies and policy areas might impose on presidential management of administrative action—and how presidents seek to minimize those costs. To do so, it uses painstakingly compiled archival data to explore the sources and formulation of executive orders over the course of nearly seven decades. Study of a sample of more than five hundred EOs shows their issuance follows extensive consultation across the executive branch and even within the White House; it finds that presidents often cajole, rather than command, departments and agencies in pursuit of an order in a given form. These new data allow us to examine how long it takes orders to be constructed and what slows or speeds that process. And, for the first time, we can look systematically at what stops them from being issued at all.

None of this means presidents are powerless. Far from it. They have clear legal and constitutional advantages in dealing with other executive branch actors. A bureau cannot get an EO issued that the president ultimately refuses to sanction. But it does mean that even in policy produced "by executive order," presidents face a management challenge linked to the broader challenge of administering the executive branch. Many models of presidential-bureaucratic relations assume a principal-agent template, with the president as boss and policy demander, seeking to prevent bureaucratic shirking. But if executive orders may originate from the bottom up, we need to complicate those models to reflect the "two-way street" between principal and agent—here, agency—bruited earlier. As George Krause argues, "In reality, the nature and degree of success of these authoritative relations will rest upon some level of agreement between relevant political and bureaucratic actors."[98]

How are these agreements reached? As explored in the rest of the book, we can perhaps conceive of a presidential policy market where the president must decide what executive orders to issue and whether to "make or buy" each. That is, should a given EO be a White House creation? Or should it be crafted in the agencies—in this case themselves perhaps the "first mover" in proposing EOs, selling their wares and requesting presidential attention to their priorities? The choice rests on the relative price of competing products: What will it cost, politically or policy-wise, to issue a given order? Are agencies trying to sell the president a pig in a poke, to achieve something that will benefit their agenda but not hers? On the other hand, are White House staffers unaware of substantive grenades their order might explode? Again, the president is often at an informational disadvantage in such dealings. I will argue below that the creation of the enduring "central clearance" process run by OMB since the 1930s is a structural approach to counteracting that imbalance.

Another test is whether different characteristics of EOs—or of the agencies that influence their substance—are associated with different loci of policy formulation. What kinds of EOs are most likely to be created by centralized staff? Conversely, what order or agency characteristics seem to grant agencies more sway in the formulation process? If my focus here has merit, the answer should be tied less to external political circumstances and more to the complex contingencies of managing the executive branch.

The Plan of the Book

The rest of the book expands and tests these arguments. The next chapter builds on the brief discussion above to explore the strands of public administration scholarship stressing the organizational complexity of the executive branch and the difficulty of imposing centralized leadership upon it. It considers the transaction costs involved in managing the executive branch—and seeks to situate presidents as they both respond to the administrative products of the agencies and create their own within the Executive Office of the President. The notion of contingent centralization, used in other research on policy formulation, is adapted here to the president's decision to "make or buy" a given executive order. What characteristics of an order, or an agency, shape presidential decisions about where to formulate an executive order? When will EOP intervention be most required; when will agencies be given freer rein? The vantage is largely presidential here in asking how presidents can lower their managerial transaction costs. But that frame allows for agencies to have influence over the provision of information and thus scope to shape presidents' cost-benefit analysis.

Two chapters then lay out different aspects of the data used. Chapter 3 provides some background on the collation of executive orders generally, then details the creation of the institution of "central clearance" in the Office of Management and Budget. Central clearance has served as both a proactive and protective process for presidents since the 1930s, especially after OMB (then known as the Bureau of the Budget) moved into the Executive Office of the President from the Treasury Department in 1939. It matches well with the kind of "governance structure" an information-seeking president might rationally construct in order to evaluate and winnow proposals for executive action.[99] These come at him from all directions, as chapter 4 shows: it lays out the data set of EOs created for this book, drawn from archival sources spanning the Roosevelt to George W. Bush administrations. It provides comprehensive data regarding the making of those orders and a scheme coding their relative centralization. In so doing it answers a basic empirical question: How are executive orders actually formulated? The most frequent answer is, with lots of participation by different agencies.

The next chapters take a more systematic approach to these descriptive statistics, from either end of the "two-way street" running between president and agency. Chapter 5 returns to the question of the conditions that underlie decisions to use a centralized EO versus a decentralized one. For presidents seeking to minimize their managerial transaction costs, what matters in that calculation? Do the same factors that influence the decision to issue an executive order (the focus of the literature in this area to date) affect the manner in which that order is formulated? According to the approach taken here, characteristics specific to individual orders and the agencies linked to them should instead be the primary influences over how presidents manage the process of policy development.

Chapter 6 examines to another aspect of that management. It turns out that the average executive order takes some seventy-five days to move from draft proposal to the *Federal Register*, with huge variation around that figure. What affects that timing? What makes an EO take longer to issue? What characteristics of orders and agencies, of interagency interaction and requirements of the management process itself, are associated with delay? Quantitative analysis, elaborated by case studies, helps us explore these questions for the first time as the duration of the formulation process is tested as a proxy for executive collective action problems.

Finally, of course, some proposed EOs are never issued at all. Chapter 7 presents a new data set of more than two hundred executive orders never signed by the president. However that is interpreted—as good management or as gridlock—something that could have been done "with the stroke of a pen" was not. Here, too, quantitative and archival analysis pair to help us understand why. The results highlight the fact that unilateral action has costs, which at some point outweigh the benefits. Those costs may be rung up in Congress, or the courts, or by public opinion. But as the exploration here shows, they may also be imposed by the executive branch.

That leads to the concluding chapter, which summarizes the overall findings and pushes them toward related topics in sore need of additional study. This book examines what happens before an executive order is issued, but we know little about what happens afterward. Do executive orders actually get implemented? How might the formulation process—and the path dependence imposed by past EOs—matter to that? Another topic for future research is the plural nature of the Executive Office of the President itself, qualitatively evident in the cases above (and many others to follow) but quantitatively far less tractable. How do divisions within the president's closest staff units affect the notion of centralization?

The conclusion is also a chance to explore the question of bureaucratic capacity and autonomy as it runs up against presidential desires to control that bureaucracy—a claim bolstered by electoral legitimacy. Presidential hostility to the permanent government is hardly new, of course. But the Trump administration's amplification of that contention—with frequent, personal attacks on agencies and even individual civil servants on the one hand, and "resistance" to presidential preferences on the other—raised its salience, and its stakes. The argument of this book rests in part on the value presidents

derive—substantively but also politically—from astute management of a bureaucracy that can provide expert advice on solving pressing national problems. Undermining its ability to do so is therefore counterproductive.

In the end, the cases traced at the outset of this introductory chapter are
only slightly extreme examples of everyday reality: presidents use executive
orders to manage the executive branch, but that requires they manage the process of issuing executive orders themselves. Exploring these questions matters,
not least in understanding the complexities of "a world of extraordinary administrative complexity and near-incalculable presidential responsibilities"—
and how presidents can best achieve their preferences in that environment.[100]
They can help us understand how the executive branch both underwrites and
bounds presidential unilateralism. In doing so, it helps us consider what unilateralism means, and how that matters for presidential power itself.

Appendix

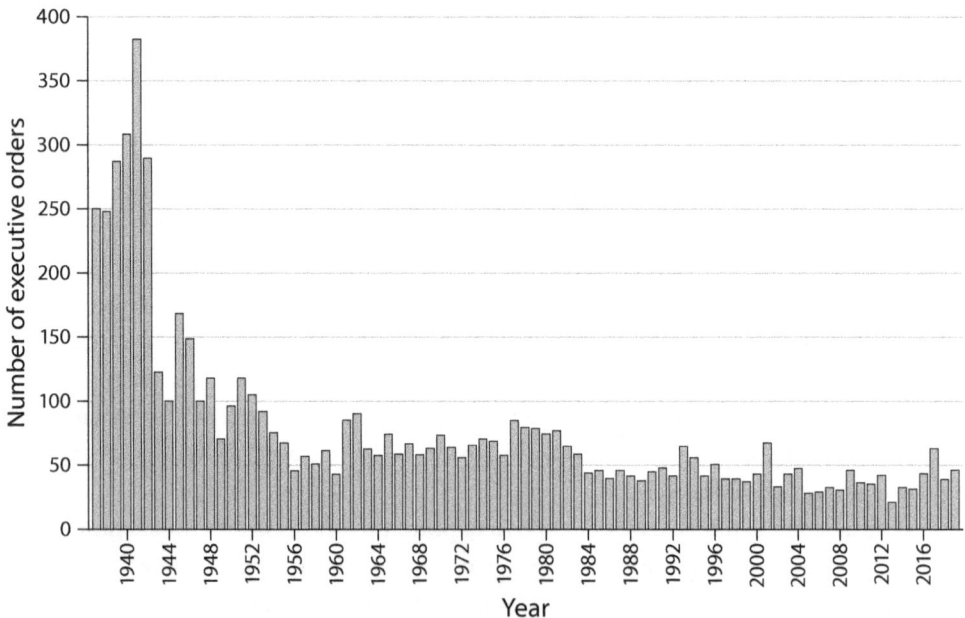

FIGURE A1.1. Executive Orders Issued by Year, 1937–2019.

2

Bargaining with the Bureaucracy

PRESIDENTIAL MANAGEMENT AND
UNILATERAL POLICY FORMULATION

SCHOLARSHIP ON THE RELATIONSHIP between the president and the executive branch bureaucracy frequently seems imported from the annals of foreign policy. Harold Seidman and Robert Gilmour argue that the executive branch is really "an alliance," "a confederation of sovereigns."[1] Francis Rourke frames relations between the president and the bureaucracy as "diplomacy."[2] More recently and in more martial tones, Daniel Farber and Anne Joseph O'Connell portray "agencies as adversaries," noting that "beneath the surface of the administrative state are constant battles, between and within agencies."[3] From the vantage of those agencies, another study stresses, even the White House is divided as it seeks to conquer: "presidential control [is] not a unified enterprise but coalitions of different offices competing for influence."[4] Former defense secretary (and OMB director) Leon Panetta, asked to describe the Pentagon's relationship with the president's staff, had a yet more pugnacious response. "Hand to hand combat," he replied.[5]

Presidents themselves often frame the matter in self-pitying tones. "I agree with you," John F. Kennedy reportedly told one confidant, "but I don't know if the government will." George W. Bush complained to an Egyptian opposition leader that "I too am a dissident in Washington. Bureaucracy in the United States does not help change." Barack Obama vowed to reform "bureaucratic hoop jumping." Donald Trump, of course, routinely accused the "Deep State" of seeking to undermine his presidency. Asked about a recent initiative in March 2020 Trump replied, "I didn't do it. . . . I don't know anything about it. It's the administration."[6] As the Bureau of the Budget lamented seventy-five years ago, while the "president's management of public policy" required getting the agencies to heed his preferences, most observers "do not gener-ally understand the extent to which [the president] lacks adequate legal au-thority, organization, and procedures to do the job." Thus: "He does so . . . if he can."[7]

Most scholarship on presidential unilateralism, by contrast, accepts that the president straightforwardly "can," and does. In practice, it has (quite accu-rately) highlighted directive tools as an important component of presidents' ability to shape governmental outcomes: new laws are hard to pass, but old laws can be implemented in new ways. In theory, it has built on the assumption of a unitary executive: that the president acts alone, controls the outputs of the executive branch, and does not need to worry about collective action or transaction cost concerns arising within that branch.

It makes sense for studies centered on the interbranch political context of executive order issuance—notably on the presidential incentives and con-straints imposed by Congress and the courts—to build on logic relevant to the president's placement vis-à-vis those institutions. Relative to Congress, presidents can use the "unity" Hamilton stressed as far back as the *Federalist* to move policy closer to their preferences, relying on Congress's collective action problems to undermine legislators' capacity to retaliate. Relative to the courts, they can likewise rely on a "first mover" advantage and the reactive nature of judicial intervention.

But as discussed in chapter 1, the new data presented in this book allow us to track what happens when the assumption of a singular, and singularly co-hesive, executive branch is relaxed. Obviously the president's relationship with executive agencies *is* quite different than it is with legislators or judges. Presi-dents bargain with the bureaucracy from a distinctive vantage point, as "chief executive." They reside atop the formal hierarchy and have a clear claim to powers of command derived from the vesting clause and beyond. Still, as the references to intrabranch "combat" that opened the chapter imply, presidents themselves rarely assume frictionless interaction within the executive branch nor see it as a monolithic entity. There are innumerable stories of recalcitrance, perhaps most famously Richard Neustadt's portrayal of Harry Truman envi-sioning a frustrated Dwight Eisenhower in the Oval Office: "he'll say 'do this! Do that!' *And nothing will happen.*" Neustadt's own take on the matter, devel-oped as a midcentury EOP functionary, was to warn against the "illusion" that "administrative agencies comprise a single structure, 'the' executive branch, where presidential word is law, or ought to be."[8] More recently, Daniel Car-penter and George Krause have focused on the role of "transactional authority" rather than "principal authority" in defining presidential relations with the wider bureaucracy.[9]

This chapter picks up on both points: on the frequently plural nature of the executive branch and on the transactions—and transaction costs—imposed upon the president as a result. New questions quickly arise. What do presidents and agencies want, and need, when it comes to administrative policymaking? What sort of presidential advising market might be posited by conceiving the executive branch in this manner? More specifically, what does it imply for how presidents might seek to manage the policymaking process, specifically that driving the formulation of executive orders? How do they bargain with the bureaucracy?

The discussion mirrors both older and ongoing research into the complexities of political control over—and delegation to—the bureaucracy. The broader literature on executive branch complexity and agency autonomy, spanning the borders of public administration, administrative law, and political science, argues for a more complicated notion of the principal-agent relationship than expressed in the models that dominated the first wave of empirical research into presidential-bureaucratic relations. Those are top-down; but the process of producing executive orders, as a descriptive fact, is frequently bottom-up. (As noted in chapter 1 and detailed in chapter 4, some 60 percent of EOs ultimately issued by the president are preponderantly the product of staff outside the Executive Office of the President.) How do presidents manage the traffic on the "two-way street" posited not just by Krause but by scholars as distinct as Neustadt and Terry Moe?[10]

"Manage" is the right word given the approach taken here. I will assume presidents are proactive within their institutional constraints, investing their resources for policy formulation in ways consistent with the informational environment in which they work. "Every president wants to make policy," and as discussed below we can imagine a mix of legislative and unilateral proposals that make up a given policy portfolio.[11] In either category we can derive insight from a different strand of literature, largely from transaction cost economics, that builds on the theory of the firm and when executives should "make" or "buy" the products they need. For presidents seeking to manage the formulation of unilateral directives, these theories highlight the notion of minimizing managerial costs and offsetting the informational advantages agencies possess. When do they utilize centralized, White House staff for policymaking, and when can they rely on decentralized agencies to provide what they need? As Richard Nathan's seminal work on the administrative presidency put it, the point is not "to lament the fact that the president cannot exercise full control over the bureaucracy, but rather to demonstrate that explicit effort is required if the president is to exert *greater* influence over the bureaucracy on administrative matters."[12] How does the formulation of executive orders reflect that state of the world?

"Tugging and Hauling": Transaction Costs in the Executive Branch

Nixon aide William Safire called the executive branch a "lethargic behemoth. . . . The so-called Chief Executive can tug and haul all day and never rip up the bureaucracy."[13] Professor turned departmental assistant secretary, White House counselor, and U.S. senator Daniel Patrick Moynihan agreed that it is "quite mistaken" to see the executive branch as "a more or less passive executor of policies made on high": after all, "a very great portion of policy ideas 'bubble up' from the bureaucracy."[14] As a State Department official said in 2007, "Policy is not what the president says in speeches. Policy is what emerges from interagency meetings."[15]

There is of course a rich literature exploring these dynamics—the tugging and the hauling and the non-ripping, the bubbling and the interagency. The executive branch is vast, fragmented, and possessed of as many voices as it has constituent agencies. The result is cacophony. The *Sourcebook of United States Executive Agencies* identifies 15 Cabinet departments (with 173 bureaus within them) and nearly 80 agencies outside those departments, using the term "federal executive establishment" rather than "executive branch" to emphasize that some agencies were created precisely to resist hierarchical political control.[16] The distinction between line departments and independent regulatory commissions is one clear example, but within each of those categories, too, each agency has its own bespoke incentives and resources. And many policy arenas are under the jurisdiction of multiple agencies, either because legislators have little incentive to create an efficient bureaucratic structure or (as former DOJ official Neal Katyal argues) because "well-functioning bureaucracy contains agencies with differing missions and objectives that intentionally overlap to create friction."[17] The attribution of intentionality may be overly generous, but even Justice Antonin Scalia's dissent in *Morrison v. Olson*—something of a love letter to a hypothetical unitary executive—refers to "the Executive Branch and the internal checks and balances it supplies."[18]

Study of intra–executive branch friction tracks the historical rise of the American "administrative state" generally. One recent study suggests that already by the 1860s "the executive branch was not easily managed or controlled by a single person or office."[19] Twenty years later, as a pre-presidential Woodrow Wilson observed, "new conceptions of state duty" meant that "at the same time that the functions of government are every day becoming more complex and difficult, they are also vastly multiplying in number."[20] Soon "the central issue" became, as John Huber and Charles Shipan summarize, "whether politicians can effectively harness bureaucrats' knowledge and expertise, or whether this very knowledge and expertise allow bureaucrats to usurp the rightful role of politicians in policymaking."[21]

Progressives themselves assumed away this problem, exalting the presidency in theory and downplaying any notion of bureaucratic independence in practice.[22] Wilson famously commented that "the field of administration is a field of business," whereby bureaucratic technicians simply oversaw the translation of the decisions made by political actors in government into their most efficient tangible form. Bureaucracy was thus "a part of political life only as . . . machinery is part of the manufactured product."[23]

But however true at the time (spoiler: not very), a fiftieth anniversary assessment of Wilson's essay in 1937 concluded that politics had a lot to do with agency behavior, and indeed that bureaus were largely attuned to the demands of various interest group constituencies.[24] By the time the New Deal, World War II, the Cold War, and the Great Society had exploded the size and scope of the federal establishment, theories of bureaucratic dominance had turned Wilson's model on its head. Now an administrative state challenged Congress and the president "for hegemony in the national political system" and "on equal, and sometimes superior, terms" to those political actors.[25] A wave of twentieth-century literature studying bureaucratic politics generally attributed this to executive branch "disunity," to what Clinton Rossiter described in the 1950s as "pluralism in fact" if not in theory.[26] Allison's *Essence of Decision* saw American government acting as the "conglomerate of semi-feudal, loosely allied organizations" far more frequently than as a singular rational actor, even in the national security arena.[27] In this view, while presidents have clear legal and constitutional advantages in dealing with others in the executive branch, they are something like the rulers of a far-flung empire nominally under their control but whose constituent states in practice exercise a good deal of discretion—and on which their capitol depends for its very subsistence. "A president is not self-sufficient," Seidman and Gilmour wrote. "It is the agency heads, not the president, who have the men, money, materiel, and legal powers."[28]

In general, following from Allison's example in his sequential explications of the Cuban Missile Crisis, these works stressed two main aspects of executive branch decision making. One drew on organization theory, especially that of the Carnegie school, to stress the limits of bounded rationality and the subsequent creation of standard operating procedures within agencies.[29] The other focused on interbureaucratic politicking, tracking key actors in multiple organizations as they jostled for influence on behalf of their respective institutional interests.[30] Any resulting policy constituted a "collage" built by piecemeal negotiation rather than a centrally directed artistic vision.

If these models convincingly rendered the complexities of a burgeoning bureaucracy, they implied a sort of helplessness on the part of elected officials generally that went beyond real-world constraints; empirical studies found plenty of evidence for "active political control."[31] Scholarly efforts to fill in the gap centered on principal-agent models, accounting for how elected principals could indeed govern the behavior of their bureaucratic agents. At first this work largely ignored the president, creating a model of "congressional dominance": legislators were seen as the repository of administrative authority, if not always through proactive policy "patrols" then through their ability to leap into action when a "fire alarm" was pulled by someone (an interest group, a constituent, a journalist) observing agency misdeeds.[32] The latter meant that even when Congress seemed dormant, the actions of prudent bureaus would remain within the bounds of legislative preferences to avoid budgetary retaliation or embarrassing public oversight hearings.[33] Either way "the legislative arena [was] central"; indeed, from the congressional vantage, presidential efforts to control the agencies were a "problem."[34] For presidents, of course, the problem was being left out of the administrative equation. And other scholars soon pointed out that presidents, and for that matter the courts, had their own authority both to take part in shaping these ostensibly legislative decisions and to assert their own influence over bureaucratic behavior. Most important were the presidential appointment power and a larger White House "counterbureaucracy" providing staffing resources for independent action and executive branch coordination.[35] (These dynamics—politicization and centralization, respectively—are discussed in more detail below.)[36]

The principal-agent models developed to assess political control of the bureaucracy, then, quickly sprouted multiple principals. They also called more attention to the agents; modeling bureaucratic control, Terry Moe reasoned, was problematic if one paid "precious little attention to the bureaucracy."[37] Executive branch agencies had their own internal dynamics, which dictated how they responded to any given request, and their actions were shaped at least partly by the ways in which they could use their own resources to bound or even block efforts at external control.

A wave of recent studies straddling the borderlands of public administration, administrative law, and political science flesh out these points, detailing agencies' own abilities and motivations. This scholarship extends the older bureaucratic politics literature to account both for agencies' own agency and for principals' motivation to nurture and manage their agents' resources.[38]

Key among those resources remains specialized policy knowledge and expertise. If, as in Seidman and Gilmour's observation above, agencies have personnel, appropriations, legal powers, and "materiel" to hand, they have those things toward a particular substantive purpose: "its advice on the 'how to.'"[39] As the discussion of the "Keating Five" scandal that begins Gary Miller and Andrew Whitford's *Above Politics* shows, the deployment of bureaucratic expertise and legal standing (along with a timely leak to the press) turned what seems at first to be a classic case of "congressional dominance" into something quite different.[40] Miller and Whitford's broader point, though, is that political decision makers themselves have incentives to provide bureaucrats with discretion and enough autonomy to be able to cultivate their specialized competence. This echoes in other work that stresses the delegation of authority to executive agencies: "That expertise is something that is valued by political principals," Gailmard and Patty note, is "a foundational presumption" of their research.[41]

Daniel Carpenter's research on bureaucratic autonomy shows that autonomy may not be given so much as earned, achieved via a reputation for substantive policy work that prompts politicians to give the agency more independence.[42] That in turn leads to power, which in turn helps burnish reputation; the two become institutionalized in a reciprocal way.[43] Autonomy can transmute to policy as well: "working within a set of established constraints," Rachel Potter writes, regarding the development of regulations, "bureaucrats can use administrative tools to strategically and systematically insulate their rulemaking proposals from political scrutiny and interference."[44] This "procedural politicking" includes the way in which a proposed regulation is written; the scope of public input it receives; and the timing of its promulgation.

In fact—and crucially, given arguments regarding the unitary executive—she and other scholars argue that agencies have the chance to be "first movers" in the rulemaking domain, giving themselves "considerable latitude in the particulars of the policy they advance."[45] Promulgating regulations differs from producing executive orders, of course: statute normally vests authority for the former in the departments themselves, not in the president. Still, the analogy is a useful one given that agencies can themselves propose EOs, and that presidents have created a centralized regulatory review function in the Office of Information and Regulatory Analysis to attain de facto authority over rulemaking. More generally, Miller and Whitford argue that agencies can take advantage of divisions among political overseers: "bureaucratic discretion is enhanced by disagreements among other political actors and constrained by political consensus."[46]

Bureaus do not usually have formal veto power over what a president proposes. But given the resources noted above, they may be able to raise the costs of policy issuance, perhaps beyond its benefits. In part, they can do so by providing substantive information not yet under consideration. But they also have the ability to slow the pace of consideration via various mechanisms of delay, from flat-out "shirking" to what Jennifer Nou calls "record-building" via the additional gathering of evidence and demands for enhanced deliberation, perhaps recruiting allies in other agencies along the way.[47] (Agencies can also leak information to the press, or share it with inspectors general or with Congress; they can sue, or help others to; and individual appointees or civil servants can resign in protest to raise the salience and political costs of a given course of action.)[48] At the very least, as Kagan noted, a pluralistic system produces "a welter of cross-pressures, forcing all manner of trade-offs and compromises and offering a wealth of opportunities for strategic machination."[49]

We might think that different agencies have different default levels of resources along these lines—Francis Rourke holds that "one of the best measures of an agency's strength in dealing with the president is the extent to which the president has to bargain with it in order to secure its cooperation."[50] Picking up on agency-specific characteristics, another set of scholars has sought to provide taxonomies of executive branch pluralism. They define the differences between agencies in various ways. Some detail agencies' divergent structural features and their level of insulation from political oversight.[51] Some create measures of agency ideology, tracking both the distinctions between agencies and the distance between a given agency and a given president.[52] Other studies survey federal personnel to unearth how they gauge their own agency as well as others—in terms of autonomy, ideology, interagency influence, or organizational competence. Measuring the last, for instance, gives the National Institutes of Health and Federal Reserve high scores for their workforces' skills; peer agencies are rather less impressed with the Bureau of Indian Affairs or, perhaps more ominously, the Transportation Security Administration.[53]

Thus both older studies of bureaucratic politics and newer explorations of institutionalism and administrative law converge on the same basic points: namely, the pluralistic nature of the executive branch, the authority and sometimes autonomy vested in its component agencies, and the resultant "two-way street" between bureaucracy and president that shapes policy development and even preferences. As Krause points out, "Analyses grounded exclusively in formal executive powers understate organizational complexity, and thus overstate presidential capacity for controlling the bureaucracy."[54] In short, executive branch decisions—and presidential decisions—carry with them their own burdens of collective action.

Constructing Unilateral Action:
A Theory of the White House Firm

What does this mean for unilateral action? As Adam Warber observed over a decade ago, "The presidency literature contains no studies addressing the importance of persuasion in relation to the president's executive order authority because scholars consider executive orders as a tool of command."[55] But as the discussion and case studies in chapter 1 suggest, executive orders are part and parcel of the fragmented bureaucratic politics and policymaking processes sketched above. Whether an order exists, and what it says, is affected not just by a president's personal preferences but by multiple actors reaching far beyond the Oval Office. As early as 1925, in a rather more tractable administrative environment, James Hart already thought presidents would struggle for control. "In theory, but only in theory, the President controls all executive formulation of policy, all ordinance making," he wrote. "In practice the heads of departments may themselves merely accept ordinances drawn up by bureau chiefs, while the President may have only passing knowledge of the whole affair."[56] And if that provocative observation should not be taken literally with regard to "ordinances" requiring presidential signature, it still highlights the relative advantages of bureaucratic agencies versus their political overseers, not least in informational terms. In fact executive orders are a particularly interesting test of how presidents deal with the components of the executive branch, given that EOs' substance is aimed directly at departments and agencies.[57] Thus bureaus care deeply about what executive orders are issued and have a real incentive to shape their content.

Stepping back a bit, we can consider the supply and demand sides of a presidential policy market of sorts. For their part, presidents need an agenda: indeed, the notion that they will provide an affirmative policy direction to the federal government is arguably part of the very definition of the modern presidency.[58] They must act. As Terry Moe and Scott Wilson note, "Presidents are held responsible by the public for virtually every aspect of national performance," and when the government falters in any way "it is the president who gets the blame, and whose popularity and historical legacy are on the line."[59]

The "president's program" is partly legislative, of course, and sometimes predominantly so; the choice of whether to pursue formulation of a bill or an executive action is analytically prior to the questions posed in this book.[60] Of course, as we have already seen and as detailed further below, the predominant strand of EO research deals with factors affecting that choice, many of them linked to the partisan makeup of Congress. In 1961 BoB pointed out to the White House that "executive orders . . . can occasionally cause more of a stir than legislation, and they can have a lot to do with the President's legislative relations."[61]

For present purposes, though, we can posit a swirling "policy primeval soup," with presidents always open to initiatives that will advance their agenda or illustrate their leadership, and that those initiatives can be by executive order.[62] Sometimes presidents will be proactive, driven by their own key policy priorities: "bring me my tariffs!" Donald Trump repeatedly demanded of his White House staff.[63] Other proposals will be internally generated from party platforms and campaign pledges. Some will be driven by ongoing events or sudden crisis. Some will be discretionary. In this rather open marketplace—as discussed in chapter 3, anyone in government can proffer a proposed order—EOs will come from a variety of actors seeking to sell their preferred options for Oval Office consumption. Indeed, sometimes an open audition might be held: Bill Clinton's staff put out a "request for a list of possible upcoming executive actions" within a week of his taking office, a practice that continued to the end of his term (an April 2000 memo "lists and categorizes proposals for executive actions that we have received from relevant federal agencies and offices within the White House").[64]

It's worth noting, in this regard, that presidents cannot rely on the White House for the entirety of their policy development, even if they wanted to: their personal staff simply lacks the capacity. The striking growth of the Executive Office of the President over time is driven in part by the creation of substantive policy councils and their staffs but also by multiple offices devoted to political calculus and its communication. Thus the number of staff devoted to policy production is bounded (and the number capable of doing it well even lower). But if a wider net is to be cast, as with Clinton's request for proposals, that requires thinking about the agencies' part of the supply side equation—what agencies want as they generate positive proposals of their own. In some cases, agencies affirmatively need EOs in order to give them authority to act—perhaps as a result of recent statute requiring implementation, or to coordinate across departmental lines. In others they might seek presidential sanction for their own efforts to promote policy, or to drive that coordination. (Though of course the boundary between need and want may not always be obvious, or clearly presented, to the president.) As succeeding chapters will show, many agency concerns are internally driven, operating on a timeline independent of the political calendar and moved forward irrespective of who occupies the White House. But presumably agencies may also await the opening of the right policy window and a sympathetic incumbent, perhaps taking advantage of a change in presidents to seek the reversal of past action.[65] Where agency strategy links to ideological alignment with the current president—for instance, withholding orders it thinks will not find favor with the incumbent—that should affect our theoretical expectations and empirical interpretation. Finally, another aspect of agencies' behavior is preventative: as noted above, delay is a non-negligible bureaucratic resource. So we expect them to desire to shape (or block) proposals they did not themselves offer.

All this presents presidents as part policymaker, part traffic cop, with issues potentially arriving in the Oval Office from many sources. Problems, solutions, participants, and their opportunities for choice may be variable and even free-flowing, but this is not a "garbage can" model, exactly—those factors are not random, nor exogenous to the organization.[66] Indeed, they flow from the organization. They are, by default at least, guided toward the president's desk not by chance or idiosyncratic presidential inventiveness but by advisory institutions. Organization is policy; but in the modern presidency, at least, organization is information, which makes policy.[67] Dwight Eisenhower's de facto response to the Neustadt anecdote above was in a letter to his own eventual successor, Richard Nixon: "the secret is adequate and skillful organization . . . so that necessary information and opinion come to [the president] in usable form."[68]

That makes the key question facing presidents what that organization should look like: how they can structure the policymaking process to receive sufficient information to protect their own substantive and political interests as they build an executive policy program. "We do not want one supplier of information to the President," Katyal writes; "a competitive market better supplies clients than a monopolist."[69] But presumably its vendors still want an edge. If a bureau is proposing an EO that suits its own agenda, presidents need to be able to evaluate whether that agenda should be theirs, too: again, does an agency *need* authority?—or only want it? Nor does the president want to be spun, told an option is substantively impossible when in fact the agency merely considers it undesirable. At the same time, proposals generated by White House staffers might be ineffective or have unanticipated consequences, their authors lacking the specialized knowledge to play out the technical aspects of implementing a given policy choice. In short, the president needs a mechanism for learning about the relative features and "price" of the policy products he could issue. This is less a function of their fiscal impact, though this could matter, than their overall costs and benefits in terms of their policy, political, and administrative impact. Such information could alter his own preferences (to his pleasure or anger; the two are observationally equivalent in most cases) by shaping his knowledge of the costs and benefits of given options, within the range of possibilities that he prefers to the status quo. (Of course, new information could also make it clear that no such possibility exists at an acceptable price.)

Framed that way—in terms of the president seeking to lower the managerial costs of doing (policy) business—the questions are similar to those at the heart of informational economics. There, the black box portraying a unitary rational actor was not the state, or the executive branch, but the firm, "in which inputs are transformed into outputs without reference to organization."[70] The internal makeup of the firm did not matter in the purest reaches of economic theory, where every transaction is a spot-contract—carried out at one time for every one thing exchanged, each purchaser and supplier meeting at the idyllic intersection of supply and demand. But in the 1930s, Ronald Coase pointed out that contracting in the real world was not friction-free. Each transaction came with costs, whether in the currency of time or expertise or information; the parties' bargaining preferences might be difficult to calculate and repeated bargains easier to institutionalize than renegotiate. Coase's insight became a branch of economics focusing on transaction costs—defined by James Q. Wilson as "the costs of planning, negotiating, directing, and evaluating the activities necessary to produce something"—and how they might be minimized.[71] The basic question became the "make or buy" question facing private sector executives: when should a firm purchase a product on the open market, and when should it make that product itself? The answer depended on the nature of the transaction, or set of transactions. The frequency of a given exchange might govern the appropriate choice, as would the "asset specificity" involved. The more repeated the need for a particular technology or form of expertise, and the more uncertainty inherent in the outcome, the more sense it made to impose ongoing hierarchy rather than rely on spot-contracting.[72]

The metaphor is inexact, of course. Yet its insights carry over to the president's policymaking process in two useful ways. First is the notion of "governance structures," in which transactions are "embedded."[73] As Oliver Williamson writes, governance structures exist to "attenuate incentives to exploit information impactedness opportunistically."[74] Translated out of economese, if only into political sciencese: well-designed institutions can help protect buyers from a combination of ubiquitous uncertainty and bounded rationality on the one hand, and sellers' desire to hide negative information, on the other. Uncertainty itself might arise from the nature of the problem requiring solution, but also from the "strategic non-disclosure, disguise, or distortion of information."[75] In this a governance structure mirrors the kind of monitoring system set up to ameliorate the informational advantages of agents in principal-agent models generally. In the private sector, such a structure might include labor-management fora, including collective bargaining; auditing requirements; arbitration mechanisms; various sorts of vertical integration; and even differently structured boards of directors that reflect various forms of expertise or impose behavioral safeguards.[76] For presidents it involves building a process for that same sort of auditing of, and learning about, proposed policies, from whatever source: what is a policy's expected utility, broadly speaking? Asset specificity, as for Williamson, is perhaps the fundamental quality—here, not so much factory machinery but knowledge of the finer points of soybeans and the social safety net, of substantive capacities, political impacts, and legal limits.[77] When the president demands that someone "draft an executive order and repeal that law," all are required.[78]

Second, for present purposes, the make or buy question is less the choice of governance structure itself but rather the calculation of where—with such a structure in place to integrate information about the "transaction"—the president might logically invest policymaking resources in order to reduce its managerial costs. In order to reduce their uncertainty about the expected utility of a given proposal, presidents should choose on a case-by-case basis the source of policy production providing the optimal combination of reliability and cost. The "cheaper" (in a managerial sense) the information is, the better. Of course, minimizing transaction costs does not mean eliminating them; again, the formulation process may actually add to uncertainty by highlighting objections to a given initiative, perhaps raising the price of issuance beyond its benefits.

In assessing the managerial cost of a given proposal's preparation, we return to the questions of politicization and centralization noted earlier. These flow originally from Terry Moe's highly influential 1985 article "The Politicized Presidency," which noted the huge gap between the "formidable expectations" of presidents and the "limited constitutional powers" available to meet them.[79] Given a separated system stacked against their needs as political leaders, rational presidents—irrespective of their personal qualities or partisan leanings or policy positions—will bring as much as possible under their direct control, indeed are "destined" to do so.[80] The two most prominent tools for this purpose are politicization and centralization.

Politicization occurs with the seeding of the wider bureaucracy with presidential loyalists who can act as proxies for the White House, allowing presidents to "implant their DNA throughout the government."[81] Centralization, for its part, describes the shift of functions from the wider executive bureaucracy to the Executive Office of the President (EOP), especially to the White House Office (WHO) itself. It "generally refers to the division of power over major decisions, both in making them and advising on them, as distributed among the president's inner circle, EOP staff, and the Cabinet secretaries."[82] This draws a line between the Cabinet departments and independent agencies, and the president's personal staff located in the WHO and EOP: centralization moves authority from the former to the latter.

As such, it is particularly relevant to the make or buy question. In earlier work examining presidents' task in producing a particular piece of legislation, I argued that presidents must choose whether to "make" that legislation, inside the EOP, "buy" it from the wider executive branch, or utilize some hybrid of the two. Theoretic expectations about the likely conditions under which information would be "cheaper" from centralized sources versus the executive branch agencies were tied to the characteristics of each programmatic proposal: presidents would draw upon the staff resources, or the blend of them, that minimized their own informational transaction costs for a given pro-posal.[83] The goal is to calculate what factors are associated with a given formu-lation process, all else equal. It's worth noting, perhaps, that centralization does not automatically lower transaction costs. Instead, this lens assumes whatever process is chosen does aim to lower them.

To be sure, the specific nature of the transaction costs involved in the for-mulation of executive orders surely varies from those stemming from the pro-duction of legislative proposals. These distinctions are explored below, and tested in chapter 5. Nonetheless, the processes should be similar in kind from a managerial viewpoint: the proper unit of analysis would seem to be each individual EO itself, with production of each hinging on its characteristics and on the nature of a president's assessments of various parts of the executive branch. Different kinds of orders should carry with them different kinds and levels of costs. Thus the key elements predicting a centralized or decentralized venue for EO formulation should be linked less to external political circum-stances than to managerial factors.

Before describing those, two caveats are in order. One is that while central-ization, in the literature and in this book, does not treat the executive branch as unitary or for that matter unified, it does treat the president's immediate personal and institutional staff in the EOP as such. The "presidential branch" is disaggregated descriptively in some of what follows, but not systematically. As such it takes the view Rossiter espoused long ago: "The President is still one man, but he is also, like any man with a thousand helpers, an institution."[84]

This is defensible as analytic assumption and in fact inevitable given avail-able data, but it is far from ideal. As the Clinton case traced in chapter 1—or, frankly, any published account of the Trump White House—makes clear, even within the EOP different staff units are often contending for the president's ear with competing policy views. As a result our theories may underestimate the benefits of delegation to the agencies, to the degree fragmentation within the EOP raises the cost of centralized policymaking.[85] I return to this point in the concluding chapter.

A second caveat that does receive attention throughout the book is the role of the bureaus on their own end of the street. The policymaking market model used here dramatically complicates the notion of a unified executive branch; it requires presidents to bargain with the bureaucracy rather than to command it. Even so it places the president very much at the center of determinations about administrative policy development. This seems reasonable given a focus on executive orders—which, after all, a president must sign. But it should be clear from the discussion above both that individual agencies have their own resources and that, collectively, the competition *between* agencies may impose its own constraints over presidential decision making. For instance, as noted above, such friction may provide new information that, perversely, increases the uncertainty surrounding the expected utility of a given EO. For that matter it may clarify that agency resistance will make faithful implementation of the order problematic, thus elongating the formulation process to seek consensus or short-circuiting it entirely. The conditions affecting the relative impact of bureaucratic behavior of this sort on transaction costs will be discussed below, but in more detail in chapters 6 and 7, which track agencies' roles in the politics of EO delay and its extreme cousin, outright non-issuance. The vantage is one on presidential management, and the effects of the bureaucracy thereon, rather than a quantitative taxonomy of bureaucratic "resistance." Still, readers will find many specific examples of the latter in what follows.

Synthesis and Hypothesis

What behavior should we expect of presidents seeking to lower the managerial costs of producing executive orders? Most generally, they should put in place a governance structure that allows them to vet policy proposals from whatever source, protecting against the chronic uncertainty and potential opportunism (while taking advantage of the specific expertise) stressed by Williamson. The next chapter explores this in some depth, focusing on the institution of "central clearance" established by presidents with the Office of Management and Budget starting in the 1930s. This structure allows variation in the formulation of EOs, as presidents delegate EO policymaking in some cases and centralize it in others depending on factors that affect transaction costs and thus raise the relative benefits of centralization or lower the cost of alternate strategies.

The remainder of this chapter, then, turns to consideration of those factors, with the empirics reserved to chapter 5. They can be loosely grouped into three categories.

Expertise

The provision of subject-matter expertise on specific issues is fundamental to why bureaucracy exists in the first place. What are an EO's technical complications, its legal implications, its consequences for policy change, its interaction with other parts of the executive branch and the outside world? All else equal, the more complex and technically involved is a proposed EO the more agency involvement is needed, to ensure it is substantively sound and can be implemented in a way that brings about the desired result.

All else may not be equal. As noted above, agencies vary in the level of substantive competence they bring to bear. Some agencies have a reputation for excellence in this regard; others are considered far less able. But even in the former case presidents may fear departmental control of technical details, wondering if a pig is hidden in the provided poke. That in turn may vary with presidential trust in a given agency, as discussed in the next section. An irony lurks here: if an agency's appointees are deemed sufficiently loyal to the president, its output may be less questioned but also of lower quality. A variety of studies suggest that responsiveness and competence vary inversely.[86]

Trust and Congruence

The underlying question is the perceived distance between presidential preferences and agency outputs. As just suggested, the president's appointment power can help stock the bureaucracy with ideologically like-minded, loyal appointees. This implies a relationship between centralization and politicization in which one substitutes for the other: if the latter has been successful, the former is less necessary.[87] Indeed, Nixon chief of staff H. R. Haldeman's notes record his boss's emphasis that "loyalty up is the most imp[ortan]t thing" and his order that "as we dismantle [EOP] offices use the *loyal* people out thru agencies."[88]

Of course, political appointees may be hopelessly unprepared to actually govern. According to Haldeman's notes, Nixon went on to say, "loyalty much more imp[ortan]t than competence"; Donald Trump's promise to bring "the best people" to Washington was likewise premised on a definition of virtue closely linked to obeisance, not administrative ability.[89] Further, as Clinton and Lewis note, "even if we could measure the preferences of every political appointee, agency preferences are not solely, or even largely, the product of appointee preferences."[90]

Trust, then, cannot be metered simply by the reliability of the secretarial suite. For one thing, appointees normally comprise a small proportion of agency personnel. Trump secretary of state Mike Pompeo highlighted the point by using it as an excuse: facing a president angry at State Department testimony regarding Trump's self-serving dealings with Ukraine, Pompeo "defended himself . . . by telling Trump he doesn't know who half of these State

Department officials are" and noting "there are thousands of employees at the agency, explaining that he can't control them."[91] And without another dimension of trust, that between political appointees and civil servants, presidents may find it hard to fully exploit the expertise that resides in the latter.[92] This is hardly a new issue. As an Eisenhower administration memo considering "Suggestions for the Department of Agriculture" warned, "the place is saturated below high levels with people who do not want the department to succeed. . . . These people can sabotage any Secretary without the Secretary even knowing about it."[93]

Another aspect of this dynamic flows from the multiple principals issue. Since bureaus are necessarily responsive to Congress as well as to the president, we should expect presidents to be more trusting of agency advice when legislative and presidential preferences align.[94] By implication, presidents should be more suspicious of departmental expertise during divided government. Further, while party identification and ideology are quite tightly aligned in present-day politics—with a paucity of liberal Republicans or conservative Democrats—that is not true during long segments of the seven decades under study here. Thus it may be helpful to look not just at the number of presidential co-partisans in Congress but at the congruence of legislative and presidential "preferenceship" as well.[95]

At the same time, and with an even larger impact, agencies also have their own long-standing internal identities, grounded in their statutory mission, their functional tasks, and the ethos of the profession(s) from which their staff are primarily drawn.[96] The political coalitions that create agencies also seek to embed their own preferences within the organization and insulate it against later efforts by competing coalitions to rework its structure and outputs.[97] These structural factors have their own impact on agency policy preferences across administrations, and thus on any given president's attitude toward that agency. Most broadly we can think of clashes between liberal agencies and conservative presidents, or vice versa; as Joel Aberbach and Bert Rockman's famous survey of Nixon-era civil servants concluded, even paranoids might well have enemies.[98] In recent years renewed efforts have been made to measure these distinctions more systematically, as noted earlier and operationalized later.

In short, as a former CEA chair once put it, "there was bureaucracy and bureaucracy."[99] The centralization decision will hinge in part on what kind of bureaucracy the White House perceives: we would expect more leeway for trusted agencies. But what the agency perceives may matter too. As suggested above, a strategic agency sensing a proposed EO may find a hostile reception in the White House could decide not to proffer it.[100] That, or for that matter the reverse dynamic, could have implications for the empirical impact of variables measuring trust, as discussed in chapter 5. That is, a less trusted agency could send forward only orders it feels are likely to win issuance, while a more trusted agency might be emboldened to send forward substantively worse orders that require remedial work by other agencies or the EOP.

Learning

A quick addendum to the trust issue might include trust over time. In principle, presidents have the same choices about centralization on their first day in office as on their last. But in practice their informational environments vary over time. At the outset of their term, for instance, presidents do not have a fully staffed executive branch. The Trump administration became infamous for its spate of unfilled vacancies, but the broader phenomenon is hardly unique: months into the Obama administration, confronting a historic economic challenge, Secretary Tim Geithner was "home alone" as the only confirmed denizen of the seventeen most senior posts in the Treasury Department.[101]

Geithner was far from literally alone, of course—that year more than 98,000 people worked for Treasury—but early term presidents may not yet trust (or even be aware of) the broad executive branch resources they suddenly command. They may also have a backlog of EOs they promised during the campaign to issue "on day one of my administration." By contrast, as presidential appointments are selected and confirmed, the president should trust a broader array of departmental staff. And presidents should normally become more expert in their utilization of a wider range of far-flung staff resources, simply through experiential learning; Krause and O'Connell find that "when it comes to agency appointments, presidents place less emphasis on loyalty (compared to competence) over time."[102] Thus, all else equal—a key caveat for all of these hypotheses—we should expect presidents to centralize more early in their tenure, especially very early.

Policy Scope and Significance

EO-specific attributes—for instance, the scope, purpose, and importance of a given order—also seem likely to affect the managerial and informational dynamics of their formulation process. These include whether an order falls within the jurisdiction of multiple agencies (and how many); whether it deals with reorganizational matters; whether it flows directly from specific statutory delegation; and whether it is substantively important and/or a presidential priority. The timing of its development within the president's term might also have managerial implications.

Crosscutting Issues. Many issues—perhaps most issues of interest—cut across the jurisdictions of multiple executive branch agencies. From environmental protection to job training, consumer safety to international trade, slivers and sections of the broad arenas of public policy are assigned to different bureaus. A department's narrow vantage complicates its ability to give presidents objective analysis of subjects that cross jurisdictional lines. As public administration scholar Eugene Bardach has observed, "almost nothing about the bureaucratic ethos makes it hospitable to interagency collaboration."[103]

Thus the president needs a point of coordination that can assess and integrate the wide range of (potentially self-serving) advice being offered by the executive agencies. One result has been the use of White House "czars," as presidents seek mechanisms that can provide a "coordinating leadership role" to "collaborate in a way that maximizes agency values and expertise in the most effective and efficient manner for moving the president's policy agenda forward."[104] Along similar lines, the Office of Management and Budget has long held "crosscutting" exercises as part of the budget process. Dwight Eisenhower captured the dynamic in a letter to budget director Rowland Hughes in 1954, discussing the need for an executive order creating a White House–led interagency committee to address questions of agricultural surpluses as a mechanism of foreign aid. "The very fact that a number of agencies have a responsibility in one or another aspect of surplus disposition makes effective coordination absolutely essential," the president wrote. Central leadership could bring "into harmonious action, consistent with the overall policy objectives of this government, the various . . . activities vested in" the multiple agencies concerned.[105]

In short, the more departments affected by the scope of an executive order, the less likely the president can rely on an individual department's assessment of the matters at hand. In such cases, more centralization is likely to lower the transaction costs of the interagency wrangling involved.

Reorganization. Issues dealing with reorganizational matters should tend to produce more centralization too, and for similar reasons. Since individual bureaus fiercely protect their turf, their advice on proposals that affect their own structure or other agencies' staff is unlikely to be fully trusted by the EOP. Departments tend to resist organizational changes that infringe on their autonomy, particularly those that require their decisions to flow through other departments; conversely, as detailed in chapter 3, they frequently propose changes that will give them a leg up over their executive branch rivals. Either way, a more centralized process is usually necessary for presidents to obtain unbiased information on the rationale for (or against) reorganization.

"Clerkship." Some EOs, however, are linked specifically to a given department because they are prompted by a recently passed law that either requires changes by a particular bureau or delegates authority to the president that is then routinely re-delegated to a specific agency. "In this capacity," Michelle Belco and Brandon Rottinghaus note, "the president fulfills a central, but rather benign, executive function of administering governmental maintenance by carrying out laws that have been passed or initiating the policy implementation process."[106] Such EOs, especially when they flow from specific provisions of statute and involve a single agency, usually present few informational hazards; and agencies have an interest in making them effective. Thus they are likely to originate from the departments most affected by the new law.

A related group of "benign" EOs relates to what Neustadt famously called the president's "clerkship"—implementing duties imposed on the presidential office in the past, sometimes decades ago. These EOs involve presidential discretion as to triggering and timing but are largely routine in nature. For instance, until 1978, when the Civil Service Reform Act permitted Jimmy Carter to delegate this power to the new Office of Personnel Management, presidents were responsible for personally issuing exemptions from the civil service laws governing mandatory retirement ages and the like.[107] Pleas for acts "of Executive benevolence" were therefore frequent, though rarely as melodramatic as a 1940 case where Franklin Roosevelt was asked to allow the debt-laden widow of an Agriculture employee to take over his job despite her mediocre performance on the relevant civil service exam. (USDA's letter assured FDR "it is our policy to request executive orders of this character very rarely and only in what appear to be really warranted cases.")[108] Other early twentieth-century statutes such the Pickett Act and the Taylor Grazing Act delegated power to the president over the designation and withdrawal of public lands. Kenneth Mayer found that by the 1920s land matters accounted for over half of all EOs.[109] But in 1943, Franklin Roosevelt delegated this task to the secretary of the interior, and in 1952 Harry Truman used the new Presidential Subdelegation Act to make that transfer of authority more permanent.

Some of these sorts of lasting responsibilities remain, though, for instance in the regular EOs relating to "adjustments of certain rates of pay." And a third category of clerkship still commonly represented in EOs is the creation of mediation panels to cool off labor disputes when strikes threaten the rail or airline industry. A key actor here is the National Mediation Board, created in 1934, which produces standardized executive orders for presidential use when such cases develop.

Here, too, we might expect EOs issued under long-standing statutory authority to become routinized form letters that require little new information and are outsourced to the agencies. Transaction costs economics research on firms' ability to generate knowledge ranks any given problem on two dimensions: the additive value of the solution, and the cost of discovering a particularly valuable one.[110] For these sorts of orders the average effort involved in uncovering a novel approach would be high, given its low likelihood and the relatively low value of the "solution" generally.

Significance. But across EOs generally this calculation will vary by the weightiness of the problem; any differentiation among types of orders implies the need for attention to their relative importance. The first generation of literature on unilateral directives was driven by the aggregate number of EOs issued, treating all equally: an observation shuffling the order of secretarial succession in the Commerce Department was the same, for this purpose, as Franklin Roosevelt's infamous EO directing the internment of Japanese American citizens during World War II.[111] Likewise, a simple count of orders would perhaps exaggerate the importance to American history of G. Joseph Minetti's tenure at the Civil Aeronautics Board. His delayed retirement was the subject of five separate executive orders in 1977.[112]

Subsequent scholarship honed in on those orders' crucial differences instead. Researchers argued it made intuitive sense generally to care more about orders that had a major impact, and found that the number of significant orders was on the rise even as the number of overall orders declined.[113]

Empirical efforts to measure EO significance are deferred to chapter 5. But theoretically, it makes sense that presidents would find additional centralized attention to higher-priority or higher-impact directives desirable. That does not imply, however, that their formulation should be fully centralized within the EOP. A substantively important order is likely to be technically complex, requiring the infusion of bureaucratic expertise if it is to achieve its ends. But a wholly decentralized approach seems equally unlikely. An important order likely implicates multiple agencies, and thus the coordination issues noted earlier; and its very complexities raise informational asymmetries requiring EOP monitoring. For priority items, the increased managerial costs are worth the investment.

If so, should we care about "insignificant" orders at all? Given present purposes, the answer is yes, largely because those purposes diverge from the extant literature. It makes sense to exclude less significant EOs from an analysis centered on interbranch relations; it is less helpful to do so when analyzing the mechanisms that produce EOs inside the executive branch. Indeed, if the parameters of intra-executive management vary according to the importance of the EO in question, removing variation on that variable is problematic. Depending on how significance is defined, doing so would discard as much as 90 percent of the universe of orders actually produced. Some of those might prove intriguing. Exempting an over-age employee from mandatory retirement is generally unexciting—but what if that employee is J. Edgar Hoover?[114]

Next Steps

It is often useful for scholarly purposes to assume the executive branch is unitary. But in practice, political authority is not solely a matter of hierarchical command. That applies even to unilateral directives: as one George W. Bush staffer memorably put it, moving an executive order from idea to issuance can be "like giving birth to a pineapple."[115] More broadly, as Barry Friedman observes, "the relationship between the president and his subordinates is not that of the supremely powerful with the despairingly powerless." Instead it represents "a balancing of needs, interests, and conciliations between worthy competitors for leverage."[116]

This chapter has examined ways in which the president may seek to lessen the transaction costs generated by that balancing act. First, it outlines the logic behind the creation of enduring governance structures that give presidents an informational, institutional resource in the metaphorical policymaking market that helps populate their agenda.

Second, managerial dynamics guide when presidents "buy" their executive actions from this wider market or "make" them in-house. When do they choose to delegate, and when to centralize? As with legislative policy, I argue, these choices are predictably contingent. Restated in conditional terms, we should expect relatively more centralization when:

- an executive order's subject matter cuts across multiple agencies' jurisdictions;
- the EO carries out reorganizational or broad personnel functions;

- the EO is substantively significant and/or a presidential priority (though with a hybrid process most likely here); or
- the EO is issued very early in the president's term.

Less centralization, thus more agency autonomy, is expected when:

- the EO is more complex and technically involved, requiring agency expertise;
- the preferences of the agency with substantive jurisdiction over a potential EO are closer to those of the president—that is, it is viewed as more "loyal";
- the preferences of Congress are close to those of the president; or
- the EO involves clear delegation in statute, or the routine use of authority delegated sometime in the past.

Third, agency behavior will itself affect transaction costs. Past behavior, of course, affects its reputation for competence and the president's trust in its products. But agency participation within the formulation process for a given EO may either enhance or limit uncertainty about the utility of that order in ways that prolong its deliberation or even prevent its issuance.

The following chapters test these hypotheses by tracing different aspects of the executive order formulation process. The next chapter focuses on central clearance, the long-standing governance structure designed to provide presidents with basic information about proposed EOs and their likely outcomes. Chapter 4 then presents a wider data set of issued (and unissued) orders, drawn from extensive archival research, presents a methodology for analyzing the centralization or decentralization of a given formulation process, specifies what cases in each category look like in practice, and summarizes what the formulation data look like in the aggregate. Chapter 5 probes the hypotheses of managerial centralization laid out above. Chapters 6 and 7 return to factors that might delay or thwart the issuance of EOs.

Together, they show that presidents established and have long utilized a standard coordinating process for dealing with executive orders; that a majority of executive orders are formulated from the bottom up, rather than as centralized directives, and subject to the same intrabureaucratic (and sometimes interbranch) negotiations as other presidential actions; that formulation processes seem to be consistent with much of the managerial logic developed above; and that agency pushback is an important factor affecting EO issuance. In short, that the executive branch matters to executive orders.

3

Executive Orders

STRUCTURE AND PROCESS

MOST OF WHAT we hear about executive orders celebrates their birth. There is a press release, sometimes a signing ceremony—Donald Trump, in particular, was fond of brandishing his oversized autograph for the cameras.[1] A formal text is furnished in the *Federal Register* and, these days, on the White House website. And perhaps there is some news coverage, depending on the significance of the order and the pace of world events. Eventually the completed order is conveniently collated with its predecessors in various government publications, such as the Executive Order Disposition Tables maintained by the National Archives.[2] In their aggregation the neatly listed orders immediately transform into data.

As already noted, those data have been used extensively for quantitative analysis, with the dependent variable most often the simple fact of an order's issuance. The present project, of course, seeks to commemorate gestation rather than birth—to trace the interactions of the various parts of the Executive Office of the President and the wider bureaucracy and reveal the intricacies of the decision-making process behind the formulation of executive orders. How do presidents manage that process? Chapter 2 argued that part of the answer lies in the creation of informational institutions: that presidents should seek to impose a governance structure in which transactions are "embedded" for the purpose of gaining crucial information about the proposed directives being considered for issuance. More formally, such institutions ameliorate presidents' informational asymmetries and the transaction costs associated with collective action.[3]

The current chapter details just such a governance structure in the long-standing process of central clearance, housed in the Office of Management and

Budget since the 1930s. Its intent is to protect the president from opportunistic efforts by agencies to use their informational advantages, as well as from efforts by White House staff to push substantively problematic initiatives of their own. Central clearance is an example of what Richard Rose usefully called "institutionalizing distrust."[4] It gives wide advance notice not only to presidents but to agencies of what other parts of the executive branch are proposing, and the chance at a sort of collaborative—albeit often fiercely competitive—peer review.

This chapter provides a brief history of executive orders followed by a detailed discussion of the central clearance process and its role. The narrative here, along with the analysis in the following chapters, rests on extensive archival research exploiting the comprehensive executive order files compiled by the Office of Management and Budget. Those files cover nearly seven decades, from 1937 to 2004, and are supplemented by public documents, by interviews with relevant practitioners, and by numerous additional primary documents from presidential libraries and private holdings. In chapter 4, the OMB order files and the random sample extracted from them are described in depth, along with a coding scheme identifying the provenance of EOs in the data and presenting a variety of examples of how EOs are formulated in practice. As we will see, a majority are formulated preponderantly in the wider executive branch, making central clearance all the more important as a tool of presidential management.

Tracking Executive Orders: A Prehistory, 1789–1936

The neat packaging of executive orders just noted is very much a modern phenomenon. In the dark days of prehistory—that is, before the existence of the *Federal Register*—things were far less orderly.

It didn't help that presidents issued administrative directives long before they labeled them "executive orders." The latter did not formally occur until after the Civil War, under President Ulysses S. Grant; but the former began with George Washington.[5] A good candidate for the first official order is Washington's June 8, 1789, edict that his department heads provide "a clear account" of the matters before their agency, while Louis Fisher nominates the 1793 neutrality proclamation during the Napoleonic Wars as "the first venture into unilateral presidential lawmaking."[6] In any case, by many names and in many formats, Washington's successors consistently followed suit, issuing their orders by proclamation, "presidential regulation," letter, or memorandum, or simply via handwritten scrawl in the margins of legal briefs or even on maps.[7]

President Grant sought to standardize the form and style of executive orders in 1873, a fragile forebear of the process that would later evolve into the institution of central clearance. At the time, though, things were far from systematic. Orders were not assigned numbers until 1907, when the State Department sought to organize those already issued into a chronological sequence.[8] President Theodore Roosevelt's order of November 9, 1907, expanding a Navajo reservation in Arizona and New Mexico, became Executive Order 709, and the series went forward from there. But this was based on State having decided that an October 1862 directive from Abraham Lincoln would be Executive Order 1, disregarding anything issued earlier. Even then there were many gaps, because not all departments cooperated with State's efforts and because State itself made errors in the compilation. Orders unearthed after the fact were inserted into the sequence by giving them a suffix, adding "-A" or "-1" or even "½."[9] Odd inconsistencies of nomenclature persisted: for example, an 1868 proclamation by Andrew Johnson announcing the ratification of the Fourteenth Amendment wound up as Executive Order 6. (And also, in slightly different form eight days later, as Executive Order 7.)[10]

All this means that a large number of eighteenth- and nineteenth-century executive orders—almost certainly more than 10,000 and perhaps as many as 50,000—are not in the official count, and there is no way to know the true total.[11] James Hart complained about this in his 1925 book on presidential "ordinance-making," highlighting the difficulty in untangling substantive and hortatory proclamations, executive orders, and various flavors of departmental directive; he devoted an appendix of "technical analysis" to clarifying the types of "executive ordinances" generally, including a guide to readers as to where those might (or should) be published.[12]

That burden was seemingly eased in 1929, when President Herbert Hoover mandated that copies of all directives be sent to the State Department when they were issued.[13] But compliance was uneven, and the explosion of dozens of new agencies and thousands of associated administrative orders during the early New Deal exacerbated the problem in oddly tangible ways—since even executive departments did not always know what orders were actually in effect. Kenneth Mayer notes that when the 1934 case *United States v. Smith* approached the Supreme Court, a government attorney discovered that a poorly drafted 1933 EO had actually rescinded the regulation under which Smith was being prosecuted. No one had kept track of the new language, and dropping the charges did not save an assistant attorney general from a fifteen-minute tongue-lashing by the Justices in a related case's oral arguments a few months later.[14] As the White House admitted to the attorney general in March 1934, "the actual issuance of executive orders and regulations is accompanied with rather amazing informality."[15] Finally, in 1935, Congress passed the Federal Register Act, requiring that all executive orders and proclamations—along with many other federal documents—be officially printed in a new government publication.[16] On March 14, 1936, EO 7316 (enlarging a migratory bird refuge in South Carolina) had pride of place as the first document published in volume 1, number 1, of the *Federal Register*.[17]

The new mandate didn't solve every problem for those tracking executive orders. Not just EO 9744-A but -B and -C as well, unclassified orders all signed the same day in June 1946, had to be shoehorned into the numerical order after brief misplacement by record keepers. That same year, the Interior Department released to the *Federal Register* both a "new" 1942 order and some eighteen confidential land transfers issued under its auspices: "Withdrawing Public Lands for Use of War Department for Military Purposes" retrospectively became EO 9153-A. In the late 1950s an EO from the late 1940s dealing with the imminent diplomatic recognition of Korea (not yet South Korea) became 10026-A; as a Bureau of the Budget memo explained, the "restrictive confidential status was appended to the order to prevent possible premature release of knowledge" regarding Korea's shift to sovereignty from military occupation.[18]

Good government types in the executive branch had recurrent hopes they could rationalize the way EOs were numbered, shifting away from a cumulative list to a series denominated by year, like public laws—changing Executive Order 11073 to "Executive Order 1963–1," EO 11074 to EO 1963–2, and so on. Indeed, the BoB's Harold Seidman declared in 1962 that "the present method of numbering . . . is an utterly primitive one. . . . It is self-evident, we think, that the identification by means of a perpetual chronological numerical series is unworkable in the long run." But the Office of the Federal Register found the matter less obvious and the proposed changes were abandoned.[19] The sequential system continues to this day, and as of October 1, 2020, the official count stood at 13,951.

Central Clearance and Presidential Governance

Even with the occasional hiccups, the genesis of mandated publication solved most of the questions of defining the "universe" of executive orders (and thus made it possible to randomly sample from that universe). So the data set created for the present project begins in 1937, the first full year of the *Federal Register* and the first of Franklin D. Roosevelt's second term.

But there is another important reason to start in that era, one related not to record keeping but to developments in the institutional presidency. With the growth in the size and scope of government, and the concomitant expansion of both the executive branch and the White House staff, administrative tactics generally became more central to presidential leadership.[20] The number of executive orders grew dramatically as statute delegated more authority to the president, and through him to the executive branch. In his four years in office, Herbert Hoover issued just under 1,000 EOs; FDR exceeded that total before his first term was halfway through.

As the frequency of these sorts of transactions rose, so did the president's need for information about what they meant. Recall the earlier discussion of "governance structures": these arise to constrain opportunism and error in the face of uncertainty and bounded rationality, to take advantage of "asset specificity" (in this case, bureaucratic expertise), and generally to lessen whatever informational costs a particular recurring class of transactions imposes. Franklin Roosevelt's answer to those needs was to impose the institution of central clearance, housed in the Bureau of the Budget (BoB), which became the Office of Management and Budget (OMB) in 1970.[21] As Richard Neustadt describes it, in establishing central clearance Roosevelt "sought to protect both President from agencies and agencies from one another"—a useful intuition to which we will return.[22]

The BoB itself was created in 1921 by the Budget and Accounting Act in order to help the president prepare a comprehensive and unified executive budget each year.[23] At the time, departments and agencies sent their funding requests directly to Congress, giving little scope for unified management or, for that matter, a coherent sense of how each program fit into national needs and priorities. BoB was a nod toward the best principles of contemporary public administration, which viewed the president as a true chief executive in the sense that phrase applied in the private sector. As a 1921 business journal put it, the president must "successfully administer the biggest business in the world despite the interferences of Congress."[24]

Yet "by the standards of business," the article went on, "he cannot successfully do any such thing. . . . [A] dozen big business men combined into one could not do it—because he hasn't the instruments with which to work." The BoB was designed as such an instrument. As its first director, Charles G. Dawes, put it in a speech to executive branch officials shortly after the Bureau's creation: "the President is simply putting into effect for the first time in this country a condition which exists in any business corporation."[25]

The new Bureau resided within the Treasury Department, though as an independent entity: the president appointed its director and assistant director without Senate confirmation, and they in turn reported directly to him rather than through the Treasury secretary. BoB had the authority to "assemble, correlate, revise, reduce, or increase the estimates of the several departments or establishments" as well as to "secure greater economy and efficiency" in government through managerial reforms. Again, this was consistent with Progressive-era notions of hierarchical, non-partisan technical management. "The Basic Principles of Budget Operation in the United States" that Dawes announced in June 1921 held that "the Budget Bureau must be impartial, impersonal, and non-political." The director disavowed any power over statutory substance: he was merely an advisor "in the matter of correcting business administration" for the "Government business corporation."[26]

Even so Dawes saw the opportunity for what he called "the reorganization of the routine business of government through the use by the president of the Budget Bureau as an agency of executive pressure, and the creation . . . of coordinating machinery out of the body of the existing business organization."[27] In December 1921, a BoB Circular (already the forty-ninth such decree) told executive branch agencies that any proposal, "the effect of which would be to create a charge upon the public Treasury or commit the Government to obligations which would later require appropriation to meet them, should be first submitted" to BoB before it went to Congress. This would allow the Bureau to determine whether it was "in accord with the financial program of the President."[28] This power play, however, was implemented only intermittently for the next decade-plus.

That changed in 1934. Neustadt recounts that FDR's first budget director, Lewis Douglas, was not fully versed in the "old orders," which went unenforced in 1933—but that Roosevelt himself revived the issue the next year, giving Circular 49 new teeth in association with the flurry of new policy proposals that marked the New Deal.[29] The range of policies subject to BoB review expanded as well. In late 1935, the president directed that the Bureau should receive copies of all executive-proposed legislation.[30]

This prompted some Cabinet-level pushback. As Secretary of Labor Frances Perkins asked the president, "Why should one refer to the Bureau of the Budget a question of policy? It seems a peculiar thing to do. . . . You say the Director of the Budget passes upon the question as to whether the project is worth the price?" Roosevelt quickly denied it. Non-budgetary items would be passed on to his Cabinet-level National Emergency Council, he said: "[If] it is a fiscal matter involving the expenditure of money, one way or the other, it clears through the Director of the Budget. . . . He gives me factual information about finances, that is all."[31]

Still, FDR's disavowal didn't last long. When the NEC was phased out in 1937, BoB took over not only its records but its coordinating functions.[32] And that merely foreshadowed the expansion of BoB's duties that accompanied its shift into the new Executive Office of the President (EOP) and the appointment of Harold D. Smith as budget director, both in 1939.[33] Smith, a professional public administrator and aggressive advocate of executive-centered leadership in government, soon created a Legislative Reference Division to replace an earlier Division of Coordination. The new nomenclature was supposed to sound less threatening, hiding its new powers: but as Smith reminded FDR several years later, coordination was still the aim. "Recognition of the necessity for coordination was the basic reason for transferring the Bureau of the Budget from the Treasury Department to the Executive Office of the President," he wrote, a transfer that enhanced presidential leverage "in all fields of governmental activities."[34] This was entirely consonant with Dawes's focus on the Bureau's use as "an agency of executive pressure" and the importance of administrative "machinery"—a word that Roosevelt himself had used as early as 1919, when as assistant secretary of the Navy he had testified to Congress about strengthening presidents' ability to direct the actions of the growing executive branch.[35] That machinery was very much intended to help him determine whether a project was worth the price.

Even as FDR was hardening this philosophy into organizational form by creating the EOP, he began utilizing BoB to coordinate the preparation of executive orders. Attention to EOs' stylistic formatting had begun in the 1920s, most notably with President Hoover's 1929 directive to standardize punctuation and place-names and to require a certain number of copies on a specific kind of paper. (For the record, that paper was to be 8″ by 12½″, though some in BoB had wanted smaller sheets, to cut costs. "Immemorial custom should give way to utility and progress when an annual saving of 30 per cent is involved," pleaded one budget hawk.)[36] Recall that Hoover had also tasked the State Department with proofreading draft EOs, but without any power of substantive review.

A dramatic change came in August 1933 with Roosevelt's EO 6247, which required that "the draft of an Executive order or proclamation shall first be submitted to the Director of the Bureau of the Budget," and if approved at BoB, to the attorney general. The latter was given the job of analyzing the order "for form and legality." From Justice, the order did go to State, to check on formatting and style, before the president finally received an official copy to sign. Three years later, to State's displeasure, its role was assumed by the staff of the newly created *Federal Register*, which as noted above had become the official publisher of executive orders.[37]

That 1936 order, EO 7298, made two other more important changes as well. It required proposed EOs to cite the statutory or constitutional authority justifying their issuance. And it strengthened the veto points at Budget and Justice: "If [the proposed order] is disapproved by the Director of the Bureau of the Budget or the Attorney General," Roosevelt directed, "it shall not thereafter be presented to the President unless it is accompanied by the statement of the reasons for such disapproval." As such, BoB approval of an executive order became a standard part of the wider process of central clearance also extended to legislative proposals, agency communications with Congress, and enrolled bills ready for the president's signature or veto. (Much later, agency-issued regulations were included too.)[38] The 1939 reorganization order that moved BoB into the new Executive Office of the President specified that the executive order review process remained one of the Bureau's core duties.[39]

So it remains today. These days the governing authority is John F. Kennedy's EO 11030, "Preparation, Presentation, Filing and Publication of Executive Orders and Proclamations," issued in 1962 and still in effect sixty years later. To Roosevelt's central clearance "machinery" Kennedy added the mandate that those seeking issuance of an order had to include documentation "explaining the nature, purpose, background, and effect of the proposed Executive order or proclamation and its relationship, if any, to pertinent laws and other Executive orders or proclamations." This was needed, staff at BoB argued, because they (and thus the president) frequently did not have "from the agencies adequate information in support of the proposed order. . . . Such information has frequently been meager and has necessitated requests for additional material."[40] BoB had always tried to educate itself anyway, as this suggests. But the new directive strengthened its hand in terms of reducing presidential uncertainty and undercutting opportunities for agency opportunism.

Subsequent amendments to central clearance have been largely cosmetic. In 1987, Ronald Reagan finally removed the term "Bureau of the Budget" from operative executive orders, replacing it with "Office of Management and Budget" a mere seventeen years after the agency reorganized and changed names. In 2006 George W. Bush deleted previous orders' references to items being literally "typewritten," and allowed them to be submitted on standard legal-size paper. The only shifts in the mandated formulation procedure came in 1978, when OMB was authorized to send commemorative proclamations (honoring "National Safe Boating Week" and the like) directly to the president without requiring the attorney general to approve them, and in 2014, when preparation of the highly technical trade proclamations issued under the 1974 Trade Act was formally vested in the office of the United States Trade Representative rather than in OMB.[41]

But those changes did not alter the substantive heart of the institution, which served and serves as a key management mechanism for presidents. Again, for present purposes we want to keep central clearance in mind as an informational governance structure that provides feedback regarding the "make or buy" decision analogized in chapter 2. The process allows OMB, on behalf of the president, to tally the substantive and political costs and benefits of orders formulated in different ways, and to enforce what it sees as the president's own interests.[42] The next section traces examples and variants of that process as it applies to executive orders.[43]

Central Clearance, Step by Step

How does central clearance work, in practice? While there are exceptions to any given rule, there is a standard operating procedure, its sequence proceeding in five basic steps.

1. Does It "Smell Like an Executive Order"?

The OMB general counsel's office runs the EO central clearance process and should be the first stop for drafts of proposed EOs from whatever source. (Usually the office of the White House counsel gets some sort of early heads-up. But as new Ford counsel Phil Buchen was instructed, "OMB performs the coordinating function.")[44]

Often the counsel's office will ask personnel in OMB's subject-matter divisions, the Resource Management Offices (RMOs), for their feedback.[45] RMO staffers may already have caught wind of the order from their ongoing work with the division's assigned agencies. In some cases, depending "on the sophistication of the agency player," the originator will have worked with OMB and/or one of the White House–centered policy councils in advance of providing the draft.[46] A Reagan-era memo on this point notes that OMB staff were "working with NSC staff, White House Counsel, and the Department of Agriculture to structure" a proposed EO (on private sector aid to Polish farmers) that "will probably be submitted within a week or so."[47] Often, then, what OMB formally receives is not the very first draft of the order.

Even so, some proposals wind up rejected out of hand. When Roosevelt aide Harry Hopkins sought an executive order to create a new Farm-to-Market Roads Administration during the New Deal, for instance, BoB staff reacted strongly. "More rattle-brained thinking on administrative problems by Hopkins," one analyst grumbled in a handwritten memo to the files. "His overhead—front—call it what you will—is without a shred of justification." Thus: "NO as to issuance of EO," BoB decided: "will accomplish informally."[48] Likewise, late in the Carter administration a White House aide sent OMB a "draft EO that Stu would like to have signed as soon as possible," referring to top domestic policy advisor Stuart Eizenstat. An OMB attorney recorded subsequent phone calls with passive-aggressive pleasure: "Told him this doesn't look, smell, or read like an Executive order. . . . [He] said he would talk to 'Stu' and call back." In the return call "he says 'Stu' still wants an Executive order. I told him to dream up something to put in it and contact me next week."[49]

The first question, in short—one reprised in more detail in chapter 7—is whether a proposal should *be* an executive order.

After that comes how it should be crafted. OMB is sometimes commissioned to draft EOs outright, on behalf of other EOP staff or occasionally for an agency; it also does early editing of orders, seeking to avoid hortatory language and imprecision.[50] One overwrought Treasury draft order proposed in 1948 was met "with interest, and some amusement. . . . I have a small hunch that language of this character is slightly inappropriate."[51] In 1974, Ford White House staffer David Gergen passed along edits suggested by the OMB general counsel: "Would strongly recommend that the preamble be tightened up considerably. . . . Ordinarily, Executive Orders are fairly legal in nature and the preambles are kept very short—so short, in fact, that in a case like this you might even want to issue the preamble as a separate statement."[52] In 2001, an EO creating a new Office of Faith-Based and Community Initiatives saw the soaring rhetoric of its opening section toned down quite dramatically during its short stay in OMB. The first draft's "Government can rally a military, but it cannot put hope in our hearts or a sense of purpose in our lives. . . . The indispensable and transforming work of faith-based and other charitable service groups must be front and center," became simply: "Faith-based and other community organizations are indispensable in meeting the needs of poor

Americans." (One staffer recalled of the original: "there was a lot of eye-rolling at the time.")[53] Of course, presidents who affirmatively want flowery language will get it: the Trump administration greatly expanded EOs' hortatory preambles, incorporating effusive self-promotion more normally included in accompanying talking points into the text of the order itself. Trump's 2019 EO on collating citizenship data, for instance, ran eleven pages—eight of which were comprised of a "policy" section that doubled as a press release, complete with first-person editorial commentary.[54]

Another drafting concern is agency efforts to include self-promoting language loudly affirming their role in a given policy area, presumably with the notion of establishing a precedent for later claims. In 1948 BoB staff urged revising EOs that might spur copycat crimes, in a manner of speaking: "I feel sure approval of this Order will in turn stimulate other Departments or Agencies to develop proposals for including themselves in the party."[55] In the 1960s, complaining about a similar tactic, BoB observed that "the occupancy of a proper foreign policy role by the Department of State should not be dependent upon constant reiteration of statements of that role."[56]

Even once EOs pass these thresholds, OMB continues to evaluate them for their impact on presidential power, with a particular eye on the presidency as an office as much as on behalf of the current incumbent. Language that seeks to limit presidential discretion over appointees to a given entity (e.g., requiring a "fairly balanced" membership or overweighting a board with unpredictable public members), or that creates organizations whose mandates are not "clearly defined and bounded," is routinely shorn.[57] As the OMB general counsel has put it, "It is sufficient to achieve whatever balance the President desires . . . by the appointment of members"; more exact specification "would be an artificial and restrictive provision."[58] In discussions over whether to use an EO to create a Water Resources Council, a body promised in a legislative message John F. Kennedy had sent to Congress, BoB noted that "as a matter of policy, we believe it is preferable for such interagency coordinating bodies to be created by Executive Order rather than by statute. . . . [The] legislative route has no advantage over an Executive Order, but it has the major disadvantage of tying the President's hands with respect to establishing the most appropriate method for coordinating executive agencies and revising the method as need arises without resort to Congress."[59] In a similar vein, BoB has railed against the "so-called independence" of the regulatory agencies and urged they advise the president directly. (As one staffer commented, "I agree! . . . There is no substitute for the President!")[60]

Likewise, consider EO 9806 of November 1946, which dealt with the Inter-departmental Committee to Consider Cases of Subversive Activities on the Part of Federal Employees (mercifully, the ICCCSAPFE was later renamed the Interdepartmental Committee on Employee Investigations, or ICEI). ICEI's authority was expiring and there were substantial political demands to continue to keep the matter of "subversion" on the front burner. BoB was skep-tical of the substantive need for more permanent attention to the question. "The real problem is that of the necessity to continue any central function in this field," it concluded, given the "overemphasis on this form of unfitness due to the war" and the political dynamics that would soon enough manifest in McCarthyism. But the Bureau was even more concerned with allowing Con-gress to vest this responsibility in statute in a new agency insulated from the president.[61] After a flurry of quiet negotiation with Justice and the Civil Ser-vice Commission, BoB staff helped White House counsel Clark Clifford's of-fice seize on a House of Representatives subcommittee report recommending a study of loyalty issues. It devised a new order doing just that, via a temporary interagency group chaired by the attorney general. This at least punted the issue past the midterm elections and into 1947—when Truman, under con-tinuing pressure, issued a new EO establishing a Loyalty Review Board based on the temporary group's recommendations, largely to fend off continuing legislative interest in creating a new and very differently structured indepen-dent agency devoted to these concerns.[62]

At times OMB has to lecture other parts of the executive branch—including the White House—about the limits of presidential power. Anec-dotal evidence, at least, suggests this was a common task in the Trump years.[63] More broadly, since EOs are often used to create advisory committees, how to fund those committees becomes a key issue in their formulation: the long-standing "Russell Rider" requires that after one year they receive congressional authorization. That complication hampered a 1980 EO creating a Nuclear Safety Oversight Committee after the Three Mile Island reactor meltdown. The EOP's Office of Science and Technology Policy (OSTP) created the origi-nal draft, and a variety of White House and departmental offices were asked for comment. The Department of Energy wanted to keep the new committee under its purview, while OSTP put it under Health and Human Services (HHS) on the grounds of "optics" (since Energy might be thought to have an interest in covering up its own potential regulatory failings). For its part HHS thought the committee should be independent, to avoid "even the appearance" of conflicts of interest for the administration generally.[64] Meanwhile the White

House pushed back against any termination date for the committee, given the gravity of its task; perhaps it could be renewed before the year was up? "Is this adequate to circumvent the requirements for Congressional authorization?"

A scrawled scolding from OMB said no: "This should be done by legislation. There is no Presidential authority to renew *without* congressional approval. It is an essential administrative control that no suggestion of renewal is made." Further, if the committee were to have "real authority"—staff, subpoena power, and the like—it would also need legislation, if only to allow a department to transfer funds to it. As an advisory committee, OMB noted, it would not really be targeted toward oversight: "it needs to give advice," although admittedly it "need not have responsibility to come up with a lot of *new* recommendations."[65] In the end, the committee was created with the short termination date imposed by the Russell Rider (albeit with hopes of obtaining a legislative extension); it would advise the president ("it is not a body to advise the agencies how or what to do"); and its enforcement power would be limited to "public exposure (good and bad)."[66]

2. Agency Feedback: The Views Letter

OMB must also consider substantive questions specific to the utility and quality of the order. Will the order actually work? Who can shed light on the programmatic or technical questions involved? How will an EO affect other agencies and policies? To answer these questions, OMB requests input on the draft order from any executive agencies (including separate offices within the EOP) with potential interest in its issuance. This both supplements its own analysis and gives other political actors notice of what their colleagues are suggesting. Even the seemingly innocuous gets feedback: a proposed official seal for the EOP's Cost of Living Council got so much, in fact, that it was never issued.[67]

The formal version of OMB's request is the "views letter" (these days normally sent by email but in the past by messenger, then fax), which usually comes from the OMB general counsel "on behalf of the Director." The letter largely follows a standard format: it cites the EO 11030 clearance process, notes the title of the enclosed proposed executive order, identifies the originator of the draft, and attaches a copy thereof. It asks for "any comments you may have concerning this proposal" and gives a date by which those comments should be returned to OMB.[68]

The time allowed for comment varies greatly, contingent on the importance of the order, on whether it is being issued because of an external event or deadline, and on the degree of departmental or White House pressure. That last can be gamed—as one BoB lawyer put it in 1959, the "pressing of the State Department for rapid action should be preceded by knowledge as to actual urgency."[69] In general, as one recent OMB general counsel noted, "our least favorite" orders were "those that came out of presidential scheduling," where White House aides decide to give heft to an impending event by having the president announce the signing of a new EO.[70] In such cases the clearance process speeds up to match the motorcade. (See chapter 6 for more on the timing of EO development.)

Mostly, departments want to have their say and aggressively seek to be dealt in. The Department of Agriculture, catching word of its omission from a distribution list, scolded BoB for the oversight "in view of the fact that this department has a vital interest . . . which has not, in our view, been taken fully into account in the two drafts previously submitted."[71] Occasionally, though, departments seek a low profile on orders that might entangle them with their own constituency. In 1940, for instance, the War Department proposed an EO forbidding entry to the Panama Canal Zone to workers striking against the government. Agency personnel responsible for being solicitous toward strikers decided that discretion was the better part of valor: a BoB notation indicates that "the Department of Labor appreciates very much this matter *not* being referred to it by the Budget."[72]

The process churns on irrespective of external drama. Exactly one day after Franklin Roosevelt's sudden death, Secretary of War Henry Stimson proposed an order granting higher rental allowances for enlisted personnel; BoB put aside its mourning long enough to push back on the measure's costs and demand it receive full clearance.[73] EO 11799, for its part, arose from a proposal developed by the Department of Defense Office Personnel Management Study Group and was issued on August 17, 1974. This would not be notable except that the central clearance process bridged the rather notable events of August 9, when Richard Nixon became the first president to resign his office. The Pentagon had much to do with the second EO issued in the Ford administration; President Ford, rather less.[74]

Just as striking, perhaps, was an EO proposed on October 8, 1962, imposing "prohibitions on vessels engaged in trade with Cuba." An interagency group led by the State and Commerce Departments sought to prevent ships using Cuban ports from using U.S. ports as well. Agencies who had been asked for comment seemed to take little notice when the famous "thirteen days" of the Cuban Missile Crisis ensued barely a week later. Even after John F. Kennedy's

October 22 address announcing the naval blockade of the island their letters kept flowing back to BoB without reference to ongoing events. It would be nice, the Bureau's general counsel finally told Kennedy aide Ted Sorensen, if someone concerned with "the present Cuban situation" could pass along views "as to whether, or when, the proposed order should be issued."[75]

3. Tabulation and Assessment of Views

Agency comments return to OMB by mechanisms ranging from a formal letter over a departmental secretary's signature to a quick phone message. Back in the general counsel's office they are tabulated and assessed. Feedback might fluctuate from "unequivocally opposed" (Commerce, 1968) to "strongly recommends for signature by the President at the earliest possible time" (Defense, 1951) to a sort of baffled apathy (many, often).[76] Agency views, as Obama administration attorney John Bies notes, may provide both "policy-based" and "law-based" commentary.[77]

"No objection" is a common response, though OMB learns to read between the lines; one of its former general counsels notes that when it is clear that the political winds are blowing against an agency's preferences this can mean "no *formal* objection."[78] Agencies certainly try to read the tea leaves as to a particular proposal's standing in the intra-administration balance of power. In May 2002, for instance, the chair of the Interior Department's Advisory Council on Historic Preservation submitted a proposed order that would "promote the preservation and effective use of the many historic properties held by Federal agencies." Substantive pushback against the idea of more "use" came from the Army, which pointed out that the Corps of Engineers had oversight of some 45,000 prehistoric archaeological sites meant to be protected from tourists, not attract them. But for its part the Commerce Department raised the question of why Interior was making this move: "*we* already have a place that this could go," OMB's handwritten notes of a meeting with the department record. Commerce went on to say "our econ[omic] development people say this isn't needed"—careful to note this was an "unofficial" view pending the answer to another query: "Is there some W[hite] H[ouse] interest[?]" As the OMB note-taker put it, "They will go if *WH* staff wants it. But if it's staff at [the Interior Department's] Council then . . . much less concerned." The assistant counsel checked to find "there *is* senior WH staff interest": enough, it seems, to keep the process going. After additional revisions and meetings into the spring of 2003, EO 13287 was finally issued that March.[79]

In general, then, agency consultation can result in rapid internal sign-off of the EO; in more edits, light or heavy; or in a request that the originator defend the extant draft against criticism, perhaps with a revised draft sent out once more for repeated clearance. Multiple drafts, and multiple rounds of comments, are not uncommon.

As the Clinton child health order case in chapter 1 made clear (and as emphasized again in chapter 4), that is because agency feedback throws up new information and spurs a good deal of negotiation. In many ways the clearance process is a bargaining mechanism seeking both to reach agreement between departmental and presidential interests and to understand what those interests are or should be. Whether an EO originates in the department or the White House—recall that EOP drafts are not systematically privileged in the process—OMB has generally emphasized gaining consensus, on ensuring where possible that the entire executive branch agrees on the text of an order moving forward. Acting BoB director Percival Brundage summed up this goal nicely in 1954. In the preparation of a current EO, he said, "the comments of the various affected agencies with respect to earlier drafts of these documents have been taken into consideration and have been accommodated as far as appears to be practicable, bearing in mind particularly the sum total of agency views and the sometimes opposed views of agencies upon the same point."[80]

Achieving that outcome can spur a long process of sequential appeasement. "We have been actively negotiating for the past three weeks or more with OPM [Office of Production Management], OPA [Office of Price Administration], War, Navy, Agriculture, the Economic Defense Board, and other interested agencies, in an effort to reconcile the many conflicting proposals originally presented to us," Harold Smith told FDR in late 1941, sending along the fruits of that effort.[81] A series of reports updating the Reagan White House on "changes in the status of executive orders" document morph progress from agency "concerns" to "we expect to resolve those concerns" to "we have resolved the concerns" (and thus to "forwarded to Justice") over the course of weeks or months.[82]

In an even more extended 1962 case the Department of the Interior produced a draft order (appended to a draft letter it had prepared, having the president direct the secretary of the interior to submit such an order) in mid-February. The order gave Interior the authority to coordinate administration policy regarding outdoor recreation. Rather than suggest the president sign Interior's instructions to itself, BoB produced a rival draft and wound up sending out both that and Interior's original for clearance. Other agencies, most vehemently the Department of Agriculture, quickly objected to what they saw as Interior's effort to grab additional authority: "this Department has consistently opposed" such proposals, shot back Agriculture Secretary Orville Freeman, attaching yet another draft order that downgraded Interior and elevated Agriculture instead. "We believe our position to be fundamental."[83]

A long back-and-forth ensued; by the end of March, Bureau staff reported that all objections had been met except for Agriculture's—and that Agriculture was, to be blunt, wrong. Even so BoB leadership continued to soothe various agency feelings and asked for another set of revisions. When that did not resolve matters, the next offer was of a BoB-brokered summit meeting between Freeman and Interior Secretary Stewart Udall—meanwhile a placating letter from BoB deputy director Elmer Staats to Udall sent yet another version of the EO, in the "hope that something along the lines of the attached might meet as far as possible the different views of the two agencies in this order." And by mid-April the logjam was finally broken, by having Agriculture and Interior rotate the chair of the new coordinating committee the order established. As well he might have, Freeman sent Staats an appreciative note: "Thank you for your patience and thoughtful consideration of our points of view." EO 11017 was finally issued on April 27.

At times, of course, gridlock must be resolved by a definitive ruling on the side of one agency over another. Regarding one Ford administration EO dealing with the delegation of functions under the Foreign Assistance Act, an OMB staffer noted that "this matter is at such a relative impasse between State and Treasury that we recommend the following course: Return the file to Treasury, with agency letters, indicating State's counter proposal and requesting Treasury's reaction thereto. Then, let's see what happens." Two months later, nothing had; OMB noted, rather wistfully, "we could, of course, kill the whole matter by requesting [the Defense Department] to come up with a complete rewrite . . . it is highly unlikely that State, DOD, and Treasury would be able to agree upon a clean Order." The EO was finally issued three months later, after political decision makers ruled in Treasury's favor.[84]

As all of this makes clear, both the thrust and exact wording of EOs receive substantial agency—and OMB—attention. Not all input is created equal: even agency staff concede that some is "crazy" and some "not-so-crazy."[85] But even the crazy gets sorted through. C. Boyden Gray, George H. W. Bush's White House counsel, told one scholar that "a lot of care [goes] into the drafting. . . . You could get into heated arguments over the use of a particular word."[86] Likewise a deputy White House counsel in the Obama administration recently noted that "an incredible amount of work" goes into "resolving differences" to craft an order that reflects agencies' input.[87]

4. Form and Legality

A draft order negotiated, it must gain approval as to "form and legality" from the Justice Department. The attorney general normally delegates this work to the Office of Legal Counsel (OLC), which prepares a memorandum certifying the order.[88] That memo can consist of one substantive sentence ("the proposed Executive order is acceptable as to form and legality") or, in the case of Ronald Reagan's famous 1981 EO formalizing regulatory review in OMB, eighteen single-spaced pages defending its constitutionality.[89] It can mean no substantial change—or, as the attorney general told the president in 1958, it can mean an EO "completely revised in the interest of form and legality" (though Ike was assured that "no change has been made to its basic purpose").[90]

"Form" simply means the EO adheres to stylistic norms and standards (some of which are required by additional EOs, as detailed earlier) and that it makes correct reference to the statutes or constitutional authorities on which it relies.[91] William Rehnquist, then in charge of OLC, told White House counsel John Dean in 1971 that "we will review orders and proclamations with avoidance of unnecessary legal gobbledygook in mind." He noted the "requirements respecting the style of executive orders" but assured Dean that "ponderous language" was not actually mandated.[92]

Questions of "legality" are far less standardized. They range widely, depending on the scope and salience of the order. Still, as Clinton administration OLC attorney Beth Nolan noted, almost all orders other than those "kind of copying another executive order" have "some legal issue that goes beyond the form part."[93] At the least this requires a review of relevant statutory text and judicial precedent. George W. Bush's efforts to expand faith-based initiatives, for instance, meant vetting a variety of constitutional issues governing the relationship of church and state.[94] One of Bush's orders that seemed to implement a major change to the definition of discriminatory employment policy was quickly reined in with what his aide John DiIulio called "black-letter language reiterating" existing law: this was meant as a "hedge or loophole against any possible court challenge," another White House staffer explained.[95]

The steps laid out here are not always purely sequential. It is not uncommon for legal analysis to be occurring simultaneously with other stages of central clearance, or even for an agency to approach OLC for guidance before starting to haggle over an order's politics. After all, it makes little sense to go through the effort of selling the EO to other agencies and the White House only for Justice to determine the order is on shaky legal ground. Charles Cooper, who headed OLC in Reagan's second term, held that "typically executive orders don't make it even to the drafting stage unless legal issues have been identified and pretty well-thought through."[96] Handwritten notes by Elena Kagan, then in the Clinton White House Counsel's office, reminded herself of just this: "EPA draft—late aft[ernoon]. *Comments back from OLC*. Then to OMB—formal distribution. Final draft. Then WD [Walter Dellinger, at OLC] formally approves."[97]

Tobias Gibson's research into OLC's role argues that the key reason few executive orders are overturned in court is the legal vetting done prior to their issuance. As a former OLC attorney notes, "If we felt the order was going beyond the president's power, it was our obligation to point that out and suggest ways that we could rein it in and make it consistent with the statute or Constitution."[98] As that suggests, the default position of OLC, as for most attorneys who work for the president, is to find a legally supportable way of taking the action desired.[99] That dynamic has arguably been enhanced in recent years—especially as partisan polarization makes passing new laws harder—but it is hardly a new development. As far back as 1938, an internal BoB memo refers to an order where DOJ "finally stretched a point and approved it."[100]

Still, Douglas Kmiec, who worked in Reagan's OLC, stresses the opposite, citing a sweeping draft order seeking to ban the sale of obscene material on federal lands or properties (for instance, at retail stores in government office buildings). This proposal ran up against jurisprudence protecting publications like *Playboy* as protected speech under the First Amendment.[101] An earlier proposed EO gives a similar flavor: back in 1956, OLC's J. Lee Rankin wrote to BoB saying he could not sign off on a proposed order "because I feel that certain of its provisions are legally questionable." The way it delegated presidential power seemed to override statutory language: "I have been unable to find anything in [the law] which would legally justify the conclusion that statutory functions of this type may be eliminated by executive order."[102]

Technically, as acting attorney general Sally Yates put it in 2017, "OLC's review is limited to the narrow question of whether, in OLC's view, a proposed Executive Order is lawful on its face and properly drafted. . . . [It] does not address whether any policy choice embodied in an Executive Order is wise or just."[103] But it is worth noting that the Department of Justice also acts as, well, a department—offering advice in line with its institutional interests, sometimes alongside its legal commentary. Perhaps for tactical reasons, it does not always make the distinction clear. In 1962, for instance, DOJ refused to approve a draft order flowing from the new Federal Salary Reform Act. Here its objections were driven more by projections of its own workload than by cautious statutory interpretation. The proposal would have required that each agency position subject to the Classification Act was, in fact, properly classified; it became clear that Justice's take on what it called an "extremely questionable" clause was based on its imposition of "an almost impossible administrative burden upon this Department." After a meeting that the BoB counsel called an opportunity for Justice "to blow off steam," the provision was dropped.[104]

5. Memo to the President

Finally, in accord with EO 11030, OMB formally approves the order. These communications have evolved stylistically over time but give the same basic information to the president.

A 2003 memo from OMB director Mitch Daniels to George W. Bush regarding what would become EO 13293 provides a template. It begins by "forwarding for your consideration a proposed executive order that was prepared by" (in this case) the Department of Defense and by summarizing the order's text (expanding the population of reservists eligible for a service medal). A second section gives background information on the topic, noting two prior EOs relevant to the medal in question going back to 1953. The memo then presents the views of "affected agencies and staff." In this case, given the nature of the order, this section consists of noting that a long list of executive departments, agencies, and White House offices "do not object." As dull as it is, the list nevertheless highlights the rigorous, even paranoiac, nature of the clearance process: it includes forty-two staff units, nineteen of them within the EOP, ranging from the Department of State to the White House Office of Administration. A final section cuts to the chase: "I recommend," says the director, "that you sign the proposed executive order."[105]

Any given iteration of this memo will differ slightly, depending on the details and salience of the proposed order. At times departments may want their continuing objections put on the record, and OMB will justify why those were not dispositive. In other cases OMB provides a long blow-by-blow history of the order in the background information section. Even the director's endorsement can be fervent or lukewarm. In 1944, for instance, Harold Smith complained to FDR that time pressures had curtailed analysis: "Under the existing circumstances I think the draft is reasonably satisfactory. Under other circumstances the concept . . . might have been more fully developed and the delineation of its functions more fully matured before the issuance of the Order."[106] However, since an order that does not receive OMB approval is not (under EO 11030) supposed to make its way to the president, at this stage the formal recommendation is invariably favorable.[107]

Before this memo is sent, there is often an additional round of clearance, within the West Wing itself. This last check is usually coordinated by the staff secretary, ensuring that "relevant constituencies in the White House" are on board with the EO's final text.[108]

Even so, the president doesn't always choose to sign the proposed order. Here, as at any of the other steps above, the EO could move forward, or terminate. The latter happens often enough that the fate of unissued EOs is detailed in chapter 7.

Central Clearance as Information and Negotiation

Is the process of central clearance universally honored and unfailingly effective? Of course not. In some cases parts of it are skipped—perhaps most commonly, formal OLC review.[109] In others it is rushed to meet a real or artificial deadline and becomes (as a BoB staffer put it in 1957) "a rather pro forma ratification of action already announced."[110] The Trump travel ban order that begins this book provides a good example.

There are also instances where central clearance is evaded, by negligence or craft—it is sometimes hard to tell the two apart. JFK staffer Richard Goodwin sent what became the EO establishing the president's committee on equal employment opportunity to BoB on a Saturday morning, demanding immediate approval. Even under the circumstances BoB managed by 2:00 p.m. to get comments back from every affected agency (most of which were, naturally, prefaced by "would like more time to study"). At 2:15 p.m., BoB general counsel Arthur Focke and Assistant Attorney General Nick Katzenbach were called to the White House to meet with Goodwin. The draft was finalized at that meeting, and transmitted to the president via Goodwin at 8:00 p.m. that same Saturday. It was signed by Kennedy on Monday.[111]

More recently, a former OMB manager told his boss, Deputy Associate Director Barry Clendenin, that into the early 1990s those who "didn't want to deal with the executive order process, which had become so ritualized and process-oriented," found it "easiest to just issue a memorandum, which didn't go through [the same] processes." Clendenin himself recalls reviewing multiple drafts of EOs related to his division; when it came to the final draft, OMB associate general counsel Mac Reed "would personally walk around for sign-off on a cover sheet. For the memoranda, it was more of a pickup game."[112] (OMB higher-ups took notice: by the time of the Clinton administration, at least some presidential memoranda had been folded into the formal clearance process. This continued under Bush and by 2010 memoranda were specifically included with EOs in OMB's formal description of its clearance duties.)[113]

Canny agency heads may also take their case directly to the president. In 2001, Vice President Cheney famously gave "emphatic instructions to bypass staff review" as a military order issued by George W. Bush took shape in a matter of hours without input even from the national security advisor. "What the hell just happened?" Secretary of State Colin Powell fumed.[114] Fifty years before, Secretary of Defense Robert McNamara did much the same thing: the archival file for EO 11058, modifying eligibility for the armed services' reserves, consists of a single index card. The card's plaintive text reads, in its entirety,

> The Secretary of Defense brought the order to the White House on October 23rd and took it back to the Pentagon with him after obtaining the President's signature. Someone in his office then transmitted it to the *Federal Register* the next morning, when we became aware of its existence for the first time. A request has been made of the Defense Department for any file or papers that may have accompanied it but as yet none have been received. This constitutes the file so far.[115]

In this instance, McNamara and Defense bypassed the long months of clearance that had been part of an earlier effort by Treasury to amend the Ready Reserve rules as they pertained to the Coast Guard. But central clearance exists to prevent just such an outcome. Recall Neustadt's summary of the process as a talisman of presidential "protection." That word echoes frequently in the relevant record. As BoB general counsel Arthur Focke lobbied for what would become EO 11030, he stressed to Kennedy aide Ted Sorensen the need for an orderly process that would allow all aspects of an issue to be considered before an order was "presented to the President. In most cases," Focke went on, "a proposed order . . . handled under this procedure can be issued more expeditiously, and with greater protection to the President, than one which is presented and processed outside the normal channels."[116] Some two decades later, OLC head Theodore Olson emphasized the "protection this process offers" in helping the president "minimize his exposure to the type of problems which distract disproportionately from the implementation of his policy objectives."[117] For that matter, in a former life, Dick Cheney had underlined to incoming Reagan chief of staff James Baker the importance of "an orderly paper flow" as "the way you protect the President." He told Baker, in comments he later echoed at a public symposium, that "it's not in anyone's interest to get an 'oh by the way' decision"—one made on the fly in an informal bilateral encounter with a single advisor—"and all have to understand that. Can hurt the President."[118]

Here, again, the travel ban order comes to mind—and Richard Goodwin's rush job did not prove out well either. Katzenbach told Goodwin that "although the Attorney General would give his approval to the order, this should not be construed as indicating that the order contained no legal problems." BoB told him that having short-circuited the process—"insufficient to permit thorough consideration" by "either the policy-making officials or the staffs of the agencies concerned"—substantive issues might well remain. Indeed, a warning about the commission's funding soon proved prescient. In a detailed note written for the files, BoB counsel Focke wrote that the White House had concerned itself only with the form of clearance, not its reality. But "a proper clearance, with adequate time for consideration by agency staff members having an interest in the matter, would likely have produced some resolution of the financing problem before the order was issued."[119]

However, the "oh by the way" anecdotes tend to be the exceptions that prove the rule of fidelity to central clearance. As early as 1943 a telephone message slip in the BoB files records a White House staffer calling to say the State Department had sent over an EO—but "I don't know whether it's been to 'you people.' I wonder if I could send it over to you and you see that it goes to the proper people." Subsequent clearance efforts ensued with the Departments of Navy and War.[120] In 1961, Robert F. Kennedy attempted his own end run on behalf of an EO establishing the Administrative Conference of the United States (ACUS). The attorney general sent the EO directly to his brother, saying since it had already been approved by RFK's own staff at Justice it could avoid the clearance process—but the BoB staff pushed back, hard. There were "special reasons" for clearing this order in particular, the Bureau's Hazel Guffey said. Key were informational concerns: the results of a past iteration of ACUS "were never visible to the Bureau," and clearance would help uncover "what agencies think of the benefits" of that prototype. Further, "the president doesn't like inter-agency committees. This is a colossal inter-agency committee, complicated by outside members and numerous subcommittees." And in the end, the draft was cleared.[121] That is, as Lyndon Johnson would later reassure a concerned senator, "the usual way."[122]

Continuity is enforced by regular reminders to incoming administrations about the importance of the institution to the president. In early 1969, Focke stressed to new Nixon aides the role of central clearance in helping the White House learn of budgetary, managerial, and organizational implications raised by a draft order, providing "the best judgment of the Administration as a whole." The process would also avoid "the confusion and embarrassment" that could result from endorsing a request without the key information wider co-ordination and consultation would generate. White House chief of staff H. R. Haldeman certainly did not believe that the executive branch, left to its own devices, would blindly mirror presidential preferences: "the procedure out-lined by Mr. Focke . . . should become standard procedure immediately," he announced. Haldeman even drew a reminder on an affixed Post-it note, in flow-chart form: "Originator" went to "Budget" (as in Bureau of) went to "AG" (the attorney general) went to Counsel (in the White House) went "to Pres."[123]

Twelve years later budget director David Stockman reminded department and agency heads that "EO 11030 continues in effect" and that every proposal for an EO needed to include an explanation of its substance, a rationale for its necessity, and "a recitation of the president's authority to issue" it.[124] And Bill Clinton's transition team sent out similar instructions even before Clinton took office, since "President Clinton might sign one or more executive orders either on Inauguration Day or shortly thereafter." Therefore policymakers needed to keep in mind "the formalities and practicalities of the clearance and approval of proposed Executive Orders before they are transmitted to the President," practicalities the remainder of the document laid out.[125] For its part, as the Bush administration took office in 2001, a five-tab binder was created to guide officials to the documents needed for the "Executive Order Process." These mirrored the steps tracked above, starting with the "White House Office or Executive Agency Request for Executive Order," moving through the gathering of comments and OLC's legal judgment, and providing for the collation of an "OMB Executive Order Package" which contained, among other things, an "abstract of OMB officials approving the order" and the OMB director's memo to the president requesting final signature.[126] Even the Trump administration, where clearance was somewhat haphazard during what one OMB observer called the "totally batshit stuff that was flying in those very early days," was largely if not invariably corralled by the process over time.

Indeed, officials "threw their bodies" on draft EOs to ensure their wider review.[127] Another OMB staffer noted that political officials at the agency had no problems working with careerists there even when White House staffers did; over time, the latter realized that directives failed precisely as OMB had predicted they might, helping them understand the value of the interagency process.[128]

Again, such institutionalization reflects the key elements of the governance structures posited in transaction cost economics. As noted in chapter 2, these are utilized to reduce "friction" in cases where transactions are frequent, providing a recurring interaction that lessens the cost of each iteration. Governance structures are also used where there is significant uncertainty regarding the expected utility of a given action or even regarding its characteristics, where the seller of a given item might mislead, or where there is asset specificity associated with the good being produced. Like a solution to a traditional principal-agent puzzle, they seek to reduce "large demands against cognitive competence," given that actors are self-interested (and perhaps even deceptive) and accurate information is expensive (in terms of time and attention—which are themselves scarce resources).[129]

The production of executive orders fits these criteria quite cleanly. This is clearly a recurring transaction. While the number of EOs issued annually has declined since the 1930s, in part as demands originally placed upon presidential action by statute have been delegated to other bureaucratic actors, there were still an average of 86 orders per year across the 1937–2004 time frame under study here and some 77 orders per year if that chronology is extended through 2019. In most recent years between 30 and 60 EOs have been issued, and this is of course only a subset of the EOs under consideration via central clearance. (As we will see, perhaps a fifth of proposed orders wind up unissued.)

Uncertainty is also rife when it comes to EOs—both about the likely outcome of an order's issuance and about the intentions (and/or competence) of the actor proposing it. Presidents need to be aware of the intended and potential unintended consequences of a proposed EO. Is the substance consistent with presidential preferences? What are the political implications, inside and outside the administration? Is the government capable of implementing it as written? Answering these questions is tied to the management of asset specificity, in terms of targeted subject-matter expertise, which of course is agencies' perpetual edge vis-à-vis their political principals.[130] Along the way, the president obtains the data required to calculate an order's costs and benefits and to determine whether its formulation is best assigned to a given agency or to the EOP, or some mix of both.

All this means that the presidential "protection" urged above rests predominantly on the provision of information. This is the founding purpose of OMB: as Charles Dawes told department and agency representatives back in 1921 that "the first thing which must be clear is the absolute right of the President, through his Budget machinery, to have immediate access to information. . . . I am entitled, because I represent the President, to information, and entitled to that information over the head of any independent department from now on."[131] As the Budget Bureau developed, according to veteran Bureau official Roger Jones, its units became established "in a very firm way as institutional arms of the White House straight across the board from the President on down."[132]

Thus it matters that the central clearance of executive orders is vested in OMB rather than in the White House staff proper—and that EOs proposed by White House staffers are subject to the process as well. The White House, staffed overwhelmingly by short-time political appointees, does not have the substantive expertise or ongoing relationship with the agencies needed; as longtime White House executive clerk William Hopkins scolded Nixon aide Ken Cole, who had tried to run his own clearance process from the West Wing, "the customary way of handling such a request . . . is to refer the request to Budget. . . . In that way," Hopkins concluded, "you get a coordinated recommendation, which you do not have here after nearly three weeks of effort."[133] Utilizing OMB, more than 90 percent of whose 500-person staff is made up of civil servants, takes advantage of one of the EOP's few pockets of institutional memory. Here OMB serves a purpose analogous to an arbitrator, created in the business world to avoid dispute resolution processes (e.g., in the courts) that lack crucial "specialized knowledge of the industry."[134] It may be over-ridden, and on good grounds: as one Reagan-era appointee scrawled, an EO could be "a terrible policy decision—but the correct political decision."[135] Or it may reveal that bureaus do have the resources and will to constrain a presidential initiative. But the president will have the information needed to make that choice.

Conclusions: "Quite Proper as a Presidential Requirement"

The aims of central clearance were summarized nicely in a memo BoB attorney Fred Levi wrote to his counterpart at the Pentagon in 1959, describing what he hoped a newly vetted version of a Defense-drafted EO could achieve. The revision, he said, "represents an attempt to supply text which (1) the Department of Defense can live with, (2) recognizes in some degree the GAO [General Accounting Office] position, and (3) is quite proper as a Presidential requirement."[136] That sort of accommodation, within the bounds of presidential preferences, is key to formulating executive orders.

As Neustadt noted six decades ago, the standard distribution of draft EOs to other agencies helps convince the agencies generally to buy into the process, as an early warning system regarding their counterparts' intentions. But in so doing it brings information to bear that protects the president. It enforces a peer review of sorts that both undercuts the proposing agency's incentive to mislead (given that it is likely to be caught) and allows for objective improvements in quality in the finished product. Of course, in a truly unitary executive it would surely be notable that the president needed "protection" from the agencies, or that he needed procedural insulation against being manipulated by his own executive branch. But the institution of central clearance, which has not changed substantially since the 1930s, meets those very needs.

As a governance structure, central clearance serves a key information-distribution purpose; as a practical matter, it serves as a fulcrum for record keeping. This allows a more systematic evaluation of where executive orders actually come from. Recall that a basic assumption of the process is that EOs will often—perhaps even mostly—be proposed by actors outside the Executive Office of the President. Is this true? That question comes next.

4

Executive Orders

BIRDS, BEES, AND DATA

MANY OF THE EXAMPLES just used to illustrate the stages of central clearance were drawn from the Office of Management and Budget's own files, going back to the 1930s. These files provide rich color commentary on EOs as they traverse the bureaucracy and EOP, detailing the vagaries of executive politics. But with careful coding they also enable us to aggregate anecdotes into data, allowing in-depth analysis of a random sample of more than five hundred EOs issued over a period of nearly seventy years—not to mention more than two hundred additional EOs proposed but never issued during that time.

The central clearance process is based on the notion that the originator of a given executive order can come from anywhere in the executive branch (and occasionally beyond)—indeed, recall that a key assumption of Kennedy's EO 11030 was that proposed executive orders will normally *not* come from the president or White House. The new data here help us assess that assumption far more systematically than has previously been possible. In a perfect world, we could track the pre-issuance history of any given order—who proposed it, whose feedback altered or even stymied it, what combination of input was represented in its final draft. And while the world is far from perfect, this is the approach taken here, as bounded by statistical sampling and real-life record-keeping practices. Where *do* EOs come from? This chapter starts to quantify their provenance, and thus to delineate the "birds and bees" of executive orders.

The OMB Executive Order Files

Even before it became part of the EOP, OMB kept records of proposed executive orders and proclamations, documenting the formulation and clearance of each proposal. These were rapidly systematized and over time were held in sequential files kept by the OMB general counsel's office. When an EO is issued, the file concludes with the order's publication in the *Federal Register*; if it is unissued, the end point of a file is normally some notice of the decision to abandon it.

OMB executive order files dating from the 1930s to the 1980s are housed in the immense National Archives and Records Administration (NARA) facility in College Park, Maryland, as part of NARA's Record Group 51. From the 1930s until the middle of the Reagan administration the EO files are more or less complete, if not always well indexed. (As with most NARA records, the availability and accuracy of relevant finding aids vary inversely with time.) Some classified or otherwise sensitive EO files dating as far back as the 1950s, along with most of the standard files from the late Reagan administration to the George W. Bush years, are currently stored in the Washington National Records Center (WNRC), a NARA facility in Suitland, Maryland. The WNRC is where records go when agencies lack space to keep them on-site but do not want to cede control of them. In short it represents archival purgatory: the records will someday ascend to the glories of College Park, but until that time can be recalled to the less celestial environs of the agency that created them and viewed by others only with permission.

With the help of OMB records officers, I was granted access to OMB executive order files ranging from the mid-1980s through 2004 at the WNRC.[1] Orders more recent than that—and those still considered active or relevant to current work—are still held by OMB itself and were not made available. A Freedom of Information Act request for a number of additional files dating from the 1950s to the 1990s, also held at WNRC, has been pending for more than eighteen months as of this writing, with no substantive response.

Where possible, I supplemented the OMB executive order files with additional archival material held in the Eisenhower, Kennedy, Johnson, Nixon, Ford, Carter, Reagan, and Clinton Presidential Libraries. I also conducted numerous interviews with practitioners and consulted oral histories. Still other relevant documents came from the Library of Congress, from other OMB files and the records of specific departments and agencies housed at NARA,[2] and from private collections, notably the Hoover Institution Archives at Stanford University (especially for the Nixon and Reagan presidencies) and (for Clinton) the Leon Panetta Institute Archives at California State University–Monterey Bay.

The EOs under study here cover the period 1937 through 2004, beginning with the first full year of the *Federal Register* and continuing to the most recent year for which substantial archival data could be obtained. This includes orders from the (second to fourth) F. D. Roosevelt, Truman, Eisenhower, Kennedy, Johnson, Nixon, Ford, Carter, Reagan, G.H.W. Bush, Clinton, and (first) G. W. Bush administrations. Material from the Obama and Trump administrations is incorporated into the analysis as available and appropriate, but not included in the database of EOs. Even so the historical sweep captured here provides a wide range of potential variation, in terms of partisan affiliation and the scope of the presidential agenda. Institutionally, it covers the pre-"imperial" presidency as well as the "imperiled" version of the late 1970s, and includes the later resurgence of presidential efforts to assert unilateral authority.[3]

Over the sixty-eight-year period under study, presidents issued just under 5,850 executive orders. To make archival analysis and coding possible, a random sample of 544 EOs was drawn from that universe of orders.[4] The sampled orders were then located in the OMB files and, as described below, coded for centralization and other relevant variables.

Since the formulation process—not the overall number of orders—is the element of interest, the sample was stratified by administration in order to ensure a steady number of initiatives over time and to avoid oversampling from more active presidents. It also allows reliable generalizations across administrations; there is no theoretical reason to think that the managerial cost-benefit analysis of EO formulation will vary by individual president, but that assumption can be tested. The target sampling frame was 32 orders per four-year presidential term—thus, 32 for a one-term president like Jimmy Carter, and 64 for someone who served eight years, such as Dwight Eisenhower.[5] That figure was prorated for partial terms, where those were cut short by death (FDR, JFK) or resignation (Nixon).

This approach means that summary statistics for the sample will be presented both weighted and unweighted. If stratification avoids oversampling from more active presidents, weighting avoids too much stress on the output of less active presidents. That is, it corrects for the fact that some proposals were more likely to have been included in the sample than others, since an equal number were selected per presidential term and the number of EOs issued per term varies by president (recall from chapter 1 that the annual number of issued EOs generally declines during the period under study). Weighting thus allows us to draw more accurate generalizations about the entire population of EOs over time.[6]

In the analyses below, of course, n will vary quite widely across various specifications, since where insufficient facts were available regarding a given

TABLE 4.1. Coded Executive Orders, by Administration

Years	President	# Orders in Sample	# Orders Coded
1937–45	Franklin D. Roosevelt	67	66
1945–53	Harry S. Truman	61	61
1953–61	Dwight D. Eisenhower	64	64
1961–63	John F. Kennedy	23	23
1963–69	Lyndon B. Johnson	41	41
1969–74	Richard M. Nixon	45	44
1974–77	Gerald Ford	19	19
1977–81	Jimmy Carter	32	32
1981–89	Ronald Reagan	64	64
1989–93	George H. W. Bush	32	32
1993–2001	Bill Clinton	64	37
2001–4	George W. Bush	32	32
Total		544	515

variable associated with a given observation, no code was assigned. Table 4.1 summarizes the number of orders whose files yielded enough information to code the formulation process with some confidence. The total is 515 orders, with the largest discrepancy coming from the Clinton years. Even so, more than 35 orders from the Clinton administration are included in the analysis.[7]

Two additional collections of data from the OMB files were also used at different times. During the early stages of this research, systematic EO files from the Kennedy and Reagan administrations were the first to be unearthed. I coded as many of these as possible, since it was not then clear that a wider historical sweep would be possible. Thus, data are available for a total of 42 JFK orders and 70 Reagan orders, rather than the 23 and 64 orders, respectively, required for the sampling frame ultimately chosen. Some scattered EO files located in those early research visits were also coded, even though the EOs in question were not in the final sample; these represent another 16 EOs in total, scattered across administrations.

To obtain the smaller number of EOs, the collection of EOs coded for a given president was itself sampled. Thus the "correct" number of 23 and 64 orders, for Kennedy and Reagan, respectively, can readily be utilized. But the sin of discarding data can be avoided when looking at just the Kennedy or Reagan administration, or when cross-administration comparisons are not being drawn. This brings the total n as high as 556 in some of the aggregate analysis presented below and in future chapters. As discussed there, the additional observations do not change the descriptive statistics associated with any given administration and make no substantive differences to the quantitative analysis.

A second trove of data is more intriguing, and more consequential. My archival excavations unearthed some 238 unissued orders that could be coded along the same dimensions as the issued EOs. Because the scope of the universe of unissued orders is unknown—as detailed later, it may represent 20 percent of all proposed EOs—the collection of unissued EOs here cannot be assumed to be a representative sample of that universe. That said, there is no evidence they are consistently distinct from the broader pool on any particular dimension. All we know is that they were not rejected out of hand: they "lived" long enough to be worthy of a file in the first place. And they are numerous enough be systematically as well as substantively useful.

All told these previously unstudied records, of both issued and unissued EOs, allow for numerous new avenues of inquiry. Primarily, of course, they enable a far richer narrative of executive order formulation, from the EO's origin somewhere in the executive branch—or occasionally outside it—to its issuance or abandonment. They trace various vectors of influence: who had a say, and with what outcome? In short, they track the provenance of a given order—and thus help us understand the ways presidents interact with the wider bureaucracy in producing these directives. We can create a taxonomy of orders that sheds light on the dynamic principal-agent models outlined earlier, on both ends of the street. What is the relative sway of departments and agencies vis-à-vis the EOP in any given case? Since each EO can be coded according to how centralized its formulation process was—that is, how much involvement the president's closest advisors had in its creation and development—we can utilize that information as a variable in concert with a range of other political and managerial contexts. This in turn allows qualitative, archival data to be used as the basis of large-n quantitative analysis. Such multivariate analysis makes up the heart of chapters 5 and 6.

The remainder of the present chapter describes the coding of the order formulation process and provides numerous examples of what each assigned code looks like in practice. Then it calculates some broad descriptive statistics for the level of centralization utilized by different administrations over time. The approach is similar to previous work on legislative policy formulation, likewise based on utilizing archival records to fuel data-driven theory-testing.[8]

As there, key qualifications should be stressed early and often. After all, any translation of the real-world policymaking process into a blunt numerical assessment will misapprehend that process to some degree. In using archival records, another caveat is necessary: it requires waiting for those records to be open. And even with rigorous crosschecks, we may never know what is *not* in the files. It is possible that the memo tracing an EO's background is skewed by its author's self-justifying bias. It is possible that the presidential command that appears in black and white one day was softened by a phone call or amended in a hallway conversation the next. It is possible that the key document that would explicate an agency's reasoning was suppressed, discarded— or simply slipped into the wrong folder, for a bemused scholar of another topic altogether to one day encounter and ignore. (Perhaps it should be conceded too that the occasional 5¼" MS-DOS floppy disk found in the archives went unread.) Not all coding decisions can be made on the basis of equivalent information, or made at all.

Further, as noted in the opening chapter, executive orders are not the only kind of presidential directive and, as one staffer told the national security advisor in 1965, "Executive Orders can be issued by the President any way he wants."[9] But what any given president chose to call an "executive order" instead of a proclamation or memorandum or guidance document will affect the universe from which the sample here derives. If certain kinds of directives are systematically labeled EOs at some times but not others, that could skew the analysis.[10]

Yet despite these caveats, these data represent a substantial step forward in our understanding of the executive politics of executive orders. OMB's comprehensive curation of the EOP's institutional memory is a hugely valuable resource. The executive order files contain rich historical details not available from any other source, from the systematic cataloguing of those consulted regarding a given EO and their replies to scribbled and sometimes profane marginal commentary. Even where the minutiae must be lost in their translation to discrete categorization, their essence remains, infusing confidence in the validity of the hypotheses developed and conclusions drawn. And in any case the simplification carried out by coding of this sort is unavoidable if we are to draw, and test, generalizations about presidents' relationship to this policymaking process. Importantly, the aim is to identify not the precise locus but the relative centralization of the process in question—to be ordinal rather than exact.

To be sure, as already discussed, the kinds of administrative action requiring EOs have been shifted by statute over time; for instance, presidents no longer need to exempt individual civil servants from a mandatory retirement age. And there is occasional evidence that presidents have sought to use fewer (or more) EOs for some discrete period of time, in order to make a political point—recall Barack Obama's claim that his low order count in 2013 proved that he was not the "dictator" congressional critics charged, or Trump's that a larger number of EOs proved his effectiveness. But these were short-term effects.[11] More broadly, the population of EOs may be somewhat randomly birthed, but that randomness in itself curbs the chances of problematic bias, even as the aggregation of so many individual cases grants protection against an error made in interpreting any given example.

Coding Centralization: Provenance and Preponderance

The OMB executive order files identify who took the initiative in proposing or presenting a given EO and what parts of the executive branch took part and had the influence to prevail in arguments over its thrust and drafting. Together these shape a given EO's provenance—a useful word most often associated with the art world as a record of ownership or custody—and allow us to describe the nature of the formulation process. Another key concept comes from an early study of the source of major laws, Lawrence Chamberlain's 1946 book *The President, Congress, and Legislation*, which gauged statutes' "preponderant" origin.[12] Because executive orders need not be approved by another branch of government, the *management* task facing presidents is somewhat different than it is for the formulation of legislative proposals. But the *research* task facing scholars is quite similar.[13]

Chamberlain's aim was to judge whether a given bill was mainly a legislative or executive product. Here, though, as in my earlier book on legislative program formulation, those branches shift to the executive and "presidential."[14] The latter includes the immediate, centralized staff surrounding the Oval Office, as opposed to the plethora of departments and agencies that populate the wider bureaucracy. The level of centralization serves as a rough proxy for the level of influence exerted by that bureaucracy over the content of executive orders generally. To be sure, the Executive Office of the President itself has expanded greatly over time, importing its own managerial challenges and potential transaction costs. Nor are the denizens of the EOP always united in their preferences.[15] Still, "White House staff" generally can be accurately distinguished from those who reside in the many agencies scattered across the executive branch. The idea of provenance here is not to simply identify the author of the first draft of the EO but to assess the relative influence of the wider executive branch relative to the EOP throughout the formulation process. Where did the president (metaphorically) choose to make or buy a given policy proposal? How did the different actors weigh in, and have weight? As made clear below, that starts with the first draft but even an EO proposed by a particular department may wind up fully centralized by the time it is issued. The site of origination matters but is not determinative.

From OMB's archived EO files, then, I coded each proposed executive order, taking into account how their pedigrees are combined and revised throughout the formulation process. The subsequent index of centralization takes on one of four values, from least to most centralized:

- Decentralized (coded as "0"): the product of the Cabinet departments and/or executive agencies outside the Executive Office of the President;
- Mixed, departments preponderant (coded as "1"): both the White House or EOP and the wider bureaucracy involved, but with the departments taking the lead role;
- Mixed, EOP preponderant (coded as "2"): again, with both the White House or EOP and departments involved, but with the former taking the lead role; and
- Centralized (coded as "3"): predominantly the product of centralized staff, within the White House or EOP.

Again, this measure is ordinal, not absolute; it does not assume that each category is equidistant from its neighbors. The distance between orders coded "1" and orders coded "2" may not be exactly the same as that between orders coded "2" and those coded "3"; nor is every EO coded "1" at exactly the same level of centralization. (These relaxed assumptions underlie the later use of ordered probit to analyze factors contributing to different levels of centralization.) Thus, to give a better sense of how EOs were sorted into these categories, the next sections provide broad guidelines and specific examples of how given codes were assigned. What does a centralized, or decentralized, or mixed process actually look like, across different administrations and policy arenas? A number of narrative cases drawn from the OMB/BoB archives help explain.[16]

Decentralized Formulation Processes

A three-year process to amend military draft regulations kicked off in 1953 when the Selective Service System sent a proposed executive order to the Bureau of the Budget on May 1. The Bureau's first reaction was that "these amendments are all of a technical, non-policy nature," but decided "the regulations should probably be checked with the Department of State" even so. This proved fortunate since within days the secretary of state had sent a competing version of the EO. Selective Service objected to State ("I must oppose this proposal") and State renewed its objection to Selective Service.[17]

At the heart of the dispute were contradictory legal interpretations over the status of non-citizens and the draft, and BoB, finding itself over its head, asked the Justice Department for help in sorting out the two agencies' positions. Lawyers there replied that it was "an extremely close and complicated question" and vaguely hoped that pending court decisions would solve the problem for them. "My sympathies are entirely with the S.S.S. brief," scrawled longtime Bureau official Roger Jones on an April 1954 memo concerning one such case, but when the opinion did come down in a way supporting Selective Service, Justice remained reluctant to accept it as definitive. Selective Service protested—"in the state of this [court] record, we feel that it is only fair to release our EO without waiting"—but Justice refused to sign off until a different court case it felt was more on point was decided. That did not happen until February 1955, at which point Jones wrote happily that the "State Department has been informed of the Attorney General's views [on the EO] . . . and has withdrawn objection to its issuance."

But a week later, the assistant secretary of state was back, yodeling a new problem at BoB. "As a result of conversations with representatives of the Swiss Legation," he wrote, "it is now the Department's view that the proposed executive order . . . should not be issued until the interested agencies have had an opportunity to work out a substitute for that portion of the regulations dealing with treaty aliens." Jones made clear he "doesn't agree with State on this" but additional negotiations ensued anyway. In March State thought a new draft was "more satisfactory." Yet before a deal could be finalized, Congress changed the law on which the EO was based.[18] Thus in September the Selective Service agreed that further revisions were necessary. A newly revamped EO went out for clearance again, this time to a wider swath of eleven agencies ranging all the way to the Department of Agriculture.

State, by now, had decided to live with things: despite continuing concerns, it replied, this version is "more satisfactory than some alternatives" and "the Department is not prepared to object to it." But now others *were* prepared to do so—by mid-November, proposed amendments from the Civil Service Commission and Defense had prompted BoB to host a conference with Selective Service to resolve things. With the Pentagon still insistent on changes to the EO, and with another summit at BoB "unable to resolve this matter," the BoB finally punted again and sent the long-suffering order back to Justice, along with a three-plus-page summary of its history: "it was agreed that the matter was for legal consideration." It was not until January 25, 1956, that the Pentagon settled on language with Selective Service and DOJ. Finally, on February 15, EO 10659 was issued.

During this fray, the Selective Service System, State, Defense, and Justice were the key actors; the BoB role was as a referee who had long since lost control of the game. White House staff were kept informed throughout, but there is no sign in the thick file that they had any particular substantive views that became part of the debate.

More broadly, decentralized orders normally originate outside the Executive Office of the President. They may in fact arise from outside the executive branch itself; in one case the great Langston Hughes credited in verse the key role of labor leader A. Philip Randolph in Franklin Roosevelt's 1941 issuance of EO 8802, which prohibited discrimination in defense industries and related government activities during World War II. Hughes hailed Randolph's ability to play "the checkered game / Of king jumps king / And jumps a President / That order 8802 / For me and you."[19]

True, poetry and executive orders rarely coincide. Far more common are prosaic legislative requests such as those from congressional committees seeking access to tax data. In 1950, for instance, Estes Kefauver's Senate investigation of organized crime in interstate commerce asked to inspect income, excess-profits, capital stock, estate, and gift tax returns: "the Executive order . . . [is] submitted pursuant to the request of the Special Committee," wrote Treasury Secretary John Snyder.[20] Sometimes, as with Kefauver, requests were time-limited; but in 1973, having received a letter from Rep. Jim Wright of the House Committee on Public Works, OMB reminded the attorney general that "similar authority has been granted to the Committee biennially since 1961," in order to allow Congress to delve into questions of potential corruption in construction projects.[21] Individual legislators may also prompt EOs, as when Sen. John Warner proposed in 1984 that military personnel killed by acts of terrorism be eligible for the Purple Heart.[22] Other requests are less public-minded. Sen. John Stennis, for example, asked Richard Nixon to make sure the senator's "close personal friend since high school days" was exempted from mandatory retirement. Stennis, an important committee chair and potential "Democrat for Nixon" in an election year, got what he wanted.[23]

Agency-initiated actions may be prompted by need, recent statute, internal housekeeping, or external ambition—the last usually linked to an expansion of turf or autonomy that effectively asks the president to bind other agencies on the proposer's behalf. The first category, need, includes EOs driven by events, such as the long series of orders proposed by the National Mediation Board to establish emergency investigative boards in the case of transportation-related labor disputes.[24] More dramatic was Harry Truman's decision to suspend the eight-hour workday for employees of the armed services. In terms that would surely get any White House to take notice, the War Department framed its request by warning that "an extreme shortage of 'Mortuary Cars' requires that the unloading and shipment of military remains be carried on at maximum speed. Since this activity depends on ship arrivals and the availability of cars, mandatory application of an eight hour day will have seriously adverse effects in delaying shipments to burial points."[25] Not surprisingly, BoB's instinctive objections to the overtime costs involved gained little traction.

Similarly, a 1956 order arrived courtesy of Panama Canal Zone governor William E. Potter, via the Panama Canal Company, via the secretary of defense. It suspended a statutory provision requiring both that certain positions be filled only by American or Panamanian citizens and that Panamanians not outnumber Americans in those jobs. But not only did numerous citizens of other countries work in the Canal Zone (many actually brought there by the United States), the balancing requirement would require firing "a significant number of citizens of Panama." Doing that would not only anger Panama, as the State Department agreed, but raise labor costs as well. Unions protested—"we do not believe it in the public interest to suspend any part of these sections"— but even the Department of Labor quietly assented to the new order.[26]

Though far from all EOs required by statute are wholly decentralized (for instance, see the discussion of EO 12968 below), recent changes in the law are a frequent motivation for proposed EOs drafted by departments invested in those changes. The Interest Equalization Tax Act of 1964 prompted the Treasury Department to draft what became EO 11206, along with associated regulations implementing it. The Defense Department formulated Ronald Reagan's EO 12340 to amend court-martial procedures and regulations consistent with the Military Justice Amendments of 1981. A 2003 order issued by George W. Bush—the "Brownfields EO," in OMB shorthand—flowed from the Small Business Liability Relief and Brownfields Revitalization Act.[27] The EPA took the lead on the last, working with Interior and Agriculture to replicate older language linked to Superfund implementation.[28]

Often these sorts of EOs propose narrow technical changes. But even minutiae may be manipulated by departments in ways they see as useful to managing their policy tasks. For example, a subsequent Treasury order on the interest equalization tax issue modified the tax rate slightly, but also dealt with a special Japanese debt exemption. As the assistant secretary of the treasury noted, "we propose to put these two changes in a single executive order in an effort to 'bury' insofar as possible" the provision affecting Japan.[29] That burial went forward as Treasury desired. (Without a mortuary car.)

Internal organizational matters with a decentralized formulation process include EOs designating a line of succession within a given department. EO 10791 did this for State in 1958, EO 12514 the same for the secretaries of the Army, Navy, and Air Force in 1985. Note, though, that not all order of succession orders are wholly decentralized either; the OMB files help distinguish between the two EOs just noted and something like EO 10941, coded as "1"— mixed but with the Treasury Department in the lead—or EO 13242 regarding Commerce, which was largely coordinated by the White House Counsel and properly coded as "2."[30]

EOs that affect only the proposing agency normally attract less critical attention from others in government, but not always. Even then external actors may see implications for their own activities, especially when their competitors propose to add themselves to interagency advisory groups. They are even more concerned, of course, when the proposal changes who runs those committees. And yet a third level of agency ambition is achieved when they propose receiving a delegation of statutory authority that might also be logically given to a different agency. Often agencies request language requiring other agencies to report to them or to receive their blessing to act: this prompts frequent arguments over the exact phrasing of "coordination," "supervision," and "direction," among other terms. In one such case, Defense sought to limit State to supervision, while State—seeking to direct—complained that "we have attempted without success to learn from Defense the precise nature and scope of the problem which it seeks to meet." The final phrasing instead allowed State to "exercise . . . affirmative responsibility for the coordination and supervision over."[31]

Where OMB coordinates—but does not or cannot rewrite—the terms of these arguments, the EOs in which they are contained are normally coded as wholly decentralized. Where it or other presidential staff get substantively involved, though, they are appropriately coded higher on the index of centralization.

The "o" code also houses interesting cases of agency entrepreneurship. For instance, in January 1993, outgoing president George H. W. Bush declined to issue an executive order banning smoking in federal workplaces—which seemed to end a long process of lobbying from the Department of Health and Human Services (HHS). As early as June 1990, HHS had pushed for this policy—and in February 1991 OMB official Tom Scully told his boss, director Richard Darman, that "HHS won't give up on this."[32] Indeed they did not, despite strong pushback—coming from the Department of Defense, even though a second HHS draft excluded work space used by uniformed personnel; from Agriculture and Interior, who feared the EO's definition of "work space" was so broad that it encompassed not just federally owned buildings but parks and even the National Mall; from Justice, who worried about burgeoning lawsuits alleging the infringement of privacy rights; from OMB, who worried the EO would serve as a legal rationale to force EPA or OSHA to regulate "indoor air pollution"; and even from public sector unions, who didn't necessarily like smoking but were angry at having an executive order preempt their right to bargain over the matter.[33] Scully added that "I totally agree with [HHS] on the merits, but this will be very tough to do in the real world. I think that it could potentially be a big embarrassment for the Administration." A year later HHS was pushing Draft #3, including new exceptions, and two years later—five days before Bush was to leave office—Darman sent the EO to the White House. In violation of EO 11030, it did not have his endorsement. Though "this order has undergone lengthy consideration and careful revision," he wrote, "views are split on this issue. . . . If you wish to approve the order, it is attached for your signature."[34]

Normally this would have sent the EO to the scrap heap (or, in this book, to chapter 7). But HHS quickly realized that a new administration might be in the market for their old idea. Weeks later, in early February 1993, the department had sold it to their incoming secretary, Donna Shalala. HHS and EPA sent their draft back to the White House, noting that "HHS's Office of Smoking and Health is reworking the order now, and copies of the draft will be sent to GSA, OPM, and the Labor Department for their comments. These steps will take only a short time, correct mistakes within the draft and avoid unnecessary delays by including the interested parties."[35]

That draft would become EO 13058—though not until August 1997. Thus "a short time" would prove to be more than four years. Continued skirmishes with Defense, OPM, and federal unions (with whom the Clinton administration sympathized more than had their predecessors) held up issuance—even as piecemeal agency-specific bans drained some of the urgency for the broader EO. HHS, though, with EPA—and aided by the evidence gathered from the large-scale tobacco settlement against cigarette manufacturers—continued to revise and sell its proposal, winning out after six years and two presidents. Amusingly, DPC's Elena Kagan, editing a draft set of FAQs to accompany the new EO, crossed out one question entirely: the one asking "why did it take you so long to issue this order?"[36]

Mixed Formulation Processes, Led by Department(s)

The final draft of Executive Order 12968, a 1995 directive specifying the ground rules for gaining access to classified information, went to President Clinton with a covering memo noting that it had "been extensively negotiated and reviewed by 26 executive agencies, industry representatives, the [American Bar Association], federal employees unions and interested members of Congress. All support the proposed Order, as do OMB and relevant White House staff." National security advisor Anthony Lake weighed in, telling the president that congressional intelligence committees were "particularly involved" and that deputy attorney general Jamie Gorelick, along with White House counsel Abe Mikva, "took particular care" to make sure the new EO "reflects this Administration's views on due process and sexual orientation in the clearance process." The prior guidelines on classified information were outdated, having been written in the 1950s, though the immediate need to revise the order had arisen from the fiscal 1995 Intelligence Authorization Act (IAA), which required that an EO or regulation be issued within six months of its enactment. That provision of the IAA had itself been prompted by the Aldrich Ames spy scandal.[37]

A working group already convened by the National Security Council prior to the passage of the IAA was placed under a new Security Policy Board made up largely of departmental representatives in the wake of the new law, which expanded the parameters of the EO under consideration.[38] From October 1994, drafting was led by the Justice Department, with other "drafting team" members drawn from Energy, Defense, the NSA, OPM, Treasury, FBI, and CIA. Ultimately the NSC received the draft order, praising the Security Policy Board's work overall for having "significantly enhanced the initial draft" and asking for some changes to strengthen its financial disclosure requirements, along with others reflecting concerns from Sen. Arlen Specter, chair of the Senate Intelligence Committee.[39] Another team of departmental drafters was convened to "address the NSC's concern without creating an untenable cost and management burden." Finally, in the summer of 1995 departmental and congressional concerns had been met, albeit in compromise fashion ("many of the most difficult issues have simply been postponed," one analyst carped). The EO was issued exactly 180 days after enactment of the IAA.[40]

As this suggests, EOs in this "mixed" category feature involvement from both one or more departments and agencies, and one or more parts of the Executive Office of the President. They may originate from either side of that divide, though more commonly they are proposed by the agencies and then tweaked by OMB or other presidential staff. In 1961, for instance, State proposed what seemed to be a simple delegation order, asking for the authority to manage foreign aid funds earmarked for Latin America generally and Chilean disaster relief specifically. Treasury, which already ran an inter-American development bank, questioned why a new mechanism was necessary. BoB, with its wider perspective on the president's entire legislative program, thought Treasury was overreaching and urged State to hold firm even as the administration's hopes for a single cohesive foreign aid program under a new Agency for International Development (AID) risked foundering on the shoals quickly accreting from numerous inter- and intra-agency committees. These "overly-elaborate and extremely cumbersome" programmatic arrangements, BoB director David Bell wrote to the president, "constitute, in my view, a wholly unsatisfactory approach to the problem of administering the programs." Ultimately BoB was able to reduce Treasury's role in aid distribution to something "ministerial. . . . The matter will, in any event, be appropriately assigned as soon as the AID agency is established."[41]

Another useful example of a department-leaning mixed process comes from the Reagan administration and the implementation of the 1988 Trade and Competitiveness Act, with OMB as the coordinator but not the substantive driver of a complex multi-agency EO.[42] In mid-October, as the administration wound down, OMB general counsel Alan Raul provided various officials with a "booklet" (approximating the size of the space shuttle's owner's manual) made up of "the source materials that my office will use to prepare a draft omnibus order" that would "synthesize the various agency submissions." Early consultation with the agencies had identified fifteen areas in the law as "executive order candidates."[43]

Key elements of the proposed order ranged from export control sanctions to the role of a Competitiveness Council, and from presidential reporting requirements to the management of steel and superconductors. Each came with a list of "policy issues," affected agencies, and a "drafting agency." For instance, the question of vetting acquisitions of American firms by foreign ones involved Treasury, Justice, Commerce, Defense, the United States Trade Representative (USTR), State, Labor, and OPIC (the Overseas Private Investment Corporation), as well as OMB and CEA; Treasury was the designated "drafting agency."[44] One issue that drew OMB into the fray was in refereeing the role of the USTR, to whom the new law directly delegated substantial authority, vis-à-vis the president and his Cabinet councils, notably the Economic Policy Council (EPC).[45] Raul reported that "the White House wants to ensure that the USTR continues to consult with the EPC on investigations" while trade representative Clayton Yeutter was "concerned that the President's executive order will flout the congressional will by attempting to take back this authority for the President." Raul, of course, did what the White House asked, "drafting language at their request that would continue the EPC role." That itself went through different iterations, including one that created EPC formally within the EO itself to give it more institutional heft (it had previously been established only by press release).[46]

A mid-November draft was sent back to the agencies, but despite Raul's assurances that "we attempted to take a consistent approach . . . in favor of maximum inter-agency consultation," this version attracted even less consensus.[47] EOP agencies were also unhappy, for different reasons: the NSC complained that "the largest difficulty with the draft E.O. is that its conceptual framework is exactly backwards," delegating too much power to department heads.[48] Still more attempts to placate not just the White House but other agencies peeved with USTR thus followed, including a December 8 draft that resuscitated an older body called the Trade Policy Committee and required it to report directly to the president. That didn't work either. As OMB discovered, "USTR objects strongly to this" while "Defense wants to be included as [an] agency to be consulted" and, for good measure, "Justice wants to be included" too ("if Justice is not included, they would prefer deleting agency names" altogether).[49] The issue from OMB's point of view was "sensitive considerations regarding the preservation of Presidential flexibility and the prerogative of the President to name his own Executive Branch advisers on trade policy issues." To this end drafters considered ignoring entirely the congressional designations included in the language of the statute.[50]

After yet another iteration in mid-December ("the proposed order has been extensively revised from the one previously submitted for your review and comment in an effort to reflect, reconcile, or resolve agency comments and requests")—to which Secretary of State George Shultz's immediate reaction was "worse than the original"—the combatants finally wore each other down. USTR's continued warning against "unnecessarily tweaking the nose of the Congress" with the Trade Policy Committee language won out. In return USTR pledged that "we recognize the President's constitutional power to organize his economic decision-making . . . as he chooses" and that "we have not, and do not plan to, change the way we conduct business among agencies."[51] The final language was broad but vague, specifying that "any actions or determinations taken or made by an officer or agency" under the law or the EO "shall be undertaken after appropriate inter-agency consultation as established by the President." This, OMB director Joe Wright told President Reagan, "preserves the Presidential prerogative . . . , while preserving maximum flexibility for President-elect Bush. It also avoids directly confronting Congress on the question of which agencies should be included."[52]

More generally, Wright had to concede, given that the statute itself had taken fifteen months and twenty-four congressional committees to finalize, and given "such a broad inter-agency consultation process involving such a complex order, not all the commenting agencies were completely satisfied with all provisions." He tallied their continuing objections in an appendix to the approval memo. But "the various agency differences have been reduced to a minimum, with the major issues being successfully resolved by consensus. Accordingly," he concluded, central clearance had done its job. The president had been apprised of key issues, the office's prerogatives had been protected, and "I believe the proposed Executive Order is largely acceptable to all of the affected agencies."[53]

Mixed Formulation Processes, led by EOP

The third category along the centralization index includes cases of orders proposed by departments that subsequently attract a good deal of EOP intervention, as well as the reverse: those originated by EOP actors and then modified by departmental input.

In the former category is a 1958 case that started life in decentralized fashion before drawing increasing BoB involvement. Amendments to the Atomic Energy Act passed that July led to an EO jointly proposed by the Atomic Energy Commission (AEC) and the Pentagon. Their draft promptly drew complaints from CIA and State, who both sought to deal themselves into the new regime. (State wrote that "the executive order, if silent on the responsibility of the

Secretary of State, might contribute to misconceptions on the part of foreign governments with respect to assignment of basic responsibilities within the Executive.") By October, BoB had rewritten the draft and the CIA and State had accepted the changes. But after a long silence Defense did not—five months later, in March 1959, it rejected the revisions; a month later, AEC too inveighed against what it snarkily labeled BoB's "tentative substitute draft." Another five months of work followed, with BoB ultimately ruling for State and against CIA (and, by favoring State, against Defense and AEC). "Regarded from the point of view of the President," general counsel Arthur Focke told the attorney general, "we think that the . . . transmitted draft is proper." To CIA head Allen Dulles, the message was, instead, better luck next time.[54]

The 1999 agreement between the Pentagon and the Food and Drug Administration (FDA) over the military's use of "investigational" drug treatments is another example of OMB—in this case, its Office of Information and Regulatory Affairs (OIRA)—as the driving force behind interagency negotiations. The idea was to allow the Defense Department to issue drugs not yet approved by FDA in case service members were exposed to chemical, biological, or radiological weapons. The 1999 Defense Authorization Act had given the president authority to waive the necessity for informed consent for military personnel undergoing medical treatment in certain circumstances, one of which was linked to FDA standards and criteria. The draft EO was designed to work, and be issued in conjunction, with those regulatory criteria—hence the involvement of OIRA, whose job is to review the costs and benefits of new regulations in its own central clearance process.[55] A draft in early April developed by Defense and FDA, with input from OMB, OSTP, and NSC staff, was cleared to State, Justice, Treasury, HHS, Transportation, and CIA, as well as several EOP offices. Extensive feedback on the legalities came from OLC. The EO "has been carefully negotiated," OMB's Health Division reported in August, allowing for military flexibility without sacrificing FDA's "sound scientific analysis." Ultimately, the weight on the scales completing the deal came from OIRA. In fact OMB's Joshua Gotbaum touted a single staffer's role to his director, Jacob Lew: "you should know this is a personal accomplishment of Wendy Taylor of OIRA," who pushed a "hard-negotiated compromise between DoD and FDA."[56]

In other cases OMB seizes on an agency proposal—jumping aboard a moving train—to advance the presidency's agenda. In 1965, Civil Service Commission (CSC) chair John Macy proposed repealing an Eisenhower EO that had created a new special assistant to the president for personnel management and replacing it with a new order that would formally give the CSC chair this job (something Macy already did, in practice). Other language in the proposed order greatly expanded the CSC chair's broader remit, including the authority to "coordinate" the entirety of executive branch personnel programs. BoB's antennae went up: "the draft order raises as many questions as it answers," staffer Harold Seidman warned. For one thing, "attempts to formalize the role of the Chairman as special assistant to the president for personnel management . . . are likely to complicate the Chairman's relationships with his colleagues on the Commission and with . . . Congress." Higher-ups agreed: "while I don't see ghosts in the closet," one noted, this EO would be "unfortunate. It would be another volley in a long game of ping-pong, and it would give a future President an awkward problem if he wished to organize his office and duties differently."[57] BoB also worried that an expanded CSC would wander into the Bureau's own "already assigned fields." Thus, it replaced Macy's draft with one simply repealing the Eisenhower order, omitting the new, capacious authority CSC had proposed. In the letter it drafted for LBJ to send to Macy, the Bureau sold this as an upgrade. "It is my wish that you continue to serve" in both roles, LBJ was to say, "but without the restrictions in this latter role which are inherent in the delegation of responsibilities by executive order. I prefer a less formal arrangement."[58] BoB did, too.

An EOP-centered example comes from 2001 and an NSC-proposed order entitled "Critical Infrastructure Protection in the Information Age." The drafting process began in the late spring of 2001 (long before the September 11 attacks that fall) with a wide range of input "from the interagency," as an NSC memo on the "penultimate draft" observed on July 5; by July 11 an OMB note made overly optimistic reference to "the *final* draft of the famous EO." A week later, another not-yet-final draft went back to eighteen departments and agencies, as well as a dozen aides and entities within the EOP. At this stage it sought to create the President's Critical Infrastructure Protection and Continuity Board "to coordinate and have cognizance of federal efforts and programs" regarding physical and cyber assets requiring particular attention.[59]

An August meeting was convened by OMB, bringing together EOP staff from OSTP, NSC, DPC, and the vice president's office to review the agency feedback. Revisions—regarding funding for the new Board (one OMB counsel noted "pass-the-hat concerns"), its hierarchy, and very name—continued through the summer. On August 29 Vice President Dick Cheney's counsel, David Addington, weighed in with eight pages of detailed comments, generally rejecting the whole idea; he thought creation of a separate board was superfluous and urged that the NSC or some other extant agency with "the requisite authority, responsibility, and accountability" do the job.[60] But most of those proposed edits, including the existential one, were not ultimately adopted. Indeed, when the September 11 terrorist attacks suddenly made the need for infrastructure protection more tangible, Justice Department lawyers and OMB worked quickly to finalize the EO's language.[61] With new language taking the attacks into account—for example, the Board's chair would now report both to the national security advisor and to the head of the just-created Office of Homeland Security—EO 13231 was issued on October 16, 2001.

A final type of a mixed EO in this category is a White House suggestion to a Cabinet department that the latter decides to heed. For instance, in April 1957 Eisenhower aide Gerald Morgan thought the Interior Department should look into a matter concerning bonds issued by the territory (not yet state) of Hawaii. If Interior decided this was important, it should "please transmit a draft of an executive order designed to accomplish the delegation." Five months later, Interior did so, throwing in new material on Alaska and the U.S. Virgin Islands for good measure. After BoB made some additional changes, the Bureau told the attorney general that the EO now represented "a revision of a proposal presented by the Under Secretary of the Interior. The order draft has evolved out of the original suggestion of a representative of the White House Office that an exploration be made."[62]

Centralized Formulation Processes, within the EOP

Those sorts of "explorations" may also be wholly powered by the White House; the final, fully centralized category includes orders that were drafted by a department or agency but on the clear directions of the White House rather than on their own initiative. In 1982, for instance, the Department of Transportation (DOT) submitted an assigned draft of what became EO 12358 creating a Commission on Drunk Driving, "in response to a request from the President." OMB director David Stockman reminded the president after the order was finalized, with additional OMB and WHO input, that it "was proposed by [DOT] to implement your decision to establish such a Commission."[63]

OMB itself carries out similar drafting assignments: EO 12412 in 1983, which reconstituted a Peace Corps Advisory Council, was, Stockman noted, drafted "in this office, at the request of the White House Office."[64] And orders that revoke previous EOs are often in this category as well. A 1982 EO terminated the Urban Impact Statements imposed on agencies by Jimmy Carter in 1979. This had the benefit of having the president demand that OMB do less: the new EO allowed OMB to revoke a requirement it thought had "not made a useful contribution to the decision process and is redundant of other agency or OMB analysis."[65]

Sometimes, of course, the White House overrules agency objection in straightforward fashion. In late 1980, for example, White House aide Esther Peterson produced a complex EO to regulate the export of materials that were labeled hazardous domestically but not abroad. What became EO 12264 would publicize such exports, relying on regular notification and reporting procedures, while in some cases requiring them to undergo additional analysis and acquire a special export license. Peterson claimed there was wide enthusiasm for these initiatives, but the Commerce Department told OMB that her summary "conveys a misleading impression of general support for these policies. . . . The overwhelming number of comments, from industry and Congress, raised strenuous objections. . . . This is typical of the manner in which the summary was drafted." Other agencies argued the benefits of the proposal did not outweigh the administrative burden it imposed; the U.S. Trade Representative's office suggested a formal economic impact report be conducted (with the clear hope that this would delay the EO past Carter's time in office).[66]

While OMB had some sympathy for the agencies' objections—"the draft order could be the biggest single piece of the alleged 'regulatory explosion,' taking place right under our noses here in the Executive Office," wrote one analyst—the president did not.[67] On January 9, 1981, Peterson told the OMB counsel that she was sending along a final draft "in accordance with the President's decision yesterday." OMB complained, internally, that without "a copy of the [Carter] decision memo" it is "pointless to review the document based on agency comments which are in opposition to it." In the end the OMB general counsel told the attorney general that "we have not attempted to reconcile agency objections because Esther Peterson represented that the President's decision rejected those positions."[68]

The order issued on January 15, five days before Carter left office. The only immediate consolation for OMB staff was that a related, second EO, "even more complicated than the first," was "fortunately . . . destroyed before signature."[69] But with Ronald Reagan's inauguration, the agencies had the immediate opportunity to relitigate the matter, painting the Carter EO as "excessive regulation." It was revoked less than a month later, in an EO drafted directly (and rather gleefully) by OMB.[70]

EO 12264 represents a case where the president overrode the cautionary feedback gathered by the central clearance process, preferring to trust his centralized staff to translate his preferences to policy. This is not necessarily bad management, though it is hard to know how well the new export requirements would have worked, or how fervently the EO would have been implemented, had it been issued earlier in Carter's term. This is also a useful example of intra-EOP argumentation, something difficult to analyze systematically but that deserves discussion. A code of "3" indicates an EO formulated by the president's centralized staff; as noted in chapter 2, this implies that the "presidential branch," at least, as opposed to the wider executive branch, is uniform in its perspectives and preferences. But that sometimes oversimplifies. OMB's career staff has its own long-term views on presidential interests differing from those of the White House policy councils and even more dramatically from the president's political staff. The White House counsel's office may disagree with a counsel to the president, NSC with NEC with CEQ.

The Clinton child health order detailed in chapter 1 serves as one useful example. Similarly, in the process that led to EO 13078 in 1998, the Clinton DPC clashed with OMB in a battle over budgetary directives to the agencies that OMB won by attrition. (One DPC staffer told Elena Kagan that "if OMB were under instructions to do this because it's a priority, I am sure they would find a way. Without that, there's a million reasons why it can't be done.")[71] In a different Carter case, OMB's effort to derail an executive order, seeking at least to convert it into a less formal presidential directive, ran up against others in the White House "not receptive to further accommodation"; it ultimately decided "not to bother with cleaning up the language . . . the goal is to get it out of here as soon as possible."[72] George H. W. Bush budget director Richard Darman demanded that such interventions go on the record. Responding to a request from "the White House" that OMB change the text of an EO it had already approved, Darman carped, "I do not like this approach!" He asked that a memo be included in the file holding "some named party" accountable, that is, noting changes "requested by 'the White House' (some named party) on behalf of the president along w/our concurrence in the changes."[73]

Finally, though, presidential branch unity vis-à-vis the wider bureaucracy is hardly impossible to attain. President Reagan's approach to regulatory review serves as a telling example. Reagan had announced the formation of a Presidential Task Force on Regulatory Relief, to be chaired by Vice President Bush, just two days into his term; a week later he announced a freeze on pending regulations. On February 17, he issued EO 12291, which created the template for the process of regulatory review still used today.[74] As issued, it required all executive branch line agencies to submit both proposed and final draft regulations to OMB, linking their issuance to analysis that showed "the potential benefits to society from the regulation outweigh the potential costs to society."

Prior to issuance the new text was tightly held among a small group of OMB and White House staff, who sought to work out key questions dealing with the president's authority to control the content of rules issued by the agencies.[75] The first draft distributed for wider review went to the departments around 8 p.m. on Friday, February 13. Feedback was due by 11 a.m. on Monday—Presidents' Day. More than one new Cabinet secretary had trouble tracking down needed staff over the three-day weekend, and many did not respond until Tuesday.[76]

Those that responded (on time, or not) were largely critical. A memo to the new secretary of agriculture warned that the proposal placed "considerably more of the management function at OMB." Another department told the White House that "the Secretary of Transportation is strongly opposed to the proposal as written": that it would lead to lengthy delays, that OMB was not competent to review regulations anyway, and that it represented "over-centralization" (contrary to the "Cabinet government" the president claimed to want).[77]

But the deal was done, in fully centralized fashion. Department lawyers, summoned to the White House on Tuesday, February 17, assumed the text was a draft still ripe for revision. When they reached the last page, they found President Reagan's signature already affixed.[78]

Descriptive Statistics

With these illustrations in mind, we can collect the observations together and turn to more comprehensive analysis. What do the more than 500 executive orders coded here look like in terms of their aggregate formulation process? The shortest answer is in Tables 4.2a and 4.2b. Table 4.2a shows where EOs in the main random sample fall along the centralization index, while Table 4.2b folds in the 41 additional observations described earlier and supplementary to

TABLE 4.2A. Formulation of Executive Orders by Level of Centralization, 1937–2004

[Main sample only] Centralization Code	Weighted % of Total	Frequency in Sample (%) ($n = 515$)
0 (decentralized)	49.4	226 (43.9%)
1 (mixed, dept.-centered)	16.1	87 (16.9%)
2 (mixed, EOP-centered)	16.4	103 (20.0%)
3 (centralized)	18.2	99 (19.2%)
Mean	*1.03 (s.e. = .06)*	*1.15 (s.d. = 1.18)*

TABLE 4.2B. Formulation of Executive Orders by Level of Centralization, 1937–2004

[All coded observations] Centralization Code	Weighted % of Total	Frequency in Sample (%) ($n = 556$)
0 (decentralized)	49.4	245 (44.1%)
1 (mixed, dept.-centered)	16.1	94 (16.9%)
2 (mixed, EOP-centered)	16.0	107 (19.2%)
3 (centralized)	18.5	110 (19.8%)
Mean	*1.04 (s.e. = .06)*	*1.15 (s.d. = 1.19)*

the original sample. As noted, the added observations make no difference to the results.

Note that the weighted results in Table 4.2 vary slightly from the unweighted totals, with the proportion of fully decentralized items somewhat higher in the estimated population than in the sampled observations (49 percent of the total versus 44 percent). That brings the weighted mean for the population of all coded items to 1.04, compared to 1.15 for the sample—not a huge difference, though an interesting one. Either way, one quick conclusion is clear: some 6 in 10 EOs are formulated primarily outside the Executive Office of the President, and more than 4 in 10 preponderantly by the departments and agencies with little EOP intervention. Some 20 percent are fully centralized—are "unilateral" in the colloquial, albeit not scholarly, sense. These findings raise intriguing questions about the provenance of presidential directives and the role of the wider executive branch in their issuance.

The degree to and conditions under which unilateralism is plural will be followed up more systematically in the chapters that follow. In the meantime, the difference between weighted and unweighted results does call attention to potential questions of temporality. The divergence seems likely to reflect the

TABLE 4.3. Formulation of Executive Orders by Level of Centralization, 1945–2004

[All coded observations] Centralization Code	Weighted % of Total	Frequency in Sample (%) ($n = 492$)
0 (decentralized)	43.1	206 (41.9%)
1 (mixed, dept.-centered)	16.8	85 (17.3%)
2 (mixed, EOP-centered)	20.5	102 (20.7%)
3 (centralized)	19.6	99 (20.1%)
Mean	*1.17 (s.e. = .05)*	*1.19 (s.d. = 1.18)*

very large number of EOs issued by Franklin Roosevelt relative to later presidents, and the subsequent statistical stress the weighting places on observations drawn from FDR's time in office. The shift in presidential output, noted in chapter 1, is especially emphatic from the Eisenhower administration on: FDR issued 995 EOs per four-year term from 1937 to 1945; Truman 726; Eisenhower 242; and all presidents from Kennedy through George W. Bush, an average of 194. As a quick check, consider a similar comparison that includes only 1945–2004. As Table 4.3 indicates, the sample frequencies and mean become nearly identical to those of the estimated population.

Does centralization increase over the years? Figure 4.1 provides one quick answer: slightly. It divides the data into roughly decade-long blocks, to check on developments not associated with specific administrations. (Again, the drivers of centralization are hypothesized to be managerial dynamics not reliant on the personality of the individual in office.)[79] Here we see a small but clear upward trend, from a mean figure of just under 0.9 in 1937–45 to just over 1.4 by 1996–2004.[80]

Even the end point of the timeline, of course, is at the midpoint of the measure—well below where a pure measure of unilateralism, formulation dominated by centralization, would be. That suggests a wide range of actors and processes involved in EO policy development across all the administrations under study. We can also see this another way, by separating out fully centralized EOs from the rest. The cases coded "3" represent the conventional view of unilateral action. Do we see more of them over time? As shown in Figure 4.2, we do not. Fully centralized orders—the bottom line—are quite stable as a proportion of EOs issued over time. They start and end the time series at one-fifth of issued orders, remarkably close to their overall frequency in the data as a whole.

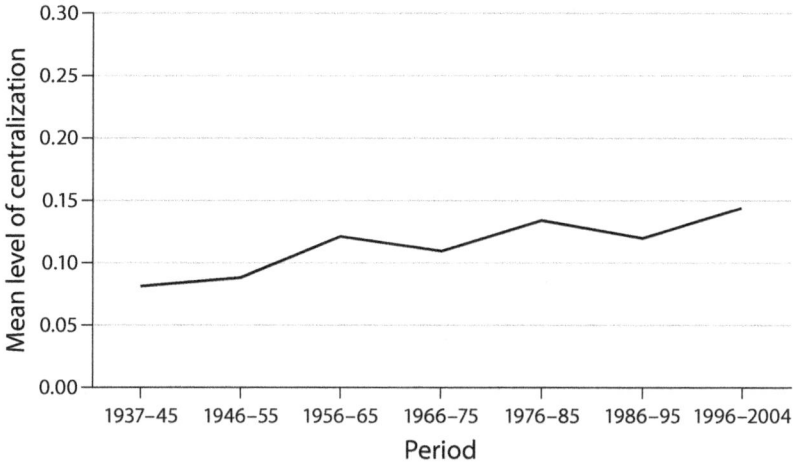

FIGURE 4.1. Mean Level of Centralization, by Time Period, 1937–2004.

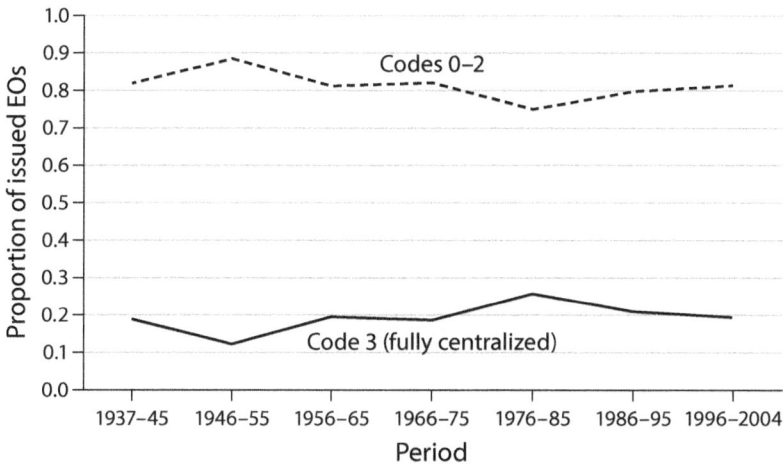

FIGURE 4.2. Proportion of Fully Centralized EOs, by Time Period, 1937–2004.

It's worth breaking down the data further to explore the variation in both figures. As it turns out, for example, the small bump in fully centralized orders from 1976–85 is attributable not to Ronald Reagan but Jimmy Carter. Returning to the average centralization figures, broken down by the more intuitive category of presidential administration, the underlying data are included in Table 4.4 and graphed in Figure 4.3.

TABLE 4.4. Mean Level of Centralization, by President (weighted means)

	[Sample]			[All coded observations]		
	Mean	S.e.	n	Mean	S.e.	n
FDR	0.83	.133	66	0.83	.133	66
Truman	0.86	.136	61	0.83	.132	63
Eisenhower	1.14	.141	64	1.14	.141	64
Kennedy/Johnson	0.95	.121	64	1.05	.113	83
Kennedy	1.39	.239	23	1.40	.184	42
Johnson	0.73	.137	41	0.73	.137	41
Nixon/Ford	1.27	.142	63	1.27	.142	63
Nixon	1.43	.173	44	1.43	.173	44
Ford	0.89	.246	19	0.89	.246	19
Carter	1.72	.196	32	1.58	.184	38
Reagan	1.24	.142	64	1.19	.137	70
G.H.W. Bush	1.09	.207	32	1.09	.207	32
Clinton	1.52	.141	37	1.52	.141	37
G. W. Bush	1.28	.183	32	1.35	.161	40

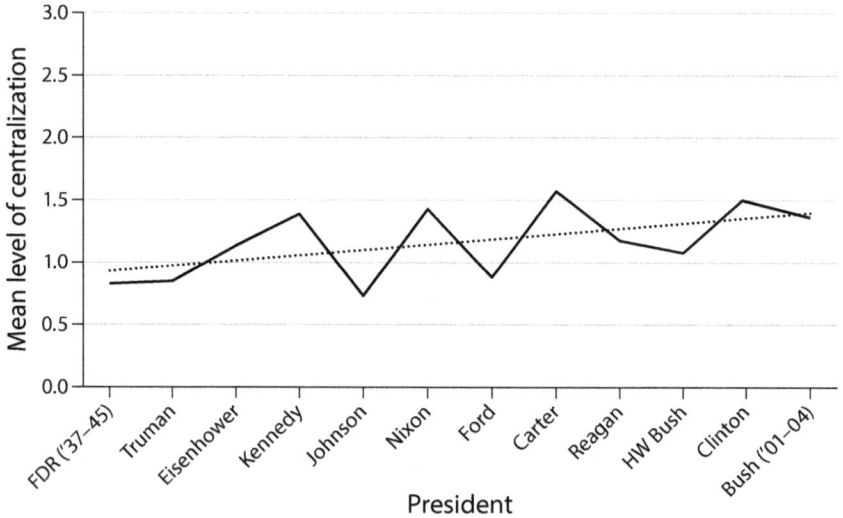

FIGURE 4.3. Mean Level of Centralization, by President, 1937–2004.

As those indicate, the means bounce up with Kennedy but then down again with Johnson, up with Nixon, down with Ford (since the truncated term presidents' figures are based on less data, combined figures for Kennedy/Johnson and Nixon/Ford are also provided, as well as the additional Kennedy observations). As just noted, it is actually the unlikely Jimmy Carter who serves as centralizing powerhouse here, largely driven by Carter's preoccupation with government reorganization—which, as discussed in chapter 5, is a management factor heavily associated with centralization. As that suggests, president-by-president results might vary even if presidents' decisions regarding formulation of a given executive order with a given set of characteristics are consistent across administrations, if particular periods prompt more EOs with a particular set of characteristics.

By contrast, the figures for Reagan—often presented as the exemplar of the centralizing presidency—are basically the same as for Eisenhower, usually associated with "Cabinet government." The latter title here seems to go to Lyndon Johnson. It is possible that Reagan, and for that matter Johnson, was more effective than Carter at the other side of centralization—politicization. As such they likely relied more readily on a responsive set of departmental officials than did Carter, another factor investigated in chapter 5.

Does the higher average level of centralization under Clinton and George W. Bush pull up the fitted line in a way that portends an enhanced "new normal" for White House involvement in the executive order process? To shed light on that, Figure 4.4 presents presidential variation graphically via the distribution of centralization for each administration using kernel density estimation. Seven of the ten administrative groupings are extremely similar, with decentralized orders dominant. However, Carter, Clinton, and George W. Bush stand out as providing a flatter distribution. In each case (and most notably for Clinton), there is an emphasis on mixed processes, ensuring that EOP staff have involvement in the formulation of orders. Kennedy and Nixon are presented here combined with their vice presidential successors, to ensure sufficient observations in the analysis; if they are separated out, their individual distributions are also distinct in that they are bimodal, with more density on the poles than in the "mixed" middle categories (see Figures A4.2(a) and (b) in the appendix to this chapter for details). But even those individual distributions do not diverge statistically from the broader distribution of the EO population.

In fact, by that measure only Carter (barely) and Clinton (with a small n) present a blend of formulation processes distinct from their peers.[81] In general, then, the consistency of the distributions over nearly seventy years suggests that time is not the key factor in determining centralization.

What is? The previous chapter laid out expectations along those lines, and the next returns to them. But before doing so, it is worth providing one more piece of descriptive data. If executive branch agencies play a key role in the production of executive orders, what agencies are most frequently

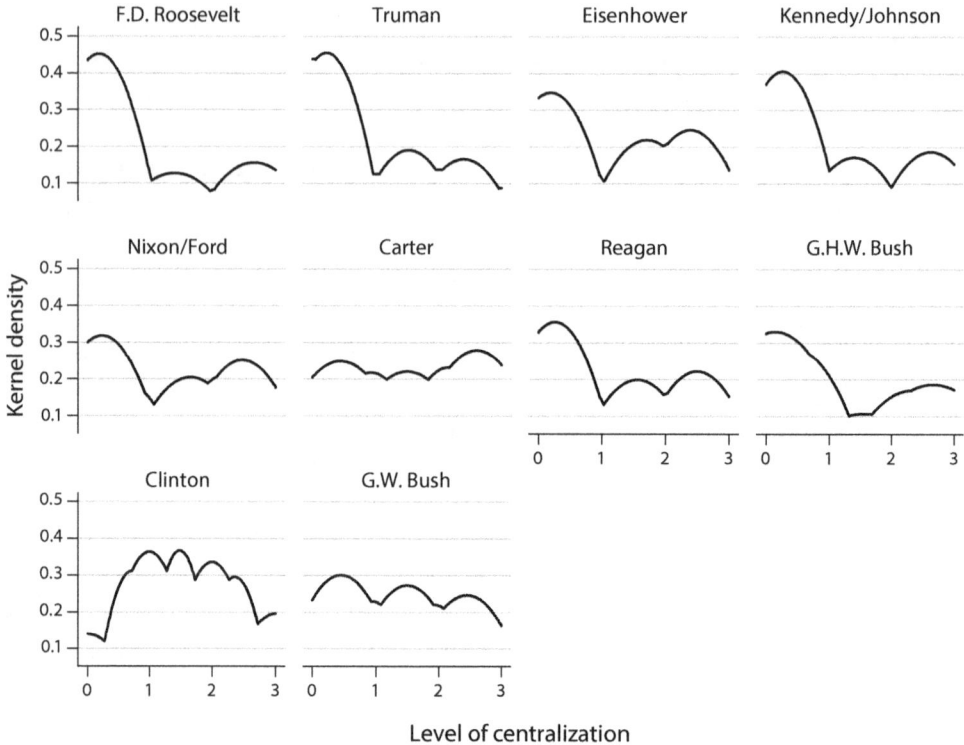

FIGURE 4.4. Centralization by Administration: Kernel Density Estimation.

involved? To find out, each EO in the sample was coded to identify its "lead agency."[82]

This designation is a matter of substance rather than authorship. The lead agency is, indeed, frequently the agency that proposed the order—that sent it to OMB in the first place, as recorded in OMB's executive order files—on the presumption this identifies the agency most concerned with its issuance. But that may shift if the EO's main effect is on a different bureau. This most commonly occurs in one of two circumstances: when the White House or OMB staff specifically direct a department to draft it, or when those centralized staffs wrote the EO themselves but where its sole or primary impact is on a specific department. In such cases the EO formulation would be coded as centralized, but with the affected department coded as lead agency (thus, not the White House or OMB). Occasionally, too, an agency proposes something that primarily affects another (for instance, to remove them from an interagency group); there, the displaced rival would be the lead agency.

Fifty-nine different agencies appear in the sixty-eight years of data here as the lead agency associated with at least one issued executive order. Sixteen of them are linked to only one EO: these include the Department of Homeland Security (DHS), the National Science Foundation, and the Office of National Drug Control Policy. On the flip side the Department of Defense is associated with 81 EOs, 14 percent of the total. These examples immediately raise the question of organizational change. Since DHS did not exist until January 2003, my data include just two years of its life span; prior to that its component parts are coded either independently or with their then-hierarchical superiors (as with immigration policy, previously housed in the Justice Department, or with the Coast Guard, part of Treasury or Transportation depending on the year of the EO). The Department of Defense itself came into being with the 1949 amendments to the National Security Act of 1947, which had already combined the separate departments of War and Navy and the new Air Force department under the umbrella of a single national military establishment. So before World War II my data would count the Navy as a separate department but afterward as part of the Pentagon.

To track substantive continuity across these changes, agencies subject to reorganization during the time series were also coded under a consolidated category—in this variant the Navy Department and other military agencies are counted under DoD throughout. (Doing so brings the Defense total to 100 EOs within the sample, 17.6 percent of all orders.) This also brings together like policy with like: Labor, for instance, considered as broad topical umbrella, includes the National Mediation Board, and so on.

This is inexact, of course, and even more so when there is multistage institutional evolution: as when, for example, the Federal Emergency Management Agency, itself a descendant of the Office of Civil and Defense Mobilization, the Office of Emergency Planning, and the Office of Emergency Preparedness (to give only a partial genealogy), becomes part of DHS. Still, the consolidated coding helps keep substantive subject matter together over seven decades of organizational evolution.

With all this in mind, Table 4.5 presents the full and consolidated versions of lead agencies, for all agencies with at least five EOs linked to them. These make up just under 90 percent of the issued orders in the expanded list and more than 95 percent in the consolidated account.

We can also determine agencies' link to centralization in these data: the "average" process varies widely by lead agency. The small number of observations in most cases means wide confidence intervals around these estimates,

TABLE 4.5. Sampled Executive Orders by Lead Agency

Agency	Full Listing		Consolidated		
	N	Pct. of Total	N	Pct. of Total	
Defense	81	14.2	100	17.6	[inc. War, Navy]
State	56	9.8	56	9.8	
Treasury	43	7.6	44	7.7	
Interior	37	6.5	38	6.7	
Justice	31	5.5	31	5.5	
Civ. Svc. Comm.	30	5.3	[see OPM]		
Commerce	30	5.3	30	5.3	
Agriculture	20	3.5	20	3.5	
National Mediation Board	20	3.5	[see Labor]		
White House Office	16	2.8	16	2.8	
Transportation	14	2.5	23	4.0	[inc. FAA, CAB]
GSA	13	2.3	13	2.3	
Health & Human Svcs.	13	2.3	21	3.7	[inc. HEW]
OPM	13	2.3	43	7.6	[inc. CSC]
OMB	11	1.9	11	1.9	
USTR	10	1.8	10	1.8	
War	10	1.8	[see Defense]		
EPA	9	1.6	9	1.6	
Labor	9	1.6	29	5.0	[inc. NMB]
Energy	8	1.4	9	1.6	
HUD	7	1.2	11	1.9	[inc. HHFA]
CIA	6	1.1	6	1.1	
Ofc. Emergency Mgmt.	6	1.1	[see DHS]		
Education	5	0.9	6	1.1	
Health, Ed., Welfare	5	0.9	[see HHS]		
Navy	5	0.9	[see Defense]		
Homeland Security			16	2.8	[inc. OEM, FEMA]
Nuclear Regulatory Comm.			5	0.9	[inc. AEC]
Other	61	10.7	22	3.9	
Total	*569*	*100.0*	*569*	*100.0*	

of course, but Figure 4.5 displays all agencies with more than 10 EOs linked to them. The mean centralization levels of EOs linked to those agencies range from a paltry 0.05 for the National Mediation Board (NMB) to over 2.5 for both the White House Office and OMB. Neither extreme is surprising; indeed, for the most centralized agencies it is true almost by definition.

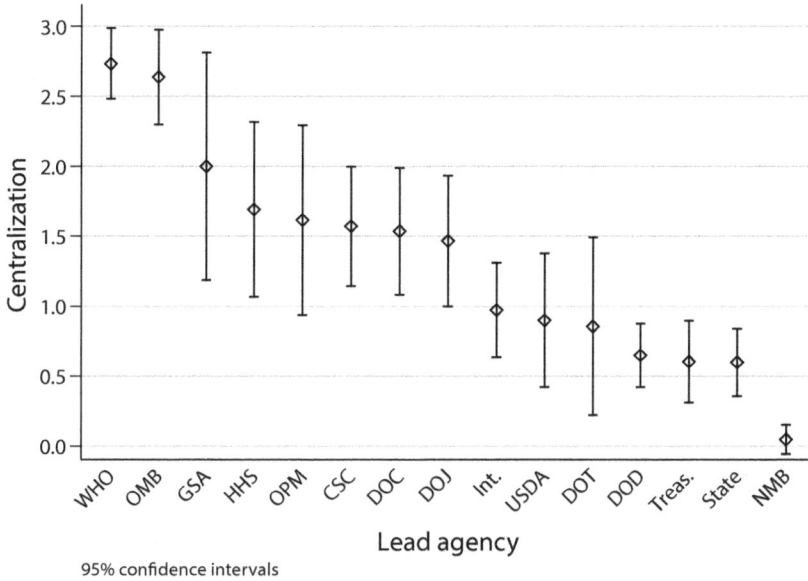

FIGURE 4.5. Mean Centralization, by Lead Agency.

The NMB, for its part, was created in 1934 and provides help resolving labor disputes within the airline and railroad industries. Its EOs nearly uniformly use standard pre-drafted language creating a temporary arbitration board to help settle strikes. Additional input is rarely needed: a strike happens, or does not.

More intriguing is the placement of the so-called "inner Cabinet," which also clusters near the decentralized end of the scale—with the glaring exception of the Department of Justice. State, Treasury, and Defense each have formulation processes with a mean of approximately 0.6 on the 0 to 3 scale of centralization. Along with relatively compact confidence intervals, that suggests they are given a fair bit of leeway in crafting relevant EOs. This may of course depend on the kind of EOs they craft: as discussed in the next chapter, many of the foreign policy issues that arise as executive orders rather than as different kinds of national security directives are less likely to incent centralized supervision. Perhaps just as importantly, as the extended examples traced earlier in this chapter should make clear, a decentralized process hardly means the process was nonconflictual—only that centralized staff were generally uninvolved. State, Treasury, and Defense are often at loggerheads with each other, and with outer Cabinet departments as well.

Testing Contingencies

It is said that the goddess Athena sprang fully formed direct from the brow of Zeus. Presidential brows may furrow, but rarely do they produce executive orders in quite the same manner. As we've seen, those orders come from many sources within the executive branch, and only a minority are preponderantly the product of the presidential branch. Presidents seek information to ensure they are aware of agency motives and policy consequences while asserting their own priorities. Agencies, for their part, seek to infuse the formulation process with arguments that help improve EOs substantively but also in ways that achieve their own ends, vis-à-vis both other agencies and, at least sometimes, presidents' preferences.

Given these data, the next chapters return to the hypotheses laid out in chapter 2 to examine the dynamics that shape any given formulation process. For instance, as Figure 4.5 showed, agencies dealing with government-wide matters of property, procurement, and personnel (thus, the General Services Administration, the Civil Service Commission, the Office of Personnel Management) tend to be associated with more centralized EOs—as does a traditionally politicized agency such as Health and Human Services. Are those factors systematically important in determining how presidents seek to manage EO formulation? What order-specific or agency-specific factors matter most in driving centralization, or in empowering agency autonomy? The answer, again, will prove to be managerial in nature.

Appendix

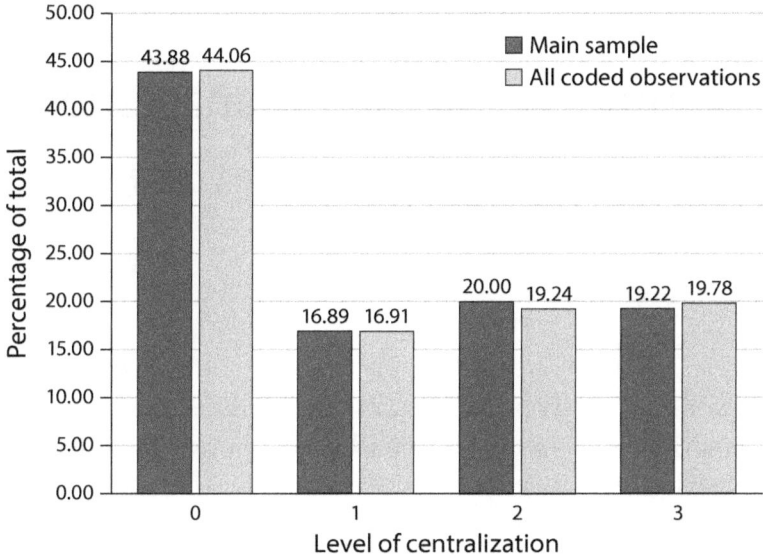

FIGURE A4.1. Executive Orders: Formulation by Level of Centralization, 1937–2004 (unweighted).

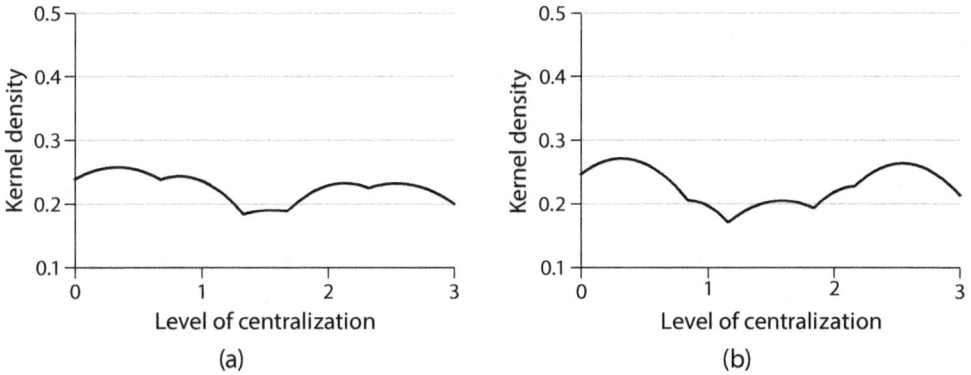

FIGURE A4.2. (a) Kernel Density Estimate: Kennedy Administration Only. (b) Kernel Density Estimate: Nixon Administration Only.

5

Testing Presidential Management

THE CONDITIONS OF CENTRALIZATION

"THE LORD AND THE FOUNDING FATHERS created executive orders," Trump advisor Peter Navarro proclaimed in August 2020.[1] The history, narrative examples, and descriptive statistics presented thus far suggest otherwise. The provenance of any given executive order is unlikely to be either divinely ordained or wholly centered in the White House—two contingencies presidents as well as their aides may sometimes confuse.

But neither the process of central clearance itself nor the aggregate numbers tell us why certain orders remain largely decentralized while others attract intensive EOP supervision. If presidents are indeed seeking to minimize their transaction costs regarding bureaucratic policymaking, the distribution of EO formulation processes should reflect that management.

To test that premise, we return to the hypotheses advanced in chapter 2 to discover whether there are regularities in the conditions under which the formulation of EOs is likely to be more or less centralized or decentralized. The first section of this chapter will review and operationalize these. The second assesses the relative strength of various contributing factors to the management of EOs' formulation process, using the more than five hundred executive orders detailed in chapter 4 along with a wide range of additional variables. Recall that the argument here is that central clearance should (at least on average) help presidents get the most from a far-from-unified executive branch, protecting themselves against informational end runs by bureaucratic actors and allowing them to invest their limited managerial resources in ways that minimize the transaction costs of that management. In turn, the attributes and managerial demands specific to a given EO should drive its provenance.

Of course, as we will see in subsequent chapters, this is not the end of the story. For one thing it does not account for how long the formulation process takes, where prolonged delays might themselves reflect the interagency transaction costs associated with an order's issuance, nor does it address the instances in which bargaining with the bureaucracy led to an EO remaining unissued. These explorations of potential negative power vested in the bureaucracy, and how presidents might negotiate them, are reserved for chapters 6 and 7. For now, we examine presidents' ability to shape EO formulation in a way that serves their informational needs.

Centralization and Context

To reprise the observable implications suggested in chapter 2, we should expect relatively more centralization when:

- the EO cuts across multiple agencies' jurisdictions;
- it carries out reorganizational or broad personnel functions; or
- it is significant and/or a presidential priority. (Here, we might expect a mixed process, but not something fully decentralized.)

By the same logic, we would expect less centralization—more delegation—as:

- the EO grows increasingly complex and technically involved;
- it is responding to a statutory assignment or reflects an older delegated "clerkship" function of the presidency;
- the agency with substantive jurisdiction over a potential EO is considered more "loyal" to the president, that is, its preferences are closer to those of the president;
- the preferences of an agency's other principals (notably in Congress) are closer to those of the president; or
- the EO is issued later in a president's term (reflecting a more trusting relationship with the bureaucracy over time).

In the discussion below, these hypotheses are fleshed out and supplemented with additional variables derived from the extant literature on executive orders and unilateralism. When it comes to the issuance of EOs, incentives and constraints imposed by external actors and events are given crucial weight: "the frequency of executive orders," Kenneth Mayer concluded, "is . . . a function of the president's political environment."[2] It turns out, though, that this matters less for their formation. There, the management context within which a given EO resides is the key. We begin by reviewing what that means in practice.

Management Contexts

Crosscutting Jurisdictions. The narrow vantage of departments makes it difficult for them to give presidents trustworthy advice on issues that cut across numerous agencies' substantive jurisdictions. Thus the more agency interests (really, self-interests) involved, the more centralized the formulation process is likely to be. A change to all agencies' personnel processes, for instance, should be very closely held indeed—as was President Trump's creation of a new schedule of political appointees just before the 2020 election.[3]

The "crosscut" variable is calculated here by utilizing the OMB clearance records identifying the bureaus asked to comment on a proposed order, or from secondary sources or the text of the EO where appropriate archival data were not available.[4] For instance, EO 10251 (a 1955 order on how to screen the armed services' ready reserve intake) was cleared through seven agencies: the Departments of Agriculture, Commerce, Defense, Labor, and Treasury, as well as the Office of Defense Mobilization (in the EOP) and the Selective Service System; EO 12789, issued in 1989 to delegate reporting functions under the Immigration Act of 1986, was considered by just two (Labor and Justice). The number of agency jurisdictions in these data range from 1 to 21, with a median figure of 3 and a mean just over 5.

Reorganization. Departments are turf-conscious, resisting organizational changes that infringe on their autonomy, and particularly those that require their decisions to flow through other departments. Conversely, as highlighted in chapter 3, they frequently propose changes that will give them a leg up over their executive branch rivals. Thus proposals that affect their own structure or require them to work with other agencies on a permanent basis are unlikely to be seen as disinterested, necessitating more centralized involvement to police opportunism. These are coded via a dichotomous variable assigning "1" to reorganizational matters and "0" otherwise.

Examples of reorganizations in this coding make up 14 percent of the total sample, about one in seven orders. They include the 1947 directive splitting the functions of the National Housing Administration into distinct agencies, and the 1980 EO creating a governmental Nuclear Safety Oversight Committee in the wake of the Three Mile Island reactor meltdown.[5]

Significance. The parameters of intra-executive management should vary according to the importance of the EO in question to the president, with significant orders likely to receive more attention from the president and his centralized staff.

Measuring significance, however, is a complicated task. As noted earlier, the question of significance serves as a dividing line of sorts in the scholarship on executive orders. Early work used a straightforward count, treating all EOs as equivalent, but subsequent scholarship sought to distinguish their relative policy weight.[6] Mayer designated 149 of his 1,028 sampled orders from 1936 to 1999 as significant, grounded in the attention they attracted and his assessment of their substantive heft.[7] Howell similarly and systematically included as significant any order mentioned in the appendix of the *Congressional Record* or in the federal judicial opinions of two or more cases, seeking to capture "the contemporary and retrospective judgment of political actors."[8] The resulting time series was then updated by including EOs mentioned by the *New York Times*, a process that also served to check on the broader public impact of the relevant EOs. Given the high correlation of orders across the sources utilized, and the improved accessibility of the *New York Times* archives in the years that followed his first study, Howell was later able to avoid the "acrobatics" of the combined time series and construct a data set based on one source across the postwar era.[9] This time series covered 1945 through 2001 and defined any non-ceremonial order that made it to the front page of the *New York Times* as significant.

Fang-Yi Chiou and Lawrence Rothenberg then expanded this approach to produce a measure of significance drawing on the form of "item-response theory" (IRT) used by congressional scholars to weight legislation by its importance.[10] They utilized nineteen "raters," sources with the expertise to distinguish between significant and less significant EOs; these include daily newspapers, political magazines (e.g., *National Journal*), congressional and court records, legal journals, and even subsequent presidential rhetoric.[11] The upshot is a continuous variable that does not rely on a dichotomous decision— "significant, or not?" Values of the measure, covering EOs issued from 1947 through 2003, range from −0.994 to 3.491.

Given the specific intra-institutional concerns of the present research, a third approach has merit too. After all, defining significance solely in terms *external* to the executive branch, whether in the media or elsewhere, may not capture the importance of that order to the internal workings of that branch. Since executive orders are by definition issued to executive branch actors, their impact on agency duties or procedures is a dimension worth capturing. For instance, EO 11602, issued by President Nixon in June 1971, would hardly attract much attention from reporters; in apparently innocuous bureaucrat-ese it simply provides for "Administration of the Clean Air Act with Respect to Federal Contracts, Grants, or Loans." But that order, when proposed, prompted a file five inches thick, full of denunciation and demands for revision. For the intended audience of government procurement officers (and as it turned out, for a wide range of private sector contractors as well) this was a hugely significant order. The Bush-Clinton smoking ban saga noted earlier serves as another good example.

The analysis here uses each of these specifications of significance, including Howell's data on *New York Times* appearances, as extended in time by Sharece Thrower for her own research, and Chiou and Rothenberg's IRT model measure covering multiple raters.[12] Since the latter covers a slightly shorter period (1947–2003) than does my sample (1937–2004), n will be smaller when the IRT measure is used. Extending through the whole time series is a measure seeking to extend Mayer's classification of orders deemed substantively significant; this includes all of the orders in his sample that overlap with mine, and others that follow his requirements. Finally, as above, I constructed a "government significance" dummy variable denoting EOs important to executive branch operations, such as the Nixon order above. Including this variable adds some fifteen observations to the pool of EOs already designated as significant in some way; it correlates with the other dichotomous variables at just .18 (for the Mayer-inspired measure of substantive significance) and .32 (for the extended *New York Times* data), respectively.[13]

While we cannot consistently measure presidential priorities separately from "significance," EOs issued in order to preempt potential or extant legislation do seem a potential avenue of insight here. In 1954, for instance, the Eisenhower administration—like its predecessor, seeking to grapple with questions around government employee loyalty—put forth an order that BoB director Rowland Hughes explained was meant to serve "in lieu of a bill which [anticommunist crusader Sen. Karl Mundt] had planned to introduce." Five decades later the George W. Bush administration wanted to blunt the legislative momentum of the 9/11 Commission recommendations regarding the coordination of information across the intelligence community. In August 2004, Bush issued EO 13355, which designated the director of the CIA as the person in charge of such coordination. (The Commission proposal for a Director of National Intelligence to supersede the DCI would nonetheless become law.)[14]

The higher political stakes of preemption suggests its own sort of significance. Thus an additional dummy variable was created to code EOs that the record shows were issued to forestall congressional action on the same topic. However, such cases are quite rare, at least in these data, representing only about 2.5 percent of issued orders (and just over 3 percent of those not issued).

Expertise. Specialized expertise is at the heart of the bureaucratic advantage vis-à-vis the president and EOP. The more technically complex the requirements for an executive order, the more a president should need to rely on agency input. Here a commonly used proxy is the length (in words) of the EO itself.[15] I will test both an absolute and logged word count measure below.[16]

Another measure comes from an imaginative approach taken by David Lewis and other scholars in recent years. They have developed extensive survey-based measures of agency attributes, as viewed by those who should know best: the rest of the executive branch.[17] In this way they measure the competence—the "workforce skill"—of a wide range of agencies, including all Cabinet agencies and other federal bureaus with more than a thousand employees as of late 2013. All else equal, competence should track with policy expertise and agency capacity; thus, again all else equal, EOs associated with more competent agencies should be relatively decentralized. Note, though, the potential interaction with agency loyalty: delegation is only likely to the degree the president feels an agency will not take advantage of their technical knowledge. (Of course, as noted in chapter 2, presidential efforts to instill loyalty via politicization may in turn lead to less competence.)

Statutory Delegation and "Clerkship." Congress, too, delegates to the bureaucracy, and some EOs respond to those kinds of statutory assignments.[18] Most passively, EOs may follow from recently passed law that affects a specific bureau or grants authorities to the president that is meant to be delegated, in turn, to one or more agencies. Occasionally the agencies squabble over who should receive the delegated autonomy; for instance, during the Korean War in 1951 agencies jostled to use the powers granted in P.L. 81–921, "amending and extending the First War Powers Act" to allow government stockpiling.[19] In most cases, though, the choice is obvious. A 1984 law required the Defense Department to shift its housing policies in Panama pursuant to the recent canal zone treaty there; EO 12520 authorized the Pentagon to issue regulations doing just that. No other agency objected.[20]

Other EOs may relate instead to Neustadt's notion of presidential clerkship, implementing routine duties long ago imposed on the presidential office. As described in chapter 2, some of these functions—affecting certain civil service personnel and land use, for instance—are no longer in force but must be accounted for in the historical timeline; other, similar responsibilities do remain, in areas ranging from statutes linking federal pay to inflation to the creation of arbitration procedures for certain labor disputes.[21] EOs issued under longstanding statutory authority should, like their functions, become mundane and thus readily outsourced to the agencies. From the informational perspective, finding an approach distinct from delegation will rarely be worth presidents' managerial effort, given the relatively low value of these items to their agenda. It is possible, of course, that a president could seize on such a routinized mandate to serve as a fig leaf covering rather bolder action. However, in practice, the powers coded under this category lend themselves to limited skullduggery.

Two dichotomous variables were created to test these hypotheses. The first tracks whether the OMB file specifies that the order was issued in response to a recent statute prompting or, often, requiring executive implementation. The second looks instead for orders issued under broad grants of past authority. Each of these constitutes just over one-fifth of the issued orders in the sample.

Preference Congruence. Agencies whose policy preferences are more congruent with the president's—less analytically, those considered more loyal—are more likely to be trusted with the formulation of executive orders.[22] That congruence might flow from the president's successful politicization of the agency; as a Clinton White House aide noted, "people make policy, and unless you look for the people who have policy visions that track with the President, you are not going to have policies emerging from the departments that track with the President."[23] President Trump's frequent attacks on the so-called "Deep State" tapped into these concerns of disloyalty.

Some agencies, of course, are more structurally independent of the president than others. Indeed, presidents fear that the centrifugal forces of agency culture and constituency pull even rabid partisans away from the White House. And agencies have their own ideological leanings that, to the degree they shift over time, do so slowly. Centralization should increase as an agency moves farther away from the president's preferences, and vice versa. More distant agencies, we might expect, are trusted less.

There are useful measures tracing the structural barriers insulating agencies from political control. Most notably, Jennifer Selin's work on "what makes an agency independent" goes well beyond a simple divergence between line agency and independent regulatory commission; she estimates both the relative buffering of agency actors from political control (decision makers within the Cabinet and especially within the EOP are less independent on this dimension) and an agency's freedom from what she calls "political review." The latter includes statutory features that remove an agency from OMB's purview when it submits legislative testimony or budget estimates or allow the agency to litigate or implement policy without outside approval. Both dimensions are tested below, again applied to the lead agencies defined earlier.[24] In general we would expect presidents to be less certain about the advice and motives of more insulated agencies, prompting a positive coefficient for centralization; a negative coefficient, by contrast, would serve as an intriguing hint that efforts to buffer agencies actually work.

If the structural insulation measures highlight that past legislators can affect a bureau's proximity to the president, that distance is linked to their contemporary Congresses too. Note that legislators have been an essential element of research into executive orders from the outset; the president's partisan support in Congress, measured in various ways, is consistently linked to the number of EOs produced. A "substitute" camp grounded in what Deering and Maltzman called "the strategic model" argued that EOs filled in for legislative action, and thus increased (decreased) levels of presidential support in Congress should lead to the issuance of fewer (more) EOs.[25] "Complement" advocates argued instead that unified government tended to produce more laws, which in turn required additional EOs to interpret and implement them. By this logic executive orders are "primarily a vehicle for reinforcing legislative victories, rather than circumventing a hostile Congress."[26] Pivotal politics models came to the same prediction from a different direction: since the anticipated reaction of other branches of government serves as one of the main constraints on the issuance of orders, the makeup of Congress matters greatly to presidential calculations in this regard. Divided government, especially when girded by ideologically cohesive opposing majorities, suggested a Congress more inclined (and able) to overturn presidential actions. In that environment rational presidents would not issue controversial orders in the first place.[27] Empirical studies using different time frames and measures of presidential strength in Congress do find contemporary unified governments associated with more, not fewer, EOs.[28]

That the makeup of Congress influences presidential reasoning regarding executive orders carries over to the formulation process, too, though via a different logic. Here the key is bureaus' multiple principals.[29] Presidents will trust the departments more if they feel that committee chairs and their partisan brethren are not urging those departments to do bad things—that is, things contrary to presidential preferences. Mixed messages are less likely under unified government, meaning that "trust" should increase with the strength of the president's party in Congress generally.[30] If so, there should be more delegation to the departments (i.e., more decentralized strategies, on average) when presidents have stronger ties to Congress than when they do not. This is likely a weaker relationship in administrative action than in legislative policy formulation, given the direct role of members of Congress in the latter. Still, as we saw in chapter 4, legislators often have an interest in executive action as well and seek to shape or even prompt it. Thus, we can hypothesize that the higher the percentage of legislative seats in House and Senate held by the president's co-partisans, the lower the level of centralization.

Scholars have used a variety of measures for presidential-legislative congruence. These include both combined and separate variables for House and Senate presidential party strength and a simple dichotomous variable for divided government. Not surprisingly, these are heavily correlated; the total co-partisans measure used below correlates at over .95 with each of the separate House and Senate variables, and at .86 with the generic divided government dummy. Presidents' ideological divergence from legislators was also tested, taking the absolute value of the difference between the president's score and the House floor median in the 75th through 108th Congresses (1937 to 2004) using the common space scores originally developed by Keith Poole and Howard Rosenthal. This correlates so significantly ($r = -.78$) with the co-partisans measure that it is not utilized in the main specification reported below, but results using this variable instead of partisan strength are reported in the appendix (Table A5.2, column C).[31]

We turn finally to more direct measures of president-agency congruence. Ideally, we could calculate the distance between a specific agency's ideological disposition and presidential preferences in any given year. And a variety of recent work has made important—even heroic—advances along these lines. Anthony Bertelli and Christian Grose's research, for instance, seeks to establish common referents between presidents and executive branch agencies via the latter's legislative testimony in different sessions of Congress.[32] At present, though, only a limited set of agencies and years have been measured in this manner. The set of lead agencies identified in chapter 4 goes well beyond available data of this kind.

For present purposes, then, we extend the imperfect assumption that agency ideology remains at least somewhat stable over time and use a fixed estimate. Here the executive branch surveys noted above provide the most comprehensive data. I will use the estimates of perceived agency ideology derived from the views of hundreds of experienced peers within the executive branch itself, as placed on a common space by Richardson, Clinton, and Lewis.[33] Since this survey does not include a direct measure of presidential ideology, however, several proxies were tested below. A dichotomous variable was developed tracking the ideological match between lead agencies and the party of the president: thus a pairing of Republican president and conservative agency (e.g., the Department of Defense) would be coded as 1, while a Democratic president's pairing with that same agency would be coded 0. Obviously this disregards the relative differences between presidents of the same party as well as between agencies, treating as it does all liberal agencies as equally liberal and vice versa. Another variable, then, includes the agency ideology estimates themselves, as interacted with a dummy for the party of the president. This also has shortcomings, since it assumes a linear effect on presidential "trust," that is, that a given president would be twice as happy with a twice-as-conservative agency.[34]

A broader caveat for variables in this category is that strategic behavior by agencies could affect the magnitude and direction of the observed effect of "trust." There is no bar to an ideologically distant or insulated agency proposing an EO—under the EO 11030 process detailed in chapter 3, their draft goes directly to OMB. But it is worth wondering whether an agency that knows it is less aligned with the president's preferences will refrain from proposing at least some subset of its draft EOs, suspecting they will not win favor. We would not be able to observe this directly.[35] Yet in constraining the shape of the EO universe it might shift the direction or magnitude of estimates of how ideology and insulation in turn affect centralization. If so, perhaps the most likely impact of such self-censorship would be to mute the importance of agency ideology and insulation on centralization (all else equal), since the kinds of EOs brought into the sample by either type of agency—"trusted," or not—would be those of a "trusted" agency. The expected empirical results, with congruence offsetting the need to centralize, might simply be inconclusive.[36]

Still, there is a coda to that caveat. A null finding might itself be read as at least consistent with strategic agencies acting on anticipated reactions, with the notion of bureaucratic autonomy this book posits.

Learning: Time in Term. New presidents rarely realize the value residing in the expertise of the permanent civil service or even in OMB; nor is every departmental political appointee in place on inauguration day. Thus a final hypothesis posited increased centralization at the outset of a president's first term. In practical terms, presidents may of course be utilizing EOs linked to their campaign pledges, drafted by transition staffers without much if any wider departmental input. These receive departmental clearance, or are supposed to— recall the Clinton team's directives noted in chapter 3—but this is likely less rigorous than normal given the brevity and chaos (not to mention the "ignorance and arrogance") of even a well-run transition.[37] As they settle into office, presidents should attain increasing awareness of what expertise resides in the permanent bureaucracy and should achieve the confirmation of their appointees in political positions across that bureaucracy. All else equal, then, presidents should centralize more earlier in their tenure.[38]

The analysis below tests two specifications of this notion. A linear variable counts the months of a president's term, from 1 to 96 for a two-term president (and up to 146 for Franklin Roosevelt).[39] An alternate measure uses a dichotomous variable denoting whether an EO is issued in a president's first hundred days in office. That is no magic interval, of course, but since the 1930s has become a symbolic benchmark for achievement drawing significant media attention and placing political pressure on presidents to create policy before it elapses.

Political and Control Contexts

Political pressure of various kinds is key to the wider literature on executive orders analyzing the scale of EO issuance. Besides the measures of congressional partisanship detailed above, they range from the state of the economy to the level of a president's public approval to the fact of an election year. Not all of these have clear implications for decisions regarding formulation but are relevant to any model of unilateralism as control variables.

For instance, *policy type* has received sustained attention in the study of executive orders and proved a useful control in measuring the centralization of legislative policy proposals.[40] Warber's content analysis led him to place

EOs into specific policy domains such as military and war policy, administrative reforms, regulatory action, and distributive or redistributive policies. Mayer's classifications divide the EO universe somewhat differently, including executive branch administration, civil service, public lands, labor, foreign affairs, defense and military, war and emergency powers, and domestic policy generally.[41]

These categories are generally descriptive as much as analytic. In legislative formulation, foreign policy proves a good predictor of a decentralized policy-making process—though this finding likely results from the fact that a skewed subset of foreign policy proposals makes its way to the legislative arena. Much foreign policy is non-legislative in nature. Still, despite Pentagon complaints of "the increasing desire of the White House to control and manage every aspect of military affairs," it is not clear such a trend would appear in the realm of numbered executive orders either.[42] As Warber concluded from his content analysis, "presidents rarely use executive orders to directly develop war policies."[43] National security directives compiled by the National Security Council, by various formal names across different administrations, are commonly used here instead. And while executive orders are not absent from the trade arena, proclamations crafted by the United States Trade Representative are the standard vehicle there.

Foreign policy matters amenable to executive order, then, may not be centered in the EOP. That suggests an agnostic approach to the likely direction of this measure's coefficient, with a tentative expectation that, as with legislative proposals, such EOs will be decentralized, given the jurisdiction of the powerful "inner Cabinet" State and Defense Departments over many of them. Indeed, in the data, two-thirds of the EOs wholly devoted to foreign policy had either State or the Pentagon as their lead agency; recall from the end of chapter 4 that EOs linked to these departments were less centralized than average. The specific measure is an index taking the values 0 through 2: 0 if purely domestic policy (this constitutes just under three-quarters of the sampled EOs), "1" if containing both domestic and foreign policy elements (such as with most trade issues), and "2" if predominantly foreign policy–oriented.[44]

A second measure is the *size of the federal government* overall. This measure is used in some previous studies on the grounds that a larger executive establishment should prompt presidents to issue more EOs: they need to, simply to control it.[45] When it comes to order formulation, size might matter in contradictory ways. On the one hand, following the same logic—and that of presidents facing increasingly crosscutting issues, as above—increased centralization might flow from presidents' need to coordinate the organizational chart chaos below them. On the other hand, a larger federal government—a deeper state?—provides more potential originators of EOs and a wider range of bureaucratic expertise to bring to bear on their development, which could prompt decentralization. Here, the size of the federal government is derived from the *Statistical Abstract of the United States* and is calculated as total civilian employment excluding postal workers.[46]

Additional political controls include a *shift in presidential party* and the approach of an *impending election*. Transitions between presidents of different parties were included by both Mayer and Howell in their analyses: given that presidents enter office with an extended list of campaign promises, early EOs provide a convenient way to winnow down that list. The early term should thus see a surge in new orders, particularly if there has just been a change in the party of the president.[47] During an election year, presidents might likewise be tempted to ramp up order issuance, to build capital for the campaign trail. And a president about to leave office, whether term-limited or defeated for reelection, might face similar incentives—especially if a successor of the other party is looming in the doorway to the Oval Office.[48]

The possible incentives of early term formulation have already been addressed and linked to increased centralization, carrying over from the president's lack of knowledge of the executive branch (and for that matter from the work of pre-term transition staff). To control for party change as well, the analysis below tests a dichotomous variable taking the value of "1" in the first year of a president's term following an administration of the opposing party (e.g., in 1969 or 1993), and otherwise 0. Likewise, it is plausible that a president coming closer to an election (and thus requiring enhanced speed or increased control, or simply desiring clearer credit claiming) may also centralize more. To the degree presidents see the agencies as sluggish, they could turn to in-house advice when time is short.[49] Such reasoning, of course, runs counter to the "learning" hypothesis. However, the measures are not quite reciprocal, since the time to an election will re-set—more than once, early in the period under study—while time in office continues to aggregate. Thus an additional measure tracks the number of months until the next presidential election, counting down from 48 to 0. Since specifications using this variable exclude EOs issued after the election by lame duck presidents not continuing in office, *n* is lower here by about 25 observations.

A president's *public standing* has also been linked to EO issuance, albeit with conflicting hypotheses as to its impact. Does an unpopular president issue more EOs, on the grounds that such presidents have more difficulty achieving legislative success? Or is it popular presidents who wear out their pen, having attained more leeway to set the agenda using administrative means?[50] More nuanced recent research examines the specific impact of public opinion on presidents' choices in this domain. Public disapproval of executive action may work directly or through other political actors sensitive to such feedback, limiting presidents' willingness to take such action.[51]

Even so it is not obvious that public standing should factor into the president's decision about the source of a given EO. Still, if Neustadt is right that additional "public prestige" generally enhances a president's bargaining position, the bureaucracy no less than Congress might account for that when considering presidential preferences. If so, less popular presidents might fear additional agency recalcitrance and act preemptively by centralizing policy formulation.

"Prestige" is measured here, however inexactly, by using the Gallup approval rating of the president. Two variables were compiled, one taking in the most recent poll conducted prior to the issuance of a given order and the other linked instead to the date the draft EO was sent to OMB. As discussed at length in chapter 6, EOs may have a long gestation period, and the start of the formulation process is more theoretically relevant given present purposes. However, while some EOs do span dramatic shifts in approval during the central clearance process—as when the unpopular Truman gives way to the well-liked Ike, or over the forty-eight hours flipping the calendar from September 10, 2001, to September 12—the two measures correlate at .87 for issued orders. Thus, since using the earlier date means losing close to forty observations for which data are not available, most of the specifications below use the approval figure timed to issuance; there is no meaningful change in the results (see Table 5.2, column (A)).

Finally, a dummy variable for each of the twelve presidents was calculated to control for any *president-specific effects* on centralization. Controlling for the other aspects of the management environment, I would not expect these to be significant in themselves but rather that institutional variables account for much of the variation often attributed to individual presidents. In fact this proves to be the case: none of the presidency dummies are individually significant, and removing them from the overall analysis has no substantive impact on the rest of the analysis (see the appendix, Table A5.1, to compare the results presented below with those including the president-specific measures). Another diagnostic control for robustness, using a year fixed-effect variable in place of the multiple measures listed above that vary by time, is discussed with the findings, and also presented in the appendix: it shows the results to be robust for the order-specific and agency-specific variables of primary interest here.

Centralization in Practice

The tables below utilize these variables to present ordered probit analysis of the level of centralization in the executive order data set. Depending on the specification used, n will vary, since coding for a different range of years or agencies may be available for different variables. For instance, using the agency survey or insulation data limits the analysis to the agencies measured by those scholars. However, dropping those variables and increasing the overall n available makes no substantive difference to the strength or impact of the remaining measures, as the last column of Table 5.1 makes clear. The appendix to the chapter presents additional alternate specifications.

Ordered probit models are designed to analyze situations where the dependent variable has discrete outcomes that can be measured ordinally. That is the case here, where the level of centralization—again, from 0 (fully decentralized) to 3 (fully centralized)—is categorical but not assumed to be evenly spaced, as would be required for an OLS model.[52] Ordered probit, however, makes a different assumption, which is that the relationship of the covariates is equivalent across the categorical outcomes—that the impact of crosscutting jurisdictions, say, is the same across all levels of centralization.[53]

A diagnostic test shows that the model overall does meet this assumption but that three variables violate it in some of the reported specifications: the crosscutting variable; the measure of significance, and the president's ideological alignment with a given agency. Thus, standard ordered probit results will be reported here (since their interpretation is familiar and relatively parsimonious, and the alternatives far from such), but analysis of the substantive shifts in variables will be augmented by an alternative analysis using a generalized ordered logit estimator.[54] The probit results themselves, of course, need to be transformed into probabilities, since a unit change in x does not lead to a unit change in y (all else equal) but rather to a shift in the probability of y being placed in one of the dependent variable's four categories. More intuitive presentations of the variables' substantive significance are therefore provided as well.

The four models presented in Table 5.1 vary mostly according to the measures of significance noted above. Three are presented here—Howell's dichotomous *New York Times* appearance marker, the continuous Chiou-Rothenberg

TABLE 5.1. Executive Order Formulation: The Contexts of Centralization

	(A)	(B)	(C)	(D)
	1937–2004	1947–2003	1937–2004	1937–2004
Crosscut	.077***	.066***	.071***	.099***
	(.015)	(.016)	(.015)	(.013)
Reorg.	1.014***	1.039***	1.023***	1.038***
	(.169)	(.195)	(.169)	(.159)
Significance	.281*			.252*
(NYT)	(.129)			(.122)
Sig. (Chiou-Roth.)		.177*		
		(.077)		
Sig. (intra-executive)			.425*	
			(.192)	
Preempt	.722*	.604	.771*	.632
	(.367)	(.401)	(.366)	(.337)
Word count	−.000	−.000	−.000	−.000
	(.000)	(.000)	(.000)	(.000)
Agency competence	−.333***	−.388***	−.319***	
	(.085)	(.092)	(.086)	
Statutory	−.468**	−.348*	−.489**	−.526***
	(.142)	(.152)	(.141)	(.136)
Clerk	−1.245***	−1.284***	−1.252***	−1.253***
	(.183)	(.204)	(.183)	(.165)
Co-partisans	−.010	−.015	−.010	−.009
(House and Senate)	(.007)	(.008)	(.007)	(.007)
Insulation (pol. review)	−.077	−.089	−.075	
	(.115)	(.124)	(.115)	
Insulation (appts.)	−.208	−.183	−.218	
	(.137)	(.150)	(.137)	
Ideological congruence	.083	.092	.083	
(distance from agency)	(.055)	(.060)	(.055)	
Month of term	−.003	−.006	−.002	−.001
	(.003)	(.003)	(.003)	(.002)
Hundred Days	−.093	−.091	−.082	−.046
	(.254)	(.279)	(.252)	(.231)
Foreign policy	−.320***	−.335**	−.327***	−.289***
	(.091)	(.099)	(.091)	(.082)
Gov. size	−.000	−.001	−.000	−.000
	(.000)	(.000)	(.000)	(.000)
Party change	−.024	−.098	−.071	−.100
	(.217)	(.228)	(.219)	(.195)

Continued on next page

TABLE 5.1. (*continued*)

	(A)	(B)	(C)	(D)
	1937–2004	1947–2003	1937–2004	1937–2004
Time to election	.004	.003	.004	
	(.005)	(.006)	(.005)	
Pres. approval	.001	−.002	.001	.000
	(.004)	(.005)	(.004)	(.004)

Note: Ordered probit analysis. Dependent variable is the 0–3 index of centralization discussed above: "0" represents an order formulated via a decentralized process, "3" a wholly centralized process. Each entry presents the variable's coefficient and standard error.

* $p < .05$; ** $p < .01$; *** $p < .001$ (two-tailed tests)

N	453	388	453	498
Pseudo-r^2	.213	.219	.213	.204
LLR	−465.3	−395.6	−465.2	−521.7
Prob>chi^2	.000	.000	.000	.000

IRT measure, and the intra-executive dummy noting items important to internal management—with the fourth (the more overarching dichotomous variable developed by Mayer) deferred to the appendix. As noted above, the fourth column streamlines the model to maximize the number of observations available. Various alternative specifications were also run, and are discussed below in connection with individual variables. But the short summary is this: the main variables of interest are robust across these different analyses and indeed very consistent in terms of their substantive and statistical significance throughout. The managerial hypotheses, not least the key role of agency competence, are largely supported. Political contexts, by contrast, generally have little impact.

There is little relationship between most of the control variables, largely associated with the EO issuance literature, and the locus of EO formulation. Party change at the outset of a term, the counter leading up to the next election, and presidential approval (however measured) are all rather impressively insignificant. More surprisingly, perhaps, so is the overall size of the federal government, which while negatively signed (implying that as government grows, centralization decreases) is not anywhere close to statistically meaningful.

As the number of presidential co-partisans rises in Congress, orders become less centralized, as predicted. But here this measure is only close to statistically significant (and only at $p < .10$, using a two-tailed test) when using the somewhat truncated timeline available with the Chiou-Rothenberg continuous measure of significance.[55]

Generally, then, the impact of Congress, even as one of agencies' multiple principals, seems muted—and so do other measures of presidential proximity to agencies. These give similar results: signed as expected, but not statistically significant. Neither of the two agency insulation variables drawn from Selin shows much impact either. Both the measure coding appointments and that tracking agencies buffer from "political review" are negative, suggesting that the more insulated the agency, the less centralized the proposal; the former is much closer to significance, but that tells us little (at best, $p < .21$). Dropping one or the other or both has little effect. The same is true for the measure of the president's ideological congruence with a given agency, derived from surveys of federal personnel. It is correctly signed. As distance between a president and an agency grows, so does centralization; the closer their preferences, the more likely the president is to delegate formulation. Again, though, neither the absolute measure of agency ideology nor the dummy variable "matching" presidents to agencies (not reported here) proves statistically significant.[56] As discussed above this may be partially due to inexact measurement of the president's own ideology, but as with insulation the non-finding may also represent agency self-censorship. As such a non-finding hints at bureaus' strategic behavior.

But there are interesting divergences here within different levels of centralization, as calculated by the generalized ordered logit analysis noted earlier. In this case president/agency congruence has no impact when examining only decentralized items, or when the two decentralized values (0 and 1) are set at 0 and the two centralized values (2 and 3) are set at 1. But when wholly centralized items are set apart as their own category compared to the rest, the president's "trust" in an agency does in fact suggest a statistically significant level of decentralization ($p < .031$). An alternate analysis using a simple probit analysis to analyze a dichotomous dependent variable indicating whether an item is fully centralized (coded 3) or not was also conducted. It also finds a stronger impact for agency "trust" on full centralization as opposed to its gradations—the larger the distance between president and agency, the more likely full centralization—albeit at $p < .101$. Table A5.3 in the appendix provides details. One tentative implication is that the most trusted agencies will rarely be shut out of the formulation process, even if they are not the sole vessels for an order's gestation.

Time does not seem to matter much to the formulation process. Neither the month of a presidential term nor a more truncated measure of the first "100 days" makes a difference to centralization, contrary to hypotheses positing experiential learning.

However, centralization is very strongly associated with the rest of the managerial contexts outlined above. Reorganizations are nearly invariably centralized. Likewise, the more agency jurisdictions an EO cuts across, the more likely it is to be centralized. Interestingly, though, generalized ordered logit shows that this effect is slightly asymmetric across levels of centralization. It is positive in all cases but weaker when considering fully centralized items as "1" and all other categories as "0." (See again Table A5.3.) This suggests that the effect of a rising number of subject-matter jurisdictions is to prompt centralized involvement while retaining agency input—moving the formulation to a mixed process. This makes sense, given that White House staff may well lack the breadth of expertise to know how a given directive will impact a wide range of different agencies. Indeed, the more agencies involved, the more likely at least some of them will have useful information (or at least lasting stubbornness) and will see their suggestions folded into the issued order.

The results strongly endorse the importance of agency expertise. Agencies' reputation for competence is a consistently significant predictor of the shape of an order's formulation process, across all specifications. The more expertise is attributed to an agency (again, by surveys of federal executives) the more EO formulation will be decentralized, all else equal ($p < .001$). The technical complexity of the EO, as measured by its word count, does not have an impact separate from this finding. However, the word count variable is far stronger in specifications omitting the expertise variable, suggesting that measuring substantive complexity does have utility.[57] It also strengthens in the analysis predicting fully centralized orders: more complex EOs are less likely to be fully centralized.[58]

The statutory delegation of powers—recent (via the "statutory" variable) and remote (via the "clerk" variable)—and its link to the "safe" provision of routine orders from the bureaucracy are also reflected in the results. Both the statutory and clerk variables are also associated with the sharp decentralization of EO formulation. Both coefficients are negative and strongly significant ($p < .001$). So is that for foreign policy. As expected, given the kinds of policy proposals contained in executive orders (versus other sorts of directives), EOs linked to international affairs are more likely to have agency input. This is yet another nod to specialized agency expertise.

Finally come two measures predicting increased centralization. One is the use of an EO to preempt congressional action, described above as a (decidedly imperfect) proxy for a presidential priority item. The other, building on the extensive work in the extant literature on unilateralism, is the substantive significance of an EO—strongly associated with increased centralization of a formulation process. Presidential attention does, indeed, elevate White House involvement in a given order—and this is true whether significance is measured by media mention (the *New York Times* measure pioneered by Howell, in column (A)), by the broader range of external attention tracked by Chiou and Rothenberg's IRT model (column (B)), or by the assessment of intragovernmental significance broached above (column (C)). It is also true for the dichotomous coding utilized by Mayer (reported in Table A5.2, column (B)).

These measures do diverge slightly when examined via generalized ordered logit for divergence across the different categories of centralization. The Chiou-Rothenberg and governmental significance measures have a constant impact across this analysis; interestingly, the *NYT* measure varies. As with the crosscut measure, these strongly predict additional centralization when considering decentralized measures versus all others, and when dividing the sample down the middle (thus, using the 0 and 1 categories as "0" and 2 and 3 as "1"). But when centralized items are isolated, the *NYT* measure of significance falls away. Indeed, as Table A5.3 shows, it is negatively signed as well in predicting fully centralized orders—indicating a tendency for significance to lead to mixed processes. Such measures, as we will see below, far more strongly predict an EO will *not* be wholly decentralized than that it *will* be wholly centralized. Again, this makes sense from a management standpoint: the more important the matter, the more crucial to get it right, substantively, garnering agency expertise while at the same time ensuring that expert advice does not mask another agenda.

In fact, simply sorting significant orders by levels of centralization shows that their highest percentage are within processes coded "2"—mixed, with the EOP in the lead. They make up just under half of the EOs formulated in that manner, compared to just under 30 percent of mixed processes with agencies preponderant, and 36 percent of fully centralized EOs. The same pattern holds if the mean IRT measure of significance is broken down by level of centralization: processes coded "2" are significantly more significant on this scale than those managed fully within the EOP (see Table A5.4 for details).

The overall findings are extremely robust to alternative specifications. The closest to a caveat on that score is reported in Table A5.1 in this chapter's appendix, which includes fixed-effect dummy variables for the dozen individual presidencies in the timeline. None of those are significant in their own right. Here, the *NYT* measure of significance drops slightly out of the range of standard statistical significance (but only to $p < .08$; and this is not true when any of the other measures of significance is used in conjunction with the presidency dummies). Other models are shown in Table A5.2, including different

measures for presidential approval, significance, and congressional congruence, as well as the impact on the main order-specific and agency-specific
variables when the variables varying by time are replaced by a simple year
fixed-effects variable. The last, presented in column (D) of Table A5.2, suggests
the multiple time-variant variables are not skewing the results. Indeed, the
coefficients of the key variables barely quiver with their removal. It is the
transaction—the combination of order and agency—that matters, not its
timing.

The impacts of the managerial variables on the formulation process are also
substantively meaningful, as Table 5.2 indicates and Figures 5.1 and 5.2 dis-
play.[59] Throughout we see that variables' impact may be uneven across
the categories of centralization. For instance, as a proposal moves from the
25th percentile on the "crosscut" variable (involving two agencies) to the
75th (ten agencies), the likelihood of a fully centralized process—holding all
other variables at their means—increases by eight percentage points, all else
equal. Such a shift similarly increases the likelihood of a predominantly centralized process (i.e., a value of "2"). And it has more impact still on the
converse side of formulation: the probability of a fully *de*centralized process
decreases by just under 18 percentage points as the crosscut variable increases.
(Moving from its 10th to the 90th percentile instead, as shown in Figures 5.1
and 5.2, the impact is even more striking. Ceteris paribus, that results in
an increase of 20 percentage points in the likelihood of centralization, and
a 33-percentage-point decrease in the chances of a fully decentralized
process.)

Reorganization proposals have even more impact. Moving from an order
that is not such a proposal to one that is increases the probability of a wholly
centralized process by some 27 percentage points (and a predominantly centralized process by 11.6 percentage points), all else equal. Preemptive proposals
also produce significantly more centralization (close to a 20-percentage-point
impact on full centralization), though across a tiny number of those cases
under study here.

Significant orders, however measured, increase the likelihood of a centralized process and—more strongly—decrease the chances of one that is fully
decentralized. For instance, moving from an EO that is not considered significant to one featured in the *New York Times* decreases the chance of that EO
being fully decentralized by more than ten percentage points, all else equal.
The continuous variable developed by Chiou and Rothenberg provides quite
similar substantive results; proposals tagged as internally significant have an

TABLE 5.2. Substantive Impact on Centralization and Decentralization, selected variables

Variable	Percentage Point Impact on Probability of Being...			
	Centralized (3)	Mixed (2)	Mixed (1)	Decentralized (0)
Reorg.	27.2	11.6	−5.9	−32.9
Preempt.	19.3	7.3	−4.7	−21.9
Sig. (Gov.)	9.4	6.5	−0.1	−15.1
Crosscut	8.0	8.2	1.5	−17.7
Sig. (NYT)	5.7	5.0	0.3	−11.0
Sig. (IRT)	3.9	4.3	0.7	−8.8
Insulation	−0.8	−0.8	−0.1	1.7
Congruence	−2.1	−2.1	−0.3	4.5
Competence	−4.4	−4.7	−1.0	10.1
Foreign pol.	−5.4	−5.8	−1.2	12.5
Statute	−7.1	−8.5	−2.7	18.3
Clerk	−14.9	−20.2	−10.9	46.0

Note: Figures indicate the percentage change in the probability of obtaining a result in one of the categories of centralization, from most to least centralized, given a shift in the independent variable from its 25th to 75th percentile (or 0 to 1, for dichotomous variables), holding all other variables at their mean. Calculations are based on Table 5.1, column (A), except for the Chiou-Roth. measure of significance ("Sig. (IRT)"), which is derived from Table 5.1, column (B). All variables significant at $p < .05$ (two-tailed tests), except those italicized.

even stronger impact. Each moves orders toward centralization and, asymmetrically, away from decentralization. These impacts are in some ways surprisingly low in absolute terms. To be sure, substantive significance is rarely isolated in the way this particular calculation assumes—it is unlikely to be the only moving part in a formulation decision. And while this particular estimator downplays the impact on middle categories as it calculates first differences, as we have seen already one effect of order significance is to make mixed processes more prominent. Still, that itself suggests that while significant EOs naturally tend to receive attention from the EOP and the president, even those—the orders that attract media and intergovernmental attention—are part of a wider bargaining process.

There are some equally striking results on the delegation side of the ledger—that is, among variables associated with more decentralized formulation processes. Indeed, an order flowing from the presidents' clerkship duties is (all else equal) 46 percentage points more likely to be wholly decentralized, and quite unlikely to be anything *but* wholly decentralized; likewise the chances of an order flowing directly from a recent statute having a decentralized process increases by some 18 percentage points compared to those orders

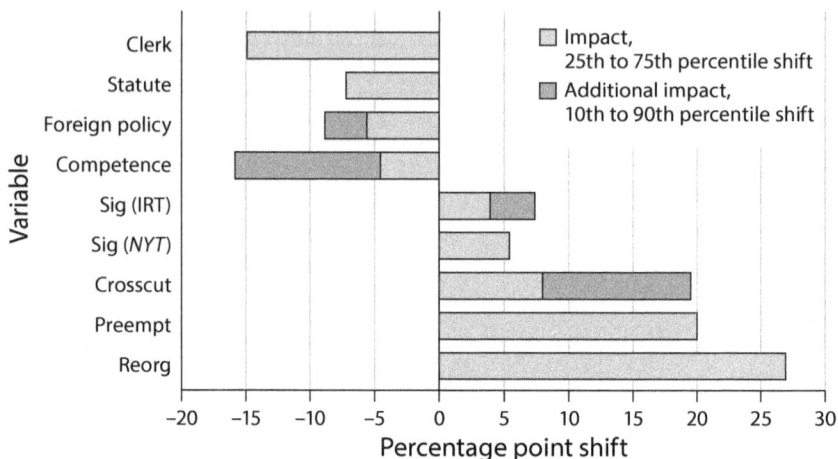

FIGURE 5.1. Impact of Determinants of Centralization. Estimated mean percentage point shift in likelihood of centralization, given specified shift in explanatory variable (other variables held constant at their means).

issued for other reasons. (As ever, all else equal.) Orders involving foreign policy have a similar effect, weighted toward the decentralization side of the scale. As suggested above, this likely reflects a sort of technical deference to (usually) the Departments of State and Defense on the sorts of issues appropriate for executive order as opposed to a decision directive controlled by the National Security Council.

Agency-centered variables also make a difference, largely driven by expertise. The insulation of agency decision makers as well as the ideological congruence of the president with the agency do seem to have modest substantive impacts on formulation—but these estimates are quite uncertain (as reflected in the original probit calculation), with the 95 percent confidence interval including both positive and negative estimates in each category for each variable. They are thus included here mainly for purposes of comparison. We can be far more confident in the agency competence variable, where moving from the 25th to 75th percentile reduces the likelihood of a wholly centralized process by 4.4 percentage points and increases that of a wholly decentralized process by more than 10 percentage points (again, all else equal). As shown in Figures 5.1 and 5.2, agencies at the high end of the competence spectrum have an even stronger impact. Moving from the 10th to the 90th percentile (instead of the 25th to 75th) increases the likelihood of increased decentralization by more than 27 percentage points, and diminishes the chance of a fully centralized

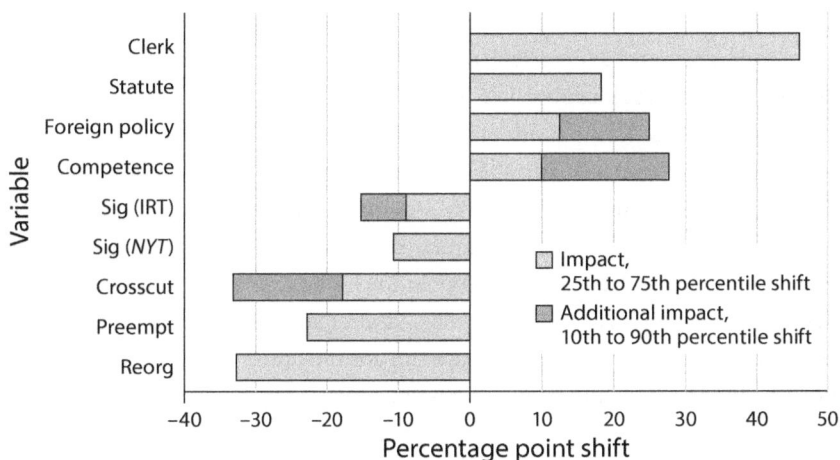

FIGURE 5.2. Impact of Determinants of Decentralization. Estimated mean percentage point shift in likelihood of decentralization, given specified shift in explanatory variable (other variables held constant at their means).

process by close to 16 percentage points. That is almost four times the impact of the smaller percentile shift, suggesting an uneven impact at the tails of the distribution.

Crossing the Street

This chapter has tested the hypotheses about presidential decisions about EO formulation laid out in chapter 2 using the data set described in chapter 4. The analysis showed strong empirical support for conceiving the management of the formulation process in informational terms. The contours of each transaction are shaped by the characteristics of the proposed order itself and the expertise of the agency with which it is associated. Formulation strategies blend departmental and EOP personnel in near-infinite combination, as the case studies throughout this book narrate. But they do not do so randomly.

Indeed, the results of this chapter suggest that chronology, presidential personality, and external political factors have minimal impact on the manner in which executive orders are crafted. Instead, presidents seek to manage EO formulation in ways that should reduce transaction costs within the executive branch. Hypotheses predicting increased centralization—substantive importance, crosscutting issues, an EO's reorganizational impact—found robust support across time, presidencies, and partisan context. So were measures incenting delegation to specific agencies, driven by a given agency's reputation for competence and expertise. Routinized functions with low informational demands were also decentralized.

These findings show presidents act as rational managers of policy formulation. But in conjunction with the data presented in chapter 4, they also confirm the utility of complicating easy assumptions about unilateral behavior: presidents manage, because they must. Even executive actions thought to reside at their end of the street—and even the highest-profile items in the president's policy agenda, as we have seen—are reliant on bureaucratic expertise and thus require presidents to finesse the complications of bureaucratic politics. The inconsistent and mostly negligible impact for the decentralizing influence of agency "loyalty" here is intriguing, along these lines: it might be read, tentatively at least, as evidence for bureaus' strategic behavior in choosing the policies they will proffer. Agency competence is crucial to crafting even unilateral policy, but presidents must sidestep the hazards of informational opportunism and channel that competence to suit their own needs. As Stephen Krasner notes, "When the President does devote time and attention to an issue, he can compel the bureaucracy to present him with alternatives."[60] But time and attention can be expensive.

How expensive? While this chapter has identified key commonalities across the EO formulation process, it does not take into account the length or difficulty of that process in any given case. The next two chapters introduce complications, shifting our perspective to the agencies' side of the "two-way street." When and why are executive orders slowed or even stopped in the midst of their path to the president's desk? In short: we turn next to delay and then doom, in the context of departmental dynamics.

Appendix

TABLE A5.1. Executive Order Formulation: The Contexts of Centralization, including Presidency Fixed-Effect Dummy Variables

Crosscut	.081	Preempt	.803
	(.016)		(.356)
	.000***		.024*
Reorg.	.981	Word count	−.000
	(.172)		(.000)
	.000***		.797
Significance (NYT)	.229	Agency competence	−.396
	(.130)		(.085)
	.078		.000***

		Individual presidents	
Statutory	−.461		
	(.142)	Pres. Roosevelt	.197
	.001**		(.638)
Clerk	−1.240		.757
	(.183)	Pres. Truman	−.074
	.000***		(.287)
Co-partisans	−.015		.796
(House and Senate)	(.020)	Pres. Eisenhower	.133
	.446		(.272)
Insulation (appts.)	−.063		.625
	(.112)	Pres. Kennedy	.460
	.572		(.352)
Insulation (decisions)	−.170		.192
	(.135)	Pres. Johnson	−.304
	.208		(.382)
Ideological congruence	−.090		.427
(distance from agency)	(.057)	Pres. Nixon	.352
	.115		(.345)
Month of term	−.002		.306
	(.003)	Pres. Ford	−.440
	.585		(.511)
Hundred Days	.130		.389
	(.258)	Pres. Carter	.500
	.614		(.361)
Foreign policy	−.252		.165
	(.089)	Pres. Reagan	−.003
	.005**		(.283)
Gov. size	−.000		.990
	(.000)	Pres. G.H.W. Bush	−.084
	.610		(.369)
Party change	−.151		.820
	(.215)	Pres. Clinton	−.181
	.481		(.290)
Pres. approval	.001		.533
	(.006)		
	.812		

[Pres. George W. Bush dummy omitted]

Note: Ordered probit analysis. Dependent variable is the 0–3 index of centralization discussed above: "0" represents an order formulated via a decentralized process, "3" a wholly centralized process. Each entry presents the variable's coefficient, standard error, and p value.

* $p < .05$; ** $p < .01$; *** $p < .001$ (two-tailed tests)

N	477
Pseudo-r^2	.224
LLR	−483.02
Prob>chi^2	.000

TABLE A5.2. The Contexts of Centralization (alternate specifications)

	(A)	(B)	(C)	(D)
Crosscut	.082	.075	.075	.078
	(.015)	(.015)	(.015)	(.015)
	.000***	.000***	.000***	.000***
Reorg.	1.095	1.018	1.010	.983
	(.177)	(.169)	(.169)	(.167)
	.000***	.000***	.000***	.000***
Significance	.271		.278	.281
(NYT)	(.135)		(.129)	(.125)
	.046*		.047*	.025*
Significance		.313		
(Mayer)		(.125)		
		.013*		
Preempt	.686	.687	.728	.744
	(.383)	(.367)	(.366)	(.347)
	.073	.061	.047*	.032*
Word count	−.000	−.000	−.000	−.000
	(.000)	(.000)	(.000)	(.000)
	.553	.449	.518	.882
Agency competence	−.376	−.347	−.336	−.361
	(.089)	(.086)	(.085)	(.083)
	.000***	.000***	.000***	.000***
Statutory	−.440	−.477	−.468	−.468
	(.148)	(.142)	(.142)	(.137)
	.003**	.001**	.001**	.001**
Clerk	−1.208	−1.228	−1.257	−1.161
	(.191)	(.183)	(.185)	(.175)
	.000***	.000***	.000***	.000***
Co-partisans	−.008	−.010		
(House and Senate)	(.008)	(.007)		
	.270	.173		
DW-Nominate distance			.428	
			(.312)	
			.170	
Insulation (pol. review)	−.159	−.081	−.075	−.048
	(.120)	(.115)	(.115)	(.108)
	.186	.482	.518	.656
Insulation (appts.)	−.198	−.224	−.193	−.164
	(.142)	(.137)	(.138)	(.131)
	.163	.103	.169	.212
Ideological congruence	.082	.086	.075	.079
(distance from agency)	(.057)	(.055)	(.055)	(.054)
	.151	.119	.169	.141

	(A)	(B)	(C)	(D)
Month of term	−.003	−.003	−.002	
	(.003)	(.003)	(.003)	
	.308	.335	.398	
Hundred Days	−.085	−.075	−.073	
	(.261)	(.253)	(.254)	
	.743	.766	.774	
Foreign policy	−.285	−.328	−.323	−.260
	(.094)	(.092)	(.091)	(.086)
	.000***	.000***	.000***	.003**
Gov. size	−.000	−.000	−.000	
	(.000)	(.000)	(.000)	
	.613	.494	.476	
Party change	−.078	−.063	−.019	
	(.225)	(.219)	(.216)	
	.729	.772	.931	
Time to election	.002	.004	.004	
	(.006)	(.005)	(.005)	
	.658	.404	.476	
Pres. approval (issuance)		.001	.001	
		(.004)	(.004)	
		.758	.825	
Pres. approval (formulation)	.006			
	(.005)			
	.219			
Year				−.000
				(.003)
				.947

Note: Ordered probit analysis. Dependent variable is the 0–3 index of centralization discussed above: "0" represents an order formulated via a decentralized process, "3" a wholly centralized process. Each entry presents the variable's coefficient, standard error, and p value.

Column (A) includes the measure of presidential approval dating from the start of the formulation process rather than the EO's date of issuance. An alternate specification dropping the time-to-election variable so as to include lame-duck orders (thus, $n=440$) made no substantial difference to any remaining variables.

Column (B) includes the Mayer-type dichotomous variable for EO significance. Again, including lame-duck orders ($n=477$) had no effect.

Column (C) includes the distance between president and the House using DW-Nominate scores instead of using co-partisans.

Column (D) drops variables that vary by time, and replaces them with a simple year fixed-effect counter, while keeping variables that are order- or agency-specific.

$^{*} p<.05;$ $^{**} p<.01;$ $^{***} p<.001$ (two-tailed tests)

N	419	453	453	477
Pseudo-r^2	.219	.214	.213	.208
LLR	−428.1	−464.6	−465.3	−493.18
Prob>chi^2	.000	.000	.000	.000

TABLE A5.3. Contributing Factors to Fully Centralized Orders

Crosscut	.035	Insulation (appts.)	−.075
	(.020)		(.198)
	.084		.706
Reorg.	.980	Ideological congruence	.133
	(.202)	(distance from agency)	(.081)
	.000***		.101
Significance	−.074	Month of term	−.000
(NYT)	(.187)		(.004)
	.691		.917
Preempt	.727	Hundred Days	.304
	(.430)		(.330)
	.087		.358
Word count	−.000	Foreign policy	−.393
	(.000)		(.150)
	.106		.009**
Agency competence	−.282	Gov. size	−.000
	(.118)		(.000)
	.017*		.993
Statutory	−.529	Party change	−.287
	(.215)		(.318)
	.014*		.366
Clerk	−1.150	Time to election	.012
	(.306)		(.007)
	.000***		.094
Co-partisans	−.002	Pres. approval	.003
(House and Senate)	(.010)	(issuance)	(.006)
	.858		.642
Insulation (pol. review)	−.143		
	(.161)		
	.374		

Note: Probit analysis. Dependent variable is dichotomous: "0" if an EO's formulation process is coded 0, 1, or 2, and "1" if the formulation process was wholly centralized (coded 3). Thus the model predicts the impact of each variable, ceteris paribus, on a wholly centralized formulation process. Each entry presents the variable's coefficient, standard error, and p value.

* $p<.05$; ** $p<.01$; *** $p<.001$ (two-tailed tests)

N	453
Pseudo-r^2	.261
LLR	−161.69
Prob>chi^2	.000

TABLE A5.4. Significant Orders and Levels of Centralization

Formulation Process, by Level of Centralization	% Coded Significant (NYT) (n)	Mean Significance (IRT) (n)
0	14.7 (245)	−0.227 (180)
1	28.7 (94)	0.203 (73)
2	49.5 (107)	0.568 (92)
3	36.4 (110)	0.362 (90)

6

A Brief History of Time
(to Issuance)

IN AUGUST 1989, OMB's top officials received a list of the executive orders the general counsel's office had been tracking since the start of the new George H. W. Bush administration.[1] There were close to forty, submitted as recently as four days prior and as long ago as September 1987. The topics on the table included everything from an advisory committee on the president's Points of Light initiative to mechanisms for providing assistance to the Nicaraguan resistance.

This "executive order log," extracted from the archives, serves as an intriguing snapshot of pending business. But it also provides useful information on the time routinely consumed by the bargaining over order issuance that takes place during the central clearance process. One EO aimed to regulate the "seismic safety" of a wide range of new building construction, raising concerns (as the general counsel put it) of "costs to the government, liability of [the Department of Housing and Urban Development], and the applicability of the order."[2] The order, proposed by the Federal Emergency Management Agency in June 1988, did not make its bow in the *Federal Register* until January 1990.[3]

That those concerns took nearly nineteen months to resolve was something of an outlier, at least compared to cases when an order was in fact ultimately issued—after all, close to a quarter of the EOs logged (including the one languishing since 1987) wound up discarded altogether. Even so, in this particular collection of EOs there were 154 days, on average, between receipt of a draft order at OMB and the president affixing his signature thereon. One EO, establishing the President's Advisory Committee on Aviation Security and Terrorism, took just two days. But eleven (of the 30 issued) took more than six months.

We tend to think of EOs as mechanisms for rapid response, indeed as nearly immediate. Barack Obama's justification for his 2011–12 campaign of executive action was that "we can't wait!"[4] But in fact a lot of waiting lurks behind even headline-level policymaking. Obama's executive order decreeing that the controversial military prison located at Guantánamo Bay, Cuba, would close within a year was issued just two days after his inauguration in 2009; but a related EO establishing systematic parole-like reviews of those detained, contemplated in the first order, was not finalized until two years later after "fits and starts" in the interagency review process.[5] "Gitmo" did not close, of course—in large part because Congress cut off funding for such a move. Neither did its associated intra-executive disputation wind down. Donald Trump's January 2018 EO rescinding Obama's 2009 order and declaring that Guantánamo Bay would remain open was bruited a full year before its issuance; pushback over its substantive and legal implications was so fierce that when presidential press secretary Sean Spicer was asked about an early draft he claimed (falsely) that it was not a White House document.[6] A revised EO on the matter prepared later in 2017 was also sent back for additional interagency deliberations by new White House chief of staff John Kelly (who as a Marine general had overseen the prison), a lengthy review that wound up removing the most controversial policy initiatives regarding terrorist detention the administration had considered along the way.[7]

A more extensive example gives a sense of the dynamics of such delays, even with apparent stakes far lower than in the war on terror. Here, by contrast—in a case that spanned parts of four years and two presidencies—the battle was over the federal role in rural development, and who should have charge of it.

In 1959, Dwight Eisenhower had created (via EO 10847) a Committee for a Rural Development Program. Its members included the Departments of Agriculture, Interior, Commerce, Labor, and HEW, as well as the Small Business Administration and the Council of Economic Advisers. The passage of the Area Redevelopment Act early in the new John F. Kennedy administration prompted Agriculture Secretary Orville Freeman to argue that such coordination was more important than ever and that a new executive order would both remove "dated" language and "reactivate the committee"—under Agriculture's leadership.[8]

So far, so New Frontier. But the unstated rationale for Agriculture's maneuver was the fact that the Redevelopment Act had created a new board, the Area Redevelopment Administration (ARA), and placed it within the Commerce

Department. Commerce, unsurprisingly, rejected the idea of renewing the 1959 board, as did Interior; the latter did "not believe revival of the Committee would be in the interest of effective government." The Bureau of the Budget was inclined to agree. "The proposal for a new Executive order and a new committee would appear to be, in effect, an attempt to enlist the President's support in circumventing the pattern of agency responsibility" embedded in the new law, wrote one analyst. Still, Agriculture had its proponents, even in other divisions of BoB. The 1959 committee had a national scope, one staffer argued, while the new law applied just to distressed redevelopment areas. Perhaps Agriculture could withdraw the draft EO and work out boundary lines bilaterally with Commerce?

No go, Freeman told BoB in August 1962. He still wanted the order. The result, as another internal BoB memo put it, was that the issue was now a test of bureaucratic dexterity. Issuance or non-issuance would have "effects on the relative bargaining strength" of Agriculture and Commerce. If issued, Agriculture would get "a status symbol for use in its negotiations"; non-issuance would bolster Commerce, if only as a denial of Agriculture's wishes. (It was unlikely, the staffer noted, that any of this would help with "the ultimate solution of the main problem.")

For many months, BoB sought to broker a cross-department deal. In October 1962, its general counsel drafted a substitute order that would make the membership of the renewed committee identical to that of the ARA, remove the word "area" from its name, and order coordination between the two bodies. This foundered on the key question of who would coordinate the coordination. As the argument dragged into the summer of 1963, Agriculture continued to hold that not all rural areas fell under ARA jurisdiction and that even in those that did, Commerce could act only when other agencies were not authorized to act on their own. Commerce conceded that there were limits to ARA's power but thought that coordination, at least, should be within its remit. BoB tended to think that Agriculture "did not make a strong, concrete case" and that no new order should be issued at this point. As an August 2 memo to BoB deputy director Charles Schultze endorsing the "staff consensus" argued, "it looks silly to abolish the existing USDA committee and then immediately set up a new one identical in membership and with only the 'whereas' language changed. If Freeman wants to get busy on rural areas, let him call a meeting of his present committee, which has been in rigor mortis for the past year or two."

Yet Schultze rejected the careerists' take. He sided with Agriculture, even asking, "Is there any real reason we can't give Freeman his heart's desire . . . ?"

by endorsing Agriculture's favored name for the body (the Rural Areas Development Committee). A new draft to that effect ensued in late August. It clarified that the reconstituted committee did not have jurisdiction over ARA-specific locations, and did hew to Commerce's demand to remove the word "areas" from the name. But Agriculture, recognizing its victory, had the good grace to sign off on the new draft despite the small departures from its heart's desire. In October 1963, in its letter to the attorney general, BoB justified the new order as follows:

> The final order draft represents an attempt, (1) to institute machinery which will be useful with respect to rural development matters which are of primary concern to the Department of Agriculture; (2) to avoid arrangements which could create undue interagency problems in the rural development field; and (3) by means of an express Presidential mandate with respect to coordination, to offer a reasonable prospect of positive benefit.

Agriculture won out in the end, then—perhaps even generating a "positive benefit" to policy overall—but only after a process that took more than 625 days from when it submitted its proposed order.

How should we think of such delays—and about time generally, in this context? That is: is there any connection between the time the issuance process takes and the "relative bargaining strength" of different parts of the executive branch? Is it simply a matter of complicated policy requiring time to work through? Of the intensity of preference in different bureaucratic camps? Of other factors entirely?

Chapter 5 explored the factors associated with different levels of agency and EOP involvement in the EO formulation process. But in summarizing their impact on presidential management it did not place a price tag on the overall effort required to move an order to issuance. By contrast, this chapter tries to do just that, adding a new assessment of the transaction costs associated with the formulation of a given EO with a given profile. It presents both descriptive and analytic data that use the length of time associated with the issuance of executive orders as an innovative—though of course incomplete—proxy for the scope of interagency bargaining surrounding a given order. Duration models help us examine the conditions that affect how long it takes for a proposed executive order to be issued (if, indeed, it is issued at all: this chapter sets the stage for systematic analysis of unissued orders as well).

What contexts speed, or slow, order issuance? Are some types of EOs—or some agencies—more "costly" for the president to manage? How is the power to delay—by all accounts a crucial part of bureaucratic sway—manifested in the EO formulation process? Agencies cannot require the president to sign an order, though they can present a strong case for doing so (presidents have at times portrayed themselves as victims in this regard).[9] More commonly and indeed almost universally, though, they can slow deliberation. Sometimes they sit on requests for input or information, sometimes they raise substantive amendments or caveats, sometimes they force complaints or questions up through several levels of hierarchy to the Oval Office itself.

But while delay can be purposeful, it may simply result from the complications of managing multiple participants in a complicated policy process. On average we might expect EOs featuring mixed formulation processes melding EOP and agency involvement to have the highest transaction costs in absolute terms and thus take the longest to formulate, even while that process simultaneously minimizes such costs for any particular EO. Such EOs have characteristics that make presidents wary of outright delegation but also make them hard to centralize fully. The Rural Development Program just traced is coded "1," a mixed process that played out in just this way. Is that experience, or those of the Bush administration detailed to start the chapter, typical? To find out, we turn to the data.

Time on Task

How long do orders take to be issued, on average? The OMB files tracking issued EOs come to the rescue here, since most of them ($n = 515$) contain the date on which the order was originally sent to OMB under the provisions of EO 11030 or its predecessors. This makes it possible to measure how long it took to issue any given order.

To be sure, such a calculation comes with caveats: an EO's official reception at OMB does not always coincide with the date the order was first drafted or discussed. As noted in chapter 3, ideas for EOs are often shared in advance with Justice, or other parts of the EOP, or OMB itself. A recent OMB general counsel noted that nearly every assistant secretary thinks the president should issue an EO on their behalf—but that "not every idea out there deserves an executive order." A "savvy" bureaucratic operator will therefore work internally with her agency and then with EOP staff to pave the way for a given draft.[10] Another former OMB general counsel pointed out that in some specific cases, such as sanctions orders, much of the key interagency review takes place as part of the National Security Council's own

TABLE 6.1. Time to Issuance: Summary Statistics

N = 515	
Range:	1–1,646 days
Mean:	76.4 days*
S.D.:	131.99
25th pctile:	11 days
Median:	33 days
75th pctile:	91 days
90th pctile:	181 days
95th pctile:	298 days
99th pctile:	629 days

* This figure is 71.4 (104.5 s.d.) without the two outlying observations of over 1,000 days.

process, prior to OMB's central clearance.[11] Even so, the OMB time stamp provides a consistent measure of the date on which a draft was officially considered for issuance. If the figure is not exact, at least it should be comparable across the sampled orders. If anything, it is likely to lowball an EO's "time to issuance."

Table 6.1 provides summary statistics for this calculation, with time to issuance measured in days. An EO received on Tuesday morning and issued that afternoon is counted as one day, with the count mounting from there.[12] The short version of the table is that EOs move quite slowly, on average, if not quite as slowly as the 1989 Bush administration collation tracked above.

The median time to issuance in these data is just over a month, at 33 days. That disguises a lot of variability, as the standard deviation of 132 makes clear: the shortest time to issuance was a single day, while the longest was more than 1,600 days (some 4.5 years). Thus the mean time to issuance was significantly higher, at 76 days. A full quarter of orders take more than 90 days to issue, and 10 percent more than six months.

Not surprisingly, delays rise further if we also analyze orders ultimately unissued, counting such EOs as pending until someone in OMB inscribes their death certificate. Details are reserved for chapter 7, but unissued orders are often under at least nominal consideration for a long period before the plug is formally pulled on their formulation process. Adding them to the issued orders in Figure 6.1 brings the average "days active" for all proposed EOs to 164 days, or five months-plus. The median in that larger data set ($n = 742$) is 55 days. (See Table A6.1 in the appendix to this chapter for a complete comparison.)

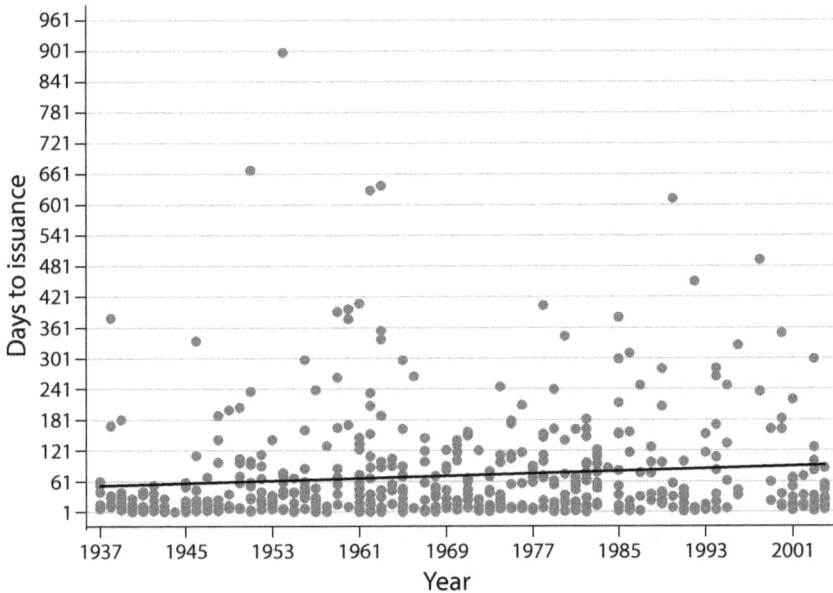

FIGURE 6.1. Days to Issuance, by Year.

Do these summary statistics disguise important changes over time? The simple fact of increased institutional complexity—growth in the number of government departments and agencies, and thickening within the EOP itself—could plausibly cause delays. As Jeffrey Pressman and Aaron Wildavsky famously demonstrated, increasing the number of actors required to sign off on a decision can postpone that decision considerably even when none of the signers are intent on delay.[13] And, of course, some of them may be. Figure 6.1, which provides a scatterplot of issuance times by year, suggests that there is indeed a small (but statistically significant, $p < .02$) upward trend across the years covered here.[14] The increased delay represents just over a half day per year, which adds up over time; all else equal, an issued EO spent forty days more under consideration in 2004 than in 1937.

However, as we will see, all else may not be equal. This simple linear relationship vanishes if we use an annual count of federal employees instead of the year and again when we control for the characteristics and contexts of individual EOs.[15] The next section discusses those variables and examines their bivariate connection to the duration of the formulation process, before we turn to multivariate survival models that allow us to draw stronger conclusions.

Internal Dynamics and External Prods

What factors dictate how long an EO will be under consideration by the president?[16] Our main interest lies, of course, in bureaucratic dynamics: the scope of the wider interagency negotiations that help produce the EO, and the friction and thus management costs they imply. The impact of the "crosscut" variable defined earlier, for example, is relevant here; that in turn is related to the kind of formulation process associated with the order. As suggested above, EOs formulated by some mix of EOP and agency input likely incur higher transaction costs than those for which a fully delegated or centralized process is feasible. As in the last chapter, characteristics of the EO itself and of the agency with which it is associated may also be important to the president's management of this process. Before turning to these variables, though, we need to consider external dynamics—notably the role of events—that may speed or slow EO issuance in ways they did not impact the shape of the process itself.

Action-Forcing Deadlines

In some cases a particular event mandates issuance of an executive order at a time certain. That could be exogenous, something outside an administration's immediate control. Remember, for example, that the Clinton administration EO on classified information traced in chapter 4 was governed by a six-month deadline set in statute.[17] Other actors besides Congress can set the calendar too: in 1947 an EO tied to the nascent organization of the United Nations required rapid completion in what the State Department's Dean Rusk called "the interests of immediate action." (However, consistent with the larger findings of this book, Rusk also noted that the resulting EO had "attendant difficulties" because it was "cleared without adequate study and analysis, and . . . now represented the narrowest margin of agreement.")[18]

More commonly, though, the spark is lit in the wider world, for instance by a labor dispute which might or might not transform into a strike enabling presidential action. In this vein the EOs proposed by the National Mediation Board (NMB), for the most part boilerplate drafts with specific transportation industry combatants filled in as needed, languish for an average of just two weeks. That is the lowest figure associated with any agency with at least five EOs in the data set. The NMB's draft orders are readied when it seems likely labor-management negotiations will founder and issued quickly if they do. EOs tied to civil unrest or national disaster may likewise be rushed along by external events. John F. Kennedy's 1963 order "Providing Assistance for the Removal of Obstructions of Justice and Suppression of Unlawful Combinations within the State of Alabama" served as rapid response to that state's refusal to allow African American university students to enroll. "The administration had laid plans well in advance of the Alabama crisis," the *New York Times* reported. "An executive order federalizing the Alabama National Guard was ready for Mr. Kennedy's signature when the White House received word of Gov. George C. Wallace's defiance."[19]

Other influences on timing are closer to endogenous, tied to White House choices. That occasionally means tactically slow-walking an EO, linked perhaps to legislative activity. In 1982, for instance, the White House wanted to "ensure the E.O. does not become a basis for the teachers union to lobby" over collective bargaining rights; therefore, OMB reported in June, "the proposal is being held until congressional action" on a relevant authorization bill. The order was issued in November.[20]

Far more often, though, action-forcing deadlines spring from political decision making, often linked to public events or announcements. Donald Trump's 2020 executive order on "preventing online censorship"—under interagency development for at least a year—was signed soon after he reacted angrily (on Twitter) about being fact-checked (by Twitter).[21] Issuance of a 1995 executive order on child support was shackled to a weekly presidential radio address in desperate search of something specific to say.[22] Likewise the president's communications staff may decide that a new EO targeted to a particular constituency is just the dramatic touch required for a speech at a veterans' or teachers' or manufacturers' convention. In January 1983, OMB asked for the attorney general's "urgent attention in light of [a] pressing deadline," a deadline made pressing only by a White House declaration "that the President wishes to sign the Executive order on Friday morning at a ceremony."[23]

This rarely makes fans across the executive branch: "You say, 'seriously?'" reported one former OMB general counsel. "'Can't you just pretend you're signing something?'" Many such proposals are diverted away from the EO process and wind up as less elevated forms of presidential mandate. But "sometimes you need something to sign."[24] Interestingly, though, executive action announced during the State of the Union Address is most often in the future tense. Barack Obama's pledge from 2012 is typical: "In the next few weeks, I will sign an executive order clearing away the red tape" surrounding infrastructure construction projects, the president said. The actual EO was not issued for close to two months.[25]

Can systematic effects be identified here? Coding EOs by whether or not they clearly responded to an external event—ranging in importance from closing federal offices for a presidential funeral, to civil rights crises, to the Gulf War—shows that such happenings do truncate the formulation process. Such EOs were issued in an average of 19.9 days, compared to 80.6 days for their less urgent counterparts in the sample ($n = 515$, $p < .01$). However, available data do not show a similar pattern linking presidential communications to the time it takes to issue EOs overall. While it is difficult to match EOs directly with a press office wish list, there are potential proxies to capture orders produced on demand, as described above, for presentation at a forum linked to a given constituency or for speeches and radio addresses generally. For example, Adam Warber has coded whether executive orders are aimed at a target group,[26] while Sharece Thrower's examination of whether EOs are revised or revoked by future presidents includes a measure of whether an EO received any public mention by a president.[27] However, neither measure links public outreach to time to issuance in a bivariate way. EOs that appear in the *Public Papers of the President* have nearly exactly the same mean formulation duration as those that do not, at 78 versus 76 days, respectively.[28]

Order-Specific Factors

As with the locus of formulation, certain order-specific factors should matter to the time that formulation takes. These include an EO's complexity and substantive significance, as markers for the information required for a successful drafting process. The more complicated that process, all else equal, the longer its duration.

Complexity. Along those lines, the more legally or technically exacting an EO's task, the longer it should take to finalize. As one Johnson administration staffer warned in 1967 in his comments on a series of "executive orders for the [military] draft," one such EO had unearthed "many complexities and we don't want to give a firm date." Another had "to be considered in connection with" overlapping policies already in place; "this system is complicated and it may take about a year to thoroughly work out."[29]

As discussed in chapter 5, the length of an executive order is commonly used as a measure of its complexity.[30] That variable did not have a strong effect on centralization, at least when controlling separately for agency expertise. But using either a raw or logged count of the words contained in an EO shows a strong bivariate relationship of complexity to the duration of a formulation process. All else equal, using a raw count, every twenty-five additional words in an EO results in one extra day being added to the formulation process.[31]

Significance. The substantive significance of an EO could also matter for its timing, though the implications are less clear-cut. On the one hand, significant orders might well be part of the administration's upper tier of policy priorities, and thus needed fast (at least in the view of the president). Further, as we saw in chapter 5, such orders tend to be associated with a more centralized management process—thus receiving EOP or even direct presidential attention, with less attendant likelihood that the proposal will fall through the bureaucratic cracks. As a former OMB general counsel notes, delay may flow from inertia or indifference or "because an agency foolishly said 'we don't need this for six months.'"[32] The energy level behind an EO itself matters.

On the flip side, though, the analysis in chapter 5 also showed that significant orders often relied on substantial agency input, even as the EOP rode herd. Intuitively an important order likely deals with the kind of complicated policy decisions that, as just noted, should tend to slow its formulation. Such an order may well also cut across multiple agency jurisdictions, another likely contributor to delay (and one discussed below).

These countervailing considerations suggest the need for the controls available in multivariate analysis, as presented in the following section. Bivariate empirics, using the measures of significance defined in chapter 5, reflect their ambivalent expectation. Using William Howell's measure of whether an EO is reported in the *New York Times*, as extended by Thrower to cover the entire timeline here ($n = 515$), reveals no important difference in terms of mean times-to-issuance between EOs coded as significant and those without that status.[33] Using the dichotomous measure tracking intragovernmental significance instead, however, shows that EOs important on that dimension do take longer to formulate (a mean of 68 days versus 133, $n = 515$).[34] This makes sense, given that this code is linked to measures most keenly affecting agencies themselves and thus those they are most likely to litigate during the formulation process.

While not a direct measure of significance, we might consider the "clerkship" EOs also discussed in chapter 5 in this broad category as well. Such orders relate to past, ongoing, and routine statutory duties placed on the presidential office by Congress; as such, their ongoing implementation should require relatively less information and intrabranch deliberation. The data bear that out: the mean days to issuance for "clerk"-type EOs is 46 days, while for others it is 86, a substantively and statistically significant difference ($n = 515$, $p < .004$).

Agency Characteristics

If the executive branch is a they, instead of an it, we might expect differential treatment across agencies engaged in the EO formulation process. Do some get "their" orders issued more quickly? If so, what kind of agency characteristics are associated with faster or slower order issuance?—incurring, at least by this imperfect proxy, lower or higher transaction costs? From a management context, more trusted agencies would seem to be the best candidates for faster formulation processes as their work should require less vetting by other agencies or EOP personnel. Again, as a proxy for trust we look at agencies closer to the president's ideological preferences—especially EOP agencies where any such divergence should be minimal—and less structurally insulated from presidential control. More trust, in principle, should involve shorter formulation processes. As before, though, if agencies are behaving strategically in terms of the kinds of EOs they propose for presidential consideration, such factors may be muted in the EOs we can actually observe.[35]

We can start with some summary statistics based on the lead agency code described earlier. Each proposed EO is matched to the agency most closely linked to its subject matter; as in chapter 4, sequential organizations were consolidated into a single code when agencies evolved over time.[36] Thus, for example, in Figure 6.2 the total for the Department of Defense includes pre-1947 observations for the Departments of War and Navy, and that for the Office of Personnel Management (OPM) includes the pre-1978 observations tied to the Civil Service Commission. The number of observations per agency in the duration data ranges from 1 (for numerous agencies, including the National Science Foundation, the Office of Production Management, the Tennessee Valley Authority, and the Veterans Administration) to 93 (the Pentagon). All seventeen agencies with at least ten observed values on the duration variable are included in Figure 6.2.[37] For comparison, the values for the overall sample are also included.

While the small number of observations for most of the individual agencies obviously limits the strength of the inferences that can be drawn, some trends do emerge. Not surprisingly, the National Mediation Board, which provides those prepackaged orders drafted in case of labor disputes, has a much shorter

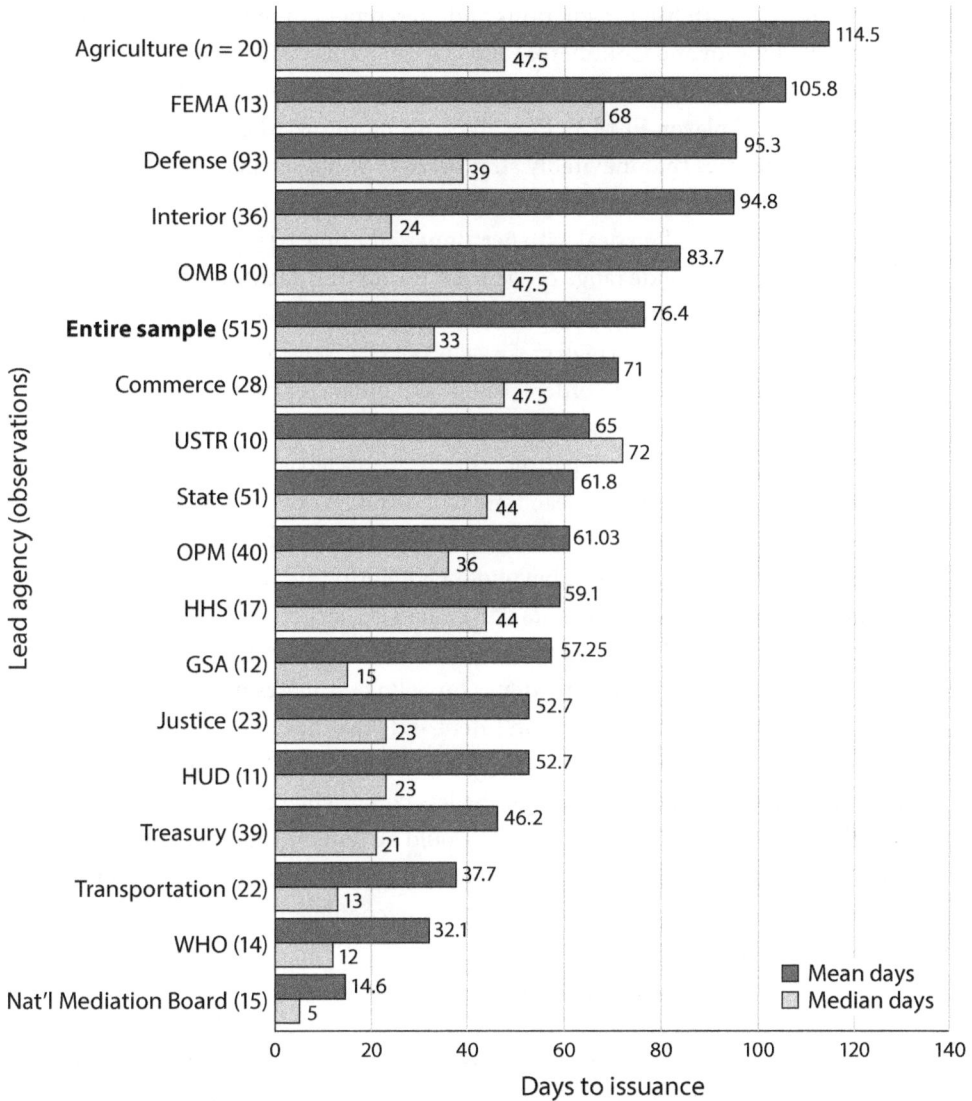

FIGURE 6.2. Mean and Median Days to Issuance, by Lead Agency.

time to issuance than any other agency. The products of the White House Office itself also get expedited attention (but remember that these EOs do not include those the WHO requests be written to manage, or on behalf of, other agencies).

Again, duration does seem intuitively to coincide with intra-executive conflict. Thus on the other end of the scale is Agriculture, whose orders nearly always overlap with the jurisdictions and preferences of other departments (especially Interior and Commerce) and inspire/require EOP intervention— at least two of the extended case studies already presented in this book feature USDA as a lead player. FEMA's EOs, likewise, tend toward emergency planning contingencies that inevitably stray across various agencies' authorities and autonomy and attract sharp feedback. And OMB's own EOs—while partly centralized—often deal with personnel, advising, or reporting requirements imposed on a wide range of agencies, prompting pushback and making an above-average time to issuance unsurprising there as well.

Interior's offerings have a high mean value but relatively low median, suggesting numerous quickly issued orders paired with others receiving extensive discussion and delay. The Defense Department's EOs have a similarly high variance. But while the inner Cabinet departments were associated with relatively decentralized EOs in general, their mean time to issuance is not statistically distinct from that of other departments and agencies (68 days versus 76 days).

To track agency dispositions beyond their identity and function, we return to the measures utilized earlier tracking agencies' structural insulation and their ideological match with the president, as well as their reputation for competence. As in chapter 5, the first draws on Selin's estimates of the insulation of agency appointments from the president and the others from the executive branch surveys conducted by Lewis and his collaborators.[38] We might expect that the more insulated an agency, or the less congruence between an agency and the White House, the more review would be required and the longer the time to issuance. Again, perhaps reflecting strategic behavior by such agencies, in bivariate analysis the signs of each of these coefficients are largely as expected but none reach statistical significance.

The same is true for an additional measure developed by Lewis and colleagues, which tracks agencies' overall influence as viewed by their executive branch peers. This intriguing variable correlates somewhat with the measure of agency competence used in chapter 5 ($r = .41$ in this sample) but clearly gets at something different. One possibility would be for such agencies to receive more deference and less micromanagement, and thus be associated with shorter formulation times. But one could imagine, too, an influential agency using that sway to reopen or prolong negotiations, shifting EO provenance from the EOP or a single department into a protracted mixed process. Thus influence here might in fact indicate the ability to impose costs on presidents (or other agencies) during order formulation—an inference supported by the general direction of the bivariate relationship, albeit one subject to a wide confidence interval.

The Formulation Process:
Crosscutting Jurisdictions and Centralization

If time to issuance is a useful proxy for the costs of managing the formulation process, it should rise as that process grows more complicated. That seems to be the case. As one BoB staffer wryly noted, summarizing an interagency dispute for a colleague who had been on an extended break from the office, "there have been times during the past week when I have seriously considered sending you a telegram . . . : 'Surplus order still unsigned; stay where you are.' . . . Remembering the conversation . . . when [you] bestowed upon me with your best wishes the problem of dealing with this executive order, you must forgive me a small amount of wicked pleasure at handing it back to you on the first morning of your return."[39]

That draft EO, ultimately issued after two months of negotiation, required nine agencies to come to terms with their role in implementing a new statute. More generally, including more agencies in the clearance process should raise the transaction costs associated with managing that process and, ceteris paribus, the longer it should take. In bivariate terms this proves out strongly: using the "crosscut" variable described in chapter 5, the addition of one new agency to the review of an EO adds five days to the formulation process ($p < .001$). Again, this relationship is explored with multivariate controls in the next section.

The crosscut figure is of course also a good predictor of whether an order's formulation process is centralized.[40] As noted above, a fully centralized EO should on average reduce the length of the formulation process, as a straightforward White House–driven episode of command with low transaction costs.[41] But the path from full decentralization to its opposite is unlikely to be a straight negative line. As suggested earlier in this chapter, a fully decentralized process represents a presidential decision that it is safe to "buy" an EO, that is, to delegate its formulation to an agency or agencies. That delegation reduces the presidential burden. But once centralized engagement is required, more management is necessary, whoever is in the lead. Thus an EO coded to reflect a mixed process with the EOP predominant could represent a hostile takeover of sorts, incurring high management costs to override uncooperative agencies; one with the agencies predominant still requires EOP resources, if only to sort through competing bureaucratic claims. If so we might expect an inverted "V" when it comes to transaction costs: that is, the middle categories ("1" and "2") should have longer formulation processes than either of the poles ("0" and "3").

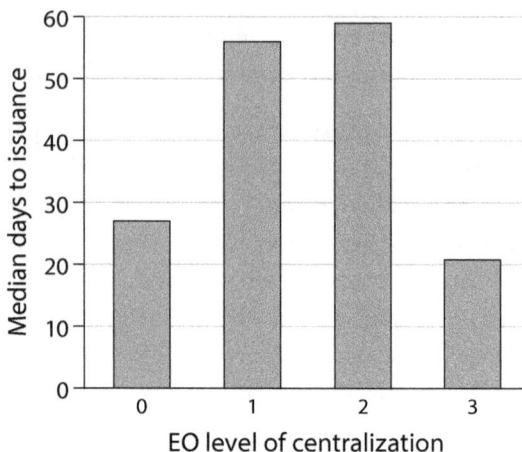

FIGURE 6.3. Median Days to Issuance, by Level of Centralization.

Figure 6.3 confirms this expectation. It shows that time to issuance is indeed shortest for fully centralized and decentralized formulation processes. The median EO in the wholly decentralized category takes 27 days to be issued; its centralized counterpart takes about 21. But the two mixed categories have median formulation times of 56 and 59 days, respectively.

The pattern remains the same for mean data (reported in the appendix to this chapter in Table A6.2).[42] The polar categories are those with the shortest formulation processes, averaging 57 to 64 days; mixed formulation processes take closer to 100 days. As the cases presented thus far make clear, even the pole categories may contain cases involving substantial disputation. Where that is the case, transaction costs and formulation times will rise. But in general, transaction costs are highest as a function of joint EOP-agency engagement, itself partly a function of bureaucratic resistance. That resistance may be driven either by EOP or agency objection to EOs driven by other agencies, or when EOP-driven orders meet sustained agency recalcitrance.

Beyond the Bivariate: "Survival" Models

If these calculations are suggestive, they are not systematic—they do not control for relationships between variables that may affect an order's time to issuance. The use of time as a key proxy here suggests use of an event history model. Such analysis focuses "on questions related to timing and duration until the occurrence of an event."[43] That approach is especially appealing since in some specifications it allows inclusion of the unissued

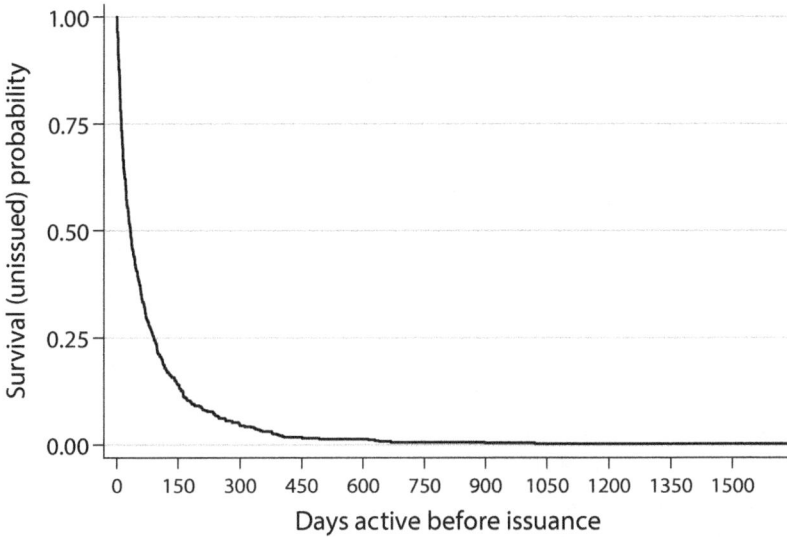

FIGURE 6.4. Kaplan-Meier Survival Curve, Issued Orders Only.

orders as censored observations in a competing risk model, as undertaken in chapter 7.

Event history approaches are often called "survival" models, because they are frequently used in epidemiological studies where the event in question is death. For present purposes this requires a bit of mental juggling; after all, normally we think of orders as being "born" on the day they are issued. They go off into the policy world, live, make a difference or fail to, and eventually die—de facto when they are no longer relevant, de jure if they are formally replaced or abrogated by subsequent presidential or congressional action. In the analysis below, however, we need to conceive of executive orders as having been born on the day they are drafted (or at least the day they reach OMB for consideration) and "dying" (or at least vanishing from the data) on the day they are issued. Their issuance is intuitively a success, but defined here as a "failure event." The higher the number of days an order is active, the longer period required for an order to be issued, and the higher the transaction costs associated with its issuance, at least by inference.

A descriptive view of the pre-issuance period uses Kaplan-Meier estimates to graph the survivor function, which is to say the probability of survival—that is, in this case, continued deliberation over EO formulation—past time t. That survival curve is presented in Figure 6.4.

The curve naturally reflects the descriptive data presented above, dropping rapidly from day 1 to day 90, at which point some three-quarters of proposed

EOs have been issued. A long tail ensues from there, with 95 percent of orders issued as the 300-day mark approaches. However, as noted earlier, including EOs that wind up not getting issued flattens that curve dramatically, with the consideration processes for more than a quarter of proposed orders exceeding 250 days (see Figure A6.1). A smoothed hazard function tells a similar story: the "risk" of issuance is highest at the outset but decreases over the course of ten months or so, with later small upward bumps reflecting the singular outliers in the data. (See Figure A6.2.)

A Cox proportional hazards model including the variables tracked above allows us to move from the descriptive to the multivariate.[44] Table 6.2 recaps the earlier discussion and the expectations associated with each variable. Not all are deployed in each specification reported below. In the table, a measure's predicted effect on duration is the reverse of its impact on the likelihood of issuance: the longer the duration, the less likely the issuance at any particular period (here, a given day). So an EO produced in response to an external event should shorten duration—if so, it will have a positive coefficient in the model, indicating that it leads to a more rapid end to the formulation process and quicker issuance of the EO.

Several specifications will be tested below. In Table 6.3 the first three columns, (A) through (C), represent the inclusion of three distinct measures of EO significance. Controls include the simple year counter noted above, as well as a measure tracking federal government employment as a proxy for the size of the overall executive branch requiring coordination here (the two correlate at .332). Dummy variables for each president in the analysis are also included. It is possible, after all, that some presidents just run a tighter EO formulation ship than others. Generally, though, as when testing for the causes of centralization, there is no theoretical expectation for these managerial dynamics to vary by president.

Again, the "hazard" here is tied to an EO's days to issuance, with orders dropping out of the data as they are issued. Recall that in Table 6.3 a positive coefficient suggests a faster issuance time (i.e., the variable is associated with fewer days to issuance), while a negative coefficient shows an association with a slower issuance time.

These results support the hypotheses that certain characteristics of a given order and formulation process matter for the duration of that formulation process, even controlling for the external context affecting the immediacy of demand for an EO. On the latter front, it is clearly the case that EOs crafted in response to external events are pulled together more rapidly.

TABLE 6.2. Time to Issuance: Variables and Expectations

Variables	Predicted Effect on Duration
Action-forcing deadlines	
External event/crisis	shorten (positive coefficient)
Produced for an external constituency?	shorten
Appears in presidential remarks?	shorten
Complexity	
Raw and logged word count	lengthen (negative coefficient)
Significance vs. routine	
Appearance in *NYT*	shorten?
Chiou-Roth. ICT measure	shorten?
Internal executive significance	lengthen
"Clerk"	shorten
Agency characteristics	
Insulation of decision makers	lengthen
Pres'l ideological congruence w/agency	shorten
Agency competence	shorten
Agency influence	lengthen?
Formulation process	
Crosscutting jurisdictions	lengthen
Centralization	offsetting:
Fully (de)centralized	shorten
Mixed	lengthen
Controls	
Year	
Federal government employment	
Presidential co-partisans in Congress	
Presidency fixed effects	

Those that by implication are linked to a presidential public appearance—
that is, those appearing in the rhetoric recorded by the *Public Papers of the
Presidents*—are also associated (in three of the four reported specifications)
with a positive and significant speeding of the formulation process. The
hazard rate associated with each variable gives us a sense of their substantive
impact, all else equal: for the external event marker in model (A), for example, that ratio is 2.27, suggesting that an EO drafted in response to such
an event faces more than twice the "hazard" of being issued on any given day
than those without such a prod. EOs later appearing in the *Public Papers* are
42 percent more likely to be issued on a given day (conditional, of course, on
not having been issued before). The link to constituencies proves less predictive. And, interestingly, in alternate specifications, the "statute" variable used

TABLE 6.3. Cox Proportional Hazards Model: Time to Issuance

	(A)	(B)	(C)	(D)
Action-forcing deadlines				
External event	.818**	1.002***	.920**	.852**
	(.260)	(.276)	(.267)	(.269)
External constituency	.060	.009	.035	.013
	(.139)	(.146)	(.141)	(.147)
Public rhetoric	.354*	.229	.463**	.407**
	(.139)	(.166)	(.136)	(.140)
Complexity				
Raw word count	−.000***	−.000***	−.000**	−.000***
	(.000)	(.000)	(.000)	(.000)
Significance vs. Routine				
NYT	.310*			.380**
(Howell, as extended)	(.124)			(.127)
IRT measure		.284**		
(Chiou-Roth.)		(.087)		
Intragov. significance			−.296	−.369*
			(.177)	(.182)
"Clerk"	.216	.419**	.213	.144
	(.129)	(.146)	(.127)	(.127)
Agency characteristics				
Insulation (appts.)	.080	.025	.067	.073
	(.112)	(.121)	(.110)	(.107)
Ideological distance	.085	.119*	.075	.079
	(.050)	(.053)	(.050)	(.051)
Agency competence	−.054	−.025	−.064	−.093
	(.089)	(.097)	(.089)	(.088)
Agency influence	.039	.117	.035	.040
	(.071)	(.080)	(.072)	(.073)
Co-partisans in Congress	−.006	.012	−.013	−.016
	(.018)	(.027)	(.018)	(.017)
Formulation process				
Crosscutting jurisdictions	−.042**	−.029*	−.032*	−.026
	(.014)	(.014)	(.014)	(.015)
Centralization	.008	.063	.023	
	(.058)	(.064)	(.058)	
Mixed centralization process				−.284**
				(.107)
Controls				
Year	−.045	.007	−.058	−.057
	(.032)	(.045)	(.033)	(.033)
Federal employment	.000	.001	.000	.000
	(.000)	(.000)	(.000)	(.000)
Presidency fixed effects	included	included	included	included
N	441	378	441	441
Log-likelihood	−2198.0	−1826.5	−2199.8	−2192.5

Note: Coefficients are from Cox proportional hazards model with robust standard errors (in parentheses) and presidential fixed effects (not shown).

* $p < .05$, ** $p < .01$, *** $p < .001$ (two-tailed tests)

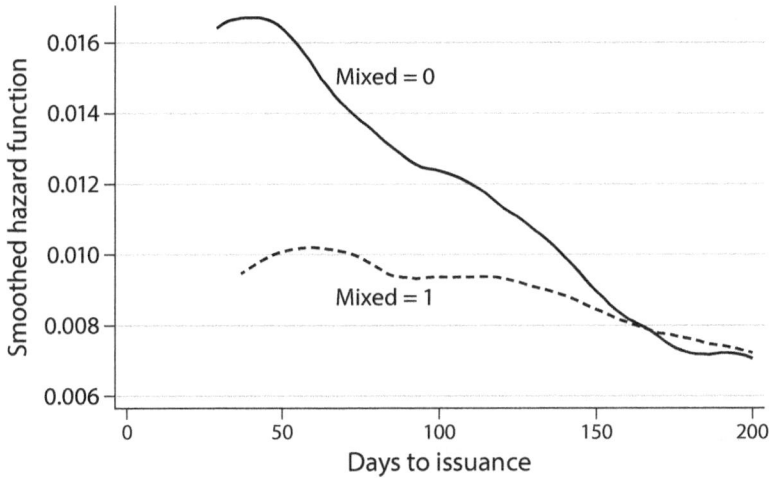

FIGURE 6.5. The Effects on Likelihood of Daily Issuance of a Mixed
Formulation Process.

in chapter 5 to represent an EO prompted by recent statute is positive but
not close to significant.

Exogenous forces matter to the schedule, then. But even controlling for
those, we see important effects for managerial constraints. As expected, centralization has no substantial impact here given its non-linear relationship with
duration. However, replacing the ordinal measure of centralization with a dichotomous variable coded 1 for a mixed process (that is, a centralization code
of 1 or 2) and 0 for fully centralized or decentralized processes does prove
significant. This is included in Table 6.3 in column (D).[45] When EOs are the
subject of more intensive negotiation between the EOP and the wider executive branch, they take longer to issue: all else equal such an EO will face about
only three-quarters of the "risk" of issuance on a given day as its centralized or
decentralized peers.

Figure 6.5 graphs the hazard function for this model when a mixed process
occurs versus when an EO is either fully centralized or decentralized. Doing
this allows us to see the difference in the "hazard rates" at different settings of
the variable, holding all others at their means: that is, showing the likelihood
of an order's being issued in the case of two different given values of a specific
variable. Here, the top line—EOs with a centralized or decentralized formulation process—is far above that representing "mixed" EOs, showing that EOs
in the polar categories have a dramatically higher chance of being issued on

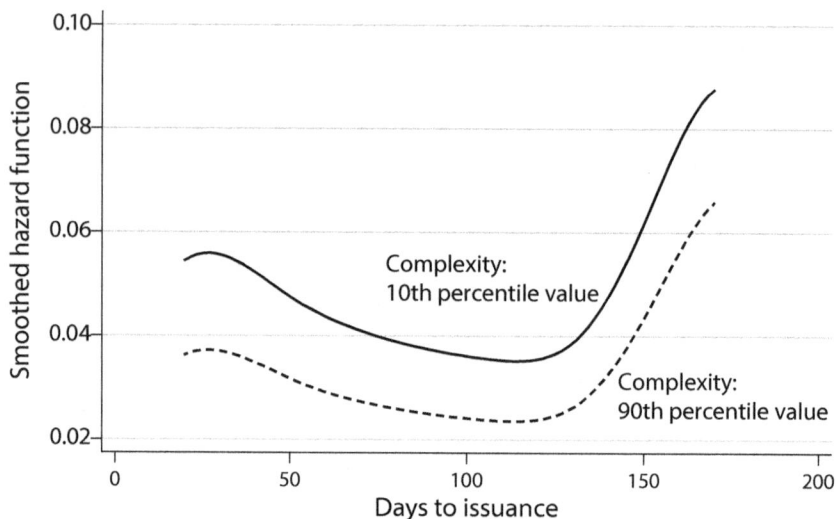

FIGURE 6.6. The Effects of EO Complexity (Word Count) on Likelihood of
Daily Issuance. Cox Proportional Hazards Regression.

any given day. The line representing the mixed processes remains flat as the
top line declines, but the two kinds of orders do not have an equivalent chance
of issuance until after the process passes the five-month mark. (This and subsequent graphs are truncated at 200 days, since more than 90 percent of orders
that are going to be issued at all have issued by then, as shown in Table 6.1. The
full data set's x-axis, stretching to more than 1,600 days even for issued orders,
simply makes it very difficult to print the graph in a way that allows one to see
much in the way of variation.)

Even controlling for this, the more complex the EO—measured by either
its raw or logged word count—the slower its formulation: the hazard rate here
suggests that the most complicated EOs on this dimension are about one-fifth
less likely to be issued on a given day than their simplest, shortest peers.[46]
Figure 6.6 again graphs the hazard function, this time when the logged word
count moves from its 10th to its 90th percentile. Here, after an early burst
both complex and simple orders have a declining chance of issuance to about
the four-month mark, then begin to move upward. But there is a wide and
consistent gap in the likelihood of order issuance between less and more
complex EOs.

A similar effect holds for orders that cross multiple departmental jurisdictions. Figure 6.7 shows the smoothed hazard function for the 10th and

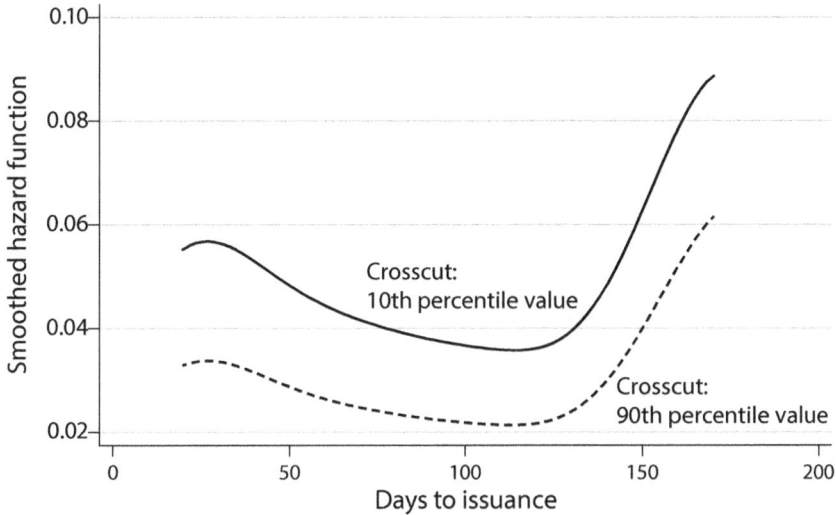

FIGURE 6.7. The Effects of Crosscutting Jurisdictions on Likelihood of Daily Issuance. Cox Proportional Hazards Regression.

90th percentile of this variable—involving 12 agencies as opposed to 1. There the likelihood of issuance early in the timeline is about 2 percentage points per day higher for the EOs requiring less cross-agency coordination, a gap that narrows slightly as formulation presses toward 150 days but never dissipates.

Both findings are solid across all three specifications of significance. Indeed, the crosscut variable holds its impact even when controlling for the measure of internal executive branch significance—a designation that itself frequently reflects an EO cutting across multiple agency jurisdictions—or when using the dichotomous variable representing mixed processes instead of centralization more broadly, which also usually signifies multiple agencies at work. However, when using all three of these variables together, as in Table 6.3's column (D), the crosscutting measure does drop away slightly.[47]

An EO's status as substantively significant proves far stronger in the multivariate analysis than in the bivariate. Both ways of using external markers for significance are positive and significant in these models—meaning an EO that attracts attention from the *New York Times* (Table 6.3 (A)) or has a higher value on the IRT scale developed by Chiou and Rothenberg ((B)) is, all else equal, likely to be issued sooner than one of its less-salient peers. Their hazard ratios both suggest that a significant order is about 20 percent more likely to be issued on a given day than a non-significant order. On the flip side, internally significant EOs (Table 6.3 (C)) are associated with a longer formulation duration—as the bivariate analysis anticipated—but in this wider context they are on the fringes of statistical significance ($p < .10$, two-tailed test). Interestingly, though, when also controlling for external salience—here, the *New York Times* measure—the internal significance variable proves both negative and strongly significant even as the *NYT* remains significant as well and continues to predict faster issuance (see Table 6.3 (D)). In such circumstances an EO that has attracted interest across the executive branch carries with it about 70 percent of the likelihood of issuance on a given day compared to its peers.

As predicted, the clerk variable proves positive, thus associated with faster formulation. It is strongly statistically significant only in Table 6.3 (B), the specification including the IRT measure of significance ($p < .10$ in the other two models in Table 6.3), and may be linked to the shorter time frame that measure covers. Still, "clerkdom" is the only change of importance if the presidential fixed-effect dummies are removed from the alternate specifications. In that case, not reported here, the variable's coefficient barely moves but its standard error decreases dramatically, bringing $p < .02$.[48] The direction of the sign may reflect that such EOs are relatively easy to draft, while the general lack of significance may indicate that they are not generally urgent or time-sensitive. Except where they have a strongly motivated sponsor—a departmental secretary, perhaps—they may await a "slow news day" before making their way fully through the process.

Agency-specific measures do not prove important here. While in the expected direction, neither agency influence nor competence, nor the level of insulation of agency appointments from the president, comes close to affecting the likelihood of EO issuance day to day. The ideology variable is positively signed, implying that the farther the president's preferences from an agency's ideological dispositions, the faster an EO will be issued. In the reported results, this is only statistically significant in conjunction with the IRT measure of significance (Table 6.3 (B)), but removing the presidential fixed-effects variables generally strengthens its impact even when using other measures of significance. While tentative, this may support the notion that agencies are strategic about the kind of orders they bring forth in the first place when they know the president may be suspicious of their products (and vice versa).[49] And as suggested above, agency influence may be used to slow orders as well as fast-track them.

The Costs (and Benefits) of Collaboration

Another possibility is that agency influence may be mostly important in achieving EO issuance in the first place: after all, that issuance is not a given. This chapter has shown that the formulation process, even when successful, takes a good deal of time—and that it varies in predictable ways. Yet as noted earlier but finally discussed in detail in the next chapter, a surprising proportion of proposed draft executive orders do not reach the promised land, a.k.a. the *Federal Register*. We will move from delay to demise.

Before turning that page, though, we should consider the results presented here as they relate to the president's unilateral power. First, EOs' managerial dynamics do play a role in expanding or contracting the transaction costs associated with their formulation. Exogenous events demanding an EO's rapid issuance—from national emergency to press office panic—do affect the duration of the formulation process. But even controlling for those, so do such factors as order complexity (or its status in "clerkdom"), agency jurisdiction, and substantive significance.

The length of the process itself was posited here as a marker for the scope of intrabranch conflict and bargaining. It bears repeating one fundamental finding: that process takes much longer than we tend to think. While EOs may outrun the legislative process, that is a low bar. They are slow. Fewer than 15 percent of issued orders take less than a week to move from OMB to the president's desk. And even in those cases, the proposal had frequently been under consideration in different parts of the executive branch long before it made its way as a formal draft ready for central clearance. The median order, as noted above, takes a month, and the average order two and a half times that. To the degree "unilateral" is equated to "instant," then, these data complicate the formula.

That is especially true when multiple agencies are involved in formulation—and that is most of the time. More than 80 percent of proposed orders cut across at least two agency jurisdictions; as noted, the time to issuance rises steeply as additional agencies are added to the mix. As they accrue, the managerial costs to the president rise. Some EOs can be delegated, some handled quickly in house, but a hefty percentage require both agency expertise and White House coordination. These "mixed" processes—which, as we have seen, apply to the majority of the most salient and significant EOs—increase intrabranch friction. Their use minimizes presidents' transaction costs in obtaining an EO that meets their needs, but within a framework of high absolute costs overall.

Yet in such cases, as the cliché goes, speed kills. When policymaking requires harnessing resources across the executive branch, its managerial costs rise, even as the benefits to the president rise too. The trade-off of accepting a longer process is the likelihood of producing an EO that will actually work. That is, an order that falls within the president's legal authority and ideological preferences, that is technically accurate, and that, not least, can be implemented as intended—because it has been substantively vetted and has allowed those who will actually do the implementing to have voice and even vote.[50] If power is defined as effective influence over governmental outcomes, then such a process enhances presidential power.[51] The catch is that it does so by collaboration as readily as by command.

Appendix

TABLE A6.1. Days under Active Consideration, All Orders

Issued Orders Only ($n = 515$)	Days Active	(Issued and Unissued) ($n = 742$)
Range:	1–1,646 days	1–2,572
Mean:	76.4 days*	163.8 days
S.D.:	131.99	286.86
25th pctile:	11 days	15 days
Median:	33 days	56 days
75th pctile:	91 days	169 days
90th pctile:	181 days	451 days
95th pctile:	298 days	719 days
99th pctile:	629 days	1,337 days

* This figure is 71.4 (104.5 s.d.) without the two outlying observations of over 1,000 days.

TABLE A6.2. Mean Days to Issuance, by Level of Centralization: With and (Excluding) Extreme Observations

Centralization	n	Mean	Median	S.d.
0	226 (225)	63.8 (59.6)	27.0 (27.0)	120.4 (102.3)
1	90	96.0	56.0	117.5
2	99 (98)	106.2 (90.5)	59.0 (57.5)	182.9 (95.4)
3	98	57.1	20.5	100.6

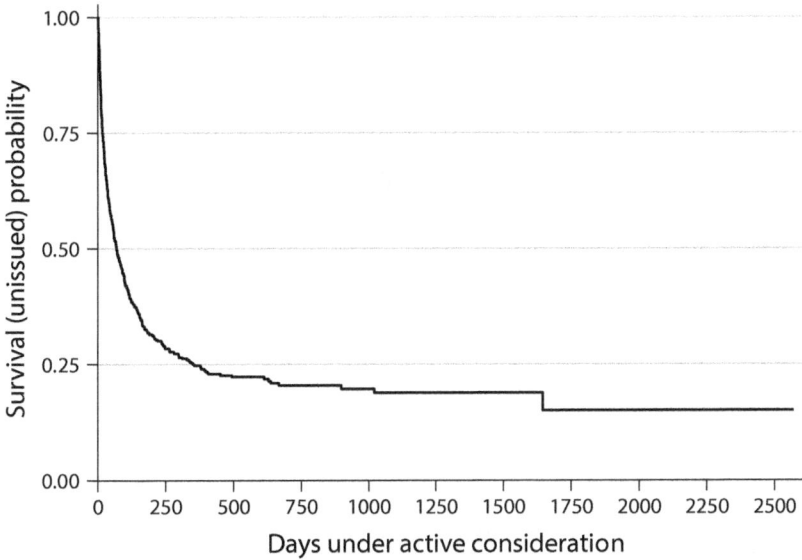

FIGURE A6.1. Kaplan-Meier Survival Curve, Issued and Unissued Orders. For unissued orders, the number of days active is measured by subtracting the date the order was received from the date that OMB records show it was no longer actively considered for issuance.

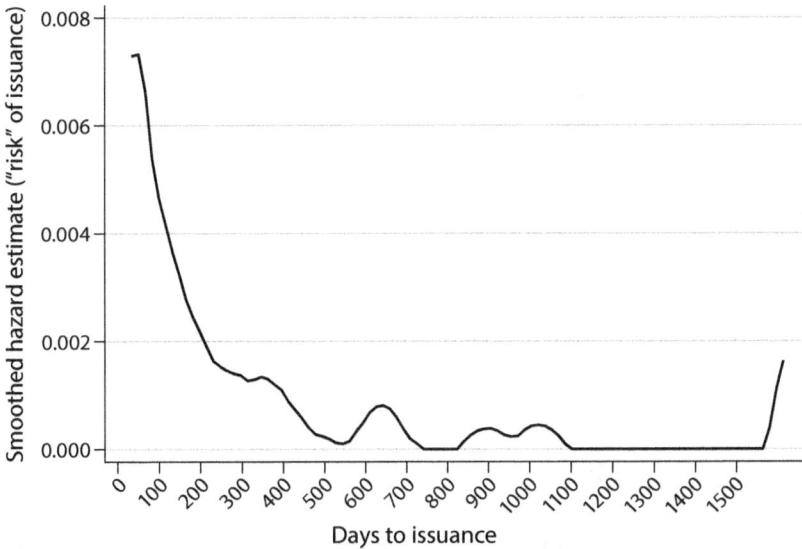

FIGURE A6.2. Smoothed Hazard Function for EO "Risk" of Issuance.

7

"Dear John"

THE ORDERS THAT NEVER WERE

IT WASN'T THAT KIND of Dear John letter. But even so it delivered bad news. "Dear John," OMB associate director Arnold Weber wrote to the secretary of transportation in August 1971. "Your executive order . . . has been carefully reviewed, and I regret to inform you that it will not be signed by the President."[1]

The file does not document Secretary Volpe's reaction. But perhaps he was not surprised. As it happens, many proposed executive orders meet the same fate.

Outside observers, though, even those who track presidential unilateralism fairly closely, may be more startled. Non-issued orders have received little scholarly attention, in part because of the invisibility of the data: it is difficult to record the dogs that did not bark. Such events, disguised as non-events, rarely catch the eye of the media—one recent exception was the revelation of a flurry of potential draft orders in the early days of the Trump administration, arising from more than two hundred possible EOs considered during the transition; only a handful of them were ever signed.[2] Nor do presidents tend to talk about the road not taken. Perhaps the exception that proves the rule is, again, President Trump. While stumping in the 2018 midterm elections, for instance, he liked to tell a story about the construction of a new American embassy in Jerusalem:

> "So I say, 'I want to build it.' . . . And they said, 'Yes, sir.' So I get this, you know, executive order—this big, beautiful piece of paper. It must have cost, like, a fortune. . . . But I have this executive—and I'm getting ready to sign it. I signed 'Donald.'"

But the president stops in mid-signature. Then:

> "I say, 'What is this, general?' I'm signing so much stuff. 'What is this, general?'
>
> "'Sir, this is the new embassy in Israel. It's for your approval, sir. The cost will be $1 billion.'
>
> "I said, 'Wait a minute. What? What?'
>
> "'$1 billion.'
>
> "I said, '$1 billion? How can it cost $1 billion? It's like a one-story building.'"

And, as the story goes on, Trump "just can't do it." He does not sign the order. Instead, he goes on to negotiate what he says is a much better deal complete with "the finest stones, the finest marbles, the best location." The triumphant conclusion: "So, instead of spending $1 billion and not having it for 20 years, we spent 400,000 bucks and it opened up in a few months. Is that good? Is that a good story?"[3]

It is, indeed, a good story (though not a true one).[4] For one thing, as noted, it is the rare narrative that features a president *not* signing an executive order. Luckily, though, more than two hundred files tucked into various presidential archives detail just that outcome, albeit largely without the braggadocio. Luckier still, they provide a great deal of variation on their path to mortality. Some proposed EOs die nearly as soon as OMB opens the envelope or email—they are "very very half-baked"[5] or, as described in the discussion of central clearance in chapter 3, don't "smell like an executive order." Some morph into different form. Some are in fact subject to Oval Office veto.

A majority, though, are crushed by the weight of dissent within the executive branch. In extreme cases, these unissued orders seem to constrain and even deny presidential preferences—a nice example of the "two-way street" discussed earlier. In 1977, for instance, Jimmy Carter's push for a newly ethical branch sought to limit the use of chauffeur-driven cars by government officials. Carter directed his staff—in writing—to "prepare an executive order. . . . Make it strict."[6] Yet no order was issued.

Do unissued orders represent a failure of presidential management, or its success? The analysis and cases detailed below suggest the answer is "both."

OMB's Unissued Order Files

The unissued order files used here were located in the course of searching for the issued EOs that were the primary target of this research. At times they are stray entries interspersed in the main series of OMB's files for a given administration, or discovered in the course of exhuming the executive order records within the White House Central Files at presidential libraries. Larger caches of unissued orders are sometimes stored separately under a particular administration's OMB filing rubric, yielding a comprehensive (though not exhaustive) collection of those EOs under consideration at a given point in time. In total, 237 unissued orders have been identified to date. This is certainly sufficient to turn "good stories" into data.

That conversion comes with caveats, of course. First, the briefer the life of a proposed order, the less documentation it accrues—not every variable of interest can be coded for every file. Thus, in the discussion below, *n* will vary. Further, and crucially, the located files are something of a convenience sample; they cannot be assumed to be representative of all unissued orders across the 1937–2004 period covered by the data set overall. We do not know exactly how wide the universe of unissued orders is or what its precise contours might be. Given the variation in OMB general counsels' record keeping over the years, there are almost certainly other EOs that did make it to OMB but that were not discovered here.[7] There is no obvious reason to think the drafts that were unearthed are skewed by substance, by significance, or by lead agency. They are certainly, though, unevenly distributed over time. As shown in Table 7.1, while at least one observation comes from each administration from Truman through Clinton, close to a third of the total originated in the Carter administration (which provided one of the caches just noted) and nearly another quarter under Lyndon Johnson.

Still, this gives us a far better understanding of just how many orders are not issued. Carter, for instance, issued 320 EOs in his four years—so if we add on the 74 unissued orders here, he considered closer to 400 draft EOs, and issued just over 80 percent of those proposed during his term. There are presumably some Carter-era unissued orders not included in my data. But even so this figure fits very well with the estimate of a recent OMB general counsel who suggested that about a fifth of "serious" EOs—those whose proposers did some groundwork to prepare—wind up falling by the wayside.[8]

Since "sophistication of the agency players" varies, that counsel continued, perhaps as many as half of all the ideas for EOs received in the general counsel's

TABLE 7.1. Identified Unissued Orders, by Administration

President	Years	# Unissued Orders	Percent of All Unissued
Truman	1945–53	1	0.4
Eisenhower	1953–61	6	2.5
Kennedy	1961–63	22	9.3
Johnson	1963–69	56	23.6
Nixon	1969–74	16	6.8
Ford	1974–77	30	12.7
Carter	1977–81	74	31.2
Reagan	1981–89	21	8.9
G.H.W. Bush	1989–93	6	2.5
Clinton	1993–2001	5	2.1
Total		237	100.0

office never made it to the president's desk, including drafts so incomplete and unpromising that they failed even to clear the bar to receive interagency review.[9] There are presumably many other ideas, presidential or otherwise, that for whatever reason do not make it as far as the word processor. As the discussion above suggests, numerous proposed orders float around during a presidential transition, some of which dissolve nearly immediately as they collide with reality. Only those adopted by incoming policymakers before abandonment will be in the data described here. By definition, proposed EOs that did not live long enough to have a file opened are not in the data described above; all those detailed in this chapter received at least some substantive consideration.

Additional descriptive information builds on the tables in chapter 6: as noted there, information on how long a proposal was under consideration before its demise is available for unissued as well as issued orders. In this case the metric is "days active" instead of time to issuance, as detailed in Table 7.2.

A small number of proposed EOs are discarded quickly—about 10 percent of them in under two weeks (and half of those within five days). But on average such proposals are under review for a full year, a figure that does not diminish much when the extreme observations (both over 2,500 days, or about seven years) are excluded.[10] Half are active for over 210 days, or approximately seven months. What is going on during that time is categorized later in this chapter.

More broadly, though, it appears that there are not systematic differences between issued and unissued orders. And this is true as well so far as their

TABLE 7.2. Days Active, Unissued Orders

n = 227	
Range:	1–2,572
Mean:	362.1 days
S.D.:	416.3
10th pctile:	12 days
25th pctile:	76 days
Median:	211 days
75th pctile:	515 days
90th pctile:	937 days
95th pctile:	1,123 days
99th pctile:	1,798 days

TABLE 7.3. Centralization and Days Active: Unissued vs. Issued Executive Orders, 1937–2004

Centralization	Unissued		Issued	
	N	%	N	%
0	100	43.7	245	44.1
1	41	17.9	94	16.9
2	32	14.0	107	19.2
3	56	24.5	110	19.8
	229		556	
	Mean = 1.19; S.D. = 1.23		Mean = 1.15; S.D. = 1.19	

formulation processes are concerned. Table 7.3 presents the level of centralization for unissued orders where this could be coded, reprising for easy comparison the data presented for issued orders in chapter 4.

As the table shows, the level of centralization for each category is close in each case, and the overall mean and standard deviation close to identical (a t-test shows the difference in means is not close to statistically distinct [$n = 785$, $p < .64$]).

The greatest divergence is between the more heavily centralized categories. Proposed EOs coded 2 and 3 (mixed, but led by staff in the Executive Office of the President, and predominantly EOP, respectively) add to the same percentage of the whole (38.5 percent for unissued, 39 percent for issued), but the unissued orders are more heavily weighted toward the fully centralized end of the index (24.5 percent for unissued, 19.8 percent for issued). One intriguing

TABLE 7.4. Unissued Executive Orders, by Proposing Agency

Agency	Unissued Orders	%
White House	54	22.8
OMB	23	9.7
Commerce/SBA	19	8.0
State	17	7.2
Defense	15	6.3
CSC/OPM	11	4.6
OEP/FEMA	11	4.6
Interior	10	4.2
Agriculture	9	3.8
GSA	8	3.4
Transportation/FAA	7	3.0
USTR	6	2.5
[Other EOP: NSC, CEQ]	6	2.5
Justice	5	2.1
Labor	5	2.1
Treasury	5	2.1
[Members of Congress]	5	2.1
Other	21	8.9

possibility—albeit one hard to state as a general rule given the non-random nature of the unissued order data set—is that EOP-driven orders are actually less likely to be issued than those proposed in the agencies.

Indeed, as Table 7.4 indicates, the White House staff itself represents just under a quarter of the unissued EOs in these data. If other parts of the EOP are added, including OMB, CEQ, and NSC, that figure rises past one-third. (The number would be higher still if the proposed EOs associated with the Office of Economic Opportunity [OEO] and the Office of Emergency Preparedness [OEP] were included in the total.)[11] Again, caveats arise regarding any claims that these figures would hold up across the universe of unissued orders. Further, the White House total includes a small number of proposed EOs the White House directly asked other agencies—often OMB or Justice—to draft. This attribution is consistent with the coding of centralization discussed earlier (see Figure A7.1 in the appendix to this chapter for a breakdown of unissued orders by the agency most directly affected, whether or not it made the proposal). Of course, since the EOs proposed by the White House and OMB vary wildly in their subject matter, another way to read these data is that their drafts are foisted upon agencies who successfully resist their imposition.

A wide range of agencies are represented here, as are assorted members of Congress (who generally appear as the proximate force requesting that agencies or the White House draft a particular EO, rather than as the direct authors). Commerce, whose tally includes the Small Business Administration, is the leading department linked to unissued orders. State and Defense are not far behind in absolute terms; however, if the rate of rejection mirrors the overall numbers of EOs proposed, the Defense and State figures are far lower than Commerce as a proportion of their overall administrative agendas. (There are 30 EOs in the sample of issued orders associated with Commerce, but 56 for State and 100 from the Pentagon and its predecessor agencies.) Are some agencies more skillful vendors of their wares than others? That is, does Commerce have a particular knack for creating EO products the president does not want to buy? Or are the key elements the characteristics of the EOs themselves, or of the interagency friction they inspire?

We can get at least a rough look at the relative impacts here by revisiting the survival analysis in chapter 6 and including unissued orders as right-censored observations in a competing risks model. These models help identify cause-specific hazards, that is, to help explain which of multiple possible factors lead to a given outcome.[12] They are sometimes used to analyze "engineering situations in which systems with many components fail when the first component fails."[13]

Which factors modify the chance that an event—in this case, EO issuance—will ever occur? Here we might at least cautiously look to several bivariate differences between the pools of issued and unissued orders.[14] For instance, in chapter 6 we saw that the larger the number of agencies involved in formulation, the longer it took. This also seems to hold for issuance itself: the mean number of "crosscutting" agencies in the issued data is 5.17, while in the unissued data that figure is 7.01. This difference is statistically significant $(n = 788, p < .001)$.

Further, while the survey data used earlier as measures of agency expertise and influence[15] did not matter for time to issuance, when including unissued EOs in the data the perceived authority of agencies seems to matter. The measure of agency influence is significantly higher in the sample of issued EOs than for those that remain unissued $(n = 758, p < .03)$, and the mean value for agency competence is likewise far higher in the issued EO data than in those unissued $(n = 756, p < .001)$. However, once again the measure of presidential ideological congruence with an agency (matching the party of the president with survey data for agency ideology) proves insignificant; it does not differ between the two pools of proposed EOs. Another hypothesized measure of agency alignment with the president, the proportion of presidential co-partisans in House and Senate, is significant, but negative ($n = 785, p < .001$). That is, issued EOs on average are associated with fewer presidential allies in Congress than are the unissued ones in this data.[16] This might suggest that expertise and influence outweigh "trust," in this context at least. But the congressional context as it applies here likely says less about formulation than about the broader question that has driven much of the extant literature on unilateralism: under what conditions does the population of the Capitol matter for EO issuance? The finding here gives at least tangential support for the "substitute" hypothesis there.

A number of variables are available for issued orders only—notably the measures of significance calculated by an EO's appearance in the media or other outlets or the action-forcing mechanism implied by an EO's mention in presidential rhetoric. Obviously external trackers of salience do not register when a proposal fails to become public. The same is true for the order's word count, standing in for EO complexity. But we can use a dichotomous measure of significance and, as a proxy for complexity, the indicator for intra-executive significance introduced earlier. Substantively important issues should (as presidential priorities) normally be issued at some point; for their part, complicated matters of internal management should be more difficult to reach consensus on, thus hindering issuance. These expectations are met in bivariate terms, at least weakly: the mean for the dummy variable tagging significance *is* higher for issued EOs, though this is on the fringes of statistical significance ($p < .06$), while the mean of the "sig gov" variable is significantly lower in the issued EO pool ($p < .001$).

Using a competing risks model to include these variables, as well as the measures and controls discussed in chapter 6 and available for unissued orders, produces Table 7.5. Here the year tracker and presidency-specific dummy variables are not included, since some presidents do not appear in the unissued orders pool and those that do are not evenly distributed over time.[17] As before, since not every agency in these data is coded for insulation or included in the agency survey data, using those variables reduces the overall n of the model somewhat. However, alternate specifications dropping those four variables (insulation, competence, influence, congruence), thus maximizing n (at 731), do not result in any changes in substantive or statistical significance for the remaining variables. Numerous other specifications were run to test the robustness of the results: all the results reported in Table 7.5 are widely supported.

TABLE 7.5. Competing Risks Regression: Days Active for Issued and Unissued Orders

	Coeff. (s.e.)	Subhazard Ratio
External event	1.381*** (.251)	3.98
Significance dummy	.634*** (.118)	1.88
Intragov. significance	−.876*** (.171)	0.42
"Clerk"	−.147 (.124)	0.86
Crosscutting jurisdictions	−.042** (.012)	0.96
Centralization	.064 (.045)	1.07
Insulation	.058 (.105)	1.06
Ideological congruence	.018 (.042)	1.02
Agency competence	−.001 (.081)	1.00
Agency influence	.169** (.062)	1.18
Co-partisans in Congress	−.013** (.005)	0.99
Federal employment	−.001** (.000)	1.00
N	699	
Log-likelihood	−2899.4	

Note: Coefficients are from competing risks regression (Stata command stcrreg) model with robust standard errors (in parentheses).

* $p < .05$, ** $p < .01$, *** $p < .001$ (two-tailed tests)

In Table 7.5, positive or negative coefficients indicate the direction of a variable's impact. That is, a positive coefficient indicates that higher values of that variable are associated with a higher likelihood of an order's issuance (thus, of its leaving the ranks of the unissued at some point). The subhazard ratio reported in the second column translates this into an estimate of the variable's actual impact on an EO's chances of issuance on any given day, contingent on it not having been issued before that time and controlling for the other factors in the model (our confidence in the estimate is, as usual, governed by the statistical significance of the coefficient). A ratio of 1.00 indicates neutrality, with a unit shift in the variable leading to no change in the probability of issuance. A ratio below 1 is associated with a negative coefficient, thus that a change in the variable makes it less likely an EO will be issued (again, on any given day). A ratio above 1 makes that outcome more likely. Taking an example from the second line in the table: a substantively significant order has an 88 percent higher chance of being issued on a given day than its non-significant brethren, suggesting such orders will less often (though not never) remain unissued, ceteris paribus.

External events, not surprisingly, have a huge effect on the daily likelihood of issuance when unissued EOs are included in the data. After all, they effectively call EOs into existence. But overall, the analysis reflects hypothesized expectations on the managerial front as well, making a strong case for the role of interagency conflict—and for the sway of individual agencies.

Significant orders are, as just noted, dramatically more likely to be issued on any given day (and by extension, issued at all). But the reverse is true for EOs coded as internally important within the executive branch; that, as noted earlier, tends to be linked to managerial complexity. Such orders face just 42 percent of the likelihood of issuance on a given day than EOs of less concern to executive branch agencies. Along those lines an increase in crosscutting jurisdictions also proves strongly negative in a wide range of specifications. Its hazard ratio suggests that each additional agency requiring coordination of this type cuts 4 percent from the "risk" of issuance in a given period (as always, contingent on it not having been issued before). Thus, a shift from the median EO in this regard (with four agencies involved) to the 75th percentile (with ten) would diminish the likelihood of its issuance by some sixteen percentage points on any given day.

Centralization, by contrast, does not prove significant here. If the level of centralization chosen reflects a president's efforts to minimize managerial transaction costs given an array of agency- and order-specific characteristics, it is unclear that the likelihood of issuance itself should vary as centralization does. In earlier studies of centralization and legislative policy formulation, centralization dragged down legislative success—that is, it was necessary inside the executive branch but problematic outside it.[18] In the context of executive orders the first dynamic seems more relevant, with centralization as a remedial mechanism of sorts ready to rescue orders that might otherwise flounder.

Still, to the extent Table 7.3 made a prediction, it suggested that EOP-driven orders might actually be less likely to be issued than those proposed in the agencies. Thus, additional checks were conducted, but showed little. Using a dichotomous measure of whether an EO was fully centralized, versus one produced by any other process, showed no effect for such orders. The same was true in reverse, examining fully decentralized formulation processes. And while a mixed formulation process has an important impact on the time it takes an order to be issued, it does not have a significant effect on whether issuance actually takes place at all.[19] Thus a centralized formulation process is not a panacea for an EO that otherwise generates unsustainable costs.

What does help an order get issued? As the bivariate analysis hinted, the impact of agency influence is quite dramatic in this context. It is strongly significant ($p < .01$) and its hazard ratio suggests an 18 percent increase in the chances of an EO being issued each day when the agency associated with the order is more influential. Removing the competence variable, which is not significant here, makes no difference to this finding. Nor does dropping the influence variable and using competence instead; the latter does not suddenly become significant. Clearly the measures are indeed, as their compilers intended, measuring different things.[20] The measures of decision-maker insulation and ideological congruence remain insignificant, as they largely have throughout the analysis.[21]

A proxy for the influence of agencies' multiple principals—the proportion of presidential co-partisans in Congress—does prove significant. The hypothesis here was that when presidents are more closely aligned with Congress they will be more likely to trust agency behavior overall, speeding issuance of EOs. In this case, though, the variable's negative coefficient indicates the reverse: that the more legislative allies a president has, the longer an EO will take to be issued. That this effect is found only when unissued EOs are included in the data suggests it is largely influenced by those unissued orders—perhaps suggesting that unified government links to a lower likelihood of order issuance overall. If so, as noted above, this might tentatively support the notion that EOs are a substitute for legislation.[22]

These findings identify factors associated with long formulation that might morph into infinite formulation. But we are not limited to these calculations and speculations. Differences of means nor even the more systematic reach of survivor models do not tell us *why* EOs that are proposed fail to be issued. OMB's files do.

Why Orders Fail

An OMB-produced cover sheet accompanying a collection of executive orders and proclamations sent to archival storage provides a list of some of the EOs that were abandoned in 1983—and briefly summarizes the causes of their mortality. "The White House took no action on this proposal," says one entry; for another, "an interagency dispute prevented processing of this order." A third was "returned to Treasury as it was decided that no useful purpose would be served by its issuance; State and Treasury will continue to resolve this issue."[23]

A close reading of the broader set of unissued order files mirrors this accounting, producing six general reasons why a proposed order might fail to make it through the process. These are not always entirely separable, as the detailed examples below make clear.

They include:

(1) a president deciding against signing an EO that had reached the White House after having been otherwise approved via the central clearance process;

(2) an EO supplanted by legislative action;

(3) a decision, often prompted by OMB (though frequently influenced by interagency comment), that the aims of the EO could be served via a different, less formal route, such as a presidential memorandum or even a press release;

(4) another kind of OMB roadblock, erected for various reasons (for instance, because the president does not have authority to issue the EO);

(5) a new administration, with new appointees, decides that a pending order is no longer on its agenda. But while changes in presidencies do often prompt review of extant EOs, the files show that most of the orders set aside via that process were already effectively dead. Normally this is because of the most prominent driver of EO mortality,

(6) inter-, and sometimes intra-, agency dissent.

Table 7.6 shows the broad distribution of the unissued EO pool across these categories. Again, some EOs suffer multiple wounds and could thus be placed in several categories; the table reflects a judgment from the file as to the primary cause of death, where that could be determined.[24] It also separates out a subcategory from "substitute action" to show the (relatively few) instances that involved rolling the subject matter of a proposed executive order into another, subsequent EO.

The relevant OMB files allow a detailed taxonomy of these categories as they work in practice. They provide intriguing highlights of bureaucratic politics at work within the executive branch and their ramifications for presidential management.

TABLE 7.6. Reasons for Non-Issuance of Executive Orders

Reason	#	%
White House inaction	26	11.8
Mooted by legislation	12	5.4
(Lesser) substitute action	38	17.2
Later EO	7	3.2
OMB objection	45	20.4
New administration	11	4.9
Bureaucratic dissent	82	37.1
Total	*221*	*100.0*

White House Inaction. Slightly more than one in nine unissued orders success-fully navigate the process of central clearance, receive approval from OMB and Justice, and stall somewhere in the White House itself.

The archival record does not always clarify why that is the case: sometimes the EO simply slips across West Executive Avenue and never reappears. In 1984, for instance, the Federal Emergency Management Agency (FEMA) wanted the president to create a new commission on fire prevention and con-trol. The departments didn't care very much, and while OMB had some con-cerns with the truncated time frame FEMA demanded, it approved the EO. Handwritten notes in the file show it vanished in the White House, probably kidnapped by Dick Darman, then an aide to chief of staff Jim Baker. Even OMB was reduced to speculation: "Any deals made with Darman? What is the reason this did not go out?"[25] The problem could have been substance, or timing, or both; as a 1963 letter from White House aide Mike Feldman to the Commerce Secretary noted, the latter's EO was not worth the flak it might attract. "I think we should avoid this kind of hassle at this time. . . . I am hold-ing the proposed executive order until such time as it might be deemed to serve a useful purpose."[26] In that instance "such time" was code for never.

Some orders are unissued because the president (or the White House com-munications staff) changes tack on an upcoming event or speech, obviating the need for an associated EO. But there are certainly instances where the president himself refuses to sign on the dotted line. One example in the John-son administration sprang from recommendations from various civil rights groups as to the placement of federal facilities: many of these were located far from low-income neighborhoods or public transit, thus foreclosing their util-ity to the War on Poverty's intended beneficiaries. Interagency discussions about this problem moved from proposing vague statements ("doomed to be forgotten . . . , to end up more 'words,'" one White House aide told Johnson counsel Harry McPherson) toward initiating a more robust directive. McPherson reported to the president in August 1968 on a long series of meetings with the General Services Administration, Justice, HUD, Defense, the Post Office, Transportation, the Equal Employment Opportunity Commission, and BoB, "trying to draft an executive order dealing with this subject." Drafts and redrafts had gone through the clearance process, "and the attached Order has the approval of all agencies concerned." It would have required most federal agencies making siting decisions to give primary consideration to a facility's accessibility to those served by it and to potential federal employees, via the availability of nearby affordable and non-discriminatory housing and mass transportation. Preference might also be given to locating facilities in areas with high unemployment rates. "We have spent more hours discussing and polishing this Order than any which has come before us this year," McPherson told the president. "The basic reason for issuing this Order is that it is sensible and right."

LBJ wasn't sold. "I have some grave doubts," he replied, likely concerned about how Congress might react to making administrative decisions on grounds other than cost and efficiency—and about Southern Democrats' potential anger at his funneling federal funds to non-segregated areas. Indeed, White House aide Jim Gaither was quite up-front about this: "I would suggest that the [order], without directly saying so, set one basic goal: the location of Federal facilities to encourage racial and economic integration." But that, LBJ knew, might have a real impact on the ongoing presidential campaign. "Let the next administration deal with this," he told his staff. McPherson continued to plead but sent the file back to BoB a few days before Richard Nixon took office. "The President does not want to take any action," he reported.[27]

In that instance, White House aides were a driving force behind the proposed order. But when a variant of the same federal siting question arose in the second term of the Nixon administration, those staffers' successors seem to have been instrumental in *preventing* its issuance. As one OMB examiner told Deputy Director Paul O'Neill in May 1974, the idea had been revived as "an OMB-inspired product" after the 1972 budget review, as a proposal "to show evidence of concern and progress in the civil rights field," not Nixon's strongest suit. It was far weaker than the order LBJ had rejected, requiring only the consideration (not the prioritization) of available affordable housing. Even so it ran into resistance from HUD, which said it needed additional funding if it were to assess local markets for agencies seeking to locate new facilities.

OMB pushed back, approved the EO, and sent it to the White House. But there, again, it was a victim of anticipated legislative reactions—and by the spring of 1974, President Nixon could not afford to lose any friends on Capitol Hill. Nixon's assistant for legislative affairs, Bill Timmons, delivered the death blow: "there is no argument made on any *need* for this Ex[ecutive] Order. . . . Seems to be flying in the face of our congressional friends. Make OMB justify draft, pros *and* cons!" (So as not to shortchange the emphasis, Timmons's note underlined "need" twice and "and" a rather dramatic five times.) O'Neill decided the best response was to "file 'til more appropriate time."[28]

Legislation. William Howell's research shows that Congress very rarely overturns executive orders once they are issued.[29] In the present data, at least, that finding can be extended: legislators do not frequently preempt EOs by new statute. This outcome accounts for only about 5 percent of unissued orders. Even then, most examples are not of direct legislative veto but merely of legislation making a pending EO unnecessary. For instance, in September 1995 Bill Clinton's Justice Department had reached "Working Draft #9" in its efforts to craft an EO making lobbying more transparent; this was superseded by the Lobbying Disclosure Act enacted that December.[30] In October 1974, Gerald Ford's Domestic Council was drafting an order creating a "President's Energy Policy Committee," but shortly thereafter OMB noted that "the new energy law eliminated any necessity for issuing the EO so it was killed." Its weary general counsel abandoned a crossed-out copy of the decision memo prepared for the president, adding the resigned heading "for file or whatever."[31]

In 1977, the mayor of Portland, Oregon, wrote to President Carter asking for help: a federal court had just closed roads and ended logging within the Bull Run National Forest, a decision based on a 1904 federal law protecting the local Bull Run watershed. The National Forest itself had been created by presidential proclamation back in 1892—so could the president please just change the boundaries? Maybe, OMB thought; but Agriculture was less enthusiastic. It would just prompt additional litigation, the latter argued, and anyway "an executive order would be an ineffective piecemeal response that would invite additional requests" for more EOs by "special interests . . . seeking to amend other National Forest boundaries for a variety of special purposes." To the relief of the administration, the Oregon congressional delegation pushed through a repeal of the 1904 act, creating a new watershed zone to be managed by USDA and mooting the draft EO.[32]

But even if Congress fails to make progress, an EO may be seen as unduly provocative. In 1968, for instance, the Johnson White House had planned "to recommend that the President deal with the subject discussed in the attached memo [Micronesia] by executive order if Congress did not act." In the end the draft was abandoned: "in conversation with Interior and State we were advised that there would be an adverse congressional reaction if we went ahead with an executive order."[33]

Sometimes, finally, an EO may prove an impediment to the progress of legislation the administration wants passed. That is, for tactical reasons the president may decide *not* to act as "first mover." In 1951, for instance, the Office of Defense Mobilization's Charles E. Wilson urged scrapping a proposed EO regarding small businesses under the Defense Production Act (DPA). While he had originally thought it important for President Truman to make a public affirmation "on behalf of small business," Wilson wrote, "the legislative situation has changed substantially in the interim." And "in view of this legislative situation, I do not believe it would be advisable to issue an executive order. . . . No action should be taken which might in any way adversely affect the passage of the DPA amendments."[34] The EO was shelved, and the Senate approved the desired statutory language.

A more extended example of that sort of dance between legislation and executive action comes from the tail end of the Johnson administration, as the president considered whether to issue an executive order greatly expanding John F. Kennedy's 1962 EO regarding racial discrimination in housing. During the 1960 campaign, Kennedy had promised to end such discrimination with a stroke of his pen, a pledge that ran headlong into political constraints— notably, Kennedy's perceived need not to offend Southern Democrats in Congress, who were well-placed to block his legislative program. As Kennedy delayed, civil rights activists sent thousands of pens to the White House in protest.[35] A relatively weak version of the EO was finally issued after the November 1962 midterms, with the congressional session coming to an end and the nation's attention still on the recent Cuban Missile Crisis.

Even so there was plenty of pushback. The records of the Public Housing Administration (PHA), for instance, show that implementation of Kennedy's EO, which barred federally funded housing agencies from discriminating on the basis of race, was spotty at best. Indeed, some local housing authorities had canceled projects so as not to comply.[36] The complaints of the housing director of Panama City, Florida, were typical of his peers: "It has NEVER been the policy of the Panama City Housing Authority to integrate the races in it's [*sic*] projects," he told his state attorney general. "It is presented for your consideration the possibility that such Order is, in fact, . . . not law, nor a legally binding promulgation, but a usurpation of power and an unconstitutional edict and mandate indefensible in a Court of legal jurisdiction."[37] White House aide Bill Moyers was later told that the Dallas housing authorities had more than five hundred vacancies owing to their unwillingness to allow African American families to move into units in "white and Latin American sections."[38] And a broader 1965 report from the Council of Economic Advisers found little enforcement, concluding that "we cannot find a noticeable effect of the Order in opening up housing markets to minorities."[39]

Housing and Home Finance Agency director Robert Weaver (who would later be the first secretary of HUD) told concerned members of Congress as early as 1963 that "the effectiveness of the order would undoubtedly be increased by broadening" its coverage to include housing underwritten by federally insured banks and other financial institutions regulated by the federal government.[40] That was also the conclusion of an advisory body on the topic LBJ had appointed under the leadership of former governor David Lawrence of Pennsylvania. The Lawrence Committee's "confidential draft" of July 1964 laid out the Kennedy order's limitations and argued a new EO should expand its coverage.[41] The committee held its peace through the 1964 campaign, but in December White House aide Lee White told the president that pressure was building: with the election past, "they will urge such action upon you in the strongest possible terms," joined by civil rights and religious groups. White suggested that senior administration figures meet with Lawrence to determine a way forward, while Justice assessed the legal issues involved—notably, whether FDIC could put these kinds of conditions on its member banks.[42] Over time, White worried, members of the commission could resign in protest, and outside groups would "get progressively noisier." Ultimately Lawrence met with Vice President Hubert Humphrey, Attorney General Nicholas Katzenbach, Weaver, and White, in hopes low-salience administrative action might do the trick without changing the EO itself.[43] But by September 1965, White was still writing to proponents of an expanded EO that it was "being reviewed by the appropriate agency officials."[44] The Justice Department complained that "the liberal members of the committee and the civil rights groups seem completely insensitive to the legal problems involved" and that only "a highly partisan view" could downplay the technical complications.[45]

One solution was to propose legislation instead. Lawrence said his committee was for that, "*if* the choice is between legislation of broad scope of success and executive action." But he conveyed "very serious reservations . . . as to the practicality of the legislative route." Johnson aide Joe Califano, for his part, didn't disagree that legislating would be hard ("people are extremely sensitive on the housing issue") but worried about an extended EO being defeated in court and especially about the ramifications of "moving in the most sensitive of civil rights areas all alone, without Congressional backup."[46] LBJ agreed. He wanted new legislation to be proposed—in January 1967, "so Cong[ress] won't get beat" over the head with the issue in the 1966 midterms. To bolster the case Johnson directed Califano to commission an opinion from Treasury Secretary Henry Fowler saying the president did not have authority to act unilaterally: "Get Fowler to get FDIC, FSLIC etc to say they can't do."[47]

Fowler's memo, saying a new EO "would not be effective and would be legally questionable," arrived in November 1965. "You might find this memorandum useful," Califano told the president, "in any discussions with Negro leaders or others pressing for an expanded executive order."[48] But others argued the president should not disavow his own authority. Lee White said that "it would be desirable to retain as much flexibility as possible. . . . [A]ny statement by the Attorney General that there is no authority to extend the order by executive action might well be embarrassing at some time in the future if the circumstances at that time would warrant considering executive action." Privately, Katzenbach thought an EO could "do savings and loans" but "that it is doubtful whether commercial banks can be included." LBJ's scrawled response was, "I think that's all right."[49]

In the end, LBJ's preferred 1967 timing for legislation had to be traded away to appease those demanding immediate executive action; he called for a fair housing law in his 1966 State of the Union Address. But even the liberal 89th Congress failed to enact his proposal, while BoB threw cold water on a series of alternative presidential directives proposed by the vice president "to cushion civil rights disappointments."[50] Only the assassination of Martin Luther King Jr. finally prodded Congress to pass the Fair Housing Act of 1968.[51] However, overall this case seems to exemplify a president getting the outcome he wanted, largely on the basis of agency expertise melded with centralized political advice. Again, an unissued order can be an example of good management rather than a failed process.

Downgrading: Substitute Action. Executive orders, as noted in the introductory chapter, are considered (as a Trump aide put it there) "very muscular," indeed, the "high[est] statement of executive direction." At times such a statement is necessary, even legally required. But in other instances what is proposed falls short of that high standard, in the eyes of OMB or other players along the way: thus, as the general counsel's office frequently notes, "an executive order is not the appropriate document."[52] Indeed, OMB may advise that "any usual format, except an Order, is acceptable."[53]

In such cases the substance of the order may wind up in different or less official form—or sometimes as an agency-issued regulation. In a 1961 case, the Civil Service Commission (CSC) proposed an order that would have prevented those appointed as "Schedule C" employees in the executive branch from continuing their employment as civil servants after the administration that appointed them left office. A clearance letter went out to every agency BoB could locate—46 in all, down to the Subversive Activities Control Board—and 44 of them registered no objection. But after some three and a half months, the Justice Department weighed in, pushing back against both the substance of the proposal ("such positions are not necessarily of a political non-career nature") and its process: "I doubt the wisdom of an absolute prohibition . . . by executive order" when "such matters are best handled by flexible Civil Service regulations which may be adapted to the changing conditions in the field of personnel management more readily than executive orders." The CSC backed down and said it would consider the issuance of such regulations instead.[54]

"The preferred format for issuing a management directive," by contrast, "is a Presidential Memorandum," as OMB advised en route to an early 1981 memo promoting programs combating alcohol and drug abuse among federal workers. White House domestic policy staff and the Office of Personnel Management had pushed for an EO, but OMB argued this amounted merely to "directing agencies to comply with [an extant] statutory mandate." While no one objected to the substance, a memorandum was the better route since "the proposed order would add nothing of legal or regulatory significance to the statutes or OPM regulations. . . . The solution to the current problem is more vigorous implementation (a management problem), rather than repetitious regulation."[55]

Other options might downgrade a proposed EO to a presidential statement or even a White House press release. For instance, the Carter administration's Council on Environmental Quality (CEQ) wanted an order that would prod rapid regulatory action by EPA and Treasury; would set up EPA as a coordinating body over a wide range of economic assistance programs designed to offset the cost of environmental regulation; and would create an interagency committee to help with that. CEQ's bland request asked OMB to "please put this executive order into circulation and arrange for an expedited review." In response, OMB counsel Ron Kienlen exploded at the agency's political appointee responsible for environmental policy with the kind of capitalized fervor presidential tweets would later make infamous: "I walked into the enclosed CEQ proposal this morning. . . . THIS IS NOT AN EXECUTIVE ORDER IN TONE. THERE IS NO APPARENT LEGAL OR ADMINISTRATIVE REQUIREMENT THAT THIS BE AN E.O. IN ORDER FOR THIS TO MEET THE STANDARDS . . . IT WOULD NEED A LOT OF WORK." And since "there are 30 E.O. ahead of this one" and "at least ¾ are better E.O. candidates," it was work he did not wish to do. Instead, he suggested a presidential statement merely urging the policy shifts CEQ described. "Please let me know today if you can't live with that."[56]

Another Carter White House–driven EO made its way to OMB in late 1980, seeking to support Vietnam-era veterans and veteran-owned businesses. In conjunction with the Domestic Policy Staff, the administrator of the Small Business Administration (SBA) noted that the president would be speaking to the American Legion's national convention in just three days' time and could announce a new EO there—conveniently addressing a resolution on the Legion's agenda that attacked Carter on this very issue. But immediate pushback from another advisory unit—the White House Veterans Federal Coordinating Committee (WHVFCC)—put paid to such rapid turnaround. "Establishing another interagency committee for veterans is duplicative," the WHVFCC told OMB. There was "insufficient time to obtain the proper clearance and to thoroughly review the content of the proposed material, which may contain questionable statements." And most damningly, the wording of SBA's letter accompanying its draft EO—designed to imply that WHVFCC supported the proposal—was at best misleading: we "did indeed react to the proposed executive order, and it was clear that this input was *not* to be viewed as approval or concurrence."[57]

A variety of other feedback, much of it negative, trickled in from other agencies too. Even the Veterans Administration thought the EO could be problematic: "the Order as drafted does not stress the particular needs of the Vietnam veterans" and had odd clashes with current law. It would burden procurement officers with massive new responsibilities, others worried, and was "technically deficient in several respects," not least in failing to define its terms properly. "Nothing is identified except the desire to assist [veteran-owned businesses] in some general and unspecified manner," complained the Office of Federal Procurement Policy within OMB, which urged "strongly that the proposed executive order not be issued, certainly not in its present state."[58]

On October 24 a revised order was delivered. White House aide Jeffrey Farrow told OMB "we would like to get this signed this month" (that is, before Election Day) since "we have resolved all issues which were noted in the original draft E.O."[59]

That proved overly optimistic. OMB hated the revised draft too, both as literature and as substantive policy. "Delete! This is hortatory, not regulatory," one staff attorney wrote on the proposed text. Where that text referred to "each department and agency of the Executive Branch," editors noted, "this is a very large universe. . . . How many . . . have any authority in these areas?" That universe was told to "take appropriate action to facilitate, preserve and strengthen veteran owned businesses and to ensure full participation by veterans, in particular those of the Vietnam Era and disabled veterans in the free enterprise system"—which prompted another flurry of criticism. "How do you 'facilitate business'?" As for participation in free enterprise, "HOW? By working, by owning business, what?" "Too broad." "Redundant and Meaningless." "Too Vague." "A lot of useless words to say the obvious."[60]

By page five of the draft OMB had been reduced to straight sarcasm, replacing the line "The Task Force shall in a manner consistent with law" with "shall not do anything illegal?" By page nine there was worry that in fact the task force *would* be asked to do something illegal: to enforce delivery of a specific quota of SBA loan funds to veteran-owned businesses ("what is the specific statutory authority vested in the President which would authorize this directive?").[61] OMB thus returned the new draft to the White House, opining that it would be better implemented as a management memo or press release. "This proposal is not regulatory in nature. Even after paring it down to the marked up version, what is left is not of sufficient specific substance to be developed into a regulatory document. *It is not the stuff of which executive orders are made.*"[62]

Defining such stuff as executive orders are made on flows ultimately, of course, from presidential dreams.[63] Presidents have a great deal of flexibility in how they define their directives; and numerous EOs over time seem likely to have received this sort of feedback but were issued nonetheless.[64] This was especially clear during the Trump administration. EO 13788, for instance, reminds the executive branch that there are various laws requiring agencies to "buy American," while EO 13879 promises that "My Administration is dedicated to advancing American kidney health."[65] In general, though, OMB seeks to resist the desire of officialdom for executive orders for their own sake, because (as one OMB general counsel put it) "they think they are more—I'm doing air-quotes—'impressive.'"

Often, the counsel noted, a letter or phone call to a relevant Cabinet member accomplishes the desired end: "just tell him!"[66]

Other OMB Objections. Though the driving force to do so often lies in the kind of interagency dissent discussed below, OMB is the most frequent conduit for recommendations that proposed EOs be converted to other sorts of policy declarations. It may also raise different sorts of objections that stop the EO rather than repurpose it. "There are lots of ideas that die on the vine, because lots of them are very poor ideas. . . . Not every idea out there deserves an executive order," said one OMB counsel.[67] Another staffer paraphrased OMB careerists' characterization of the "crazy cakes" orders proposed during the Trump transition: those concerned about what was issued, they told her, "'should see what we *stopped.*'"[68] Such input is normally founded on substantive or legal concerns, but sometimes too out of worries that a given EO will inadvertently harm presidential power.

As the veterans' business proposal just traced makes clear, there are thin boundaries between these various rationales. For instance, several months after President Reagan had eliminated a number of interdepartmental committees—symbols of the bloated size and scope of government—the National Endowment for the Arts (NEA) sought to re-create one of them. The NEA argued that its new Design Council (to replace the now defunct Design Liaison Council) was actually "very much in keeping with the Administration's philosophy" since it would "identify areas of inefficiency and waste" and promote "a dramatic saving of government funds." But OMB was unimpressed, arguing that there were additional ways to achieve these ends ("we could get work done without setting up yet another government committee," one staffer noted, and certainly not, as another had complained, "another committee . . . created with no particular power and no hope of accomplishing its objective, which is fuzzy at best").[69] Just as crucially, Deputy Director Joe Wright was warned that "reestablishing this Council might encourage other agencies to seek similar treatment for their own committees, . . . leaving the President open to challenge as to the seriousness of his announced effort to abolish federal entities."[70]

In other cases, OMB pushes against proposals it feels will undercut the presidency more generally. In 1966, for example, it resisted an EO promoted by Commerce Secretary John Connor that would have put both BoB and the Council of Economic Advisers as voting members on a Cabinet-level advisory committee; OMB director Charles Schultze was reminded that "full membership on an interagency committee tends to compromise the role of an Executive Office agency in providing staff advice to the President."[71] During the Ford administration, OMB likewise sought to block an effort to use an EO to preempt interagency arguments and constrain presidential flexibility. At that time, the Labor Department was locked in a dispute with the Department of the Interior over who should control the Mining Enforcement and Safety Administration (MESA), a battle that had escalated into distant courtrooms. The Interior secretary complained to the attorney general that "a state court is not the place to resolve policy disputes within the executive branch," and soon proposed an EO that would fend off Labor and keep MESA where it was. OMB insisted that "an executive order is not the solution." After negotiations continued for months, the general counsel's secretary finally wrote him to ask, "Do you want this killed off?" His frazzled, handwritten response: "Yes (or No?)." Ultimately the answer was yes.[72]

OMB may also "kill off" proposals based on presidential authority in a given area. LBJ aide Joe Califano drew the short straw and had to tell Lady Bird Johnson that her husband could not make permanent her committee dedicated to capital beautification (such an order "would have no real authority" over a new first lady). Some years later Sen. John Warner of Virginia was also let down gently when his (apparently serious) request for an EO mandating "the Virginia Tech Regimental Band to participate in all future Presidential Inaugural Parades" ran up against the fact that "no executive order issued by an incumbent president can dictate the details of future inaugural observances."[73] Many cases have rather weightier subjects in mind, though, and here OMB's institutional memory is a useful resource. In 1967, a State Department proposal about delegating authority over the transfer of war materials to hostile nations was ruled out based on BoB's recollection of a Justice Department objection to a parallel situation more than a decade earlier.[74]

Sometimes OMB just thinks a proposal is a bad idea. In 1981, for example, a long battle over the Office of Personnel Management's vision for a grand "charter for Federal personnel management" came crashing to a halt against a wall of opposition. "We question the totality of the delegation of Presidential authority to OPM" and the "vast regulatory authority" presumed in the draft order, warned OMB's Jim Tozzi. Another OMB staffer likewise emphasized the "major shifts of authority" from the president, OMB, and the agencies to

OPM and argued this was not required by the Civil Service Reform Act passed in 1978, "although of course OPM would so view it." A third argued that personnel was not "simply a housekeeping function" but "as important a resource as money": "no one would suggest that budget decisions be totally delegated to OMB so the President wouldn't have to be bothered."

OPM fought back, arguing that OMB just didn't get it: "In your meetings with our staff and in the correspondence we have sent you, we have tried to get across this concept," wrote the OPM deputy director, implying OMB's stupidity made such efforts fruitless. The OPM director weighed in too, complaining that "our proposal has been 'clearing' at OMB for over eight months." OMB did not bend, though, insisting that OPM instead first review the close to eighty executive orders regarding personnel already in place. "It ought to be clear that the present proposed order will never survive the review of OPM-related EOs," OMB counsel Ron Kienlen responded, adding a shot across the bows: "Unless OPM intends to do something very significant that it does not now have the authority to do."[75]

Another lengthy deliberation process—this one trying to hash out guidelines governing alcohol testing for federal employees—provides an additional example of substantive OMB recalcitrance. This saga began in 1990 when the Department of Energy proposed a regulation requiring that its contractors be tested for alcohol use. Justice responded that doing so would require an equivalent policy for direct government employees. As it transpired that no federal workers were subject to alcohol testing, not even air traffic controllers or those in nuclear facilities, an "Alcohol Work Group" was created. It ultimately included representatives from Defense, Energy, HHS, Justice, Transportation, the Nuclear Regulatory Commission, OPM, and the White House "drug czar," along with five different parts of OMB. By summer 1991 the group had a first draft of an EO. It began by proclaiming that "alcohol is used by more Americans than any other drug."

The process dragged on ("I still do not have OPM's redo of the EO," an OMB staffer griped in December 1991; a scrawled "finally . . ." greeted its ultimate appearance), and in early 1992, OMB general counsel Bob Damus pulled the plug. He held that "there has been no documentation of any widespread, or even less than widespread but significant alcohol impairment problem with Federal employees"—"do we really want to say someone can be suspended or fired for having a beer" at an office Christmas party?—"yet this order will have the President establish, out of the blue, a far-reaching, intrusive, and costly program to prevent it." Not only was the proposal "re-regulatory" (a dirty word in the Reagan-Bush years) but drafters had struggled unsuccessfully to define the employees and functions the EO would cover. "It seems undeniable," Damus noted, "that the President performs a 'function' which, if not properly discharged, could directly cause harm to public health or safety. He is Commander-in-Chief. That means, since he is Commander-in-Chief 24 hours a day, that, under this order, he cannot ever have a drink at any time." Yet at the same time the draft expressly did not apply to the armed forces. This, Damus concluded, "is not appropriate or sustainable."[76]

Changes in Presidential Administration. It seems intuitive that EOs proposed by one administration are discarded by the next. Indeed, if EOs were "unilateral" in the purest sense, they would have to be. Yet this is not the case, a finding that reinforces the institutional nature of the EO formulation process and the non-presidential provenance of most EOs. (It is worth recalling the example of Gerald Ford's second EO—proposed in July 1974, sent to the White House later that month, and issued a week after President Nixon's resignation.)[77]

There are of course examples of EOs that start too late in a given term to get full attention and that are summarily shelved by the incoming president. A draft EO "prescribing that aircraft of U.S. registry should be used when air transportation costs are paid by the U.S." was submitted to BoB on January 19, 1961—one day before Dwight Eisenhower left office. It was returned to the new leadership of the Federal Aviation Administration and never resubmitted.

And, to be sure, changes in presidencies do normally prompt review of pending EOs. In June 1977, for instance, OMB general counsel William Nichols wrote to departments with orders in the pipeline to "clarify that . . . proposed executive orders or proclamations, which were submitted prior to January 20, 1977 and not yet issued, will not be acted upon unless resubmitted for clearance and approval." Four years later, in March 1981, new OMB director David Stockman issued a similar reminder as part of his primer for Reagan appointees on the central clearance process.[78] In both cases, some draft EOs were resubmitted, while many were not: a later summary document of "Executive Orders Not Issued in 1981" lists forty-four of these, of which all but ten are annotated "submitted prior to January 20, 1981. No further action taken."[79]

For some of those proposals, a change in decision makers was indeed the cause of death. A 1974 proposal regarding the Bureau of Indian Affairs, originally delayed so that policymakers could consider data in a pending report, was tabled by the Carter administration (that report never appeared, or at least not by mid-1977). Indeed, in at least one case OMB preempted the actual transition. Carter had issued a statement on the treatment of U.S. territories back in February 1980, but it was not until after that November's election that the Interior Department sought to capitalize on this guidance with a proposed EO. OMB noted that the belated draft might be "consistent" with what Carter had said but that it "comes at an odd time" to be moving forward with new policy. Instead, the incoming Reagan administration was given the chance to make its own mark.[80]

Importantly, however, in most cases close examination of the files documenting proposed EOs indicates that inauguration day is not the actual cause of an EO's demise. The OMB date stamp on the death certificate (as it were) often ratifies events that had occurred some time past—it merely removes the deceased from cold storage long enough to formally pronounce the obvious. For instance, one of the proposed EOs withdrawn from consideration in April 1981 "pursuant to Director's Memorandum"—addressing the audit of expenditures for which security concerns prevented full disclosure—came with baggage as "a lot of unnecessary paperwork. . . . DOD and DOJ opposed." By November 1980 OMB had already decided to shelve the EO "and work to get acceptable agency procedures" in place instead.[81] Another in the same set, proposed by the SBA, was effectively dead by 1979. Agency after agency had attacked its "necessity," its "unjustified scope," its "conflict with congressional mandate[s]," its "redundancy," and even its "draftsmanship."[82]

Dissent. As that suggests, these EOs were predominantly a victim of dissent inside the executive branch—as were the vast majority of the draft orders formally set aside near the beginning of the Carter and Reagan presidencies, and many others besides. As Table 7.6 shows, bureaucratic dissent accounts for more than a third of unissued orders beyond the less direct causality just detailed. Pulling the plug on a proposed order in 1969, OMB noted it "has been opposed by two congressional committees, ten government agencies, and a number of private practitioners."[83] Five years later, similarly, an OMB staffer told the Department of Commerce that "in view of these negative comments . . . no further action to process the proposed Executive Order is contemplated."[84] Another note to the files noted sadly that after a long process of trying to bridge a gap between the Departments of State and HEW, "the two departments remained in disagreement in regard to this matter and the disagreement was never resolved."[85] While I have separated "dissent" out from the categories of OMB-specific opposition already noted, that judgment is of course somewhat subjective. OMB's issues with a given EO, after all, often coincide with agency complaints, or even anticipate them.

Intra–executive branch pushback has many pathways. Agency comments, substantive and snide, technical and tactical, decorate thousands of archival documents. The FBI's "tune doesn't change," the State Department sniffed as revisions to employment security procedures—loyalty checks—were discussed in the mid-1970s. Shift the scope of conflict! an assistant secretary counseled in the 1960s, channeling his inner E. E. Schattschneider: "From a tactical point of view, you should give the Secretary a copy of the wording you would like to see in the Executive Order."[86] In 1987, Treasury revealed to OMB that it had been engaged in a battle with State over a sanctions EO and decided to send along an eight-page "statement of [our] views, which was provided to the State Department" but ignored by the latter in its draft order. Treasury demanded OMB "convene an inter-agency meeting . . . to resolve this matter." Treasury "would be pleased to participate."[87]

Sometimes the drafter of the EO is pressured to back down. "Agency reaction was largely negative," OMB said, sending back a proposal regarding federal employment of the disabled to the Civil Service Commission; CSC chair John Macy conceded that "a number of conflicting views emerged." He wrote in 1964 that "in an effort to reconcile the differences and thereby gain greater acceptance of the proposal, a number of revisions were made." But this watered down the order so much that "after further review of the matter in light of the revisions, the Commission has decided that the benefits proposed are not such as to warrant Presidential action."[88]

Likewise, OMB noted that "various aspects" of a 1970 Interior Department proposal regarding the procurement of helium were "criticized or questioned, directly or indirectly" by three-quarters of the agencies asked for comment. Several months later Interior's revised draft "did not seem to deal quite effectively with the difficulties encountered by the order in the clearance process"; OMB thought that agency pushback, especially by the Pentagon, raised "considerable doubt . . . regarding the validity" of Interior's assertions and its "'solution.'" By April 1971, Interior "wishe[d] to reconsider the entire subject" and withdrew the proposed EO.[89]

This can occur even with EOs produced by the president's personal staff. In 1989 the White House Office of National Service wanted an EO, linked to George H. W. Bush's "thousand points of light" initiative, to "encourage federal officers and employees to engage in community service." The proposal had already been toned down from early efforts to have community service be a factor both in hiring decisions and in contracting and procurement criteria.[90] Even so it attracted much feedback—all of which claimed to eagerly support community service while asking for changes making it unlikely the EO would foment any. The Department of Education worried about "rather prescriptive" demands; HUD suggested "that its tone be softened"; Commerce thought "encourage" should replace "require."[91] Others in the EOP itself piled on. OMB staff found the EO "somewhat unrealistic in its expectations" and for that matter unneeded, given Bush's proposed Points of Light Foundation; the White House counsel's office assessment that the order was "problematic" delivered the coup de grâce.[92]

Many thwarted EOs run aground on competing jurisdictions—especially when a department complains that another department will receive unwonted advantage via presidential directive. In late 1980, for instance, the U.S. Trade Representative (USTR) proposed an EO expanding its own role in setting standards that affected international trade. Various agencies complained, notably Agriculture, which complained that the "troublesome" language "means USTR control over, for example, virtually all food quality and safety standards. Such primacy for USTR is neither contemplated by the Trade Agreements Act of 1979 nor sound policy."[93] Interestingly, USDA sent the very same letter twice—once over the signature of Carter Agriculture Secretary Bob Bergland and once from the new Reagan administration's secretary, John Block, emphasizing the strength of departmental institutional interests even across key changes in political context.[94] Either or both secretaries won out, and USTR's proposal went no further.

In a similar vein, in 1986 Secretary of Defense Caspar Weinberger personally wrote to budget director Jim Miller to complain about an EO proposed by Commerce that would have delegated export administration powers to, well, Commerce. The Pentagon objected, Weinberger said, "given the unprecedented nature of the authorities it confers on the Secretary of Commerce over critical national security and foreign policy issues." He went so far as to enclose a "preliminary point paper outlining some of Defense's most serious concerns" that he wanted to be used "as the focal point for an interagency meeting to discuss the Executive Order." OMB, if not entirely convinced, did convene such a meeting in early December. At the meeting, Commerce protested that it needed to be in charge to prevent delays in key exports: the "real dispute in their view is decision-making—how to get it escalated and decided" if multiple agencies were involved. The Pentagon held its ground: "basically, DoD asserts a concurrence right" and threatened that it would be "taking several issues directly to the President." State suggested the matter go to an NSC working group, a venue likely to favor DoD; indeed, the proposal expired there.[95] DoD does not always win, though; numerous agencies objected to a 1966 Office of Emergency Preparedness proposal that would have assigned numerous functions to the Pentagon. The OEP director backed down: "because of the issues raised by the agencies, a decision on the assignment is not appropriate at this time."[96]

Another jurisdictional hot potato started in the spring of 1988 as a FEMA proposal revising EO 10480 (from 1953) and its delegation of authorities derived from the Defense Production Act. FEMA's version, which had early support from National Security Council, gave itself an oversight role, requiring that it approve any plans and decisions made by the various agencies delegated power by the EO.

This drew fierce fire as other departments began to read the proposal. OMB circulated draft after draft across the executive branch—by the fourth, in October, the OMB counsel's office said hopefully that "substantial" revisions had been "negotiated during meetings between the proponent agency, the Federal Emergency Management Agency, and the Departments of the Treasury, Commerce, Defense, and Energy. It is our understanding that the revised document represents interagency consensus." It did not. Energy, for instance, complained that the EO gave "inappropriate" authority to FEMA—a non-Cabinet agency—over various Cabinet departments, and argued that while FEMA claimed this was for efficiency's sake, the layers of approval could slow down agencies' ability to respond rapidly to an emergency. FEMA should be a "coordinating agency" but surely not an "*overseer* or *approving authority*."[97] Arguments over these questions continued into the George H. W. Bush administration. In early 1989 FEMA reported to OMB on negotiations with Commerce, Transportation, Energy, and Defense; "some of the comments were modified after meetings were held with the agency representatives while others were rejected with a detailed explanation in our response." Those agencies rejected FEMA's rejection and the process went on. After yet another draft in December 1989, Energy expressed its "full appreciation of the importance of this proposed executive order" but said it had "made a substantial previous effort to resolve its concerns" with FEMA; that it thought "a satisfactory understanding had been reached"; and that "unfortunately, the current version . . . has proven that assumption to be incorrect." OMB also heard from Defense that one of the National Security Council's senior interagency groups had not approved

FEMA's "underlying allocation of authority."[98] At the end of January 1990 the plug was pulled: "it appears that further development of the order by the originating agency is appropriate prior to further circulation," OMB told FEMA.[99]

A case across an even longer time span dealt with convicts in state prisons—and with a 1905 executive order by Theodore Roosevelt banning the use of their labor by federal contractors.[100] State prison officials, their congressional allies, and a number of executive agencies—notably Agriculture, Interior, and the Navy—were eager to rescind the long-standing policy. In 1953, Agriculture proposed an EO doing just that, supported by Justice, but vociferous objections from the Labor Department forced the issue onto the agenda for a Cabinet meeting. President Eisenhower told the agencies "to work out a mutually satisfactory solution," the BoB general counsel recalled in 1961. "They were never able to do so."[101]

As the Kennedy administration took office, members of Congress ("importuned by State prison officials")[102] saw a chance to revive the matter. They began to lobby the White House, with some success: Kennedy counsel Myer Feldman passed along the question to Labor Secretary Arthur Goldberg asking him to get together with then assistant attorney general Nick Katzenbach "and work out a suitable modification." To Rep. Clem Miller, Feldman wrote, "I certainly agree with you . . . that a revision of this old executive order is fully warranted, and I will do what I can to expedite its consideration."[103]

What he could do was insufficient. As BoB observed, "Katzenbach has had several discussions with Labor Department representatives and is not too hopeful." Even if rescinding the EO had minimal effects on the local job market, "No one in the labor movement or in the Labor Department wants to take official responsibility for a recommendation which could be attacked as permitting displacement of free labor by convict labor." Ultimately Katzenbach had to write to nearly three dozen members of the House and Senate to apologize for the delays caused by "extensive consideration of this matter which has been undertaken in consultation with representatives of other government agencies." Those consultations, he noted, made clear that the secretary of labor was not budging. Thus revising the 1905 EO was "not presently in order."[104]

These cases emphasize that proposals arising from the Executive Office of the President are not exempt from complaint, and that actors outside the executive branch often weigh in. A colorful example of both comes from 1961, when Sen. Clinton Anderson wrote an eight-page screed to President Kennedy about a BoB proposal: "I am so shocked by its contents, as are other members of Congress who have spoken to me," Anderson chided, "that I seriously wonder if it has received your careful attention."

The draft EO in question dealt with water resource projects, a perennial favorite for legislative earmarks, and would have expanded BoB's planning authority in that area. Given the Bureau's reputation for resisting unnecessary (or at least expensive) infrastructure expansionism, one can understand why legislators wanted the president to stay far away from local pork. Noting Kennedy's legislative service, Anderson went on: "Because of your experience, you can appreciate . . . the reaction in both [chambers] to an executive order which codifies and extends the Bureau of the Budget role in policymaking, scheduling and administration of resources and public works planning and developments, and in river basin planning." The Bureau was "empire building. . . . The reach of power under the proposed executive order is not new, but its broad scope is startling." Thus, Anderson warned, "I cannot emphasize too strongly my belief that issuance of such an order will start conflicts between your Office and the Congress on the worst sort of issues for you to fight with Congress." Agencies piled on, too, perhaps seeing a chance to please legislators and take BoB down a peg. The secretary of Health, Education, and Welfare, for instance, preached of the primacy of Cabinet departments and said the EO would "define [secretaries'] responsibilities almost entirely in terms of servicing staff agencies."[105]

Kennedy had publicly placed the issuance of such an order at the center of his February 1961 special message on natural resources. That authority was invoked when the EO was drafted by BoB in April and sent out to the agencies for clearance, and the Bureau's first reaction to the attacks was to push back. One memo noted that even if the sections in the draft order referencing BoB were not needed, they should remain: "we believe that if they are dropped under the present circumstances the Bureau, as a practical matter, will be seriously weakened as a staff arm of the President." If nothing else such a retreat will "encourage executive agencies to invoke congressional pressures in the future."[106]

But the White House quickly threw the Bureau under the bus. Kennedy's legislative liaison, Larry O'Brien, stressed to members of Congress that "the language which had been circulating on the Hill was only tentative and had not been prepared, cleared, or seen by the White House staff." He assured them that offending language would be removed.[107] For his part, BoB director David Bell felt compelled to back down. He wrote to Sen. Anderson with assurance that he had "no intention of seeking to enlarge the Bureau's responsibilities or authority."[108]

As that reminds us, sometimes it is the president's own preferences that are thwarted: recall from chapter 1 the "hooray" that greeted President Carter's retreat from his lobbyist logging initiative in 1977, or his unobeyed written command noted above: to "prepare an executive order" and "make it strict."[109]

Carter, of course, was often accused of being a weak leader—not least by his successor, Ronald Reagan. And yet we can tell the same tale about Reagan with regard to a draft EO regarding affirmative action.[110] Reagan had long opposed the practice: in a 1981 press conference just ten days into his administration, the president said that he worried some civil rights programs had become "distorted in the practice" and opposed "affirmative action programs becoming quota systems" that existed "for the purpose of discrimination." Longtime aide Ed Meese, who served during the first term as one-third of the White House "troika" of key advisors, termed affirmative action "a legal, moral, and constitutional tragedy."[111]

After Reagan's landslide reelection, then—with Meese now the attorney general—the time seemed ripe to reverse Lyndon Johnson's executive orders (notably EO 11246) mandating that government contractors "take affirmative action to ensure that applicants are employed" without regard to their race, color, religion, national origin, or gender. Richard Nixon's Labor Department had used this language to require "specific goals and timetables" for hiring minorities so that the contractor workforce mirrored the local workforce overall.[112] Assistant Attorney General William Bradford Reynolds urged the president to use the "stroke of a pen" to "replace this executive order with one that makes clear that the federal government does not require, authorize, or permit" any form of "race- or gender-conscious preferential treatment by federal contractors."[113] In August 1985, Meese sent a proposed order revising EO 11246 to the White House. The White House communications office and Justice Department teamed up to produce a package of information selling the change, even drafting an address to the nation defending the president's new order.[114]

And yet, as Kenneth Mayer concludes, "despite this strong opposition and repeated efforts . . . the Reagan administration was unable to make any changes to affirmative action programs or [EO] 11246."[115] The key roadblock was the Labor Department and its ability to mobilize bureaucratic allies within the administration. Labor Secretary William Brock insisted that extant language requiring hiring goals remain in place, supported by a vocal business community reluctant to revisit now-established hiring procedures. He also garnered support from Treasury Secretary James Baker and Secretary of State George Shultz (who had been key to the Nixon policy during his own service at Labor in 1969–70). Meanwhile Sen. Thomas Eagleton put a hold on new OMB director Jim Miller's nomination over (as Reagan's legislative affairs staff reported) "his concerns . . . based on an interpretation of a draft he has seen of the revised executive order dealing with affirmative action." He "insisted Miller provide his personal interpretation of the executive order in writing," and that the secretary of labor provide additional assurances that affirmative action would continue.[116] A White House working group convened to broker compromise language could not bridge the divisions within the administration: in the end, nothing went to—or came from—the president. No order was issued.

As noted in Table 7.3, there are more than fifty proposed but unissued EOs in the data that were predominantly centralized. Given the way centralization is measured—as an assessment of the preponderant influences on the formulation process as a whole, rather than by the originator of the EO—this is not an exact proxy for presidential preferences, nor of course a random sample. Nearly a quarter of these fall short within the White House itself, after surviving the gauntlet of central clearance, and a handful were rolled over into other executive orders or were preempted by legislation. But bureaucratic dissent is the leading category in this subset of unissued orders, at 25 percent of the total. Another 23 percent were channeled into alternate (and what OMB nearly uniformly sees as less authoritative) forms of expression, which as we have seen often reflects or preempts wider executive pushback. Another 16 percent were stopped by OMB's own concerns about an order's scope or legality. Thus close to two-thirds even of this centralized subset of proposed orders hardly reflect a unitary executive in which the president's will reigns uncontested.[117]

Conclusions

That is, of course, a key theme of this book. Presidents face constraints even in their interactions across the putative hierarchy of the executive branch. Adding to the mix proposed orders that were contenders but fell short of the finish line bolsters the focus on presidential management. After all, these examples make clear that from the president's perspective, an unissued order may be the outcome of a successful management effort or, conversely, a frustrating example of the limits of unilateralism. During the clearance process, departments and agencies are given notice of a proposed order and get the chance to offer their feedback. They take full advantage. OMB does its best to referee the interagency disputes that result; the failure to negotiate consensus is by far the largest cause of an EO's demise. The information and critiques received may convince the president that issuing the order is undesirable on grounds of substance, or politics, or future Cabinet harmony.

As such, the fact of an unissued order may symbolize a well-run vetting process, making a potential EO's weaknesses evident via agency input. Additional information from a range of perspectives allows the president to come to a reasoned conclusion, even change her mind, about the merits of a given proposal. Indeed, the issuance of an EO, rather than its preemption, might be the "failure" outcome here, if the president declines to update his preferences given available but unheeded expertise—think about Trump's travel ban (in chapter 1) in this sense, or Carter's short-lived export policy EO (in chapter 4). OMB's role in assessing EOs, and its outsize sway in directing some proposals to the dustbin and others into alternate forms of presidential communication, extend its governance role on behalf of presidential management. Notably, agencies with strong reputations for influence across the executive branch tend to be significantly less prominent in the pool of unissued orders.

But in other cases the demise of a given EO is testament not to the success in managing transaction costs but the reverse. At the least, it may signal the high price in time and attention inherent in coordinating complicated directives that cut across the jurisdictions of numerous agencies. And in some cases it marks the ability of bureaus to prevent the issuance of an EO that would benefit the administration but not a given agency. A "policy market" with plentiful proposed EOs and fervent agency objection, combined with the threat of enlisting external allies—in Congress, interest groups, media— can boost the relative cost of a particular option, pushing the president toward other choices. Agencies cannot force the president to sign an EO, nor literally prevent him from doing so—but through administrative trench warfare they can raise or lower the burdens of either option, with special power on the negative side of the ledger. The qualitative record shows that agencies can on occasion constrain presidential preferences and even raise the perceived downsides of issuance high enough to deter presidential action. It's true that "to go to battle" against the White House, as one OMB counsel put it, an agency "has to be pretty fired up, to use a technical term."[118] But clearly, sometimes, they are.

Appendix

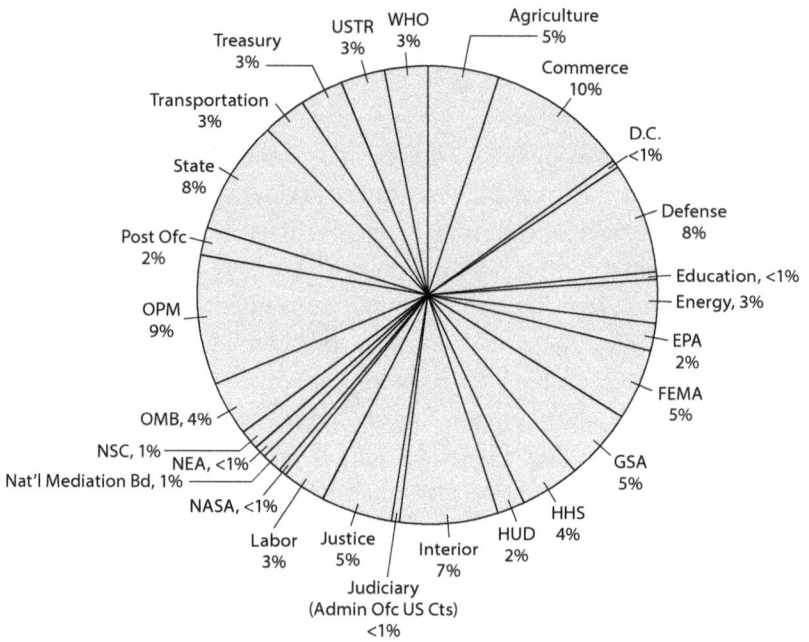

FIGURE A7.1. Unissued Orders by Consolidated Lead Agency.

8

Incorrigibly Plural

CONCLUDING THOUGHTS AND NEXT STEPS

EXECUTIVE ORDERS come from many places—and all the way from Guam.

Back in 1941, just after Pearl Harbor, Franklin Roosevelt's EO 8683 gave the U.S. Navy control over access to Guam, even for tourists.[1] Twenty years later, the threat of Japanese invasion having dramatically dissipated, the government of Guam asked John F. Kennedy for help. In a petition proposing that JFK replace the wartime order, Guam's legislature argued that the continued Naval occupation, as it saw it, gave the Soviet Union's charge of colonial dictatorship some credence. The territorial governor sent the petition on to Washington with his endorsement. Upon arrival, the Bureau of the Budget sent the proposed EO to Interior and Defense for their feedback.

Interior had no objection to emancipating Guam; but the Navy, which responded on behalf of the Pentagon, very much did. In a letter to BoB director David Bell, Captain W. S. Sampson argued that Guam remained strategically vital, and "the considerations which compelled the establishment of security restrictions in 1941 . . . remain of increasing importance today." Interior caved. While he thought the old EO should be revoked, Secretary Stewart Udall wrote, his department was "not in a position to comment on defense considerations."

BoB, for its part, thought more information was needed, preferably from someone not in dress whites. Bell wrote to national security advisor McGeorge Bundy, noting that "the determination of the proper course of action is dependent upon considerations which your office may bring to bear. While national security considerations cannot be discarded, we believe that the reasons advanced by the Guam legislature have a great deal of merit." Bundy, in turn, went over the Navy's head. He asked Deputy Secretary of Defense Roswell

Gilpatric to examine the issue. Bundy saw "no strong case for continuing the wartime executive order," he said, but wanted to know how much the Pentagon really cared. On that front, he said, "I feel that it is important to obtain a DOD view as well as the strictly Navy one."

About a month later, Gilpatric replied that Navy had overstepped: "The Department of Defense interposes no objection to the rescission of EO 8683." That conclusion, though, was quietly conditional on direct presidential announcement of the decision, loudly "emphasizing that these steps are consistent with our national policies of local self-government, and of political, economic, and social development for the people of these islands; and further, that all appropriate measures will be taken to insure that the security requirements of the US in these areas are amply safeguarded." This contingency was a clear reflection of Pentagon infighting: an unambiguous endorsement from the top of the chain of command would presumably make it harder for the Navy to fight back.

But that didn't stop the skirmishing. In August 1962, almost eleven months after Guam's original request, President Kennedy issued EO 11045. In September, letters from members of Congress started to arrive in the White House and the Pentagon. Most ominous was a sharply worded missive from the chair of the House Un-American Activities Committee (HUAC), Rep. Francis Walter, to BoB. He had heard that the Navy was upset about the executive order, Walter said, and wanted to see Navy's original response in the Bureau's files. "This information," a BoB staffer reminded Bell, "is substantially correct." It was not hard to guess who had shared it.

BoB was not interested in arousing HUAC attention even in 1962 and asked the White House to run interference. Kennedy aide Lee White passed the buck to another White House staffer, Ralph Dungan, who also "preferred not to get into it." By now it was late October. Finally, in January 1963, BoB general counsel Arthur Focke convinced White to talk with someone in Rep. Walter's office. They agreed to send a letter to Walter directly, rather than to the committee; Gilpatric insisted the letter not characterize his actions as "having 'reversed' a Defense Department position," while the White House stressed that the "security interests of the United States in the Pacific are amply safeguarded." Some anodyne word choices later, the matter was laid to rest. But it had traveled from Guam to Washington with an extended layover in Arlington, Virginia; it had fomented not just intrabranch but intradepartmental dissension; and its formulation debate had been leaked to another branch of government altogether in hopes of reversing the decision or at least casting the leakers' own superiors as embarrassingly soft on national security. "To get control of policy," wrote Herbert Kaufmann, "it is necessary to get control of administration."[2] That is readily assumed, but less readily achieved, even when it comes to unilateral action.

Indeed, as this book has sought to detail, the relationship between the president and the wider executive branch is a narrow "two-way street," where presidential management may run headlong into bureaucratic maneuvering. In itself that is not a controversial claim: as noted earlier, the metaphor has been used by scholars ranging from Richard Neustadt to Terry Moe, Herbert Simon to George Krause. But when applied to executive orders it adds intriguing complications to the current paradigm of presidential unilateralism. In this concluding chapter I reprise the key empirical findings of the book; discuss their implication for future research into other underexplored areas of the administrative presidency, especially the implementation of presidential directives; and explore the attacks on administrative expertise and the ramifications of executive branch autonomy in the era of the "Deep State."

A Summary of the Findings

This book had its origins in a multiyear data collection effort culling archival files detailing the executive order clearance and formulation process, notably those kept by the general counsel's office within the Office of Management and Budget. The original question was simple: where do executive orders come from? And that first empirical finding in some ways remains the crux of the project: a majority of EOs are formulated primarily by the departments, not by the White House. Indeed, a strong plurality—some 44–49 percent—are crafted nearly entirely by agencies outside the Executive Office of the President.[3]

This is not new news, exactly; as Ruth Morgan wrote in her 1970 book *The President and Civil Rights*, "so many active participants within the executive branch assist the Chief Executive that a Presidential pronouncement is like the most obvious part of an iceberg."[4] But for many good reasons, it has been sidelined until now in the development of theoretical foundations for the use of unilateral authority. In understanding how presidents calculate when and what executive action will succeed—in the context of a political environment populated by various independent institutional actors—the focus has been on the moment an executive order is issued. A rational president may well prefer an executive order to a legislative proposal, where such an order usefully shifts the substantive terrain on which Congress must react. Legislators, after all, face collective action problems in reacting at all. The president, it has been assumed, faces no such problems of his own. EOs appear on the scene in their final form, having been conjured by a confluence of variables springing from political circumstances external to the Oval Office.

That scenario has been the foundation for important theoretical development and scholarly progress. But there is real value in excavating even here the intra-executive intricacies that students of bureaucratic politics have long described—that is, in adding the executive to the roster of the branches of government that shape and constrain unilateral action.

First, doing so adds to our empirical knowledge of administrative process and presidential action, cracking open the black box of the wider executive branch and illuminating the activity within. How does an order go from thought to deed? And, anyway, whose thought is it? Who has influence over the substance of a given EO? This book has sought to answer these questions.

Recall Dwight Eisenhower's metaphor of a "policy hill" as he organized his national security decision making. Substantive proposals were formulated on the upward slope, via the NSC's Policy Planning Board. Decisions were taken at the hill's peak, at NSC meetings. Finally, the chosen policy instrument rolled down the other side toward its targeted destination, with the Operations Coordinating Board guiding its progress toward implementation.[5] Transferring the imagery to presidents and unilateral action, since the 1990s we have learned a lot about the very top of the hill and the view of the landscape it afforded. But we had not mapped either slope—either formulation or implementation. As discussed below, the latter remains a prime area for future research. The present project, I hope, has filled in some of the blank space moving "uphill."

Previous chapters describe the creation as early as the 1930s of the institution of central clearance, housed in OMB. They detail numerous examples of executive order development, tracing the provenance of more than five hundred proposed orders and the preponderant staff influences on their final form. These cases come in many variants but can be categorized by the level of centralization involved in their formulation process. Some are decentralized, effectively delegated to agencies; some are centralized, largely crafted within the EOP. But many others—a third or more—are the product of a mixed process, a joint effort of departmental and White House staff. That combination raises the price of managing the process, especially as the number of agencies involved increases. And at times, confrontation cannot be smoothed into collaboration and EOs wind up unissued; one useful advance in this book is simply in documenting the frequency with which this occurs. As noted in chapter 7, perhaps a fifth of serious proposed orders slide off the path as they climb toward issuance, and more than two hundred of those abandoned are analyzed here.

Bringing the bureaucracy back into executive action also requires rethinking our model of presidential unilateralism. Populating the executive branch with agencies with independent expertise, who may add new information to presidential preferences or hope to divert or even undermine them, adds transaction costs to a previously friction-free equation. As in traditional principal-agent models, presidents need to make sure their top-down authority is not subverted by agencies' informational advantage; unlike most of those models, here agencies have their own ability to act, weighing in with bottom-up policy proposals for presidential consideration. Presidents react by structuring the policymaking process to ameliorate uncertainty, to learn about the relative features and "price" of competing products and their likely substantive and political impact. Framed this way, they are faced with questions familiar to informational economics, which broke open its own black box, that of the firm. As Oliver Williamson argues, decision makers need to embed their transactions in "governance structures" that reduce the costs arising from their bounded rationality, the strategic opportunism of their bargaining partners, and the uncertainty that pervades their environment.[6] With that informational institution in place, they can calculate the relative value of making a product themselves versus buying it.

Translated to the presidency, that question becomes one of where the president logically invests policymaking resources in order to minimize the managerial costs associated with producing an executive order. (While they are not analyzed here, there is no reason similar managerial logic could not be extended to other types of unilateral directives as well.) A first step is the creation of a governance structure that serves as informational clearinghouse, allowing them to vet policy proposals from whatever source, protecting against uncertainty and opportunism—from White House staff as well as the wider bureaucracy. They can then choose on a case-by-case basis whether to delegate policy production or to keep it in house. As traced in chapter 3, the characteristics and benefits of central clearance match closely with the paradigmatic features of such a governance structure. "Information is power," as one former OMB director put it, and OMB can get the information.[7] End runs are resisted. When OMB gently rebuked the Pentagon for asking that a proposed EO go directly to the president, it invoked some of those very features: "As you know, this process provides an opportunity for all interested agencies to comment on the proposal, and then requires the approval of the Office of Management and Budget and the Department of Justice, before being presented to the President. . . . [W]e must reserve final judgment until the views of others have been considered."[8]

Seeing presidential choices through the lens of reducing managerial costs prompts hypotheses about the conditions under which presidents should use centralized versus decentralized staff in the formulation of executive orders. Using the newly coded data noted above and presented in chapter 4, chapter 5 found strong support for a series of contingent predictions: that presidents are more likely to centralize when an executive order's subject matter cuts across multiple agencies' jurisdictions; when it carries out reorganizational functions; or when it is substantively significant and thus of increased importance to the president. On the flip side, the results strongly endorsed the role of agency competence and expertise in prompting a more decentralized process. Also decentralized were EOs closely related to statutory delegation of authority to a specific agency, or the routine use of authority delegated sometime in the past, areas where a search for new information was not required. By contrast, political variables, including the partisanship of Congress or the campaign context, proved insignificant. Thus there are clear managerial contexts associated with enhanced (and decreased) levels of EOP involvement in the development of proposals for executive action. Is an order likely to be bottom-up, or top-down? As usual, it depends—and this analysis teases out at least some of what it depends upon.

All this centers on presidential decision making. But we can think too about the conditions under which those decisions have to account for increased managerial costs. Chapter 6 provided data on how long it takes to produce an executive order, starting when a first draft is sent to OMB and using that duration as an imperfect proxy for the costs of that extended transaction within the executive branch. One simple but perhaps nonintuitive finding: the average EO is far from instantaneous. Those who "can't wait!" usually have to.

Not surprisingly, EOs produced to respond to external events, be they crises or presidential speeches, do move faster through the process. Controlling for that, though, policy complexity and the scale of the interagency bargaining required in a given case are the key factors in delaying EO issuance. Orders with broad substantive significance tend to be issued in a relatively shorter time. While fully centralized EOs are quicker to formulate, so are those fully delegated for agency formulation. An important element in delay is the fact of a mixed formulation process, that is, one that utilizes both departmental and EOP resources: collaborative processes of this kind prompt a more complicated and lengthy undertaking. Negotiation—giving birth to a pineapple—takes time.[9] And as new information is accrued, or the intensity of different actors' positions made clear, preferences may shift. That includes presidential preferences. In recalling an EO he had opposed, longtime BoB official Roger Jones added: "Mr. Eisenhower didn't like that order very much either. He signed it somewhat reluctantly, I think." But "other views prevailed."[10] Thus delay—and, crucially, the interactive process it stands in for—is a key agency resource. It is a "reliable restraint" on the presidency, as Clinton Rossiter long ago observed.[11]

Indeed, that negative power can even, in extreme cases, serve to short-circuit an EO the president had desired to issue: the most common reason for abandoning a proposed EO is interagency dissent, even for fully centralized proposals. Here agencies seek to raise the cost of issuing an order well above its substantive or political benefits. That is not the only reason orders are discarded, though. Some are replaced because OMB demands another kind of directive be used instead—though that insistence often itself reflects or anticipates agency objections. Some are made moot as legislation overtakes them. But others fail because they are successfully vetted—because OMB gains new information from the clearance process that clarifies the substantive or political problems with a given proposal. Thus the fact that an order goes unissued can represent either failure or triumph in a managerial sense. Quantitative analysis suggests, too, that while agency *competence* is an important factor in whether an order's drafting process is decentralized, it is agency *influence* that matters most for issuance. EOs associated with more influential agencies are more likely to make it all the way up the policy hill.

What happens to them then is another important question. And it leads us to consider what additional research is needed in our quest to understand how, and how effectively, presidents use executive orders to further their policy goals.

Coyote Ugly: Implementation in the Long Term and Short

This book has explored in some depth what happens before an executive order is issued. It has only occasionally touched on what happens afterward. Are EOs actually carried out as written? As presidents expect? So far, where scholars have been concerned with the broad impact of presidential directives, they have tended to assume that the orders issued were effective as intended.[12] But as Bill Clinton told an interviewer several years after leaving office, "One of the things that I was frustrated about, when I was president, was that I had all these great ideas, and I'd issue all these executive orders, and then you can never be 100 percent sure that they were implemented."[13]

The record suggests the president's uncertainty was warranted. In fact, his own administration admitted—in the development of the children's health executive order described in chapter 1—that a Reagan order mandating the calculation of regulations' potential impact on families and the "marital commitment" had not been enforced for some time. (OMB actually recommended against rescinding the "Family" EO, at least while "hip-deep in [the 1996] election," since the campaign optics of backing away from "family values. . . . cut against any sort of 'hey, but the Reagan/Bush Administrations didn't comply either' response/defense.")[14] Another Clinton EO from 1996 directing the Justice Department to issue immediate guidelines on child support prompted a White House plea two years later: "can you help me find out what happened to this executive order?" Not much had: the guidelines were not formulated until 1999.[15]

Recent years provide many examples of EOs announced with great fanfare falling short on the ground, from the Obama effort to shutter Guantánamo Bay to Trump's wall- and pipeline-building.[16] Even less-than-momentous matters can stall. For example, the commission created in 1965 by EO 11256 to oversee matters of "food and fiber" foundered when the secretary of agriculture clashed with the vice president over who was going to be appointed: for months, only one of twenty-five members was agreed. ("We have waited almost a year. . . . Can't we move it along?" beseeched LBJ aide Bill Moyers.)[17] Nor is all this a new concern. Only months after the creation of the Bureau of the Budget in 1921, Director Charles Dawes complained to department and agency heads that President Warren G. Harding's executive orders were not being properly publicized or implemented.[18]

As Allison notes more generally, "formal governmental decisions are usually only way-stations along the path to action. And the opportunity for slippage between decision and action is much larger than most analysts have recognized."[19] This is true when it comes to executive orders as well. One OMB careerist commented that during his decades in the agency he "often found it interesting and perplexing that Presidential statements through Executive Orders, Memoranda, or other administrative actions were unknown, unrecognized or ignored. Sometimes OMB's role was to try to reverse such trends."[20]

The notion of "slippage" ties into the broader theme of presidential power, especially if that is defined as a president's influence over governmental outcomes. As Neustadt argues, "Not action *as* an outcome but his impact *on* the outcome is the measure of the [president]." If so, it is worth following executive directives out into the bureaucratic labyrinth. If agencies are told, "do this," do they "do that"? As noted in chapter 2, Neustadt himself suggested that "nothing will happen."[21] This exaggerates, no doubt—but how far? We don't know, as yet. Systematic research on this front has foundered on the shoals of data-gathering concerns. It remains true, as William Neighbors wrote back in 1964, that "while it is now a relatively easy task to find out what executive orders or proclamations have been issued, the problem of determining their effects remains acute."[22]

However, researchers are increasingly turning their attention in this direction. Recent work by Michelle Belco centers on executive orders issued during the "first hundred days" of a presidential term.[23] Joshua Kennedy has quantitatively explored the promulgation of new regulations flowing from executive orders across ten government agencies and conducted in-depth qualitative case studies of several environmental policy EOs.[24]

Kennedy finds that the ideology of the agency head corresponds closely to that agency's response to presidential directives. A loyalist director does indeed behave more responsively. But the ideology of the broader agency has no impact and, all else equal, increased politicization of the agency itself has a negative impact on responsiveness. As his data largely examine the likelihood of a "rule response," this suggests that expertise—in this case the expertise needed to draft regulations—remains crucial. A politicized agency may want to obey presidential prompting but not have the capacity to do so effectively. Thus, striking a balance between responsiveness and competence plays out in the implementation as well as the development of executive orders.

Sharece Thrower's innovative research tracking the conditions under which executive orders are most likely to be revoked or revised by future presidents throws some light on this, at least by implication.[25] If we can take the durability of a given EO as an indicator of its quality (granted, an assumption requiring some care), we find that EOs resulting from decentralized and mixed processes are more carefully constructed than those fully centralized. An EO coded "0" stays in effect for 29.9 years, compared to 17.4 years for one coded "3." Mixed orders fall in between, with a difference of means test indicating that the durability gap between fully centralized orders and all others combined is statistically significant. Obviously, centralized EOs may serve as the most tempting targets for later presidents seeking to mark clear distinctions from their predecessors. Interestingly, though, regressing the length of time spent formulating an order on that order's subsequent durability suggests a positive relationship: a possibility for future research is that the longer an administration spends negotiating an order, the more durable it proves.[26]

Beyond this, the material presented in this book has another key implication for implementation, flowing from our conception of presidential power. How does power work in a context where agencies have written their own marching orders? Notions of power in political science, however many "faces" are involved, generally reflect the idea that an actor is being acted upon in some way. In Robert Dahl's famous definition, "A has power over B to the extent that he can get B to do something that B would not otherwise do."[27]

But what if B wants to do something anyway, and even requests that it be done? In the context of unilateralism: if agencies do follow presidential orders, is this because those same agencies themselves are instrumental in their drafting? B says, "tell me to do X"; A says, "do X"; B does X. In this case we have some kind of influence—but do we have *power*, in Dahl's sense? Probably not. An agency that dictates the directives it is given is surely likely to carry them out.

It helps of course if an agency is *able* to carry them out. After all, as noted several times throughout the book, part of the point of the clearance process is to identify problematic drafting or demands that would prevent an EO from being effective. Formulation and implementation are directly linked, as the first Trump travel ban makes starkly clear. Something "Frankensteined together," as one OMB staffer described that order, may have monstrous consequences.[28] Reagan OLC head Theodore Olson stressed central clearance's ability to help the president "minimize his exposure to the type of problems which distract disproportionately from the implementation of his policy objectives."[29]

Likewise, Kennedy's early research along parallel lines does indeed conclude that "the generation process plays a key role in determining how agencies react to and implement an order." Ronald Reagan's EO 12630 regulating property takings, for instance, "was heavily disliked and fought every step of the way by affected agencies," and later, "for practical purposes, simply ignored." George W. Bush's EO 13352 on "Cooperative Conservation," by contrast, which flowed from Interior Secretary Gale Norton's proactive interagency negotiations, was implemented effectively. Kennedy concludes that a bottom-up process that rests on "a willingness to bargain among affected agencies" to establish shared goals is more likely to result in compliance.[30]

He also argues that presidential orders must be clear and specific to maximize agency obeisance.[31] But surely this has its own perils: successful bargaining—in any arena—often flows from resorting to vagueness. In the legislative process, the obfuscation that makes for the successful passage of a new statute is often incompatible with successful implementation.[32] Likewise, perhaps, in executive orders. For instance, negotiations over an EO implementing the Agricultural Trade Development and Assistance Act of 1954 across numerous agency lines resulted in Harold Stassen (then at the Foreign Operations Administration) commenting that "it is clear that several Government departments have an important interest in the Law, that no simple way of spelling out the precise administration of the Act is possible, and that in the final analysis the good will and friendly cooperation by departments within the Executive Branch in its actual operation will be the determining factor in its successful administration in the United States' interest."[33] But as this and many other cases make clear, "good will and friendly cooperation" must be managed rather than assumed.

A last point also springs from the EO files: formulation and implementation are intertwined in yet another way. That is because the generation of new orders is often shaped by past implementation, or its absence. EOs are developed in part because of other EOs that have served as "first mover" not just for the president vis-à-vis other branches but for agencies vis-à-vis other agencies within the executive branch. This moves our lens past short-term responsiveness to long-term effectiveness. Those studying the effect and durability of legislative enactments have begun to examine this topic, noting the role of coalitions, institutional design, and policy feedback in affecting which reforms are lasting and which fall away.[34] But it has not been a systemic focus of the literature on unilateral policy change, with important exceptions such as Thrower's work noted above.[35]

One last extended case study suggests why more extensive research into this area might be productive. It starts in April 1971, when a typically meandering Nixon conversation about crazed environmentalists took an odd swerve. "Our only big environmental problem, really," Interior Secretary Rogers Morton told the president, "is we've got a predator control problem. . . . Killing all the coyotes and stuff-like, that's got them all upset." (Morton, who spent much of his life in Kentucky, had a pronounced drawl when it came to discussing "KY-oats.")[36]

"For God's sake, what the hell good is a coyote?" asked the president, prompted to wax nostalgic about the howling "up in those hills" during his California youth and concluding that "a coyote is a mad dog. A canine, a wild dog."

"Ain't trying to argue with you, sir!" said Morton. "Just telling you what's got 'em upset. Every time [we] kills a ky-oat, I get hell at some dinner party."[37]

That would kick off extensive debate over four presidential administrations over predatory coyotes, and those who would poison them. The coyotes won more than one round—but not the final decision.

Round One. Whatever hell good a coyote might be, in February 1972, the agency version of Morton's dinner guests would convince Nixon to issue EO 11643. The new order banned poisons such as cyanide, strychnine, thallium sulfate, and sodium fluoroacetate (better known as Compound 1080) on the federal lands where many ranchers' flocks roamed. The lead advocate for this move within the administration was the Council on Environmental Quality (CEQ).[38] But CEQ's proposal, while aimed at protecting people and non-predatory wildlife from unintended poisoning, was hardly uncontested. The Department of Agriculture was fervently opposed and was mollified only by the promise that Nixon would propose legislation addressing its concerns. The jostling was stressful enough to prompt intra-OMB reassurance with all-caps emphasis: "TOMORROW WILL COME."[39]

Round Two. It did, but the new day mostly prompted those on the losing side to express their anger to the White House.[40] Ranch interests were irate, and White House aides mostly sympathetic to their concerns. As one letter-drafting staffer put it, "I don't think the man wants a recitation of why the eco-freaks think this is necessary."[41] Environmentalists' insistence on "alternative control methods" was met with scorn by the wool industry. One story making the rounds portrayed an Interior official giving a long explanation to Sen. Clifford Hansen of Wyoming about the department's proposal to sterilize male coyotes. "Hell, you don't understand," Hansen responded. "These coyotes are eating the sheep, not f—ing them."[42]

With Gerald Ford's sudden ascent to office, the EO formulation process was suddenly alive again. CEQ, Interior, and Agriculture—now joined by the EPA—pored over the question of whether to "give in to [the] demands" for repeal or revision of the EO. This was linked to a turf war between Agriculture and Interior, who argued "over which agency has a lead role to play" (and thus whose position would prevail); but given that most of the options under consideration were "merely symbolic gestures aimed at appeasing sheepgrowers" and which would make environmentalists "very upset," OMB's advice was "to avoid decisions now posed by the options."[43] White House environmental policy aide Doug Costle (who later became head of the EPA) agreed, arguing that the entire situation was a "no-win proposition for the President. . . . [O]ur principal objective," he went on, "should be to move this out of the White House." Even if the EO were amended, he pointed out, there was no "quick fix" for the ranchers. The various poisons they wanted to use, notably Compound 1080, would, by law, have to be licensed by the EPA, which would require "substantial new evidence" to do so. Thus if the president inserted himself into the situation now it would only "bring down the wrath of the organized environmental community (not just the nuts, either)."[44]

Even so, livestock groups, supported by Agriculture, still hoped for outright repeal of the Nixon EO and, indeed, for new legislation eliminating restrictions on using toxic chemicals for coyote control.[45] One draft EO produced by the National Wool Growers Association prompted a six-page denunciation from EPA administrator Russell Train. "In the opinion of this Agency," he told White House Domestic Council director Jim Cannon, "the proposed modification. . . . would no longer be a tool of administrative policy; the changes would in fact render it an empty shell of platitudes mouthing a respect for environmental integrity, but in effect removing all operational guidance of substance."[46] Agriculture, for its part, complained through its Hill allies that its policy ideas were being shut out. "I would be interested to know whether or not you ever saw that memorandum," wrote one Senate staffer to a Ford aide, "because there was a rumor that it got side-tracked before it got to the decision makers."[47]

At least some OMB staff felt no new EO was needed at all, preferring less salient regulatory action take precedence—especially given the wider politics: "the environmentalist viewpoint . . . [was] far more pervasive, effective, and influential with the public than" the ranchers.[48] For its part CEQ proposed, presumably tongue in cheek, that the best solution was for the federal government "to buy out the sheepmen in the predator prone areas and then sell the sheep to ranchers in rabbit country."[49]

In the end, OMB took the highly unusual step of sending two executive orders to the president, allowing him to choose between an amendment to the Nixon order that only authorized the use of cyanide (assuming EPA approval for experimental purposes) and one that allowed for "*any* experimental use approved by EPA." His advisors were divided, with Interior and EPA in the former camp and Agriculture and OMB in the latter. On July 18 Ford chose the narrower option, swayed perhaps by arguments that the more inclusive language would raise false hopes among ranchers.[50] At that point, as one White House staffer sighed, "I hope I never hear of coyotes again."[51]

Round Three. But that was not to be. The discussion was reopened almost immediately when in September 1975 EPA decided to allow the regular use of cyanide in spring-loaded devices used to kill predators. Ford's EO allowed that poison only as part of an experimental program, so the arguments started all over again. EPA proposed simply amending the EO to reflect its licensing decision.[52] But the forces for inaction (thus a de facto return to the Nixon ban) or full-blown repeal were strong enough that Ford did not accept the EPA position and issue his second coyote order until late May 1976.[53] In between came more departmental maneuvering, legal wrangling between OMB and the White House counsel's office, and political position-taking.[54] "I was asked to breakfast this morning by Senators Hansen and Laxalt and staff to feel again their pressures re coyotes," Domestic Council aide George Humphreys reported; CEQ chair Russell Peterson, for his part, wanted "to reiterate emphatically my position that it would be unwise in the extreme to rescind the order at this time."[55]

Round Four. Domestic advisor Jim Cannon told Ford that "further relaxation," if desired, should wait until 1977—that is, until after the 1976 election. "Rescission now," he said in April, "would not be understood properly by the public and environmentalists."[56]

But of course Ford's defeat in November only upped the pressure on the White House from ranchers and their allies, since the incoming Carter administration was expected to be more sympathetic to environmental regulation. Secretary of Agriculture John Knebel, for instance, urged the lame duck Ford in mid-November not only to rescind the various coyote orders but to transfer authority over predator control from Interior to Agriculture. CEQ's concern that Ford might bend was such that its director urged the president just after Christmas that the EO was "not simply an additional regulatory mechanism" but "an important expression of public policy regarding the public trust doctrine of public lands" that "has assumed extraordinary symbolic prominence among the environmental public." OMB director James Lynn and Cannon wrote a long joint memo to the president summarizing the issue one last time—by this point, they noted, the ranchers had soured on toxic collars containing cyanide (a "big . . . joke") and wanted to use the more effective Compound 1080. They advised against revocation. The matter made it as far as a briefing for White House chief of staff Dick Cheney two weeks before Ford left office without revisiting the matter.[57]

Round Five. As the ranchers feared, the new administration was not inclined to revisit the "predacide issue."[58] When Carter was asked directly if he would "consider rescinding" Nixon's EO, given what one rancher called "ruinous losses"—"you have it within your power with the sweep of a pen to do something about it!"—the president said no. He replied that "my present inclination would be to leave the Executive order intact. I've not made a study of it, but that's my present thought."[59]

Ranchers, and Agriculture, did not give up. And finally, in the Reagan administration, they had allies in Interior and EPA versus "Nixon's hated EO."[60] In the summer of 1981, EPA began hearings to declare a "predator loss emergency" and thus permit the wide use of Compound 1080.[61] Interior's Fish & Wildlife Service took the ranchers' side in November.[62] Sen. Paul Laxalt (R-NV), a longtime friend of the president, told Reagan counsel Ed Meese that "repeal of the Executive Order at this time is a must." He claimed that doing so immediately would "avoid a controversy" if EPA administrator Anne Gorsuch did reinstate Compound 1080.[63] The theory, as Gorsuch herself told the White House, was that the EO's "prohibition . . . prejudges the results" of EPA's review and that moving first would put the heat on EPA rather on the White House if the agency allowed use of the compound.[64] Or as White House aide Craig Fuller put it, acting now would mean that "when EPA acts, attention won't suddenly turn on the WH."[65]

Others argued just the opposite: that early repeal would "set off a controversy prematurely and impede EPA's ability to decide this question on the merits."[66] While a favorable outcome was assumed, they feared preemptive action by the president would be seen by "presently hostile environmental groups and, perhaps, the Eastern press" as an attempt to influence the agency's decision. Waiting for EPA to act would bring Reagan's action closer to Ford's precedents, simply reflecting EPA's own shifts and producing "little political heat."[67]

In January 1982, though, Interior Secretary James Watt changed the department's long-standing position and endorsed immediate repeal of EO 11643. Proponents of the move argued that "the political gains to the President will be great."[68] But not everyone was so sure. Fuller, for instance, urged taking advantage of the crowded news cycle linked to Reagan's State of the Union Address, writing on January 26 that "I think we ought to revoke it *now* and let it get lost in the heavy news coming tonight and tomorrow."[69] That advice was taken. EO 12342 was signed on January 28—the fourth coyote EO over a full decade and four presidential administrations.[70]

The decade of interagency maneuvering described here is a reminder of the general importance of elevating our knowledge of bureaucratic politics in understanding unilateral action—indeed, for most of the repeated rounds of play the president was being acted upon rather than serving as the central protagonist. It suggests too that we need to look backward not just from the issuance process but from the formulation process itself: the questions and insights regarding sequence and timing that have become central to historical institutionalism clearly transfer to executive actions, and not just those in the administration in which they occur.[71] And finally, it highlights something already noted in this book but which deserves additional emphasis: the potential role of fragmentation not just across the wider executive branch but within the EOP itself.

Inside the Presidential Branch

At least in its theoretic approach, this book has adopted the usual distinction between the "bureaucracy" and the "White House"—the executive and presidential branches. That is not unreasonable. There is much to the old adage "where you stand depends on where you sit," and institutional vantages shape individual behavior. As foreign policy veteran Leslie Gelb commented, "I have generally found that staffers from the Department of State or Defense or from the Central Intelligence Agency behave very differently if they are moved to the White House. They become far more conscious of Presidential stakes and interests."[72] Some scholars have noted distinctions between presidential staff who are "inside" and those "outside," that is, those who deal with external audiences (e.g., the Office of Public Liaison or of Legislative Affairs). Even within the White House the former staffs tend to distrust the latter; the gap between White House and department is much greater.[73]

But that doesn't mean the internal divergences are not important, especially as the size of the EOP grows and fragmentation rises. If anything, the approach of this book far *understates* "the drunkenness of things being various," as a poetically minded president might put it, quoting Louis MacNeice: "World is crazier and more of it than we think, incorrigibly plural."[74]

Indeed, at some point the "counterbureaucracy" created in the White House to serve as a controlling instrument of the wider executive branch just becomes a bureaucracy, spinning off its own problems of coordination and competing interests. There are plenty of examples of such internecine battles in the preceding chapters as well as throughout the coyote saga. Numerous more recent stories from the Trump White House relate a similar narrative: multiple factions with different policy preferences forcibly merged into a single organization but never coordinated as a cohesive unit. When it came to presidential directives, the tensions sometimes led to one set of staff seeking to undermine the others and even the president's stated desires: "to stall and delay, mention the legal roadblocks and occasionally lift the drafts from the Resolute Desk."[75]

Thus, treating the Executive Office staff, broadly speaking, as a unitary executive in its own right threatens to lose sight of complexities that might themselves have an impact on the way policies are developed. That is, they present their own management challenges that phase the binary "make or buy" question into multiple dimensions.[76]

After all, the real issue is an information question: when does it make sense to delegate? You might see the most centralization when (a) an agency is most ideologically distant from the president, and (b) the EOP is wholly unified. The latter has been held constant in this book and in almost all work on the presidency. But increasing the coordination costs inside the EOP (for instance, by increasing the number of agencies it contains) might make delegation more attractive, especially if the proposed EO is technically complex. A line agency, especially one close to the president, is a "cheaper" option when acting internally has its own managerial frictions. As this suggests, two dimensions could be in play here: EOP fragmentation and issue complexity (as linked to agency expertise and perhaps its reliability in terms of an agency's ideological alliance with the president). High requirements for expertise combined with high fragmentation would suggest decentralization/delegation, low levels of both the opposite. The other two cells in our analogical 2 × 2 table would suggest some sort of mixed formulation process.

Managing the EOP is, presumably, easier for the president than managing disagreement between the line agencies. In this sense there is yet another trade-off between management control and policy control. But all this suggests that we have tended to underestimate the benefit of delegation from the president's point of view. And that in turn provides an additional rationale for why so many executive orders are produced by the executive branch and not the chief executive.

Learning to Love Bureaucratic Management

The rapid expansion of the literature on unilateral action over the past twenty-plus years reflects the increasing importance of such tactics for presidents and for policymaking generally. Even in 1995, Bill Clinton could muse that "I had overemphasized in my first two years to some extent the importance of legislative battles as opposed to . . . the President's power of the Presidency to do things, actually accomplish things."[77] And it seems likely that the centrality of the administrative presidency to political life will only continue to intensify. The growth of government shows no sign of slowing; and partisan polarization makes substantial legislation ever harder to achieve. During the 2020 primary season, the myriad Democratic candidates seeking their party's presidential nomination sought to outdo each other in invoking the glories of unfettered unilateralism. As then senator Kamala Harris put it, "I will give the United States Congress 100 days to pull their act together . . . and put a bill on my desk for signature. And if they do not, I will take executive action. . . . There's been no action. As president, I will take action." Harris was talking about gun control, but her peers made similar promises about campaign finance reforms, immigration policy, environmental protections, the minimum wage, and climate change. By July 2020 the ultimate nominee, Joe Biden, had compiled such a long list of things to do "on day one" that even his advisors conceded a few might have to spill over to day two.[78]

Obviously, most of these matters would require legislative approbation. But the point is not to fact-check. Leaving aside the specific pledges, we can assume executive action will be fundamental to the next presidency and presidencies. As Biden transition chair Ted Kaufman put it well before his boss (with Harris as his running mate) won in November, "We are taking all the things he has said in the campaign and we are breaking it down, to find out what he can do by himself—like executive orders."[79]

Thus it is crucial that scholars continue to enhance our understanding of the contexts and constraints of executive orders, and of executive power more generally. The conceptual shifts and extensive evidence presented here take one step in that direction. By melding the insights of the new unilateralism with the realities of intrabranch policymaking we may learn where and when unilateral tools can be most effective, for presidents and polity—and when they represent wishful thinking.

This book has assessed presidents' ability to manage policy formulation processes in accordance with the incentives and constraints imposed by a far-from-unified executive branch. In so doing, without painting presidents as powerless (far from it), it has stressed the ability of agencies to constrain presidential preferences. Is that a good thing for the republic? The current frenzy of denunciations of the "Deep State" obscures the long history of this very question. "How widely different the business of government is from the speculation of it, and the energy of the imagination dealing in general propositions from that of execution in detail," Alexander Hamilton lamented in 1798.[80] That gap must be filled by someone. The president, nationally elected and expressing the will of the people, has a claim to the job. A few years earlier, after all, Hamilton had stressed the accountability inherent in a single executive, whose actions were in clear view of—and could be clearly judged by—the electorate.[81] If lawmaking is the proverbial sausage factory, "the administrative process . . . is an even more shadowy subterranean world that is inaccessible except to the most experienced, adept, and well-resourced interests."[82] Bureaucratic politics can blur lines of authority and responsibility, touting resistance but achieving subversion. Presidential attacks on executive branch autonomy invoke a normative theory of a unitary executive grounded in the enhanced legitimacy of elected officials vis-à-vis the career service.[83]

The Trump administration, of course, acted on this claim in particularly aggressive ways. Trump turned to old playbooks for bureaucratic control, and designed new plays too. He installed loyalists, shut out careerist advice, retaliated against evidence that contradicted White House preferences (in one case by physically relocating the offending bureau), developed new standards for regulatory review and scientific research, displaced inspectors general, fomented turnover, and embraced an ironic permanency of acting officials. He even amended expert analysis by Sharpie marker to ensure its consistency with presidential tweet.[84]

Yet this very experience exposes the harsh downside of such tactics. The quest to eliminate transaction costs in the short term, by bulldozing bureaucratic autonomy in favor of a sycophantic echo chamber, may be gratifying. But it is likely to raise the price of policymaking even for the most self-interested chief executives. For there is a case to be made for bureaucratic capacity, for expertise and for its own role as a "principled agent" toward the public good.[85] Scholars have long seen the broad executive as itself responsive to the populace, and pluralistic in compensating for the frequent failure of elected officials to reach beyond their base. Norton Long argued in 1952 that large swaths of the population "receive more effective and more responsible representation through administrative channels than through the legislature."[86] That might be even more true in today's polarized political world, given that recent presidents have themselves been dividers, not uniters. Nor is there any guarantee that presidents as individuals are motivated to act in a manner that respects or reflects public accountability—if draft orders are provided to the White House by special interests on their own behalf or to attack rivals, for instance.[87] And as posited earlier, the wider bureaucracy can serve as a competitive market supplying information to the presidency. "The story of the unitary executive has morphed into a myth of a President who must have seamless control over the executive branch," Neal Katyal writes. "But there is a counter-story to be told, one that emphasizes checks and balances within the executive branch. Just as bicameralism and two political branches produce better decisions, so too there is powerful evidence that presidents succeed because redundancy generates the information a president needs."[88]

Thus: management matters. Presidents who can extract information while fending off opportunism, who can harness the positive attributes of the permanent government while mitigating its problematic aspects—who can, in short, manage the executive branch—will benefit both themselves and their policy agenda. Degrading the expertise and legitimacy of federal public health agencies, to take a not-quite-random example, surely has problematic implications for a president's ability to coordinate a national response to a deadly pandemic. And that, in turn, has a downside for the claims to achievement that usually underwrite electoral accountability in the first place.

Put another way, if management is central to better policy, even better politics, presidents need to get better at it. Bargaining with the bureaucracy takes time and resources, to be sure, far more than reflexive deconstruction; but the end result is a unilateralism in name that reflects the national interest in fact. That kind of success should breed the kind of bargaining for which a thoughtful president will have affection. After all, as Paul Simon once tunefully informed us, "Negotiations and love songs / Are often mistaken for one and the same."[89] For presidents, they should be.

A NOTE ON SOURCES

MUCH OF THE DATA used in this book is drawn from archival sources, notably the executive order records compiled over time by the general counsel's office of the Bureau of the Budget and (after its 1970 reorganization) the Office of Management and Budget. These are mostly located in Record Group 51 of the National Archives and Records Administration facility in College Park, Maryland, and in the Washington National Records Center in Suitland, Maryland. Additional primary sources come from the National Archives' presidential library system and from collections of private papers as described in chapter 4.

Key abbreviations used in the notes include:

BoB	Bureau of the Budget
DDEL	Dwight D. Eisenhower Library, Abilene, Kansas
EO	Executive Order
GFL	Gerald R. Ford Library, Ann Arbor, Michigan
JCL	Jimmy Carter Library, Atlanta, Georgia
JFKL	John F. Kennedy Library, Boston, Massachusetts
LBJL	Lyndon B. Johnson Library, Austin, Texas
LPIA	Leon Panetta Institute Archives, Seaside, California
NARA	National Archives and Records Administration, College Park, Maryland
OMB	Office of Management and Budget
RG	NARA Record Group
RNL	Richard Nixon Library, Yorba Linda, California
RRL	Ronald Reagan Library, Simi Valley, California

WHCF   White House Central Files

WHORM   White House Office of Records Management

WHSF   White House Special Files: Staff Member and Office Files

WHSOF   White House Staff Office Files

WJCL   William Jefferson Clinton Library, Little Rock, Arkansas

WNRC   Washington National Records Center, Suitland, Maryland

Citations to archival material provide the information needed to pull a cited document:

Author, Recipient, Date of Document;
Archive Facility;
NARA Record Group (where applicable)
Finding Aid Entry # (if available, given at the first series cite in each chapter)
Series Name and/or Number (in *italics*; entry or series number used alone in subsequent cites)
Box Name or Number;
Folder Title [in brackets]
WHORM document number (where applicable)

NOTES

Preface and Acknowledgments

1. Edward Stanwood, *A History of the Presidency* (Boston: Houghton, Mifflin, 1904), iv.

2. Arthur M. Schlesinger Jr., *The Imperial Presidency* (Boston: Houghton Mifflin, 1973).

3. See, e.g., Louis W. Koenig, *The Chief Executive*, 3rd ed. (New York: Harcourt Brace Jovanovich, 1975).

Chapter 1. "On My Own"? Executive Orders and the Executive Branch

1. Jenna Johnson, "Trump Calls for 'Total and Complete Shutdown of Muslims Entering the United States,'" *Washington Post*, December 7, 2015, https://www.washingtonpost.com/news/post-politics/wp/2015/12/07/donald-trump-calls-for-total-and-complete-shutdown-of-muslims-entering-the-united-states/.

2. EO 13769 (January 27, 2017). The titles and text of executive orders (EOs) from 1994 to the present are available via the Office of the Federal Register at https://www.federalregister.gov/presidential-documents/executive-orders. The titles and dates of issuance of EOs going back to 1937 are available via the National Archives' Executive Order Disposition Tables at https://www.archives.gov/federal-register/executive-orders/disposition.

3. Tweet of February 4, 2017, https://twitter.com/realdonaldtrump/status/827981079042805761; Donald J. Trump, "Remarks at a Roundtable Discussion with County Sheriffs and an Exchange with Reporters," February 7, 2017, https://www.presidency.ucsb.edu/node/323696. Presidents' public statements quoted in this book, unless otherwise cited, are drawn from the invaluable *American Presidency Project* curated by Gerhard Peters and John T. Woolley and available at https://www.presidency.ucsb.edu/.

4. See, inter alia, Emanuella Grinberg and Eliott C. McLaughlin, "Travel Ban Protests Stretch into Third Day from US to UK," *CNN.com*, January 31, 2017, https://www.cnn.com/2017/01/30/politics/travel-ban-protests-immigration/index.html; Alan Taylor, "A Weekend of Protest against Trump's Immigration Ban," *The Atlantic*, January 30, 2017, https://www.theatlantic.com/photo/2017/01/a-weekend-of-protest-against-trumps-immigration-ban/514953/.

5. Major Garrett, *Mr. Trump's Wild Ride* (New York: St. Martin's Press, 2018), 109.

6. CNN reported that Trump White House aide Stephen Miller and "chief strategist" Steve Bannon overruled DHS's interpretation of the order with regard to green card holders. See Evan Perez, Pamela Brown, and Kevin Liptak, "Inside the Confusion of the Trump Executive Order

and Travel Ban," *CNN.com*, January 30, 2017, available at https://www.cnn.com/2017/01/28/politics/donald-trump-travel-ban/.

7. Nahal Toosi, "Inside the Chaotic Early Days of Trump's Foreign Policy," *Politico Magazine*, March 1, 2019, https://www.politico.com/magazine/story/2019/03/01/trump-national-security-council-225442. Julie Hirschfeld Davis and Michael D. Shear report that about fifteen people, many of them congressional staffers, took leave to work on the transition and drafted many of the early EOs considered by the administration. See *Border Wars: Inside Trump's Assault on Immigration* (New York: Simon and Schuster, 2019), 44.

8. Quoted in Bob Woodward, *Fear* (New York: Simon and Schuster, 2018), 100.

9. See Davis and Shear, *Border Wars*, 43, 57.

10. According to the IG report, "The Secretary of Homeland Security had seen two draft versions of the order, one on Tuesday and a revised draft on Thursday—the day before the order issued. But other than through media reports and a short email summary a few days before its signing, the main implementer of the EO's provisions—CBP [the Customs and Border Protection Agency]—had practically no advance notice that the order would issue, or that it would be effective upon signature. Nor did it know exactly what the EO would contain. The lack of clarity regarding critical issues required DHS and its interagency partners DOJ [Department of Justice] and the State Department to improvise policies and procedures in real time." The IG report was heavily redacted by DHS leadership at issuance and remains so; it is unlikely those redactions shield additional pages of gushing compliments from public view. See Office of the Inspector General, Department of Homeland Security, *DHS Implementation of Executive Order #13769, "Protecting the Nation From Foreign Terrorist Entry Into the United States,"* Report OIG-18–37, issued January 18, 2018.

11. Quoted in Molly O'Toole, "John F. Kelly Says His Tenure as Trump's Chief of Staff Is Best Measured by What the President Did Not Do," *Los Angeles Times*, December 30, 2018, available at https://www.latimes.com/politics/la-na-pol-john-kelly-exit-interview-20181230-story.html.

12. Quoted in ibid.

13. And called Yates, who was en route to an airport. Yates interview with Chuck Rosenberg, "The Oath" podcast, May 30, 2019, http://www.msnbc.com/msnbc/sally-yates-decisions-transcript.

14. Davis and Shear, *Border Wars*, 57; additional intra-OLC dissent is portrayed in George Packer, "How to Destroy a Government," *The Atlantic* (April 2020): 57. OLC's opinion is in Curtis Gannon, Office of Legal Counsel, Department of Justice, "Proposed Executive Order Entitled, 'Protecting the Nation from Foreign Terrorist Entry into the United States,'" January 27, 2017. OLC's memo was just over a page long, but all but one sentence of it merely summarized the text of the order. On DOJ, see Perez, Brown, and Liptak, "Inside the Confusion of the Trump Executive Order and Travel Ban."

15. "Statement by Press Secretary Sean Spicer," January 31, 2017, https://www.whitehouse.gov/briefings-statements/statement-press-secretary-sean-spicer-2/. For a useful overview of the complicated legal issues that arise in such decision making, see Jack Goldsmith, "Yates Changes Her Tune," *Lawfare*, May 8, 2017, https://www.lawfareblog.com/yates-changes-her-tune.

16. The second version was EO 13780 (March 6, 2017); the third, Proclamation 9645 (September 24, 2017). See also *Trump v. Hawaii*, 585 U.S. ___ (2018).

17. EO 13815 (October 24, 2017).

18. Quoted in James Bennet, "True to Form, Clinton Shifts Energies Back to U.S. Focus," *New York Times,* July 5, 1998; see more generally Kenneth R. Mayer, *With the Stroke of a Pen: Executive Orders and Presidential Power* (Princeton: Princeton University Press, 2001).

19. George W. Bush, "Remarks at the White House Conference on Faith-Based and Community Initiatives," March 3, 2004, available at https://www.presidency.ucsb.edu/node/211634.

20. Toosi, "Chaotic Early Days."

21. Ibid.

22. "Alexander Statement on Refugee Executive Order," January 29, 2017, archived at *VoteSmart.org,* https://votesmart.org/public-statement/1149832/alexander-statement-on-refugee-executive-order#.XCpiBs17mUk.

23. Author interview, November 12, 2019. See too Amy E. Black, Douglas L. Koopman, and David K. Ryden, *Of Little Faith: The Politics of George W. Bush's Faith-Based Initiatives* (Washington, DC: Georgetown University Press, 2004); Anne Farris, Richard P. Nathan, and David J. Wright, "The Expanding Administrative Presidency: George W. Bush and the Faith-Based Initiative" (Roundtable on Religion and Social Welfare Policy, Rockefeller Institute of Government, August 2004); David Kuo, *Tempting Faith: An Inside Story of Political Seduction* (New York: Free Press, 2006), and additional interviews with several White House and departmental staff involved in the formulation of the EO, including Office of Faith-Based and Community Initiatives director Jim Towey. Their assistance is much appreciated.

24. Quoted in Davis and Shear, *Border Wars,* 89; tweet of June 5, 2017, https://twitter.com/realdonaldtrump/status/871675245043888128.

25. The material utilized in this section is, unless otherwise noted, from the Clinton Library and available online. It is drawn from Kagan's Domestic Policy Council files, Box 22, Folders 27 and 28, and Box 23, Folders 2 and 3; from her White House Counsel files, Box 6, Folder 14; and from the "NLWJC—Kagan Hard Drive" release, Folders 5, 9, and 11.

26. EO 12606 (September 2, 1987).

27. The Sessions bill, S. 891 of 1997, never even received a hearing. However, a provision reinstating a variant of the Reagan order was eventually added to a fiscal year 1999 appropriations bill, causing OMB to dust off old guidance on the matter.

28. The memo was addressed to Secretary of Agriculture Dan Glickman, Secretary of Commerce Mickey Kantor, once and future OMB director Jacob Lew, HHS Secretary Donna Shalala, Kathryn Higgins (assistant to the president for Cabinet affairs), John Hilley (legislative affairs), Carol Rasco (head of the Domestic Policy Council), Joseph Stiglitz (chair of CEA), Laura D'Andrea Tyson (head of the National Economic Council), Ron Klain (chief of staff to Vice President Gore), Kathleen McGinty (chair of the Council on Environmental Quality), Anne Brown (chair of the Consumer Products Safety Commission), and Robert Pitofsky (chair of the Federal Trade Commission). Eventually titled *Environmental Health Risks to Children,* the report was released on September 11, 1996.

29. Emphasis added. Even at this point, CEA and NEC were at best unenthusiastic.

30. Jimmy Carter, *A Government as Good as Its People* (New York: Simon and Schuster, 1977).

31. See Carter to "Stu," handwritten note of February 7, 1977, and Carter's handwritten comments on Stu Eizenstat to President, March 10, 1977, JCL, Office of Staff Secretary: Presidential Files, Box 11, [3/16/77 (2)].

32. All documents quoted here come from the materials in the folder "Logging of Outside Contacts," NARA, RG 51, *Executive Order Files 1977–80*, Box 3. See especially Doug Huron to Ron Kienlen, "Proposed Executive Order: Logging Outside Contacts," July 13, 1977; Ron Kienlen to Doug Huron, "Proposed Executive Order Entitled 'Logging Outside Contacts,'" August 10, 1977; Rick Neustadt to Doug Huron et al., "Logging," January 16, 1978; William Nichols to Peter Petkas, "Rick Neustadt's Logging Memo," January 19, 1978.

33. See the files cited in the previous note, as well as JCL, Office of Staff Secretary: Presidential Files, Box 84, CF O/A 548, [7/13/78-Not Submitted]. Emphasis in original. Carter aide Rick Neustadt was the son of Richard E. Neustadt of *Presidential Power* fame.

34. William G. Howell, *Power without Persuasion: The Politics of Direct Presidential Action* (Princeton: Princeton University Press, 2003), 98–99.

35. George A. Krause, *A Two-Way Street: The Institutional Dynamics of the Modern Administrative State* (Pittsburgh: University of Pittsburgh Press, 1999); and see Daniel Carpenter and George A. Krause, "Transactional Authority and Bureaucratic Politics," *Journal of Public Administration Research and Theory* 25 (January 2015): 5–25.

36. See, e.g., David E. Lewis and Jennifer L. Selin, *Sourcebook of United States Executive Agencies*, 2nd ed. (Washington, DC: Administrative Conference of the United States, 2018); Paul C. Light, *The Government-Industrial Complex: The True Size of Government, 1984–2017* (New York: Oxford University Press, 2019).

37. In 1947–48, 906 public laws were enacted; 908 were enacted from 2011 through 2016, inclusive. The latter figure includes an unusual proportion of symbolic legislation, such as a surge in renaming post offices after favored deceased constituents. In 2017, only 100 public laws gained enactment. See the U.S. Senate, Resume of Congressional Activity, https://www.senate.gov/legislative/ResumesofCongressionalActivity1947present.htm. On polarization and legislation, see Nolan McCarty, *Polarization* (New York: Oxford University Press, 2019); Frances Lee, *Insecure Majorities: Congress and the Perpetual Campaign* (Chicago: University of Chicago Press, 2016).

38. Elena Kagan, "Presidential Administration," *Harvard Law Review* 114 (June 2001): 2281.

39. Richard Nathan, *The Administrative Presidency* (New York: Macmillan, 1983), 82.

40. N.a., "The President's Management of Public Policy," May 31, 1946, NARA, RG 51, *Division of Administrative Management, 1939–1952 (Series 39.32)*, Box 3, [E2–15/46.1].

41. Schlesinger, *The Imperial Presidency*; Andrew Rudalevige, *The New Imperial Presidency: Renewing Presidential Power after Watergate* (Ann Arbor: University of Michigan Press, 2006); Charlie Savage, *Takeover: The Return of the Imperial Presidency and the Subversion of American Democracy* (Boston: Little, Brown, 2007).

42. "President Trump's 100 Days of Historic Accomplishments," Office of the White House Press Secretary, April 25, 2017, available at https://www.whitehouse.gov/the-press-office/2017/04/25/president-trumps-100-days-historic-accomplishments. The claim regarding Roosevelt is accurate if starting the calculation with Harry Truman's election in his own right in 1948. But during Truman's actual first 100 days in office in 1945, following FDR's death, he issued 50 executive orders, 20 more than Trump.

43. Tweet of October 10, 2017, available at https://twitter.com/realdonaldtrump/status/917698839846576130.

44. Pres. Barack Obama, "Remarks Prior to a Cabinet Meeting and an Exchange with Reporters," January 14, 2014, available at https://www.presidency.ucsb.edu/node/305044; "Remarks in Las Vegas," October 24, 2011, available at https://www.presidency.ucsb.edu/node/297388.

45. Quoted in Alexis Simendinger, "The Paper Wars," *National Journal*, July 25, 1998, 1737.

46. Harold Bruff, *Balance of Forces: Separation of Powers Law in the Administrative State* (Durham, NC: Carolina Academic Press, 2006), 154.

47. And every president but Harrison has issued executive orders; Harrison's single venture into unilateralism took the form of a proclamation. See Graham G. Dodds, *Take Up Your Pen: Unilateral Presidential Directives in American Politics* (Philadelphia: University of Pennsylvania Press, 2013), 4.

48. House Committee on Government Operations, 85th Cong., 1st Sess., *Executive Orders and Proclamations: A Study of a Use of Presidential Powers*, published in 1957.

49. Phillip J. Cooper, *By Order of the President: The Use and Abuse of Executive Direct Action*, 2nd ed. (Lawrence: University Press of Kansas, 2014), 21.

50. Daniel Gitterman, *Calling the Shots: The President, Executive Orders, and Public Policy* (Washington, DC: Brookings Institution, 2017), 10. That figure doubtless increased greatly in fiscal 2020 as pandemic relief spending took hold.

51. Mayer, *Stroke of a Pen*, 31, 35. Other sorts of directives have more recently received their own sustained attention, as will be noted.

52. Ibid., 85. Note, though, that because many more orders were issued during the 1940s than in other decades, prompted partly by World War II, the average annual count of significant orders is higher in the 1940s than in the 1990s (see Mayer's table 3.3).

53. William G. Howell, *Power without Persuasion: The Politics of Direct Presidential Action* (Princeton: Princeton University Press, 2003), 79–85.

54. Quoted in Frank J. Murray, "Clinton's Executive Orders Still Are Packing a Punch," *Washington Times*, August 23, 1999, A1.

55. Philip Bump, "Ted Cruz Kicks Off the Obama-as-Dictator Movement," *The Atlantic*, January 29, 2014, https://www.theatlantic.com/politics/archive/2014/01/ted-cruz-kicks-obama-dictator-movement/357489/; Eugene Scott, "Maine Gov. Paul LePage: Barack Obama Is a Dictator," *CNN*, October 12, 2016, https://www.cnn.com/2016/10/12/politics/paul-lepage-donald-trump-obama-dictator/index.html; Marco Poggio and Michael McAuliff, "Trump Wants to Act Like a Dictator, Nadler Says," *New York Post*, March 5, 2019, https://www.nydailynews.com/news/politics/ny-pol-jerry-nadler-president-trump-bloviating-president-dictator-20190305-story.html.

56. Gerald White Johnson, *Roosevelt: Dictator or Democrat?* (New York: Harper, 1941), 225.

57. James Michael (of Memphis, TN) to Sen. Estes Kefauver, June 24, 1963, forwarded to the White House, in JFKL, WHCF: Subject Files, Box 100, FE 4–1, [Presidential Powers: Executive]; Lee C. White to Rep. Dominick Daniels, November 18, 1963, JFKL, WHCF: Subject Files, Box 100, FE 4–1, [Presidential Powers: General].

58. Max Friedersdorf to Rep. John Paul Hammerschmidt, letter and attached material of July 12, 1975, GFL, WHCF, Subject Files: FE 6—Executive Orders, Box 2, [FE 6 Executive Orders—general].

59. See, e.g., John A. Fairlie, "Administrative Legislation," *Michigan Law Review* 18 (January 1920): 181–200; James Hart, *The Ordinance Making Powers of the President of the United States* (Baltimore: Johns Hopkins University Press, 1925). Dodds, *Take Up Your Pen*, chap. 5, pays particular attention to TR's role in expanding the role of unilateral directives.

60. Edward S. Corwin, *The President: Office and Powers*, 3rd ed. (New York: New York University Press, 1948), 149. Emphasis in original.

61. Richard E. Neustadt, *Presidential Power* (New York: Wiley, 1960). Neustadt may also have purposefully underplayed formal powers since Corwin's textbook (then still contemporary, in its fourth edition of 1957) had cornered the market on that particular aspect of executive authority.

62. Terry M. Moe, "Presidents, Institutions, and Theory," in *Researching the Presidency: Vital Questions, New Approaches*, ed. George C. Edwards III, John H. Kessel, and Bert A. Rockman (Pittsburgh: University of Pittsburgh Press, 1993), 337–86; Terry M. Moe, "The Revolution in Presidential Studies," *Presidential Studies Quarterly* 39 (December 2009): 701–24.

63. Moe, "Revolution," 703.

64. Terry M. Moe and Scott A. Wilson, "Presidents and the Politics of Structure," *Law and Contemporary Problems* 57 (1994): 1–57; Terry M. Moe and William G. Howell, "Unilateral Action and Presidential Power: A Theory," *Presidential Studies Quarterly* 29 (1999): 850–73; Howell, *Power without Persuasion*. See also Kenneth R. Mayer, "Going Alone: The Presidential Power of Unilateral Action," in *The Oxford Handbook of the American Presidency*, ed. George C. Edwards III and William G. Howell (New York: Oxford University Press, 2009).

65. Alexander Hamilton, "Pacificus #1," June 29, 1793.

66. Mayer, *Stroke of a Pen*, 11; Mayer, "Going Alone," 433.

67. Howell, *Power without Persuasion*.

68. In April 2020, for instance, President Trump touted "my Executive Order prohibiting immigration into our Country today" when referring to a proclamation (see https://twitter .com/realdonaldtrump/status/1252418369170501639); an earlier tweet featured "Obama's Amnesty Executive Order." For a discussion of alternate directives and their confusion (intentional and otherwise) with executive orders, see Andrew Rudalevige, "The Obama Administrative Presidency: Some Late-Term Patterns," *Presidential Studies Quarterly* 46 (December 2016): 868–90.

69. Among other omissions, the CRS list does not include presidential memoranda, which seem to be in frequent use as substitutes for executive orders. See Harold Relyea, *Presidential Directives: Background and Overview*, Congressional Research Service Report 98–611 GOV (November 26, 2008).

70. "Gaggle on Background on Buy American, Hire American Executive Order," Office of the White House Press Secretary (April 18, 2017, 4:50 p.m.), available at https://www .whitehouse.gov/briefings-statements/gaggle-background-buy-american-hire-american -executive-order/.

71. See, e.g., John Hart, *The Presidential Branch*, 2nd ed. (Chatham, NJ: Chatham House, 1995); John P. Burke, "The Institutional Presidency," in *The Presidency and the Political System*, 11th ed., ed. Michael Nelson (Thousand Oaks, CA: Sage/CQ Press, 2018), 353–76.

72. Steven A. Shull, *Presidential-Congressional Relations: Policy and Time Approaches* (Ann Arbor: University of Michigan Press, 1997), 97 (in chap. 7, written with Brad T. Gomez). Note that some scholars, perhaps most notably Phillip Cooper, were calling attention to the role of unilateral directives as early as the mid-1980s. See, e.g., Cooper, "By Order of the President: Administration by Executive Order and Proclamation," *Administration and Society* 18, no. 2 (1986): 233–62.

73. Beyond Shull and Gomez's own contributions an incomplete list of such work includes Christopher J. Deering and Forrest Maltzman, "The Politics of Executive Orders: Legislative

Constraints on Presidential Power," *Political Research Quarterly* 52 (December 1999): 767–83; George A. Krause and David B. Cohen, "Presidential Use of Executive Orders, 1953–1994," *American Politics Quarterly* 25 (1997): 458–81; George A. Krause and Jeffrey E. Cohen, "Opportunity, Constraints, and the Development of the Institutional Presidency: The Issuance of Executive Orders," *Journal of Politics* 62 (2000): 88–114; Kenneth R. Mayer, "Executive Orders and Presidential Power," *Journal of Politics* 61 (May 1999): 445–66.

74. See the review in Mayer, "Going Alone," 438–43.

75. EO 13186 (December 8, 2017) and EO 13824 (February 26, 2018).

76. See, e.g., Adam L. Warber, *Executive Orders and the Modern Presidency: Legislating from the Oval Office* (Boulder, CO: Lynne Rienner, 2006).

77. As noted above, see Mayer, *Stroke of a Pen*; Howell, *Power without Persuasion*; see also Adam L. Warber, Yu Ouyang, and Richard W. Waterman, "Landmark Executive Orders: Presidential Leadership through Unilateral Action," *Presidential Studies Quarterly* 48 (March 2018): 110–26, as well as Fang-Yi Chiou and Lawrence S. Rothenberg, *The Enigma of Presidential Power: Parties, Policies, and Strategic Uses of Unilateral Action* (New York: Cambridge University Press, 2017). These data receive sustained attention in chapter 5.

78. Adam L. Warber, "Public Outreach, Executive Orders, and the Unilateral Presidency," *Congress & the Presidency* 41, no. 3 (2014): 269–88; Brandon Rottinghaus and Adam L. Warber, "Unilateral Orders as Constituency Outreach: Executive Orders, Proclamations, and the Public Presidency," *Presidential Studies Quarterly* 45 (June 2015): 289–309.

79. Michelle Belco and Brandon Rottinghaus, *The Dual Executive: Unilateral Orders in a Separated and Shared Power System* (Stanford: Stanford University Press, 2017); Chiou and Rothenberg, *Enigma of Presidential Power*; Matthew J. Dickinson and Jesse Gubb, "The Limits to Power without Persuasion," *Presidential Studies Quarterly* 46 (March 2016): 48–72; Jeffrey A. Fine and Adam L. Warber, "Circumventing Adversity: Executive Orders and Divided Government," *Presidential Studies Quarterly* 42 (June 2012): 256–74.

80. See Dino P. Christenson and Douglas L. Kriner, *The Myth of the Imperial Presidency: Political Checks on Unilateral Power* (Chicago: University of Chicago Press, 2020); Andrew Reeves and Jon C. Rogowski, *No Blank Check: Public Constraints on Presidential Unilateral Power* (New York: Cambridge University Press, forthcoming), as well as the articles each builds on, e.g., Christenson and Kriner, "Does Public Opinion Constrain Presidential Unilateralism?" *American Political Science Review* 113 (November 2019): 1071–77; Reeves and Rogowski, "The Public Cost of Unilateral Action," *American Journal of Political Science* 62 (2018): 424–40.

81. On presidential memoranda, for instance, see Kenneth S. Lowande, "After the Orders: Presidential Memoranda and Unilateral Action," *Presidential Studies Quarterly* 44 (December 2014): 724–41; Rudalevige, "Obama Administrative Presidency." Research on other unilateral directives includes Alexander Bolton and Sharece Thrower, "Legislative Capacity and Executive Unilateralism," *American Journal of Political Science* 60 (July 2016): 649–63; Dodds, *Take Up Your Pen*; Christopher Kelley and Bryan Marshall, "The Last Word: Presidential Power and the Role of Signing Statements," *Presidential Studies Quarterly* 38 (2008): 248–67; Brandon Rottinghaus and Jason Maier, "The Power of Decree: Presidential Use of Executive Proclamations," *Political Research Quarterly* 60, no. 2 (2007): 338–43.

82. Howell, *Power without Persuasion*, 78; and see Keith Krehbiel, *Pivotal Politics: A Theory of U.S. Lawmaking* (Chicago: University of Chicago Press, 1998).

83. Howell, *Power without Persuasion*, 65.

84. Ibid., 14–15, and see Moe and Howell, "Unilateral Action and Presidential Power."

85. Terry M. Moe, "The Presidency and Bureaucracy: The Presidential Advantage," in *The Presidency and the Political System*, 4th ed., ed. Michael Nelson (Washington, DC: CQ Press, 1995), 417.

86. Howell, *Power without Persuasion*, 204n9.

87. For a collection of both, see Jeffrey P. Crouch, Mark J. Rozell, and Mitchel A. Sollenberger, *The Unitary Executive Theory: A Danger to Constitutional Government* (Lawrence: University Press of Kansas, 2020). One example is Trump attorney general William Barr's statement that "it is wrong to conceive of the President as simply the highest officer within the Executive branch hierarchy. He alone *is* the Executive branch." Quoted in Donald Ayer, "Bill Barr's Dangerous Pursuit of Executive Power," *The Atlantic*, June 30, 2019, https://www.theatlantic.com /ideas/archive/2019/06/bill-barrs-dangerous-pursuit-executive-power/592951/.

88. The economist Milton Friedman, in fact, argued against confusing "descriptive accuracy with analytic relevance." See *Essays in Positive Economics* (Chicago: University of Chicago Press, 1953), 34, and see 14.

89. Hugh Heclo, *A Government of Strangers: Executive Politics in Washington* (Washington, DC: Brookings Institution, 1977), 34. In another work, Heclo noted presidents' "constant struggle" to forge "a 'oneness' they cannot achieve and a 'manyness' they cannot accept." See "One Executive Branch or Many?" in *Both Ends of the Avenue: The Presidency, the Executive Branch, and Congress in the 1980s*, ed. Anthony King (Washington, DC: AEI Press, 1983), 27.

90. Graham T. Allison, *Essence of Decision: Explaining the Cuban Missile Crisis* (Boston: Little, Brown, 1971), 67; the second edition, published in 1999 with coauthor Philip Zelikow, adds "vast" to describe the "conglomerate."

91. Howell, *Power without Persuasion*, 98–99.

92. See Andrew Rudalevige, *Managing the President's Program: Presidential Leadership and Legislative Policy Formulation* (Princeton: Princeton University Press, 2002).

93. Christenson and Kriner, *Myth*, 6. Emphasis in original. See also Christenson and Kriner, "Does Public Opinion Constrain Presidential Unilateralism?"; Reeves and Rogowski, "The Public Cost of Unilateral Action."

94. Howell, *Power without Persuasion*, 204n9.

95. See, e.g., Ruth P. Morgan, *The President and Civil Rights: Policy-making by Executive Order* (New York: St. Martin's Press, 1970); Ricardo J. P. Rodrigues, *The Preeminence of Politics: Executive Orders from Eisenhower to Clinton* (New York: LFB Scholarly Publishing, 2009); Greg Robinson, *By Order of the President: FDR and the Internment of Japanese Americans* (Cambridge, MA: Harvard University Press, 2001).

96. Mayer, *Stroke of a Pen*, 61, and see 61–65 generally. I discuss this EO in chapter 4.

97. Mayer, "Going Alone," 448.

98. Krause, *Two-Way Street*, 10.

99. As discussed in detail in chapter 2, the phrase is economist Oliver Williamson's. See, e.g., "The Theory of the Firm as Governance Structure: From Choice to Contract," *Journal of Economic Perspectives* 16 (Summer 2002): 171–95.

100. Kagan, "Presidential Administration," 2273.

Chapter 2. Bargaining with the Bureaucracy: Presidential Management and Unilateral Policy Formulation

1. Harold Seidman and Robert Gilmour, *Politics, Position, and Power: From the Positive to the Regulatory State*, 4th ed. (New York: Oxford University Press, 1986), 78.

2. Francis E. Rourke, *Bureaucracy, Politics, and Public Policy*, 3rd ed. (Boston: Little, Brown, 1984), 130.

3. Daniel A. Farber and Anne Joseph O'Connell, "Agencies as Adversaries," *California Law Review* 105 (2017): 1378.

4. Lisa Schultz-Bressman and Michael P. Vandebergh, "Inside the Administrative State: A Critical Look at the Practice of Presidential Control," *Michigan Law Review* 105 (October 2006): 93; and see 68–69, 91.

5. Leon Panetta, interview by the author, August 9, 2016.

6. Kennedy quoted in Nathan, *Administrative Presidency*, 1; Bush quoted in Peter Baker, "As Democracy Push Falters, Bush Feels Like a 'Dissident,'" *Washington Post*, August 20, 2007, http://www.washingtonpost.com/wp-dyn/content/article/2007/08/19/AR2007081901720 .html; Barack Obama, "Remarks on Government Reform," July 8, 2013, https://www.presidency .ucsb.edu/node/304989; Donald Trump, "The President's News Conference," March 13, 2020, https://www.govinfo.gov/content/pkg/DCPD-202000153/pdf/DCPD-202000153.pdf.

7. "The President's Management of Public Policy," May 31, 1946, NARA, RG 51, *Division of Administrative Management, 1939–1952 (Series 39.32)*, Box 3, [E2–15/46.1].

8. Richard E. Neustadt, *Presidential Power and the Modern Presidents* (New York: Free Press, 1990), 10, 33. Emphasis in the original. Matthew Dickinson similarly argues that "policymaking through administrative action is no less subject to bargaining and compromise than is policymaking through the legislative process." Dickinson, "We All Want a Revolution: Neustadt, New Institutionalism, and the Future of Presidency Research," *Presidential Studies Quarterly* 39 (December 2009): 757.

9. Carpenter and Krause, "Transactional Authority and Bureaucratic Politics."

10. Krause, *Two-Way Street*, 10–11. The phrase "two-way street" is used in Neustadt, *Presidential Power*, 31, and Terry M. Moe, "An Assessment of the Positive Theory of 'Congressional Dominance,'" *Legislative Studies Quarterly* 12 (November 1987): 482. Krause himself attributes the idea to Herbert Simon's 1947 classic book *Administrative Behavior*.

11. Laurence E. Lynn Jr. and David DeF. Whitman, *The President as Policymaker: Jimmy Carter and Welfare Reform* (Philadelphia: Temple University Press, 1981), 3.

12. Nathan, *Administrative Presidency*, 85.

13. William Safire, *Before the Fall: An Inside View of the Pre-Watergate White House* (New York: DaCapo Press, 1975), 246–47.

14. Daniel Patrick Moynihan, *Coping: Essays on the Practice of Government* (New York: Random House, 1973), 322.

15. Quoted in Baker, "Bush Feels Like a 'Dissident.'"

16. See Lewis and Selin, *Sourcebook of United States Executive Agencies*, 2n3, 5–6, 10. An even larger population of agencies comes from the General Service Administration's *USA.gov* website, which lists more than 600 separate governmental organizations. See ibid.,12.

17. Neil Kumar Katyal, "Internal Separation of Powers: Checking Today's Most Dangerous Branch from Within," *Yale Law Journal* 115 (September 2006): 2317. Katyal was principal deputy solicitor general and then acting solicitor general in the Obama administration.

18. *Morrison v. Olson*, 487 U.S. 731 (1988). For a less exalted view of why bureaucratic friction might exist, see Morris Fiorina, *Congress: Keystone of the Washington Establishment*, 2nd ed. (New Haven: Yale University Press, 1989); Terry M. Moe, "The Politics of Bureaucratic Structure," in *Can the Government Govern?*, ed. John E. Chubb and Paul E. Peterson (Washington, DC: Brookings Institution, 1989).

19. Crouch, Rozell, and Sollenberger, *The Unitary Executive Theory*, 35. See also Leonard D. White, *The Jacksonians: 1829–1861* (New York: Macmillan, 1954) and *The Republican Era, 1869–1901* (New York: Macmillan, 1958).

20. Woodrow Wilson, "The Study of Administration," *Political Science Quarterly* 2 (June 1887): 200–201.

21. John D. Huber and Charles R. Shipan, *Deliberate Discretion? The Institutional Foundations of Bureaucratic Autonomy* (New York: Cambridge University Press, 2002), 42.

22. Note, for instance, Theodore Roosevelt's view of "the executive power as the steward of the public welfare." The era's public administrators saw executive power as the legitimate mechanism for implementing the will of the public—as against the fragmented, particularistic, ironically unrepresentative members of Congress. Quoted in Peri E. Arnold, *Remaking the Presidency: Roosevelt, Taft, and Wilson, 1901–1916* (Lawrence: University Press of Kansas, 2009), 1.

23. Wilson, "Study of Administration," 209–10, 212. This reflected Max Weber's classic take on the neutral, expertise-driven character of bureaucracy.

24. Marshall E. Dimock, "The Study of Administration," *American Political Science Review* 31 (February 1937): 32.

25. Lawrence C. Dodd and Richard L. Schott, *Congress and the Administrative State* (New York: Macmillan, 1986), 2. See also the useful review in Krause, *Two-Way Street*, chap. 1.

26. Dimock, "The Study of Administration," 39; Clinton Rossiter, *The American Presidency* (London: Hamish Hamilton, 1957), 6–7.

27. Allison, *Essence of Decision*, 67. Morton Halperin likewise argued that the executive branch could not be treated as "a single individual with a single purpose and an ability to control completely his actions." See Morton Halperin, with the assistance of Patricia Clapp and Arnold Kanter, *Bureaucratic Politics and Foreign Policy* (Washington, DC: Brookings Institution, 1974), 311. Other similar literature from this period includes, inter alia, Alan A. Altshuler, ed., *The Politics of the Federal Bureaucracy* (New York: Dodd, Mead, 1968); I. M. Destler, *Presidents, Bureaucrats, and Foreign Policy: The Politics of Organizational Reform* (Princeton: Princeton University Press, 1972); Roger Hilsman, *The Politics of Policy Making in Defense and Foreign Affairs* (New York: Harper & Row, 1971). More recently see Michael Glennon, *National Security and Double Government* (New York: Oxford University Press, 2015).

28. Seidman and Gilmour, *Politics, Position, and Power*, 78.

29. Key scholars in the Carnegie school include Herbert Simon, James March, and Richard Cyert. For a useful review, and a discussion of the intellectual context of Allison's work, see Sophie Vanhoonacker and Patrice Wangen, "Graham T. Allison, *The Essence of Decision: Explaining the Cuban Missile Crisis*," in *The Oxford Handbook of Classics in Public Policy and*

Administration, ed. Martin Lodge, Edward C. Page, and Steven J. Balla (New York: Oxford University Press, 2015), 272–86.

30. Allison's model of "governmental politics" relies heavily on Neustadt's *Presidential Power*; see *Essence of Decision*, 147–53.

31. The quote is from B. Dan Wood and Richard Waterman, "The Dynamics of Political Control of the Bureaucracy," *American Political Science Review* 85 (1991): 822. For theoretical critiques, see Stephen D. Krasner, "Are Bureaucracies Important? (Or Allison Wonderland)," *Foreign Policy* 7 (Summer 1972): 159–79; Jonathan Bendor and Thomas Hammond, "Rethinking Allison's Models," *American Political Science Review* 86 (June 1992): 301–22.

32. Moe, "An Assessment," 515n3, 489. See also Cynthia Farina, "The 'Chief Executive' and the Quiet Constitutional Revolution," *Administrative Law Review* 49 (Winter 1997): 179–86.

33. See especially Mathew McCubbins and Thomas Schwartz, "Congressional Oversight Overlooked: Police Patrols versus Fire Alarms," *American Journal of Political Science* 28 (1984): 165–79; Barry R. Weingast and Mark J. Moran, "Bureaucratic Discretion or Congressional Control?" *Journal of Political Economy* 91 (1983): 765–800.

34. Huber and Shipan, *Deliberate Discretion?*, 39, 34.

35. Moe, "An Assessment"; Nathan, *Administrative Presidency*.

36. Terry M. Moe, "The Politicized Presidency," in *New Directions in American Politics*, ed. John E. Chubb and Paul E. Peterson (Washington, DC: Brookings Institution, 1985).

37. Moe, "An Assessment," 476, and see 481–82. For a more recent indictment of the same literature along similar lines, see Robert F. Durant and William G. Resh, "Administrative Strategies and the Bureaucracy," in *The Oxford Handbook of the American Presidency*, ed. George Edwards III and William G. Howell (New York: Oxford University Press, 2009), 593.

38. In speaking of agencies' agency I am adapting Miranda Yaver's insight and phrasing: see "When Do Agencies Have Agency? The Limits of Compliance in the EPA," working paper, March 19, 2015, https://dornsife.usc.edu/assets/sites/741/docs/Panel_1b_paper1_Yaver_When_Do_Agencies_Have_Agency_EPA_Compliance_SoCLASS_USC_2015.pdf.

39. Seidman and Gilmour, *Politics, Position, and Power*, 78, 81.

40. Gary J. Miller and Andrew B. Whitford, *Above Politics: Bureaucratic Discretion and Credible Commitment* (New York: Cambridge University Press, 2016), 1–9.

41. Sean Gailmard and John W. Patty, *Learning while Governing: Expertise and Accountability in the Executive Branch* (Chicago: University of Chicago Press, 2013), 55. See also Kathleen Bawn, "Political Control versus Expertise: Congressional Choices about Administrative Procedures," *American Political Science Review* 89 (1995): 62–73; Huber and Shipan, *Deliberate Discretion?*; David Epstein and Sharyn O'Halloran, *Delegating Powers: A Transaction Cost Politics Approach to Policy Making under Separate Powers* (New York: Cambridge University Press, 1999); William G. Resh, *Rethinking the Administrative Presidency* (Baltimore: Johns Hopkins University Press, 2015).

42. Daniel P. Carpenter, *The Forging of Bureaucratic Autonomy: Reputation, Networks, and Policy Innovation in Executive Agencies, 1862–1928* (Princeton: Princeton University Press, 2001); Carpenter, *Reputation and Power: Organizational Image and Pharmaceutical Regulation at the FDA* (Princeton: Princeton University Press, 2010). On autonomy, see also James Q. Wilson, *Bureaucracy* (New York: Basic Books, 1989), chap. 10.

43. Carpenter, *Reputation and Power*, 298.

44. Rachel Augustine Potter, *Bending the Rules: Procedural Politicking in the Bureaucracy* (Chicago: University of Chicago Press, 2019), 5.

45. Ibid., 13, and see 62. See also Jennifer Nou, "Agency Self-Insulation under Presidential Review," *Harvard Law Review* 126 (May 2013): 1755–1837; Nou and Edward H. Stiglitz, "Strategic Rulemaking Disclosure," *Southern California Law Review* 89 (May 2016): 733–92; Miranda Yaver, "Inter-Agency Learning in United States Regulatory Policymaking," working paper, September 13, 2016, https://papers.ssrn.com/sol3/papers.cfm?abstract_id=2838457.

46. Miller and Whitford, *Above Politics*, 104, and see 118–19.

47. See, e.g., Jennifer Nou, "Bureaucratic Resistance from Below," Notice & Comment blog, *Yale Journal of Regulation*, November 16, 2016, http://yalejreg.com/nc/bureaucratic-resistance-from-below-by-jennifer-nou/; John Brehm and Scott Gates, *Working, Shirking, and Sabotage: Bureaucratic Response to a Democratic Public* (Ann Arbor: University of Michigan Press, 1999).

48. Nou, "Bureaucratic Resistance." See also Jennifer Nou, "Civil Servant Disobedience," *Chicago-Kent Law Review* 94, no. 2 (2019): 349–81.

49. Kagan, "Presidential Administration," 2273.

50. Rourke, *Bureaucracy, Politics, and Public Policy*, 74. "Differentials in agency power," Rourke argued, flowed from the nature of a bureau's expertise (for instance, scientists and soldiers had an advantage over generalists); from the strength and support of its constituency groups; from its "organizational vitality" driven by mission and personnel; and from its current leadership (81–91).

51. Jennifer L. Selin, "What Makes an Agency Independent?" *American Journal of Political Science* 59 (October 2015): 971–87; David E. Lewis, *Presidents and the Politics of Agency Design* (Stanford: Stanford University Press, 2003); Lewis and Selin, *Sourcebook of United States Executive Agencies*.

52. See, for instance, Mark D. Richardson, Joshua D. Clinton, and David E. Lewis, "Elite Perceptions of Agency Ideology and Workforce Skill," *Journal of Politics* 80 (January 2018): 303–8; George Krause and Anne Joseph O'Connell, "Experiential Learning and Presidential Management of the U.S. Federal Bureaucracy: Logic and Evidence from Agency Leadership Appointments," *American Journal of Political Science* 60 (October 2016): 914–31; George A. Krause and Anne Joseph O'Connell, "Measuring Bureaucratic Leadership in the Administrative Presidency" (paper presented at Annual Meeting of the American Political Science Association, Washington, DC, September 2014); Joshua D. Clinton, Anthony Bertelli, Christian R. Grose, David E. Lewis, and David C. Nixon, "Separated Powers in the United States: The Ideology of Agencies, Presidents, and Congress," *American Journal of Political Science* 56 (April 2012): 341–54; Anthony M. Bertelli and Christian R. Grose, "The Lengthened Shadow of Another Institution? Ideal Point Estimates for the Executive Branch and Congress," *American Journal of Political Science* 55 (October 2011): 767–81; Joshua D. Clinton and David E. Lewis, "Expert Opinion, Agency Characteristics, and Agency Preferences," *Political Analysis* 16 (Winter 2008): 3–20.

53. Richardson, Clinton, and Lewis, "Elite Perceptions," table A-11; David E. Lewis, Mark D. Richardson, and Eric Rosenthal, "OMB in Its Management Role: Evidence from Surveys of Federal Executives," in *Executive Policymaking: The Role of the OMB in the Presidency*, ed. Meena Bose and Andrew Rudalevige (Washington, DC: Brookings Institution Press, 2020); Anthony M. Bertelli, Dyana P. Mason, Jennifer M. Connolly, and David A. Gastwirth, "Measuring Agency Attributes with Attitudes across Time: A Method and Examples Using Large-Scale Federal Surveys," *Journal of Public Administration Research and Theory* 25 (April 2015): 513–44.

54. George A. Krause, "Organizational Complexity and Coordination Dilemmas in U.S. Executive Politics," *Presidential Studies Quarterly* 39 (March 2009): 75.

55. Warber, *Executive Orders and the Modern Presidency*, 8.

56. Hart, *The Ordinance Making Powers of the President of the United States*, 297.

57. Recall the congressional report's definition of EOs cited in chapter 1: "Executive orders are generally directed to, and govern actions by, Government officials and agencies. They usually affect private individuals only indirectly."

58. Fred I. Greenstein, "Toward a Modern Presidency," in *Leadership in the Modern Presidency*, ed. Greenstein (Cambridge, MA: Harvard University Press, 1988), 4.

59. Moe and Wilson, "Presidents and the Politics of Structure," 11.

60. Rudalevige, *Managing the President's Program*, 158–62.

61. William Carey to Lawrence O'Brien, "Congressional Liaison, Bureau of the Budget," March 10, 1961, NARA, RG 51, *Legislative Reference Division Subject Files, 1939–70 (Series 39.39)*, Box 10, [White House Correspondence—1961]. Further, the game has repeated moves: as we will see, statutes can require the issuance of EOs. And EOs can prompt new law.

62. John Kingdon, *Agendas, Alternatives, and Public Policies*, 2nd ed. (New York: Harper-Collins, 1995), 116.

63. Bob Woodward, *Fear* (New York: Simon and Schuster, 2018), 175.

64. John Podesta and Todd Stern to Mack McLarty, Mark Gearan, George Stephanopoulos, Rahm Emanuel, et al., "Upcoming Presidential Actions and Initiatives," memo of January 28, 1993, WJCL, FOIA 2006–0466-F, WHSOF: Office of Speechwriting: Jonathan Prince, OA/ ID 10440 [1/93 Executive Actions]; Karen Tramontano and Thomas Freedman, "Status Report on Executive Actions for April 11 Meeting," memo of April 10, 2000, WJCL, Domestic Policy Council: Bruce Reed Subject Files, Box 109, "Executive Orders [1]," https://clinton .presidentiallibraries.us/items/show/31315. Sometimes this process produced "thin gruel," as Podesta and Stern complained; sometimes the president would "commandeer" the work product of "the bureaucratic trenches" (Kagan, "Presidential Administration," 2301).

65. See, for example, the case in chapter 4 where agencies lobbied the Reagan administration to change a late-term Carter order. Another instance might be when agencies ask for reconsideration of previous proposals that fell short, as with the G.H.W. Bush-Clinton saga over a smoking ban for government buildings presented in chapter 6. Yet since that kind of case shows an agency first presenting an EO to an unsympathetic White House, it seems better classed as dogged perseverance twinned with good fortune rather than as strategy.

66. Michael Cohen, James March, and Johan Olsen, "A Garbage Can Model of Organizational Choice," *Administrative Studies Quarterly* (March 1972): 1–25; Jonathan Bendor, Terry M. Moe, and Kenneth Shotts, "Recycling the Garbage Can: An Assessment of the Research Program," *American Political Science Review* 95 (March 2001): 169–90.

67. Moe, "The Politics of Bureaucratic Structure," 268; Andrew Rudalevige, "The Structure of Leadership: Presidents, Hierarchies, and Information Flow," *Presidential Studies Quarterly* 35 (March 2005): 333–60.

68. Eisenhower to Nixon, November 15, 1967, quoted in Jeffrey Frank, *Ike and Dick* (New York: Simon and Schuster, 2013), 281.

69. Katyal, "Internal Separation of Powers," 2317.

70. Oliver Williamson, *The Mechanisms of Governance* (New York: Oxford University Press, 1996), 7.

71. Wilson, *Bureaucracy*, 358. More generally see Ronald Coase, "The Nature of the Firm," *Economica* 4 (November 1937): 386–405. See, too, Harold Demsetz, "The Theory of the Firm Revisited," *Journal of Law, Economics, and Organization* 4 (1988): 141–61; Oliver Hart, "An Economist's Perspective on the Theory of the Firm," in *Organization Theory: From Chester Barnard to the Present and Beyond*, expanded ed., ed Oliver Williamson (New York: Oxford University Press, 1995); Paul Milgrom and John Roberts, "Bargaining Costs, Influence Costs, and the Organization of Economic Activity," in *Perspectives on Positive Political Economy*, ed. James E. Alt and Kenneth A. Shepsle (New York: Cambridge University Press, 1990); Steven Tadelis and Oliver E. Williamson, "Transaction Cost Economics," in *The Handbook of Organizational Economics*, ed. Robert Gibbons and John Roberts (Princeton: Princeton University Press, 2012), 159–89.

72. Williamson, *Mechanisms of Governance*, 59. In the context of a private sector firm the asset might well be physical rather than informational. Elsewhere, Williamson argues that transactions vary by "asset specificity, uncertainty, and frequency." See *The Economic Institutions of Capitalism* (New York: Free Press, 1985), 72.

73. Williamson, *Economic Institutions of Capitalism*, 35. See also Williamson, "Theory of the Firm as Governance Structure." Note that the phrase is sometimes used to refer to the simple choice of a free market versus hierarchical firm, sometimes to internal adaptations within that hierarchy (or some hybrid model, where a particular company or industry might create institutions to ameliorate uncertainty). I adopt the latter use, again metaphorically.

74. Oliver Williamson, *Markets and Hierarchies* (New York: Free Press, 1975), 35; see also Williamson, *Economic Institutions of Capitalism*, 63 and 56–63 generally.

75. Williamson, *Economic Institutions of Capitalism*, 57.

76. See, e.g., Williamson, *Economic Institutions of Capitalism*, 20–22, chaps. 5, 10; Williamson, *Mechanisms of Governance*, 131–32, 313–15; Williamson, "Theory of the Firm as Governance Structure," 185–86; Tadelis and Williamson, "Transaction Cost Economics," 165–68. As noted, there is also a wave of "hybrid" approaches between simple market exchange and pure hierarchy; see Tadelis and Williamson, "Transaction Cost Economics," 179.

77. Tadelis and Williamson call asset specificity "a crucial defining attribute of transactions." See "Transaction Cost Economics," 164; Williamson, "Theory of the Firm as Governance Structure," 180, 189.

78. In the spring of 2017 the law in question was the Foreign Corrupt Practices Act. The president's command was to aide Stephen Miller; to be fair, even the sycophantic Miller knew that was not something that could be done by executive order. See Philip Rucker and Carol Leonnig, *A Very Stable Genius: Donald J. Trump's Testing of America* (New York: Penguin, 2020), 171.

79. Moe, "Politicized Presidency," 239.

80. Ibid., 246.

81. Unnamed George W. Bush aide quoted in Mike Allen, "Bush to Change Economic Team," *Washington Post*, November 29, 2004, A1. More generally, see David E. Lewis, *The Politics of Presidential Appointments: Political Control and Bureaucratic Performance* (Princeton: Princeton University Press, 2008).

82. Walter Williams, "George Bush and Executive Branch Domestic Policymaking Competence," *Policy Studies Journal* 21 (Winter 1993): 703.

83. See especially Rudalevige, *Managing the President's Program*. Other research in this general area also includes, inter alia, José D. Villalobos, "Agency Input as a Policy-Making Tool," *Administration and Society* 45, no. 7 (2013): 837–74; Daniel E. Ponder, *Presidential Leverage: Presidents, Approval, and the American State* (Stanford: Stanford University Press, 2017).

84. Rossiter, *American Presidency*, 103.

85. For an admirable exception, see Krause, "Organizational Complexity and Coordination Dilemmas." Thanks to Prof. Krause for his patient guidance on this front in personal conversations as well.

86. See, e.g., John B. Gilmour and David E. Lewis, "Political Appointees and the Competence of Federal Program Management," *American Politics Research* 34, no. 1 (2006): 34–50; Lewis, *Politics of Presidential Appointments*.

87. See Andrew Rudalevige and David E. Lewis, "Parsing the Politicized Presidency: Centralization and Politicization as Presidential Strategies for Bureaucratic Control" (paper presented at the Annual Meeting of the American Political Science Association, Washington, DC, 2005). Another study that grapples with both politicization and centralization is Justin S. Vaughn and José D. Villalobos, *Czars in the White House: The Rise of Policy Czars as Presidential Management Tools* (Ann Arbor: University of Michigan Press, 2015). Note that while the two are substitutes in any given area/agency, both tactics are likely used simultaneously across the breadth of any presidential administration.

88. Notes from meeting of November 17, 1972, 10 a.m., RNL, WHSF, Haldeman Notes Files, [Oct. 1, 1972–Nov. 17, 1972, Part I]. Emphasis in original.

89. Ibid.; Alexander Nazaryan, *The Best People: Trump's Cabinet and the Siege on Washington* (New York: Hachette, 2019). Nazaryan concludes this "led him to select people who were far more likely to subvert his agenda than to execute it" (51).

90. Clinton and Lewis, "Expert Opinion, Agency Characteristics, and Agency Preferences," 4.

91. Carol Lee, Courtney Kube, and Andrea Mitchell, "Trump's Impeachment Ire Turns on Pompeo," *NBC News*, November 18, 2019, https://www.nbcnews.com/politics/trump-impeachment-inquiry/trump-s-impeachment-ire-turns-pompeo-amid-diplomats-starring-roles-n1082716.

92. See especially Resh, *Rethinking the Administrative Presidency*.

93. Victor Johnston to Wilton Persons et al., "Suggestions for the Department of Agriculture," October 23, 1953, DDEL, Gerald D. Morgan Records, 1953–61 (Acc. A67–19), Box 1, [Agriculture Legislation no. 2].

94. Congressional preferences can also be considered representative of another potential bureaucratic principal, relevant interest groups.

95. Keith Krehbiel, "Where's the Party?" *British Journal of Political Science* 23 (1993): 235–66.

96. Wilson, *Bureaucracy*.

97. See especially Moe, "The Politics of Bureaucratic Structure."

98. Joel D. Aberbach and Bert A. Rockman, *In the Web of Politics: Three Decades of the U.S. Federal Executive* (Washington, DC: Brookings Institution Press, 2000), 101–3.

99. Art Okun, quoted in Rudalevige, *Managing the President's Program*, 36.

100. Such tactical non-proposals would not show up in a sample of issued EOs, of course, nor even in the collection of unissued EOs examined later in this book, since as discussed in chapter 7 those did at least make it as far as the proposal stage.

101. William A. Galston and E. J. Dionne Jr., "A Half-Empty Government Can't Govern," *Governance Studies at Brookings* (December 14, 2010), Brookings Institution, Washington, DC.

102. Krause and O'Connell, "Experiential Learning," 914.

103. Eugene Bardach, *Getting Agencies to Work Together: The Practice and Theory of Managerial Craftsmanship* (Washington, DC: Brookings Institution Press, 1998), 232. See also Kingdon, *Agendas, Alternatives, and Public Policies*, for a treatment of the difficulty of multiple agencies sharing policy responsibility.

104. Vaughn and Villalobos, *Czars in the White House*, 35.

105. Eisenhower to Rowland Hughes, September 9, 1954, NARA, RG 51, *Executive Orders and Proclamations, 1953–1961 (Series 53.2E)*, Box 25, [EO 10560].

106. Belco and Rottinghaus, *Dual Executive*, 18.

107. See Mayer, *Stroke of a Pen*, 74–75.

108. Department of Agriculture to President, June 27, 1939; Harold Smith to President, February 29, 1940, both in NARA, RG 51, Entry 24-A, *Division of Legislative Reference: History of Executive Orders, 1939–1946 (Series 39.1a)*, Box 4, [EO 8365].

109. Mayer, *Stroke of a Pen*, 75.

110. Jack A. Nickerson and Todd R. Zenger, "A Knowledge-Based Theory of the Firm," *Organization Science* 15 (November–December 2004): 618.

111. See, respectively, EO 13242 and EO 9066.

112. See EO 12006 (July 29, 1977); EO 12011 (September 30, 1977); EO 12016 (October 31, 1977); EO 12037 (January 31, 1978); EO 12056 (April 28, 1978). I mean no offense to Mr. Minetti or his heirs!

113. As noted in chapter 1, see especially Howell, *Power without Persuasion*; Mayer, *Stroke of a Pen*; Warber, *Executive Orders and the Modern Presidency*. Case study approaches to EOs, of course, had always reflected at least a tacit judgment that only select orders were worthy of sustained scholarly attention, from the internment order just noted to those advancing the cause of civil rights. See, e.g., Morgan, *The President and Civil Rights*; Robinson, *By Order of the President*.

114. See EO 11154 (May 8, 1964); alas, the file in the Johnson Library provided little detail on this case. Mayer omitted these sorts of orders entirely from his sampling—again, a perfectly reasonable step given his different research aims. See *Stroke of a Pen*, 85.

115. Fred Fielding Oral History, Miller Center, University of Virginia, March 11, 2011, https://millercenter.org/the-presidency/presidential-oral-histories/fred-fielding-oral-history. Quote is at p. 99 of the PDF version of the interview.

116. Barry D. Friedman, *Regulation in the Reagan-Bush Era* (Pittsburgh: University of Pittsburgh Press, 1995), 189.

Chapter 3. Executive Orders: Structure and Process

1. As reporter Bob Woodward comments: "Trump liked signing. It meant he was doing things, and he had an up-and-down penmanship that looked authoritative in black magic marker." See *Fear* (New York: Simon and Schuster, 2018), 263.

2. These are available at https://www.archives.gov/federal-register/executive-orders/disposition; see also the *Federal Register*'s own collation of orders since 1994, including their full text, at https://www.federalregister.gov/presidential-documents/executive-orders.

3. See Williamson, *Economic Institutions of Capitalism*, 35, and the citations in chapter 2; on structures generally as "recurring interactions in organizations," see Karen M. Hult and Charles Walcott, *Governing Public Organizations: Politics, Structures, and Institutional Design* (Pacific Grove, CA: Brooks/Cole, 1990), 34.

4. Richard Rose, "Organizing Issues In and Organizing Problems Out," in *The Managerial Presidency*, ed. James P. Pfiffner (Pacific Grove, CA: Brooks/Cole, 1991), 108.

5. Richard J. Ellis, *The Development of the American Presidency*, 2nd ed. (New York: Routledge, 2015), 283; see too the invaluable Work Projects Administration (WPA) historical surveys edited by Clifford L. Lord and published as *List and Index of Presidential Executive Orders: Unnumbered Series, 1789–1941* (Newark, NJ: WPA, 1943) and *Presidential Executive Orders: Numbered 1–8030, 1862–1938* (New York: Archives Publishing Company, 1944).

6. At any rate this is the first the WPA researchers were able to locate. See Lord, *List and Index*, 1; Louis Fisher, *The Law of the Executive Branch: Presidential Power* (New York: Oxford University Press, 2014), 103.

7. Lord, *Presidential Executive Orders*, v; U.S. Senate, Special Committee on National Emergencies and Delegated Emergency Powers, *Executive Orders in Times of War and National Emergency*, 93rd Cong., 2nd Sess. (1974), 2; Cooper, *By Order of the President*, 21.

8. There had been an effort via the 1895 General Printing Act to catalog any directive that had been printed by the Government Printing Office, but this was far from comprehensive. State began asking agencies to provide the orders from their files in 1905. See Dodds, *Take Up Your Pen*, 15–17; William Neighbors, "Presidential Legislation by Executive Order," *University of Colorado Law Review* 37 (Fall 1964): 107; Mayer, *Stroke of a Pen*, 67.

9. A May 1905 executive order restricting the use of convict labor to carry out federal contracts, for instance, became EO 325-A.

10. Lord, *Presidential Executive Orders*, 1–2.

11. Mayer, *Stroke of a Pen*, 67; U.S. Senate, *Executive Orders*, 2.

12. Hart, *The Ordinance Making Powers of the President of the United States*, 315–23.

13. EO 5220 (November 8, 1929).

14. Mayer, *Stroke of a Pen*, 68–69.

15. Quoted in ibid., 69–70.

16. P.L. 74-220, codified at 44 U.S.C. §1501 et seq. The Federal Register Act required the publication of "all Presidential proclamations and Executive orders, except such as have no general applicability or legal effect or are effective only against Federal agencies or persons in their capacity as officers, agents, or employees thereof." Publication of proposed regulations was not mandated until passage of the 1946 Administrative Procedure Act.

17. Lissa Snyders, "Exploring the First Federal Register," *Office of the Federal Register Blog* (April 2015), https://www.federalregister.gov/reader-aids/office-of-the-federal-register-blog/2015/04/exploring-the-first-federal-register.

18. Harold Ickes to the President, April 25, 1942; F. J. Bailey to Mr. Miller, July 25, 1946, and attached material, both in NARA, RG 51, Entry 24-A, *Division of Legislative Reference: History of Executive Orders, 1939–1946 (Series 39.1a)*, Box 12, [EO 9153-A]; H. H. Titus to R. W. Jones, "Lost

File," August 9, 1957, NARA, RG 51, *General Legislation: History of Executive Orders Numbered from 9818 to 10431 (Series 47.1d)*, Box 19A, [EO 10026-A].

19. See Lee White to Arthur Focke, no title, June 5, 1962, finding the "arguments advanced by the director of the office of the Federal Register meritorious"; Focke to Ted Sorensen, April 19, 1962; Seidman to Focke, "Executive Order Superseding E.O. 10006," February 21, 1962, all in NARA, RG 51, *Executive Orders and Proclamations, January 20, 1961–January 19, 1965 (Series 61.4)*, Box 4, [EO 11030; E5–3/62.1 (E18–4/60.1)].

20. Hart, *The Presidential Branch*; Peri Arnold, *Making the Managerial Presidency: Comprehensive Reorganization Planning, 1905–1996*, 2nd rev. ed. (Lawrence: University Press of Kansas, 1998).

21. I use the current name, OMB, to refer to the agency overall, and in specific references after 1970, but will use BoB or "the Bureau" or "Budget Bureau" when that is historically accurate, that is, when referring to agency actions or staff prior to the July 1, 1970, reorganization.

22. Richard E. Neustadt, "Presidency and Legislation: The Growth of Central Clearance," *American Political Science Review* 48 (September 1954): 650.

23. P.L. 67–13. For a broader discussion of the history leading to the Budget and Accounting Act, see Arnold, *Making the Managerial Presidency*; John A. Dearborn, "The 'Proper Organs' for Presidential Representation: A Fresh Look at the Budget and Accounting Act of 1921," *Journal of Policy History* 31 (January 2019): 1–41.

24. Quoted in Matthew J. Dickinson and Andrew Rudalevige, "'Worked Out in Fractions': Neutral Competence, FDR, and the Bureau of the Budget," *Congress and the Presidency* 34 (Spring 2007): 3.

25. Charles G. Dawes, *The First Year of the Budget of the United States* (New York: Harper & Brothers, 1923), 9.

26. Charles Dawes, "The Basic Principles of Budget Operation in the United States," June 29, 1921, NARA, RG 51, Entry 7A, *Records of the Bureau of the Budget, General Subject File (Series 21.1)*, Box 30, [Budget Bureau—General, 1–6].

27. Dawes, *First Year of the Budget*, ix.

28. Neustadt, "Growth of Central Clearance," 644–46. Budget Circular 49 (December 19, 1921) and related materials can be found in NARA, RG 51, Entry A1–27, *General Records (Additional Series), 1921–40 and Records Regarding the Clearance of Legislation and Executive Orders, 1929–39 (Series 21.6e)*, Box 1, [Procedures for Handling Clearance of Proposed and Pending Legislation and Executive Orders].

29. See Neustadt, "Growth of Central Clearance," 648.

30. Budget Circular 336 (December 21, 1935). FDR had already directed in 1934 that BoB receive copies of all fiscally related legislative proposals.

31. Quoted in Lester G. Seligman and Elmer E. Cornwell Jr., eds., *New Deal Mosaic: Roosevelt Confers with His National Emergency Council, 1933–1936* (Eugene: University of Oregon Books, 1965), 492–93.

32. See EO 7709-A (September 16, 1937).

33. EO 8248 (September 8, 1939). For more detail on this evolution, see Dickinson and Rudalevige, "'Worked Out in Fractions'"; Andrew Rudalevige, "Inventing the Institutional Presidency: Entrepreneurship and the Rise of the Bureau of the Budget, 1939–1949," in *Formative Acts: American Politics in the Making*, ed. Stephen Skowronek and Matthew Glassman (Philadelphia: University of Pennsylvania Press, 2007).

34. Harold Smith to the President, "Section 4 of August 28 Draft of Executive Order," September 1, 1942, NARA, RG 51, Entry 24-A, *Series 39.1a*, Box 14, [EO 9250].

35. Dickinson and Rudalevige, "'Worked Out in Fractions,'" 8–9.

36. See EO 5220 (November 8, 1929); in June 1931 the guidelines were updated slightly via EO 5658, for instance by requiring each EO to have "a suitable title." The official paper size had been set by the State Department back in 1921; the quote is from a May 18, 1925, memo from Charles Harbaugh to BoB director Herbert M. Lord, NARA, RG 51, *Series 21.1*, Box 95, [Executive Orders—General]. Not until 2006 were official copies of EOs technically allowed to be printed on standard legal-sized paper.

37. See EO 7298 (February 18, 1936). For State's objections, see Cordell Hull to Daniel Bell, February 4, 1936, NARA, RG 51, *Series 21.1*, Box 95, [Executive Orders—General].

38. Neustadt, "Growth of Central Clearance"; Rudalevige, *Managing the President's Program*, chap. 3; Andrew Rudalevige, "Beyond Structure and Process: The Early Institutionalization of Regulatory Review," *Journal of Policy History* 30 (October 2018): 577–608.

39. EO 8248 (September 8, 1939).

40. Arthur Focke to Director, "Proposed Executive Order," memo of February 4, 1962; see also Arthur Focke to Ted Sorensen, memo of April 19, 1962, both in NARA, RG 51, *Executive Orders and Proclamations, 1961–1965 (Series 61.4)*, Box 4, [E5–3/62.1 (E18–4/60.1)]. Note that EO 11030 made three other changes, largely codifying existing practice. First, the attorney general (AG) was specifically authorized to delegate approval of a given EO for form and legality to a subordinate, such as the assistant attorney general in charge of OLC. This was already standard procedure. Second, the AG was authorized to send an approved order directly to the president instead of to the staff of the *Federal Register*, if time was tight. Third, the process for ceremonial proclamations—those noting National Something Month or Destroy a Disease Day—was loosened, allowing BoB to assign the drafting of such proclamations to an agency of its choosing, with a hard deadline. This, the general counsel of BoB explained to the director in the memo cited above, would help avoid departmental shirking and the many times they were forced to "obtai[n] draft proclamations by a certain amount of cajolery."

41. Respectively: EO 12608 (September 9, 1987); EO 13403 (May 12, 2006); EO 12080 (September 18, 1978); EO 13683 (December 11, 2014). For the sake of completeness, reference should be made to EO 10006 (October 9, 1948) and EO 11354 (May 23, 1967), which made minor technical changes regarding spelling, printing, formatting, and the treatment of proclamations to the Roosevelt and Kennedy orders, respectively. Note that commemorative proclamations nearly always follow passage of a congressional mandate to issue them.

42. However, as we will see, OMB sees a particular president's interests in institutional terms, through the lens of the presidency more broadly—thus its preferences may vary from those of other White House staffers.

43. Again, there are parallel but not identical processes in place for managing legislative proposals, enrolled bills, and, since the 1980s, draft regulations.

44. However, the memo to Buchen went on, OMB "used to include this office routinely before Watergate made too heavy demands on the staff here, and OMB got out of the habit. It should be revived." Dudley Chapman to Philip Buchen, "Office of the Counsel to the President: Checklist of Functions," August 29, 1974, GFL, Chapman files, Box 13, [Chron

Files—Chapman—August 9 to September 30, 1974]. Cooperation was in fact generally revived over time, though its extent varies with the personalities occupying the different offices.

45. There are currently five Resource Management Offices, organized around groupings of related executive branch agencies: Natural Resources Programs; Education, Income Maintenance, and Labor Programs; Health Programs; General Government Programs; and National Security Programs.

46. Former OMB general counsel, interview by the author, September 2, 2016.

47. Michael J. Horowitz to Richard Darman and Craig Fuller, September 10, 1982, RRL, WHORM Subject Files, FE 003 (Executive Orders), Box 7, [FE003 (090000–139999)], #097598. The Department of Agriculture wound up submitting two proposals on this matter, according to a similar memo dated September 24, 1982, and available in the same folder.

48. "Digest of Proposed Executive Order" and J. L. Keddy, memo to file of November 21, 1935, NARA, RG 51, Series 21.1, Box 91, [Emergency Work Relief—Emergency Orders #1]. Note that since Hopkins's proposal predates the 1937 start of the data set created for this book, it (alas) does not appear as an "unissued order" in the data set summarized in chapter 7.

49. William Nichols, memoranda to the record, December 9 and 12, 1980, NARA, RG 51, Entry UD-WW 63, Executive Order Files FY81, Box 3, [Small Business Conference Commission].

50. For instance, Eisenhower national security aide Robert Cutler wrote to the BoB director on February 4, 1957, thanking him for the drafting assistance of counsel Fred Levi and others in what became EO 10700. NARA, RG 51, Executive Orders and Proclamations, 1953–1961 (Series 53.2E), Box 20, [EO 10700].

51. Charles B. Stauffacher to Elmer Staats, "Attached Proposed Executive Order," July 20, 1948, NARA, RG 51, Series 47.1d, Box 19, [V4–20/48.1].

52. David Gergen to Paul Theis, "Olympic Sports Commission—Executive Order," memo of September 27, 1974, GFL, WHCF: Subject Files, FE 6—Executive Orders, Box 2, [8/9/74–12/31/74].

53. John Bridgeland to Mitch Daniels, "Office of Faith-Based Executive Orders," January 26, 2001, and attached material, WNRC, OMB: OGC: Ex. Orders/Proc. 2001–2004, Box 3, [EO 13199]. Comment quoted from personal communication to author, August 27, 2019.

54. EO 13880 (July 11, 2019). Such "policy" sections were a rule rather than an exception during the Trump administration; it remains to be seen if the shift is permanent. In 1971, as what would become EO 11613 took shape, OMB even fought with DOJ over the matter of adding preambles to EOs generally, arguing that EO 11030 sets out specific rules and that OLC would need to amend that order if it wanted preambles. See OMB's letter transmitting the order to the attorney general, July 20, 1971, RNL, WHCF: NR, Box 2, [EX NR 1 Commissions–Committees]. See also the file for EO 11532.

55. Stauffacher to Staats, "Attached Proposed Executive Order," July 20, 1948.

56. F. E. Levi, "Foreign Policy Role of the Secretary of States," January 9, 1963, NARA, RG 51, Series 61.4, Box 12, [EO 11077/R6–5.65.2].

57. For an example of both, see the discussion of the "seriously deficient" White House Coal Advisory Council, e.g., Ron Kienlen to R. D. Folsom, March 11, 1980; Hugh Loweth to Ron Kienlen, "Coal Advisory Committee," March 12, 1980, both in NARA, RG 51, OMB Office of the Director, Executive Order Files 1977–80, Box 1, [EO 12229].

58. William Nichols to Benjamin Civiletti, July 24, 1980, NARA, RG 51, *OMB Office of the Director, Executive Order Files 1977–80*, Box 1, [EO 12229].

59. Schwartz and Seidman to Elmer Staats, "Proposed Executive Order Creating a Water Resources Council," May 3, 1962, and attached material, NARA, RG 51, *Series 61.4*, Box 18, [Creating a Water Resources Council—EO Proposed—P4–6/62.1].

60. Comments on route slip of March 30, 1961, NARA, RG 51, *Series 61.4*, Box 4, [EO 10934/E6–8/61.1].

61. Arnold Miles to Mr. Winslow, "Justice Proposal," January 21, 1946, NARA, RG 51, *Series 39.1a*, Box 24, [EO 9806].

62. EO 9835 (March 21, 1947). Operations of Truman's new board were held up for months when Republicans in Congress refused to appropriate funds for it; however, efforts to pass a different board in statute failed in the Senate after winning House approval in July 1947. See generally B. W. Patch, "Loyalty and Security," in *Editorial Research Reports 1950*, vol. 1 (Washington, DC: CQ Press, 1950).

63. See, e.g., Andrew Duehren and Gordon Lubold, "White House Shifted Authority over Ukraine Aid amid Legal Concerns," *Wall Street Journal*, October 10, 2019, https://www.wsj.com/articles/white-house-shifted-authority-over-ukraine-aid-amid-legal-concerns-11570717571; Margot Sanger-Katz and Noah Weiland, "Trump Promised Seniors Drug Discount Cards; They May Be Illegal," *New York Times*, October 22, 2020, https://www.nytimes.com/2020/10/22/us/politics/trump-prescription-drugs.html.

64. Dick Meserve (OSTP) to William Nichols, "Executive Order for Oversight Committee," memo of February 1, 1980; Secretary Patricia Harris to James McIntyre, February 19, 1980, both in NARA, *OMB Office of the Director, Executive Order Files 1977–80*, Box 2, [EO 12202].

65. Meserve to Ron Kienlen, "Oversight Committee on Nuclear Safety," February 4, 1980, and Kienlen's handwritten response; Kienlen to Meserve, "Funding for Oversight Committee," February 4, 1980, all in NARA, *OMB Office of the Director, Executive Order Files 1977–80*, Box 2, [EO 12202]. Emphases in originals.

66. William Nichols to Benjamin Civiletti, letter of February 29, 1980, NARA, *OMB Office of the Director, Executive Order Files 1977–80*, Box 2, [EO 12202].

67. See the material in WNRC, *OMB: General Counsel 1959–1993*, Box 18, [EO Draft 1973: Establishing a Seal for the Economic Stabilization Program].

68. The letter quoted here is John Carley to Distribution, October 10, 1986, concerning the second iteration of a proposed order titled "Implementation of the Comprehensive Anti-Apartheid Act."

69. Fred Levi, handwritten note, November 2, 1959, NARA, RG 51, *Series 53.2E*, Box 17, [EO 10893].

70. Former OMB general counsel, interview by the author, September 23, 2016.

71. Claude Wickard to Harold Smith, October 20, 1941, and related material, NARA, RG 51, *Series 39.1a*, Box 9, [EO 8942].

72. The rules also excluded "imbeciles, or feeble minded persons, epileptics. . . . Paupers or professional beggars . . . persons of notoriously bad character, anarchists." See Johannes, May 4, 1940, NARA, RG 51, *Series 39.1a*, Box 4, [EO 8417]. Emphasis in original.

73. Stimson wanted the allowance to rise to a princely $2.25 per day; the EO, with some amendments from BoB, was signed by President Truman on June 1, 1945. See NARA, RG 51, *Series 39.1a*, Box 20, [EO 9561].

74. See the materials in NARA, RG 51, *Executive Orders and Proclamations, FY 1969–1976 (Series 69.4)*, Box 24, [EO 11799].

75. Arthur Focke to Sorensen, October 26, 1962, and other materials in NARA, RG 51, *Series 61.4*, Box 18, [EO proposed—T3–11/62.2].

76. Department of Commerce to Charles Zwick, June 28, 1968, NARA, RG 51, *Executive Orders and Proclamations, 1965–69 (Series 65.4)*, Box 15, [EO 11420]; Department of Defense to Fred Lawton, July 3, 1951, NARA, RG 51, *Series 47.1d*, Box 10, [EO 10270].

77. OLC attorney John Bies, interview by Tara Leigh Grove, May 2018, quoted in Grove, "Presidential Laws and the Missing Interpretive Theory," *University of Pennsylvania Law Review* 168, no. 4 (2020): 902n121.

78. Interview by the author, September 2, 2016.

79. John L. Nau III to Mitch Daniels, May 9, 2002; George S. Dunlop to Mac Reed, "Revised Draft Executive Order," December 19, 2002; Philip J. Perry to Director, "Proposed Executive Order Entitled 'Preserving America's Heritage,'" February 25, 2003; and additional notes and documents in WNRC, 51-06-0013, *OMB: OGC: Ex. Orders/Proc. 2001–2004*, Box 4, [EO 13287—Preserving America's Heritage]. Emphasis in original.

80. Percival Brundage (acting director) to nine agency heads, August 25, 1954, NARA, RG 51, *Executive Orders and Proclamations, 1953–1961 (Series 53.2E)*, Box 25, [EO 10560].

81. Harold Smith to President, no title, memo of November 19, 1941, NARA, RG 51, Entry 24-A, *Division of Legislative Reference: History of Executive Orders, 1939–1946 (Series 39.1a)*, Box 9, [EO 8942].

82. Those from June to November 1982 may be found in the RRL, WHORM Subject Files, FE 003 (Executive Orders), Box 7, [FE 003 (070000–089999)] and [FE003 (090000–139999)]. Those cited here are Mike Horowitz to Richard Darman and Craig Fuller, June 11, 1982, #083158; June 25, 1982, #086804; and July 23, 1982, #090260.

83. The material cited in this case study comes from NARA, RG 51, *Series 61.4*, Box 10, [EO 11017, Providing for Coordination with Respect to Outdoor Recreation Resources and Establishing the Recreation Advisory Council].

84. Edward Strait to Charles Simms, May 3, 1974, and Simms to Strait, July 22, 1974, both in NARA, RG 51, *Executive Orders and Proclamations, FY 1969–1976 (Series 69.4)*, Box 12, [E2–13/74.10].

85. Interview with Brian Egan, counsel in the State and Treasury Departments as well as the deputy White House counsel for national security, quoted in Grove, "Presidential Laws," 904n135.

86. Gray interview of June 2018, quoted in Grove, "Presidential Laws," 902.

87. Fonzone interview of May 2018, quoted in Grove, "Presidential Laws," 902n123. Other administration attorneys from the George H. W. Bush to Trump administrations, including Trump White House counsel Don McGahn, reinforced this conclusion in their own interviews with Grove.

88. For more details on OLC's role here, see Frank M. Wozencraft, "OLC: The Unfamiliar Acronym," *American Bar Association Journal* 57 (January 1971): 33–37; Douglas Kmiec, "OLC's Opinion Writing Function: The Legal Adhesive for a Unitary Executive," *Cardozo Law Review* 15 (October 1993): 347–59; Tobias T. Gibson, "The Office of Legal Counsel and the Presidency: The Legal Strategy of Executive Orders" (PhD diss., Washington University, 2006).

89. Larry Simms to David Stockman, "Proposed Executive Order on Federal Regulation," February 12, 1981, NARA, RG 51, *Records of the Office of the General Counsel—Executive Order Files FY81*, Box 1, [EO 12291]. It is exceedingly rare to see OLC announce a position that is later disavowed by higher-ups at Justice—as occurred in the saga of the 2017 "travel ban" EO discussed in chapter 1. Even there the subsequent acting attorney general appointed in Sally Yates's place accepted OLC's conclusion. More likely is pressure from higher-ups on OLC to accept or justify an EO as constitutional. See George Packer, "How to Destroy a Government," *The Atlantic* (April 2020): 57–60; Shalev Roisman, "The Real Decline of OLC," *Just Security* (October 8, 2019), https://www.justsecurity.org/66495/the-real-decline-of-olc/.

90. William Rogers to the President, July 23, 1958, NARA, RG 51, *Series 53.2E*, Box 21, [EO 10776].

91. Gibson, "Office of Legal Counsel and the Presidency," 62.

92. William Rehnquist to John Dean III, "Wording of Executive Orders," February 16, 1971, GFL, Office of the Counsel to the President: Kenneth A. Lazarus Files, Box 2, [FE 6—Executive Orders (1)].

93. Beth Nolan, interview by Tobias Gibson, September 12, 2005, quoted in Gibson, "Office of Legal Counsel and the Presidency," 64.

94. This reasoning carried across a series of Bush-issued EOs on the topic: see EO 13198 (January 29, 2001), EO 13199 (January 29, 2001), EO 13279 (December 12, 2002), EO 13280 (December 12, 2002), EO 13342 (June 1, 2004), and EO 13397 (March 7, 2006). For a critique, see Ira C. Lupu and Robert W. Tuttle, "The Faith-Based Initiative and the Constitution," *DePaul Law Review* 55 (Fall 2005): 1–118.

95. Quoted in John J. DiIulio Jr., *Godly Republic* (Berkeley: University of California Press, 2007), 138.

96. Charles Cooper, interview by Tobias Gibson, September 21, 2005, quoted in Gibson, "Office of Legal Counsel and the Presidency," 63. An early example comes from the process that produced EO 9701 in 1946. There, BoB, as an advance check on a proposal sent by the Interior Department—intended to undercut a competing proposal from Agriculture—sent the entire package to Justice before asking for full clearance. See NARA, RG 51, *Series 39.1a*, Box 22, [EO 9701]. See also Wozencraft, "OLC."

97. Elena Kagan, handwritten notes on fax cover sheet of August 2, 1995, 9:30 a.m., in WJCL, *White House Staff and Office Files: WH Counsel: Kagan*, Box 22, Folder 10, [EPA Executive Order [2]]. Emphasis added.

98. Quoted in Gibson, "Office of Legal Counsel and the Presidency," 58.

99. George H. W. Bush OLC head Michael Luttig says that "OLC culture is to offer an 'expansive understanding' of presidential power." Quoted in Grove, "Presidential Laws," 903n129. See also Bruce Ackerman, *Decline and Fall of the American Republic* (Cambridge, MA: Harvard University Press, 2010), 99 and chap. 4 generally; Charlie Savage, *Power Wars* (New York: Back Bay Books, 2017), chap. 2; Packer, "How to Destroy a Government."

100. This became EO 7839 (March 12, 1938). But this case had interesting intra-administration politics of its own: BoB, which had its own objections, was somewhat irritated with Justice's bending the rules. DOJ responded that the attorney in question had not realized BoB's concerns. "Had he done so the order would not have been sent forward." See F. J. Bailey to David Bell, no title, memo of March 17, 1938 and attached material, NARA, RG 51, *Series 21.1*, Box 9, [Emergency (Work) Relief, Executive Orders #2].

101. Kmiec himself thought he had been too cautious in that instance; but, he argued, the opinion flowed from "OLC's institutionalized reluctance to sanction practices other than those that are so thoroughly established as to be beyond all legal question." Kmiec, "OLC's Opinion Writing Function," 359–62. Others report more recent degradation of that reluctance; see Roisman, "Real Decline of OLC."

102. J. Lee Rankin to Percival Brundage, May 8, 1956, NARA, RG 51, *Series 65.4*, Box 18, [K4–3/66.2].

103. Sally Yates, letter of January 30, 2017, available at https://www.washingtonpost.com /news/volokh-conspiracy/wp/2017/01/30/acting-attorney-general-orders-justice-department -attorneys-not-to-defend-immigration-executive-order/.

104. To its credit BoB had already identified this red flag ("I anticipate that the agencies might react strongly to this provision"), only to see its concerns waved away by the Civil Service Commission. See Norman Schlei to Arthur Focke, December 14, 1962; Focke to Elmer Staats, memo of December 17, 1962; Focke to Ted Sorensen, memo of December 27, 1962, all in NARA, RG 51, *Series 61.4*, Box 4, [EO 11073—F4–1/62.2].

105. Mitchell Daniels to the President, "Proposed Executive Order Entitled 'Amendment to Executive Order 10448, Establishing the National Defense Service Medal,'" WNRC, *OMB: OGC: Ex. Orders/Proc. 2001–2004*, Box 4, [EO 13293].

106. Harold Smith to President, "Reemployment and Retraining of Veterans and War Workers," memo of February 24, 1944, NARA, RG 51, *Series 39.1a*, Box 17, [EO 9427].

107. However, informal recommendations may undercut this finality. And in a 1975 case described in detail in chapter 8, OMB sent two different approved EOs to President Ford and asked him to choose between them.

108. Grove, "Presidential Laws," 904, quoting Obama White House staff secretary Rajesh De.

109. When the attorney general complained about a short-circuited assessment of an agricultural proclamation, one Reagan staffer lamented, "I don't think we would have drowned in sugar if we'd given Justice till close of business." (The AG had grumbled: "We have had a number of executive orders . . . thrust upon us with very short notice in the last few months. Fortunately, most of them have been relatively routine, but even the routine ones must be examined carefully to make sure that we do not certify that the President can do something which is not legal.") OMB counsel Mike Horowitz shot back that "you should know that expedited Justice Department review has been sought only in response to demands from the White House for expedited submissions to the President." See Horowitz to Joe Wright and Craig Fuller, "Attorney General Letter," May 11, 1982; Jim Cicconi, handwritten notes of May 12, 1982, on the Horowitz memo; William French Smith to James A. Baker III, "Department of Justice Review and Approval of Proposed Executive Orders and Presidential Proclamation," May 7, 1982, all in RRL, WHORM Subject Files, FE 003 (Executive Orders), Box 7, [FE003 (090000–139999)]. More broadly, see Mayer, *Stroke of a Pen*, 60–61.

110. Mr. Titus to Mr. Ellington, December 17, 1957, NARA, RG 51, *Series 53.2E*, Box 22, [EO 10747].

111. Arthur Focke, memorandum to the file of March 8, 1961, WNRC, *OMB General Counsel: Executive Orders and Proclamations: 1959–1993*, Box 7, [EO 10925].

112. Personal communication, December 17, 2014, passing along an excerpted email from "a branch chief who worked for me." For far earlier examples of evasion, see Neustadt, "Growth of Central Clearance," 651–52.

113. See OMB, *Open Government Plan*, April 7, 2010, p. 4, available at https://obamawhitehouse .archives.gov/sites/default/files/microsites/100407-omb-opengov-plan.pdf. Files for Clinton-era presidential memoranda can be found in WNRC, *OMB: OGC: Executive Orders 1986–2003*, Box 4, [Two Proposed Executive Orders]; for George W. Bush, see WNRC, *OMB: OGC: Ex. Orders/Proc 2001–2004*, Box 1, folders marked "MR."

114. Barton Gellman and Jo Becker, "A Different Understanding with the President," *Washington Post*, June 24, 2007, http://voices.washingtonpost.com/cheney/chapters/chapter_1/.

115. Memorandum [or index card] for the file, October 27, 1962, JFKL, WHCF, Box 599, [ND 4–1 Manpower]. Commentary on EO 11247 (September 27, 1965) is similarly distraught; the September 24, 1965, memo for the record observes that "the attached carbon copy and press release will have to serve as [the file] until any other papers appear, if ever." See LBJL, WHCF: EX FE 6 (11/23/63–), Box 8, [FE6 Executive Orders 1/26/65–10/10/65].

116. Arthur Focke to Ted Sorensen, April 19, 1962, NARA, RG 51, *Series 61.4*, Box 4, [EO11030: E5–3/62.1 (E18–4/60.1)].

117. Olson was, naturally, most concerned with the "legal protection" that taking "*every* precaution to make sure that the President meets *all* technical legal requirements" would ensure. Emphasis in original. Deputy Attorney General Edward C. Schmults then sent the memo to White House aide Craig Fuller as a warning that "mistakes may occur" if "the appropriate procedures for the preparation and review of presidential executive orders . . . have not been followed." Schmults to Fuller, September 26, 1983; Olson to Schmults, September 7, 1983, both in RRL, WHORM Subject Files, FE 003 (Executive Orders), Box 8, [FE003 (170000–294999)], item #179187.

118. Baker's archived notes on his 1980 conversation with Cheney are held by Princeton's Seeley Mudd library and quoted in Gellman and Becker, "Different Understanding." See also Cheney's comments in Terry Sullivan, ed., *The Nerve Center: Lessons in Governing from the White House Chiefs of Staff* (College Station: Texas A&M Press, 2004), 104.

119. Focke added that when BoB raised its concerns, "Mr. Goodwin's reply was to the effect that he was satisfied with the statements that the order had been approved by the Department of Justice and cleared by the Bureau of the Budget, and that he was not concerned with minor reservations or qualifications." Even though most agencies concerned had registered "no objection," Focke noted, he did not consider that "customary clearance with the agencies had been obtained." Arthur Focke, memorandum to the file of March 8, 1961, WNRC, *OMB General Counsel: Executive Orders and Proclamations: 1959–1993* (051-2012-0088), Box 7, [EO 10925].

120. Mr. Titus, record of call from Mr. Forster, March 24, 1943, 3:50 p.m., NARA, RG 51, *Series 39.1a*, Box 16, [EO 9331].

121. Robert Kennedy did succeed in getting a rapid turnaround: agencies were given only one day to reply to BoB before the order was issued. Interior missed this part of the memo and replied five days after the EO was issued. Luckily, the department had "no suggestions to make." Harold Seidman to Elmer Staats, "Conference on Administrative Procedure," February 2, 1961; Robert F. Kennedy to John F. Kennedy, March 27, 1961; Hazel Guffey to Fred Levi, no title, March 28, 1961; Arthur Focke, memo to the files of April 13, 1961; and other documents in NARA, RG 51, *Series 61.4*, Box 4, [EO 10934/ E6–8/61.1].

122. LBJ told Sen. Clinton Anderson in an April 6, 1965, letter that a potential EO "Clint" was concerned about was, at this point, "a rough draft which was sent to the agencies in the usual way to obtain their comments, suggestions, and criticisms. . . . I think that you will find that the

Bureau of the Budget is very open minded as to the specific arrangements." LBJL, WHCF: EX FE 6, Box 8, [FE6 Executive Orders 1/26/65–10/10/65].

123. Arthur Focke to Robert Mayo et al., "Pending Executive Orders," January 17, 1969, and H. R. Haldeman to Ken Cole, January 27, 1969, both in RNL, WHCF: Subject Files, Box 7, [EX FE6 Executive Orders]. And the Post-it note, of course, is in the same file.

124. David Stockman, *Memorandum to Heads of Executive Departments and Establishments: Proposed Executive Orders and Proclamations* (M-81-8), March 9, 1981. Thanks to Jeffrey Weinberg for providing this document.

125. Cynthia Lebow and Larry Simms, "Guidelines for Consideration of Potential Executive Orders to be signed by President Clinton on or shortly after Inauguration Day," transition memo, n.d. [early January 1993], LPIA, Box 21, [File 33]. Any early EO, they went on, "*should be of the utmost urgency* and reflect a singular commitment by the President during the campaign to take immediate action upon coming into office—action that can *only* be taken by executive order." Emphasis in original.

126. "Executive Order Process—Documents," n.d. [January 2001], in WNRC, *OMB: OGC: Ex. Orders/Proc. 2001–2004*, [MR 2001: Faith-based initiatives].

127. Author interview with former OMB staffer, April 25, 2019.

128. Author interview with former OMB staffer, April 11, 2019. White House or direct presidential intervention could of course deviate from that norm in individual cases, but then that is true throughout the history detailed here. Trump executive orders did frequently include prefatory material not common in EOs of past administrations; it remains to be seen whether that practice or other elements of what Doug Kriner has termed "Trumpian exceptionalism" will remain in place after his presidency.

129. Williamson, *Economic Institutions of Capitalism*, 46.

130. Recall that Oliver Williamson specifically notes "human asset specificity" as an element in deciding how to manage transactions. Ibid., 242–43.

131. Dawes, *First Year of the Budget*, 7–8. Dawes went on, "The President of the corporation bears a responsibility for the whole institution, and he has the right to get information where he pleases and from any source in that corporation, whether it is from a washer-woman scrubbing the floor, or his first vice-president" (9).

132. Roger W. Jones, Oral History Interview, August 14, 1969, Harry S. Truman Library, p. 20.

133. Bill Hopkins to Ken Cole, September 11, 1969, RNL, WHCF: Subject Files, Box 65, [EX FI 11–4 (4)].

134. Williamson, *Mechanisms of Governance*, 132.

135. "JW" [Joseph Wright] note of December 30, 1985, WNRC, *OMB General Counsel: Executive Orders and Proclamations 1959–1993*, Box 4, [Grazing Fees Correspondence].

136. F. E. Levi to M. Sherlock, route slip and attached material of August 24, 1959, NARA, RG 51, *Series 53.2E*, Box 17, [EO 10845—K12–4/59.5]. Note that GAO was renamed the Government Accountability Office in 2004.

Chapter 4. Executive Orders: Birds, Bees, and Data

1. Special thanks to OMB's Falisa Peoples-Tittle and the contractors working with her office for their repeated assistance with this effort.

2. Departmental records did prove useful in rounding out the narrative record in some cases. However, the archival Holy Grail—a full range of departmental memoranda tracking intradepartmental discussion of EOs and interdepartmental negotiations—proved, like its Arthurian forebear, to be out of reach. Finding the documentary history of specific EOs within departments' massive archival holdings was close to impossible, given limited finding aids. For instance, one file on an obscure EO concerning governance of the Ryukyu Islands held out great hope as an index entry. But in the flesh (*sic*) it wound up containing dozens of copies of the text of the EO, and nothing else.

3. See Rudalevige, *The New Imperial Presidency*, for a treatment of this trajectory.

4. Orders were sampled using a random number generator from the universe of orders issued by each administration.

5. Sixty-eight years equals 17 four-year terms; 17×32 gives us the overall sample size of 544. But the overall *n* in some analyses is higher, as described later.

6. Such weighting is common in survey research. In the present case the probability of a given item being sampled was $32/($EOs issued during a given four-year term$)$, adjusted for any truncated presidential term. Sampling here was conducted without replacement, but results were nearly identical to those obtained using a finite population correction mechanism adjusting for the difference in sampling with and without replacement.

7. The relative lack of Clinton orders seems to be an artifact of the way they were filed and sent to the Suitland WNRC facility. The former seems to reflect the stereotypes of distinct presidential personalities almost eerily—Clinton's files are scattered and like materials frequently separated, while George W. Bush's files are in numerical order in sequential boxes. More importantly, a disproportionate number of Clinton EOs were sent to WRNC in an "accession" which OMB would not make available without a Freedom of Information Act request. As noted in chapter 3, I filed that request more than eighteen months (and counting!) before this writing without receiving a substantive response. Even so, the type of EOs and the agencies and processes represented in the available Clinton files do not seem skewed or truncated.

8. Rudalevige, *Managing the President's Program*, chap. 4.

9. Memo to McGeorge Bundy, June 17, 1965, LBJL, WHCF: EX FE 6, Box 8, [FE6 Executive Orders 1/26/65–10/10/65].

10. This does not seem to be the case here, but as cataloged in chapters 1 and 2 and noted in chapter 8, there is a growing literature on directives other than EOs. Future research might be able to extend the analysis here to see if there is a systematic difference between types of directives. The discussion of central clearance of presidential memoranda (PM) in chapter 3 suggests that this might already be feasible for PMs, at least over a limited time span.

11. Rudalevige, "Obama Administrative Presidency"; Rachel Potter et al., "Continuity Trumps Change: The First Year of Trump's Administrative Presidency," *PS: Political Science and Politics* 52 (October 2019): 613–19.

12. Lawrence Chamberlain, *The President, Congress, and Legislation* (New York: Columbia University Press, 1946).

13. Thus the present project owes a substantial debt to scholarship tracking the development of the president's program in Congress. See Rudalevige, *Managing the President's Program*; but also, inter alia, Daniel E. Ponder, *Good Advice: Information and Policy Making in the White House*

(College Station: Texas A&M University Press, 2000) and Villalobos, "Agency Input as a Policy-Making Tool."

14. Hart, *The Presidential Branch*.

15. This is clear from the Clinton child health order detailed in chapter 1 and receives discussion in chapter 2, as well as in the concluding chapter.

16. As throughout this book, the chronologically appropriate term for the agency—BoB to mid-1970, OMB thereafter—is used in the case studies.

17. Hugh Loweth to Milton Stewart, "Amendment of Selective Service Regulations," May 4, 1953. All documents cited in this section come from NARA, RG 51, *Executive Orders and Proclamations, 1953–1961 (Series 53.2E)*, Box 21, [EO 10659].

18. The Universal Military Training and Service Act. The 1955 amendments were P.L. 84–118.

19. Langston Hughes, "Poem for a Man," unearthed by and quoted in Sidney M. Milkis and Daniel J. Tichenor, *Rivalry and Reform: Presidents, Social Movements, and the Transformation of American Politics* (Chicago: University of Chicago Press, 2019), 1–2. Hughes wrote the poem to honor Randolph on his seventieth birthday.

20. See, e.g., John Snyder to the President, June 9, 1950, and other materials in NARA, RG 51, *General Legislation: History of Executive Orders, 1947–52 (Series 47.1d)*, Box 5, [EO 10132].

21. See Stan Ebner to Attorney General, April 13, 1973, NARA, RG 51, *Executive Orders and Proclamations, FY 1969–1976 (Series 69.4)*, Box 19, [EO 11719]. For an earlier example, see EO 11370 (August 30, 1967). Sometimes committees do substantive groundwork for an EO: in 1965, for instance, Lyndon Johnson wrote to a House chair to say that "the fine work done by you and your Subcommittee on Natural Resources and Power has been a major force in bringing this [water pollution] order into being, and your advice on the contents of the order was most helpful." Johnson to Robert E. Jones, November 17, 1965, LBJL, WHCF: EX FE 6, Box 8, [FE6 Executive Orders 10/11/65–10/16/66].

22. EO 12464 (February 23, 1984). See Robert Kimmitt to Frederick Ryan, "Signing Ceremony of Executive Order," February 18, 1984, and Reagan to Warner, n.d., RRL, WHORM Subject Files, FE 003 (Executive Orders), Box 8, [FE003 (170000–294999)], #208852.

23. EO 11653 (March 9, 1972). See NARA, RG 51, *Series 69.4*, Box 12, [F4–2/72.2].

24. See, among others, EO 10969 (October 11, 1961), EO 12384 (October 1, 1982), or EO 13205 (March 9, 2001).

25. Kenneth Royall to James E. Webb, August 7, 1947, NARA, RG 51, *Series 47.1d*, Box 17, [EO 9898—S2–2/47.10].

26. The statute was known as the McCarran Provision after Sen. Pat McCarran of Nevada. Roger W. Jones to the Attorney General, November 6, 1956; Robert C. Hill to Percival Brundage, October 30, 1956; W. M. Whitman to Phillip S. Hughes, August 8, 1956; and other materials in NARA, RG 51, *Series 53.2E*, Box 7, [EO 10690].

27. Public Laws 88–563, 97–81, and 107–118, respectively.

28. [Mac Reed], "Brownfields EO Meeting 5/9/03"; Augustine "Austin" Smythe to President, June 18, 2003, and related material in WNRC, *OMB: OGC: Ex. Orders/Proc. 2001–2004*, Box 1, [EO 13308—Further Amendment to EO 12580 re Superfund Implementation—6/18/03].

29. Winthrop Knowlton to Charles Schultze, August 24, 1967, and related material in NARA, RG 51, *Executive Orders and Proclamations, 1965–69 (Series 65.4)*, Box 7, [EO 11368].

30. I.e., mixed with the EOP in the lead. In the case of EO 10941 (May 15, 1961), BoB's suggestions for revising the order to make it more flexible were sold to Treasury on the basis that "the substitute order would be preferable to the original proposal, from the point of view of the President," without really saying why, at least in the written record. EO 13242, issued December 18, 2001, reacted to a statutory change limiting secretaries' ability to set the order of succession if that authority wasn't in their department's founding statute. See, respectively, Fred Levi to Treasury, "Acting Secretary of the Treasury," April 24, 1961, NARA, RG 51, *Executive Orders and Proclamations, January 20, 1961–January 19, 1965 (Series 61.4)*, Box 6, [G1–1/61.1]; Jay Lefkowitz to John Ashcroft, October 31, 2001, WNRC, *OMB: OGC: Ex. Orders/Proc. 2001–2004*, Box 5, [EO 13244].

31. Douglas Dillon to Maurice Stans, March 18, 1960; Loy Henderson to Robert Macy, "Mutual Security Program Executive Order," August 10, 1960; Thomas D. Morris to the Director, August 26, 1960; Arthur Focke to the Attorney General, August 31, 1960; Fred Levi, memorandum for the file of October 31, 1960, all in NARA, RG 51, *Series 53.2E*, Box 17, [EO 10893—K12–4/60.2].

32. Scully to Darman, "HHS Smoking Order," February 14, 1991, NARA, RG 51, Entry 396, *OMB Director Chronological Files, 1989–92*, Box 7, [General Counsel Jan.–Dec. 1991].

33. Robert Damus to Director, "HHS Proposed Executive Order Banning Smoking in All Federally Controlled Work Space," February 11, 1991, NARA, RG 51, Entry 396, *OMB Director Chronological Files, 1989–92*, Box 7, [General Counsel Jan.–Dec. 1991].

34. Scully to Darman, "HHS Smoking Order"; Damus to Director, "HHS Letter to Skinner on Proposed Smoking EO," January 31, 1992, both in NARA, RG 51, Entry 396, *OMB Director Chronological Files, 1989–92*, Box 16, [General Counsel, Jan.–July 1992]; Darman to President, "Proposed Executive Order Entitled 'Smoking in the Federal Workplace,'" January 15, 1993, NARA, RG 51, Entry 388, *Director's Office Files, 1989–92*, Box 12, [January 1–15, 1993].

35. Kevin Thurm to George Stephanopoulos, "Executive Order Banning Smoking in Federal Workplaces," February 5, 1993, WJCL, NSC: Speechwriting Office: Robert Boorstin, [Executive Order—Workplace Smoking], available at https://clinton.presidentiallibraries.us/items/show/10029.

36. Draft Q&A headed "Executive Order," n.d. [August 1997], WJCL, DPC: Elena Kagan, Box 45, [Folder 7: Tobacco-Tobacco Settlement: Government Building Executive Order], available at https://clinton.presidentiallibraries.us/items/show/26521.

37. Todd Stern to President, August 2, 1995; Anthony Lake to President, "Access to Classified Information," August 1, 1995; Alice Rivlin to President, "Proposed Executive Order Entitled 'Access to Classified Information,'" July 31, 1995, all in WJCL, WHORM Subject Files ND011–01, [123556SS [1]], available via the Clinton Digital Library at https://clinton.presidentiallibraries.us/items/show/52955. The Intelligence Authorization Act was P.L. 103–59, passed on October 14, 1994. See Title VIII, Section 801(a). For more on the Ames affair, see Tim Weiner et al., *Betrayal* (New York: Random House, 1995).

38. The Security Policy Board was created by Presidential Decision Directive (PDD)-29 in September 1994. It was comprised of the deputy secretary of defense and Director of Central Intelligence as co-chairs, the vice chair of the Joint Chiefs of Staff, the deputy secretary of state, the undersecretary of energy, the deputy secretary of commerce, the deputy attorney general, one deputy secretary from a non-defense agency, one person from OMB, and one person from

the NSC staff. See Raymond Mislock Jr., through George Tenet to Anthony Lake, "Draft Executive Order on Access to Classified Information," January 18, 1995, WJCL, WHORM Subject Files ND011–01, [123556SS [2]], https://clinton.presidentiallibraries.us/items/show/52956.

39. Security Policy Board, n.d. [but early 1995], "Talking Point: Producing an Executive Order on Access to Classified Information"; George Tenet to William Studeman and John Deutch, January 10, 1995; Peter Saderholm (director of SPB staff) to Distribution, "Draft EO— financial disclosure suggestions from NSC," January 12, 1995; Arlen Specter to Anthony Lake, April 20, 1995, all in WJCL, National Security Council, Intelligence Programs (Edward Appel), OA/Box 2537, [Executive Order 12968—Access to Classified Information]. Note: this folder is in three parts, marked [1]–[3], available at https://clinton.presidentiallibraries.us/items/show/52967, https://clinton.presidentiallibraries.us/items/show/52968, and https://clinton.presidentiallibraries.us/items/show/52969.

40. N.a., n.d., "Executive Order on Access to Classified Information," in WJCL, National Security Council, Intelligence Programs (Edward Appel), OA/Box 2537, [Executive Order 12968—Access to Classified Information] [1].

41. James Frey to Fred Levi, "Alternative Draft Executive Order re: Latin America and Chile," June 12, 1961; David Bell to President, n.d. [July 1961]; Bell to President, "Latin American Aid and Chilean Reconstruction," July 31, 1961, all in NARA, RG 51, *Series 61.4*, Box 6, [EO 10955/ K4–3/61.1].

42. EO 12661 (December 28, 1988). The Omnibus Trade and Competitiveness Act was P.L. 100–418.

43. See Alan Raul to Joseph Wright, Stephen Danzansky, and L. Wayne Arny, "Trade Act Executive Orders," October 14, 1988, NARA, RG 51, Entry UD-UP 65, *OMB Records of the Office of General Counsel*, Box 3, [Trade Act Executive Orders 1988]. Another copy of these documents is available in NARA, RG 51, *Director's Office Files '85–88*, Box 42, untitled folder following [White House Legislation (general)]. Interestingly, in a separate memo the previous month, Raul had complained that the OMB general counsel's office was severely understaffed, with the result that it was not as involved in drafting the trade EO as it should have been: see Alan Raul to Director and Deputy Director, "Organizational Plan for the Office of General Counsel," September 21, 1988, NARA, RG 51, Entry UD-UP 200, *OMB Director's Office File, 1981–88*, Box 4, [General Counsel].

44. "Foreign Investment Screening," in Raul to Wright, Danzansky, and Arny, "Trade Act Executive Orders."

45. Note that while the Office of the U.S. Trade Representative is located, organizationally, within the Executive Office of the President, the USTR is operationally decentralized rather than (as BoB's Charles Schultze put it) a "presidential outfit." See Rudalevige, *Managing the President's Program*, 19.

46. Alan Raul to Joe Wright, "Trade Bill Executive Order," October 31, 1988, NARA, RG 51, Entry UD-UP 65, Box 1, [Economic Policy Council Papers]; Raul to Stephen Danzansky, "Executive Order Implementing the Trade Act," November 4, 1988, NARA, RG 51, Entry UD-UP 200, Box 2, [Trade Act Executive Order].

47. Alan Raul to Distribution, "Executive Order Implementing the Omnibus Trade Act," November 15, 1988, NARA, RG 51, Entry UD-UP 200, Box 5, [Trade Act Legislation and Executive Order 1987–88].

48. Mitchell Reiss to Nicholas Rostow, "Draft Executive Order . . . ," November 25, 1988, NARA, RG 51, Entry UD-UP 200, Box 6, [Executive Order Implementing the Omnibus Trade and Competitiveness Act (1988)].

49. Apparently the Council of Economic Advisers came up with the TPC language: see Alan Raul to Stephen Danzansky, "Executive Order Implementing the Omnibus Trade Act," December 2, 1988. For agency unrest, see Joseph Wright to Raul, "Executive Order on Trade Bill," December 6, 1988, both in NARA, RG 51, Entry UD-UP 200, Box 2, [Trade Act Executive Order].

50. Alan Raul to Steven Danzansky, "TPC Membership," December 14, 1988, NARA, RG 51, Entry UD-UP 200, Box 2, [Trade Act Executive Order].

51. Alan Raul to Designated Agency Heads, "Executive Order Implementing the Omnibus Trade Act," December 15, 1988, and attached material, including Judith Bello (general counsel, USTR) to Raul, "Draft Executive Order to Implement the 1988 Trade Act," December 16, 1988; George Shultz to Joseph Wright, December 20, 1988, all in NARA, RG 51, Entry UD-UP 65, Box 5, [Trade Act Legislation and Executive Order 1987–88].

52. Text of EO 12661; Joe Wright to President, "Proposed Executive Order Implementing the Omnibus Trade Act," n.d., [late December 1988], NARA, RG 51, Entry UD-UP 200, Box 2, [Trade Act Executive Order].

53. Wright to President, "Proposed Executive Order."

54. As compensation, Dulles was allowed to invade Cuba. (Just kidding! But kudos for reading the notes.) See, e.g., Department of State to Maurice Stans, September 30, 1958; Fischer to Focke, October 3, 1958; Defense letter of March 11, 1959; AEC letter of April 2, 1959; Focke to the Attorney General, August 13, 1959; Focke to Allen Dulles, August 13, 1959, all in NARA, RG 51, Series 53.2E, Box 23, [EO 10841]. The amendments to the AEA were P.L. 85–479.

55. For more on OIRA, see Potter, Bending the Rules, chap. 2; Cass R. Sunstein, "The Office of Information and Regulatory Affairs: Myths and Realities," Harvard Law Review 126 (2013): 1838–78.

56. Donald Arbuckle to Robert G. Damus, "Draft Informed Consent Executive Order," April 8, 1999; Matthew Vaeth to Dan Mendelson, "Executive Office on Informed Consent," August 18, 1999; Randolph D. Moss (OLC), "Proposed Executive Order Entitled 'Improving Health Protection of Military Personnel Participating in Particular Military Operations,'" September 17, 1999; Joshua Gotbaum to "Jack" [Jacob Lew], n.d., handwritten note. These and other materials in WNRC, OMB: OGC: Executive Orders 1986–2003, Box 2, [EO 13139—Improving Mental Health Protection of Military Personnel in Military Operations]. Email interviews with Vaeth and Barry Clendenin of the health Resource Management Office support the coding decision; many thanks to them both.

57. See EO 10729 (September 16, 1957); Harold Seidman to Elmer Staats, "Reestablishment of Special Assistant to the President for Personnel Management," February 1, 1965, and attached "Staff Analysis" of January 29, 1965; William D. Carey, handwritten comments on route slip from Seidman to Carey and Elmer Staats, February 1, 1965, all in NARA, RG 51, Series 65.4, Box 4, [EO 11205]. See also Thomas J. Weko, The Politicizing Presidency: The White House Personnel Office, 1948–1994 (Lawrence: University Press of Kansas, 1994), 58–62.

58. "Staff Analysis"; Jones, n.d., draft of proposed letter from the president to John Macy. A note on the draft, dated February 27, 1965, indicates that this letter was not sent: "decided to use shorter form, with no specifics." NARA, RG 51, Series 65.4, Box 4, [EO 11205].

59. Paul B. Kurtz through Richard Clarke to Steve Hadley, "Penultimate Draft of CIP Executive Order," July 5, 2001; Sean [O'Keefe] to "Robin," handwritten note of July 11, [2001]; Jay P. Lefkowitz to Designated Agency Heads, "Proposed Executive Order Entitled 'Critical Infrastructure Protection in the Information Age,'" July 19, 2001; handwritten attendance sheet for meeting on "Critical Infrastructure Protection in the Information Age, 8/8/2001," all in WNRC, *OMB: OGC: Ex. Orders/Proc 2001–2004*, Box 1, [MR 2001: Faith-based initiatives]. Emphasis in original. This material is clearly misfiled in that folder, which is otherwise about Bush's faith-based EOs. Other material on EO 13231 is contained in the separate and more relevantly named folder referenced in the next note.

60. Mac Reed, "Critical Infrastructure Board Executive Order," memorandum to the file of August 31, 2001; David Addington to Neil Patel, "Comments on 8-10-10 5 p.m. draft," August 29, 2001; Sean O'Keefe to the President, "Proposed Executive Order Entitled 'Critical Infrastructure Protection in the Information Age,'" October 16, 2001, all in WNRC, *OMB: OGC: Ex. Orders/Proc 2001–2004*, Box 3, [EO 13231—Critical Infrastructure Protection].

61. OMB general counsel Jay Lefkowitz told OMB director Mitch Daniels on September 28 that "the NSC requests that you approve the order as soon as possible." See Lefkowitz to Daniels, "Proposed Executive Order Entitled 'Critical Infrastructure Protection in the Information Age,'" September 28, 2001, in WNRC, *OMB: OGC: Ex. Orders/Proc 2001–2004*, Box 3, [EO 13231—Critical Infrastructure Protection].

62. Roger Jones to the Secretary of the Interior, April 30, 1957; Hatfield Chilson to President, letter and "covering brief" of September 1957; Jones to Attorney General, September 25, 1957. These and other materials in NARA, RG 51, *Series 53.2E*, Box 22, [EO 10732].

63. David Stockman to President, "Presidential Commission on Drunk Driving," April 14, 1982, and attached materials, in NARA, RG 51, *Executive Orders and Proclamations Issued in 1982*, Box 1, [EO 12358].

64. David Stockman to President, "Peace Corps Advisory Council," February 2, 1983, and attached materials, NARA, RG 51, *Records of the Office of General Counsel—Executive Order and Proclamation Files—1983*, Box 2, [EO 12412].

65. Michael Horowitz to Attorney General, October 14, 1981, NARA, RG 51, *Executive Orders and Proclamations Issued in 1982*, Box 1, [EO 12350].

66. Esther Peterson to Hazardous Substances Export Policy Working Group, "Completion of Policy," November 17, 1980, and OMB clearance materials, including Commerce letter of December 2, 1980, in NARA, RG 51, *Records of the Office of the General Counsel—Executive Order Files FY81*, Box 1, [EO 12290, Federal Exports and Excessive Regulation]. Note that this material is actually in the folder detailing the EO *revoking* EO 12264 in February 1981.

67. Edward Clarke to Jim Tozzi, "Hazardous Substances Export Policy," December 1, 1980, NARA, RG 51, Entry UD-WW 257, *OMB Program Records, Records of Regulatory Policy*, Box 1, [OIRA-RP-EPA-1980–4, General].

68. Esther Peterson to William Nichols, January 9, 1981; Ronald Kienlen to Wayne Granquist and Jim Tozzi, "Hazardous Substance EO," n.d.; Nichols to Attorney General, January 11, 1981, all in NARA, RG 51, *Records of the Office of the General Counsel—Executive Order Files FY81*, Box 1, [EO 12290, Federal Exports and Excessive Regulation].

69. Anita Ducca to Gail B. Coad, "The EPA's Regulation on Chemical Imports and Exports, Notification of Export," memo of April 6, 1982, NARA, RG 51, *Records of the Office of the General*

Counsel—Executive Order Files FY81, Box 1, [EO 12290, Federal Exports and Excessive Regulation].

70. EO 12290 (February 17, 1981), titled "Federal Exports and Excessive Regulation."

71. Diana Fortuna to Elena Kagan, March 12, 1997, WJCL, Domestic Policy Council files, Box 12, Folder 20, [Disabilities—Cap].

72. From, respectively, Ron Kienlen to Jim McIntyre and John White, "Proposed Executive Order Entitled 'Federal Consumer Policy,'" May 11, 1979; Ruth Greenstein to Ron Kienlen, note on route slip of July 16, 1979, both in WNRC, *OMB General Counsel: Exec. Orders and Proc.: 1959–1993*, Box 25, [EO 12160].

73. Alan Raul to Richard Darman, "Executive Order Revision," May 5, 1989, NARA, RG 51, Entry 388, *Records of the Director's Office: Director's Office Files, 1989–92*, Box 5, [Darman Notes—January–July 1989]. Emphasis added.

74. It did not, however, invent the notion of regulatory review—different processes had been put in place from the Nixon administration on, and Carter's EO 12044 was a crucial precursor to EO 12291. See Rudalevige, "Beyond Structure and Process."

75. For an early draft, see Richard Darman, White House Staffing Memorandum, Document 000089S, February 3, 1981, RRL, WHORM Subject Files: FG—Federal Government Organizations, Box 1, [FG 000089 (2)]; Peter Shane to James C. Miller III, "Draft Executive Order on Federal Regulation," January 29, 1981, NARA, RG 51, *Office of the Director: Deputy Director's Subject Files: Ed Harper, 1981–82*, Box 3, [Regulatory Relief]. See also Richard Willard to Fred Fielding, "Executive Order on Regulatory Reform," February 6, 1981, which notes that "a recurring question in regulatory review programs is the power of the President to control the actual content of rulemaking entrusted by statute to particular agencies." RRL, WHORM Subject Files: FG—Federal Government Organizations, Box 1, [FG 000089 (2)].

76. James C. Miller III, *Fix the U.S. Budget!: Urgings of an "Abominable No Man"* (Stanford: Hoover Institution Press, 1994), 3.

77. Richard Lyng to the Secretary of Agriculture, "Proposed Executive Order on Regulatory Management," January 27, 1981, RRL, WHORM Subject Files: FG—Federal Government, Organizations, Box 1, [FG (Begin-000066)]; Craig Fuller notes of telephone call from John Fowler, February 16, 1981, RRL, WHORM Subject Files: FG—Federal Government Organizations, Box 1, FG (000067 (1)], a folder that also contains additional agency comments (e.g., Samuel Pierce [the HUD secretary] to Craig Fuller, "Proposed Executive Order/Federal Regulation," February 17, 1981).

78. Peter Behr, "OMB Now a Regulator in Historic Power Shift," *Washington Post*, May 4, 1981.

79. This hypothesis is tested in the multivariate analysis in chapter 5.

80. Since there are sixty-eight years of data, the first and last blocks contain nine years; the remaining five contain ten.

81. Calculated using Kolmogorov-Smirnov tests checking the equality of the distribution for each administration versus the sample as a whole. Except for Carter ($p < .007$, though importantly only $p < .07$ if the six additional coded observations from the Carter years are also included) and Clinton ($p < .001$), none can be confidently distinguished from the overall distribution. Again, limited data availability keeps the number of Clinton-era observations lower than they should be given the design of the sample, so even his administration's stronger results should be interpreted with some caution.

82. This terminology draws from management exercises undertaken during the Reagan administration in 1981 and 1985, where extant EOs were assigned to agencies for review, in hopes of identifying orders that required modification or could be repealed. See Arlene Triplett to the President's Council on Management Improvement, "Next Steps in Study of Presidential and Central Management Directives," May 17, 1985, and the attached document "Lead Agency Assignments for Executive Orders," in RRL, WHORM Subject Files, FE 003, Box 8, [FE003 (332571)], #332571.

Chapter 5. Testing Presidential Management: The Conditions of Centralization

1. William Cummings, "'The Lord and the Founding Fathers Created Executive Orders,' Says Peter Navarro in Defending Trump Move," *USA Today*, August 9, 2020, https://www .usatoday.com/story/news/politics/2020/08/09/navarro-defends-trump-executive-orders -coronavirus-stimulus/3330605001/.

2. Mayer, *Stroke of a Pen*, 102.

3. The formulation of this EO, which created a new category of "Schedule F" employees, was highly centralized: "only a handful of senior administration officials were involved in putting it together" and even officials at OPM were not involved in its drafting. Lisa Rein, Josh Dawsey, and Toluse Olorunnipa, "Trump's Historic Assault on the Civil Service Was Four Years in the Making," *Washington Post*, October 23, 2020, https://www.washingtonpost .com/politics/trump-federal-civil-service/2020/10/23/02fbf05c-1549-11eb-ba42-ec6a580836ed _story.html.

4. For instance, if the OMB general counsel's clearance letter was not included in a given file. If, in such a case, advisory committees were under consideration, the "crosscutting" figure comprises the group's membership. For example, EO 13263 in 2002 created the President's New Freedom Commission on Mental Health, with representation from four departments (Health and Human Services, Education, Labor, and Veterans Affairs); the "crosscut" value is thus four. Note that when calculating this variable the EOP is treated as a single unit, even if multiple staff units within the EOP are listed on the letter.

5. Reporting questions internal to a single agency that do not change its structure—such as the order of secretarial succession—are not counted as reorganizational. Nor are short-term advisory commissions.

6. As noted in chapter 1, see especially Howell, *Power without Persuasion*; Mayer, *Stroke of a Pen*; Warber, *Executive Orders and the Modern Presidency*.

7. Mayer "counted an order as significant if it met at least one of the conditions outlined here: press attention, congressional notice, presidential emphasis, litigation, or creation of institutions with substantive policy responsibility." *Stroke of a Pen*, 85.

8. Howell, *Power without Persuasion*, 84.

9. William G. Howell, "Unilateral Powers: A Brief Overview," *Presidential Studies Quarterly* 35 (September 2005): 430.

10. Chiou and Rothenberg, *Enigma of Presidential Power*; Fang-Yi Chiou and Lawrence S. Rothenberg, "The Elusive Search for Presidential Power," *American Journal of Political Science* 58 (July 2014): 653–68. As motivation for this approach Chiou and Rothenberg credit Joshua D.

Clinton and John T. Lapinski, "Measuring Legislative Accomplishment, 1877–1994," *American Journal of Political Science* 50 (January 2006): 232–49.

11. A full list of the sources used to construct the measure is found in Chiou and Rothenberg, *Enigma of Presidential Power*, 70, and described in detail on 74–77.

12. Many thanks to Professors Chiou, Howell, Rothenberg, and Thrower for providing their data. See also Sharece Thrower, "To Revoke or Not Revoke? The Political Determinants of Executive Order Longevity," *American Journal of Political Science* 61 (July 2017): 642–56.

13. There are at least two potential caveats associated with this measure. One is that its coding is somewhat subjective, depending as it does on an individual coder's assessment of an EO's file. That file, in turn, leaving aside potential inconsistencies in record keeping over time, may be a function of the crosscutting jurisdiction measure already noted: the more agencies consulted, the more likely they are to comment. Still, while the crosscut variable correlates with the government significance measure at .42, that does not seem to rule out the independent impact of an estimate of internal significance generally.

14. Rowland Hughes to Bernard Shanley, "Proposed Executive Order Submitted to the Attorney General Relating to Security Requirements for Government Employees," August 4, 1954, NARA, RG 51, *Executive Orders and Proclamations, 1953–1961 (Series 53.2E)*, Box 9, [EO 10550]; Condoleezza Rice to Joshua Bolten, "Executive Order on Strengthened Management of the Intelligence Community," August 11, 2004, WNRC, *EO/Proclamations 2004*, Box 1, [EO/Proclamations 2004]. Such tactics also appear in the annals of unissued orders, as when in 1994 the Clinton administration pondered how to preempt introduction of unfavorable "takings" legislation. See "Private Property Rights," WNRC, *OMB: General Counsel's Office: 1993–1994 (Clinton Administration)*, Box 1, [Rejected Orders, Proclamations, Memos]. But it is worth noting that EOs can also be collaborative with congressional efforts, even if those legislative findings prompt executive action rather than law.

15. Thrower, "To Revoke or Not Revoke?"; Warber, Ouyang, and Waterman, "Landmark Executive Orders." The extended "policy" section (effectively an embedded press release) that has become a routine part of Trump administration EOs threatens to make this measure far less useful, a challenge to future researchers though not to the present project.

16. Many thanks to Prof. Ouyang for providing these data.

17. Many thanks to Prof. Lewis for providing these data. The specific "workforce skill" measure comes from Richardson, Clinton, and Lewis, "Elite Perceptions," as detailed in the online appendix, table A3. See also Anthony M. Bertelli and David E. Lewis, "Policy Influence, Agency-Specific Expertise, and Exit in the Federal Service," *Journal of Public Administration Research and Theory* 23 (April 2013): 223–45; Mark D. Richardson, "Politicization and Expertise: Exit, Effort, and Investment," *Journal of Politics* 81 (July 2019): 878–91; Lewis, Richardson, and Rosenthal, "OMB in Its Management Role." Another measure, of agency influence, is deferred to chapters 6 and 7.

18. See Belco and Rottinghaus, *Dual Executive*, chap. 6.

19. See, e.g., EO 10216 (February 23, 1951), titled "Extension of Provisions of Part I of EO 10210 to the AEC, National Advisory Committee for Aeronautics, the GPO, and the Dept of Agriculture."

20. Though even then State, passive-aggressively, wanted it known it would not "clear off on Defense's incoming letter transmitting the Executive Order as there are some historical

inaccuracies in it." Charles Kolb, memorandum for the record of May 10, 1985, NARA, Entry 295, *Records of the Office of the General Counsel—Executive Order Files 1984–87*, Box 1, [Quarters Allowance to Department of Defense Employees in Panama, EO 12520]. The law was P.L. 98–600, "An Act to Amend the Panama Canal Act of 1979."

21. For the former, as the Office of Personnel Management told George W. Bush in late 2002, "the pay increases in the draft executive order reflect decisions made by the President under current law for civilian federal employees, or are required by current law for members of the uniformed services." With EO 13282, Bush allowed civilian pay to increase 3.1 percent for 2003. See Kay Cole James to Mitch Daniels, December 4, 2002, and attached materials, WNRC, *OMB: OGC: Ex. Orders/Proc. 2001–2004*, Box 2, [EO 13282—Adjustments of Certain Rates of Pay—12/31/02].

22. Joshua B. Kennedy, "Who Do You Trust? Presidential Delegation in Executive Orders," *Research and Politics* (January–March 2016): 1–7.

23. On politicization generally, see Moe, "Politicized Presidency"; Lewis, *Politics of Presidential Appointments*.

24. Selin, "What Makes an Agency Independent?" and online spreadsheet of published estimates; thanks to Prof. Selin for making her data public. Note that for present purposes I have assigned the White House Office, not coded by Selin, a value of −1 (the lowest possible level of insulation from the president) on both dimensions.

25. Deering and Maltzman, "Politics of Executive Orders," 768.

26. Ibid., 769, paraphrasing Shull, *Presidential-Congressional Relations*, 103.

27. See especially Howell, *Power without Persuasion*. Deering and Maltzman ("Politics of Executive Orders") utilize a similar logic regarding the proximity of presidential preferences to legislative veto points.

28. E.g., Krause and Cohen, "Presidential Use of Executive Orders"; Krause and Cohen, "Opportunity, Constraints, and the Development of the Institutional Presidency"; Mayer, "Executive Orders and Presidential Power"; Mayer, *Stroke of a Pen*. But "contemporary" may matter here. Bolton and Thrower, for instance, argue that the role of divided government varies over time depending on the level of congressional capacity: the president's ideological distance from Congress, after all, matters less if Congress doesn't have the ability to enforce its preferences. They find it is only when facing more empowered legislators, as in the post–World War II period, that presidents issue fewer orders during divided government. See Bolton and Thrower, "Legislative Capacity and Executive Unilateralism." Still others suggest that the *kind* of orders issued under divided government and unified government might vary; see Belco and Rottinghaus, *Dual Executive*, chap. 2; Warber, *Executive Orders and the Modern Presidency*, 64–67.

29. See, e.g., Sean Gailmard, "Multiple Principals and Oversight of Bureaucratic Policy-Making," *Journal of Theoretical Politics* 21, no. 2 (2009): 161–86.

30. Bureaus may also be responsive to lawmakers from the minority party, of course, but far less systematically so. Indeed, a controversial OLC opinion from May 2017 held that "individual members of Congress, including ranking minority members, do not have the authority to conduct oversight in the absence of a specific delegation by a full house, committee, or subcommittee. Accordingly, the Executive Branch's long-standing policy has been to engage in the established process for accommodating congressional requests for information only when those requests come from a committee, subcommittee, or chairman authorized to conduct oversight."

See Office of Legal Counsel, "Authority of Individual Members of Congress to Conduct Oversight of the Executive Branch," May 1, 2017, available at https://www.justice.gov/olc/file/966326/download.

31. The House chamber support scores from 1937 through 2004 were also calculated (see https://voteview.com/articles/presidential_support_scores), but these proved similarly hard to distinguish from the co-partisans measure ($r = .69$).

32. See Bertelli and Grose, "The Lengthened Shadow of Another Institution?"; Clinton et al., "Separated Powers in the United States." See also Krause and O'Connell, "Measuring Bureaucratic Leadership in the Administrative Presidency"; Krause and O'Connell, "Experiential Learning."

33. Thanks again to David Lewis for providing the data utilized in a variety of his and his collaborators' work on these issues. See Richardson, Clinton, and Lewis, "Elite Perceptions," online appendix, section 4. Earlier research by Clinton and Lewis surveyed knowledgeable academic observers instead. The two measures correlate at .895 in my data, but the later survey includes a wider range of agencies, so it is used here. The earlier work is Clinton and Lewis, "Expert Opinion, Agency Characteristics, and Agency Preferences."

34. And, like the first variable, treats presidents of a given party as equivalent. If the DW-Nominate scores calculated for presidents are a useful guide, there is more variation among Republican presidents than Democratic ones during this period on this score. (The standard deviation of GOP scores is .145, Eisenhower to Bush II; for Democrats, FDR to Clinton, it is .073.)

35. At least not without a huge sifting of the departmental archival record and, even then, good fortune, as described in the notes to chapter 3. Even so it is an intriguing direction for future research. Interviewing agency general counsels would be another way to check on at least the plausibility of this hypothesis.

36. See the additional discussion of this point in chapter 2. Such an effect might be mitigated in these data by the fact that the agency characteristics are not linked only to the originating organization, since the "lead agency" code identifies the agency responsible for the subject matter covered by the proposed EO even if it did not draft it. We can also test whether these agency-specific measures differ systematically across the sample of issued orders used here and the set of unissued orders also collected for this project (see chapter 7). That analysis shows no statistically significant difference in the level of either measure of insulation in issued versus unissued orders. But this does not rule out the thought experiment above, since in that scenario at least some EOs would not have been put forward for issuance or abandonment in the first place. Interestingly, the "match" dummy variable noted above suggests that agencies matching presidential ideology are better represented in the ranks of the *unissued* order pool. Is this because agencies more distant from the president decline even to offer EOs they think will spur rejection? The inexact nature of the measure prevents a clear answer, but this is another direction for future research.

37. See Neustadt's chapter titled "Hazards of Transition" in the 1990 edition of *Presidential Power*.

38. See, e.g., Krause and O'Connell, "Experiential Learning," for an argument that presidents increasingly select their appointees based on competence rather than loyalty over time. One could argue, though, that this dynamic was inverted during the Trump administration.

39. A marker for the year of a presidential administration is also used in some of the order issuance literature but on very different theoretical grounds. In this view presidents have a larger legislative agenda at the start of their term and thus issue more orders linked to that legislation; this decreases over time. See, e.g., Deering and Maltzman, "Politics of Executive Orders."

40. See Rudalevige, *Managing the President's Program*, 96, 111.

41. Warber, *Executive Orders and the Modern Presidency*, chap. 3; Mayer, *Stroke of a Pen*, 81. See also Bryan W. Marshall and Richard Pacelle Jr., "Revisiting the Two Presidencies: The Strategic Use of Executive Orders," *American Politics Research* 33, no. 1 (2005): 81–105, which splits the dependent variable to distinguish between domestic and foreign policy EOs.

42. George W. Bush and Obama defense secretary Robert Gates, quoted at a January 29, 2014, forum held at the Ronald Reagan Presidential Library. See https://www.reaganfoundation .org/programs-events/webcasts-and-podcasts/podcasts/a-reagan-forum/a-reagan-forum -robert-gates/.

43. Warber, *Executive Orders and the Modern Presidency*, 77. Mayer's coding finds that foreign and military affairs have become a larger percentage of all orders issued over time, though their numbers have not changed much in absolute terms. *Stroke of a Pen*, 81–82.

44. Mayer's sample totaled 11.3 percent orders coded as "foreign affairs," 11.9 percent coded as "defense and military policy," and 7.1 percent coded as "war and emergency powers." This totals 30.3 percent, slightly higher than the 25.6 percent of my sample coded as partly or entirely foreign-policy related. But "emergency powers" may include domestic matters, such as presidents' use of EOs to call up troops to protect civil rights or quell urban riots.

45. See especially Krause and Cohen, "Presidential Use of Executive Orders"; Krause and Cohen, "Opportunity, Constraints, and the Development of the Institutional Presidency."

46. Many thanks to Prof. Jeffrey Cohen for providing these data, which were updated by the author.

47. Mayer, *Stroke of a Pen*, 88–89; Howell, *Power without Persuasion*, 85–86.

48. Different versions of these variables are utilized by Deering and Maltzman, "Politics of Executive Orders"; by Mayer, *Stroke of a Pen*; and by Warber, *Executive Orders and the Modern Presidency*.

49. However, as chapter 6 details, executive orders on average provide far from immediate gratification, and wholly decentralized orders do not in fact take longer to issue than their centralized counterparts. Empirically, mixed processes take the longest.

50. See Krause and Cohen, "Presidential Use of Executive Orders," 463–64, for an explication of both hypotheses and cites to relevant literature in both directions. It should be noted that empirical research linking presidential approval to legislative success has rarely shown a powerful, linear impact—and at least in Krause and Cohen's work, approval had no significant connection to the number of EOs issued annually. Deering and Maltzman, however, found that increased presidential approval had a statistically significant negative effect on the number of orders issued. See "Politics of Executive Orders," 778. Christenson and Kriner find the opposite: see "Does Public Opinion Constrain Presidential Unilateralism?"

51. See Christenson and Kriner, *Myth*; Andrew Reeves and Jon C. Rogowski, "The Public Cost of Unilateral Action," *American Journal of Political Science* 62 (2018): 424–40.

52. However, running the same specifications using OLS gives quite similar results.

53. Richard Williams, "Understanding and Interpreting Generalized Ordered Logit Models," *Journal of Mathematical Sociology* 40 (2016): 7–20.

54. The "omodel" function in Stata 14 was used for diagnosis of the parallel regression assumption. Other analysis here was drawn from the generalized ordered logit estimation ("Gologit2") package developed by Richard Williams. Gologit2's autofit function isolated the variables likely to violate the parallel regression assumption.

55. Substitution of the president's distance from Congress measured by DW-Nominate scores tracks both results: it is positive, suggesting that as distance rises, so does centralization, but not significant (see Table A5.2, column (C)). If the IRT measure of significance is used, the DW-Nominate distance has a stronger effect but only at $p < .08$.

56. Note that while the distance coefficient is positive (more distance leads to centralization), the dummy variable coefficient is negative: an agency "matched" to a president's ideology is associated with additional decentralization.

57. This finding is true for both the raw and logged word count. When the competence variable is removed, as in Table 5.1, column (D), the raw word count is negative and on the fringes of statistical significance in its own right. This is not visible from the results reported in Table 5.1, given the tiny coefficient linked to individual words in a given order, but the significance of the variable moves from $p < .36$ or so to $p < .109$.

58. See Table A5.3. But even here it is again significant only on the fringes of conventional measures ($p < .108$), at least using a two-tailed test: given the unidirectional hypothesis associated with the measure one might justify a one-tailed test.

59. The results presented in Table 5.2 were calculated in Stata 14 using the Clarify utility written by Michael Tomz, Jason Wittenberg, and Gary King. See King, Tomz, and Wittenberg, "Making the Most of Statistical Analyses: Improving Interpretation and Presentation," *American Journal of Political Science* 44 (April 2000): 347–61.

60. Krasner, "Are Bureaucracies Important?" 168.

Chapter 6. A Brief History of Time (to Issuance)

1. Robert G. Damus to the Director and Deputy Director, "Information: Executive Order Log," August 15, 1989, NARA, RG 51, Entry 139, *Director's Office Files 1989–90*, Box 9, [General Counsel, Feb.–Sept. 1989].

2. Ibid.

3. EO 12699 (January 5, 1990).

4. As Obama declared on October 24, 2011, "We can't wait for an increasingly dysfunctional Congress to do its job. Where they won't act, I will." The actions spurred by this initiative are archived at https://obamawhitehouse.archives.gov/economy/jobs/we-cant-wait.

5. Savage, *Power Wars*, 331; for some of the arguments that delayed issuance, see pp. 133–36. See also EO 13492 (January 22, 2009); EO 13567 (March 7, 2011).

6. EO 13823 (January 30, 2018). Spicer (and EOP emails disproving his contention) quoted in Mark Mazzetti and Charlie Savage, "Leaked Draft of Executive Order Could Revive C.I.A. Prisons," *New York Times*, January 25, 2017, https://www.nytimes.com/2017/01/25/us/politics/executive-order-leaked-draft-national-security-trump-administration.html.

7. Charlie Savage and Adam Goldman, "Trump Officials Renew Effort to Expand Use of Prison at Guantánamo," *New York Times*, August 18, 2017, https://www.nytimes.com/2017/08/18/us/politics/trump-guantanamo-executive-order.html.

8. The Area Redevelopment Act was P.L. 87–27 (May 1, 1961). All documents cited in this case can be found in NARA, RG 51, *Executive Orders and Proclamations, January 20, 1961–January 19, 1965 (Series 61.4)*, Box 12, [EO 11122, Establishing a Rural Development Committee/R4–7/63.1].

9. Recall Donald Trump's tweet of June 5, 2017, complaining that "the Justice Dept. should have stayed with the original Travel Ban, not the watered down, politically correct version they submitted to [the Supreme Court]."

10. Interview by the author, September 2, 2016.

11. Interview by the author, September 23, 2016.

12. Weekends and holidays are included in the count, given OMB's notoriously strict work ethic and expectations for agency turnaround. As one staffer told me, "There's no COB [close of business] at the OMB!" Interview by the author, April 11, 2019.

13. Jeffrey L. Pressman and Aaron Wildavsky, *Implementation*, 3rd ed. (Berkeley: University of California Press, 1984), 118–19.

14. Note that the two outlying values of over 1,000 days are deleted from Figure 6.1 but solely to make the plot more readable; including or removing them has no substantive effect on the linear trend.

15. The employee count has a positive coefficient, but at $p < .45$. The bivariate relationship of EOP staff size to time of issuance is actually negative, though consistent data on this measure begin only in 1950.

16. This is shorthand, of course, for "consideration managed by staff in the Executive Office of the President, especially those in OMB, via the central clearance process." And, as noted above, it excludes whatever pre-proposal negotiations may have taken place between an agency and OMB or OLC, or for that matter between a Cabinet secretary and the president.

17. EO 12968 (August 2, 1995).

18. EO 9844 (April 28, 1947), which was apparently pulled together in four days. See Mr. Abbott to Mr. Rusk, May 7, 1947; Byrnes, "Meeting with Dean Rusk," memo to the file of April 25, 1947, both in NARA, RG 59, *Department of State, Bureau of UN Affairs, Subject File 1941–51*, Box 25, [Legislative, Executive Orders, etc.].

19. EO 11111 (June 11, 1963); see Tom Wicker, "Alabama Admits Negro Students; Wallace Bows to Federal Force," *New York Times*, June 12, 1963, A1.

20. EO 12391 (November 4, 1982). Quotes in Mike Horowitz to Richard Darman, Craig Fuller, and Missy Hodapp, "Weekly Status Report on Executive Orders," June 4, 1982, RRL, WHORM Subject Files, FE 003, Box 7, [FE 003 (070000–089999)], #083983 (entry titled "Partial Suspension of Federal Service Labor-Management Relations").

21. EO 13925 (May 28, 2020); for details of early agency feedback on a draft of the order, see Brian Fung, "Federal Officials Raise Concerns about White House Plan to Police Alleged Social Media Censorship," *CNN.com*, August 22, 2019, https://www.cnn.com/2019/08/22/tech/ftc-fcc-trump-social-media/index.html.

22. EO 12953 (February 27, 1995). On the latter, see Jennifer O'Connor to Jeremy Ben-Ami, Bruce Reed, Rahm Emanuel, and Joel Klein, February 22, 1995, WJCL, WHSOF: Bruce Reed,

Subject File Series, Box 104, [Child Support—Executive Order], available at https://clinton .presidentiallibraries.us/items/show/31239.

23. See OMB to Justice, January 13, 1983, NARA, RG 51, *Records of the Office of General Counsel—Executive Order and Proclamation Files—1983*, Box 2, [EO 12401].

24. Interview by the author, September 23, 2016.

25. Barack Obama, "Address before a Joint Session of the Congress on the State of the Union," January 24, 2012, https://www.presidency.ucsb.edu/node/299426 and EO 13604 (March 22, 2012). See also a similar State of the Union trope on January 28, 2014, when his promised EO (regarding a "fair" minimum wage for federal contract employees) would emerge "in the coming weeks." EO 13658 was issued on February 12.

26. See Warber, "Public Outreach." Many thanks to Prof. Warber for providing his data.

27. Thrower, "To Revoke or Not Revoke?" Many thanks to Prof. Thrower for providing her data.

28. $N = 515$. If this calculation excludes the two outliers with times to issuance of over 1,000 days (one of the outliers is in each category), the average formulation duration of the EOs mentioned in the *PPP* is shorter than those that are not, at 62 days versus 74 days. Further, EOs linked to specific external constituencies, as in Warber's "Public Outreach" data, actually take longer on average to issue (89 days, versus 73 for others). But neither of these differences is statistically significant.

29. Larry Levinson to John Steadman, memo of March 16, 1967, and attached material, including n.a., "Executive Orders and the Draft," March 13, 1967, LBJL, WHCF: EX FE 6, Box 8, [FE 6 10/17/66–12/18/67].

30. Thrower, "To Revoke or Not Revoke?"; Warber, Ouyang, and Waterman, "Landmark Executive Orders." Many thanks to Prof. Ouyang for providing these data.

31. $p < .0001$. Available data do not completely overlap with my sample, so n using Ouyang's raw or logged count is 462. As noted in chapter 3, the tendency of the Trump administration to add lengthy self-promotional "policy" sections to its EOs may make this measure less useful over time.

32. Interview by the author, September 23, 2016..

33. For what it's worth, significant orders take on average a day and a half longer to issue. Using the Chiou-Rothenberg IRT index measuring an array of public sources ($n = 399$), regressed on that duration, gives a similar result.

34. In this last calculation, $p < .0002$. But since both of the lengthiest formulation processes, those over 1,000 days, are coded as significant by this measure, the t-test was rerun without them. The conclusion is substantively the same but much closer to the fringes of statistical significance ($p < .054$ for a two-tailed test).

35. See on this point the more extensive discussion in chapter 5.

36. Often, but not always, this is the agency providing the draft EO to OMB. For instance, in cases where OMB specifically directed a department to draft an executive order, that department would be the lead agency rather than OMB. See chapter 4 for additional details.

37. The calculation for HHS ($n = 17$) excludes an outlier value of 1,646 days. With that included ($n = 18$), the median value for HHS stays the same but the mean goes from 59 to 147 days.

38. In chapter 5, both dimensions of structural insulation developed by Selin were used, but that linked to political review (of budgeting, testimony, etc.) showed little impact. Likewise,

including it here makes no difference to the results. See Selin, "What Makes an Agency Independent?"; Lewis, Richardson, and Rosenthal, "OMB in Its Management Role." Again, thanks to these researchers for providing the data utilized in this analysis.

39. Arnold Miles to Mr. Belcher, "Agricultural Surpluses," August 20, 1954, NARA, RG 51, *Executive Orders and Proclamations, 1953–1961 (Series 53.2E)*, Box 25, [EO 10560].

40. Because of this there is at least some possibility the two confound each other in this model. More generally, variables that predict centralization are used with it as predictors of time to issuance. However, as discussed below, centralization is not theorized to be a linear predictor of increased time to issuance; more crucially, removing it from the analysis does not affect the direction or scope of other variables of interest. (Nor does removing those other variables matter to the impact of centralization proper.)

41. It could also reflect the outcome of substantial negotiations within the EOP itself—the costs of this process might be characterized as falling between that of command and that of direct oversight of interagency negotiation. Again, in this book only anecdotal evidence of intra-EOP strife can be presented. The concluding chapter returns to the point with a plea for future research in this direction.

42. The figure shows median data because of the vast standard deviations around the mean value, especially when the two extreme cases in the sample—one with a time to issuance of 1,021 days and the other at 1,646 days—are included. Mean data both with and without those outliers are provided in the appendix.

43. Melinda Mills, *Introducing Survival and Event History Analysis* (Los Angeles: Sage, 2011), 1; see also Janet M. Box-Steffensmeier and Bradford S. Jones, *Event History Modeling* (New York: Cambridge University Press, 2004).

44. The semi-parametric Cox model is used to estimate covariate effects in duration data, especially when those covariates are not themselves time-dependent (in the absence of hugely detailed data, we must assume this to be the case for the current variables, though this is indeed an assumption); a central feature of the model is that it makes no assumptions about the shape of the hazard function over time, except that it is the same for every observation. Fully parametric models can be utilized when the hazard function is known in advance; in practice, calculations using a generalized gamma distribution with the present data showed little substantive difference.

45. However, it is strongly negative and significant when run instead of or even with the centralization variable in any of the other specifications.

46. Both logged and raw counts were tested and give similar and statistically significant results; since changes in the raw count are literally measured by the single word the marginal difference is small. Thus this hazard rate is drawn from the logged count measure, as substituted in Table 6.3 (A).

47. In Table 6.3, model (D), the crosscut variable is not "starred" but is significant at $p < .08$. It correlates at .41 with the "sig gov" dummy and at .25 with the mixed formulation process dummy. Specifications with the mixed process variable run individually with the crosscut and government significance variables, respectively, are not reported here.

48. Removing the fixed-effects dummies from Table 6.3 (B) itself, by contrast, has no substantial effect on any of the variables tested there.

49. As a potential check on this, I calculated whether "distant" agencies were more likely than their counterparts to propose presumably non-controversial clerk-related or statutorily

prompted orders. In these data, at least, there is no strong evidence for this. One interesting result—and the only one that proved statistically significant—was that agencies "matching" the president on the ideological dummy variable described in chapter 5 *are* more likely to propose EOs prompted by recent statute, EOs that usually result in delegation of authority from that statute to the proposing agency. This could be read to imply that the president's preferred agencies have more confidence he will be willing to delegate authority to them.

50. Recall the benediction of sorts quoted in chapter 3: a long revision process, as the OMB counsel said, supplied text the lead department "can live with," took into account other agency positions, and "is quite proper as a Presidential requirement." F. E. Levi to M. Sherlock, August 24, 1959, NARA, RG 51, *Series 53.2E*, Box 17, [EO 10845—K12–4/59.5].

51. That definition is of course Richard Neustadt's. See *Presidential Power*, ix.

Chapter 7. "Dear John": The Orders That Never Were

1. Arnold Weber to Secretary John Volpe, August 19, 1971, NARA, RG 51, *OMB Office of the Director: Executive Order Files 1977–80*, Box 3, [Airport and Airway Development Act].

2. On the transition, see Michael Wolff, *Fire and Fury* (New York: Henry Holt, 2018), 61; Abigail Hauslohner and Janell Ross, "Trump Administration Circulates More Draft Immigration Restrictions," *Washington Post*, January 31, 2017, https://www.washingtonpost.com/world/national-security/trump-administration-circulates-more-draft-immigration-restrictions-focusing-on-protecting-us-jobs/2017/01/31/38529236-e741–11e6–80c2–30e57e57e05d_story.html?utm_term=.092ceb54119f.

3. Adapted from transcript of Trump speech to rally in Nashville, TN, May 29, 2018, https://factba.se/transcript/donald-trump-speech-maga-rally-nashville-may-29-2018.

4. Press coverage suggested the story was "richly embellished" (for one thing, an EO could hardly encumber a $1 billion expenditure) and noted that "the building dedicated this month was a converted consular office that is to serve as a temporary space until a new embassy, which will ultimately be more costly, can be constructed." See Julie Hirschfeld Davis, "At Rally in Nashville, Trump Links Democrats to MS-13," *New York Times*, May 29, 2018, https://www.nytimes.com/2018/05/29/us/politics/trump-rally-nashville-ms-13.html. Further, when Trump recounted this same story in December 2019 to the Israeli-American Council National Summit, the $1 billion had increased to $2 billion.

5. Author interview with former OMB official, April 11, 2019.

6. R. Hutcheson to R. Lipshutz, January 31, 1977, enclosing the president's handwritten annotation on a copy of S. 507 of 1977, NARA, RG 51, *Executive Order Files 1977–80*, Box 3, [Use of Chauffeur Driven Limousines].

7. For example, unissued orders were sometimes discovered not in OMB's executive order files but in the general counsel's own subject files. But those files are a separate series (meaning separate archival "pulls"); they are voluminous (especially since they frequently deal with legal disputes and contain a vast array of supporting material); and they are generally only vaguely described in archival finding aids. Even with better finding aids, subject-matter filing assumes the researcher knows that an order was drafted on a particular topic and thus under what subject to search for it. Unless another archival document or news coverage makes clear that was the case, that is rare. There is certainly room for additional exploration here.

8. Interview by the author, September 2, 2016.

9. The percentage of proposed EOs rejected out of hand is not uniform by counsel and administration. A former OMB general counsel said some counsels were "executive order android[s]" and simply sent out nearly all orders for clearance.

10. This figure is only reduced to 342.5 (362.3 s.d.) without the two highest (but not dramatically outlying) observations of over 2,500 days.

11. OEO has generally been considered an operating agency, despite its organizational home within the EOP. OEP, which succeeded a series of civil defense organizations in the EOP, e.g., the Office of Civil and Defense Mobilization, was the Office of Emergency Planning from 1961 to 1968, then the Office of Emergency Preparedness from 1968 to 1973, when it became part of the Federal Emergency Management Agency (FEMA). OEO's two unissued orders are in the "other" category in Table 7.4 while OEP's seven are included with FEMA's.

12. Melinda Mills, *Introducing Survival and Event History Analysis* (Los Angeles: Sage, 2011), chap. 10.

13. Mario Cleves, William W. Gould, and Yulia V. Marchenko, *An Introduction to Survival Analysis Using Stata*, rev. 3rd ed. (College Station, TX: Stata Press, 2016), 382, and see chap. 17.

14. Cautiously, since again, the issued orders represent a random sample while the unissued orders cannot be assumed to be completely representative of their population.

15. See chapters 5 and 6 for detailed discussion and citations; recall that these measures are based on 2007 and 2014 surveys of agency personnel.

16. A simple measure of divided government shows the same result, though of course flipped—divided government (so, fewer presidential co-partisans) is more likely within the sample of issued orders.

17. Estimating the model while including presidential fixed effects, not reported here, results in only one change of note: the coefficient of the influence variable diminishes, reducing its statistical significance from $p < .01$ to $p < .08$. If included, the year variable is positive and statistically significant, not surprising since so many of its observations are clustered later in the chronological sequence. But it has only a tiny substantive impact (its subhazard ratio is .991).

18. Rudalevige, *Managing the President's Program*, chap. 7.

19. Here, its coefficient is positive but quite unlikely to have been obtained by chance ($p < .57$).

20. A Doonesbury cartoon about loyalty and competence in George W. Bush administration appointees comes to mind: asked whether he would "also be looking for competence," the Bush aide replies, "not even the appearance of competence." The punchline to the punchline is "So much for [Condoleezza] Rice." See https://www.gocomics.com/doonesbury/2005/01/01.

21. Using the alternate dimension of agency insulation instead of or in addition to the appointee measure has no effect.

22. However, it does not account for the possibility that different kinds of EOs are issued under conditions of divided and unified government, as posited by Belco and Rottinghaus, *Dual Executive*.

23. The cover sheet is in NARA, RG 51, *Records of the Office of General Counsel—Executive Order and Proclamation Files—1983*, Box 1, [Finding Aid]. The unissued EOs cited were titled, respectively: "Reports on International Organizations"; "Notice to Foreign Governments of U.S. Actions Regulating Hazardous Materials"; and "Transfer of Authority to the Secretary of

State to Make Reimbursements for the Protection of Foreign Missions to International Organizations."

24. There was insufficient information in just over a dozen files to support confident coding on this dimension; such EOs are not included in Table 7.6.

25. Notes in WNRC, *OMB: General Counsel 1959–1993*, Box 30, [Draft: Pres'l Commission on Fire Prevention and Control].

26. Feldman to Luther Hodges, May 10, 1963, in JFKL, WHCF: Subject File, Box 100, [FE 6: Executive Orders: Executive: 1/1/63–6/30/63].

27. Don Furtado to Harry McPherson, "Placement of Federal Facilities," April 3, 1968; McPherson to the President, August 30, 1968 (Friday—3:00 p.m.) and LBJ note thereon; Jim Gaither to Matt Nimetz, April 26, 1968; McPherson to the BoB Director, January 17, 1969; Arthur Focke to the File, "Proposed Executive Order Entitled 'Location of Federal Facilities,'" January 21, 1969; and other attached materials, all in NARA, RG 51, *Executive Orders and Proclamations, 1965–69 (Series 65.4)*, Box 17, [F5-5/67.1 (Location of Federal Facilities)].

28. A "more appropriate time" seemed to arrive in 1975 after a change of HUD secretaries, but after a brief revival the EO failed to gain traction yet again. See Arthur D. Kallen to Paul O'Neill, "Proposed E.O. on Sites for Federal Facilities," May 8, 1974; C. R. Lane to Anne Armstrong, "Proposed Executive Order," March 27, 1974; Bill Timmons, handwritten to Staff Secretary, March 25, 1974; and other material in WNRC, *OMB: General Counsel 1959–1993*, Box 30, [Draft: Selection of Sites for Federal Facilities (1975)]. Additional documentation is located in the same box but in the folder [Draft: Selection of Sites for Federal Facilities 1972–74]. Recall that BoB (part of the proposed LBJ order) became OMB (part of the proposed Nixon order) in July 1970.

29. Howell, *Power without Persuasion*, chap. 5.

30. P.L. 104–65. Materials in WJCL, White House Staff and Office Files, Office of Speechwriting: Michael Waldman, Box 40, [Lobby Reform and Executive Order], Item 2006–0469-F, available via the Clinton Digital Library at https://clinton.presidentiallibraries.us/items/show /44974.

31. P.L. 93–438. See Ken Cole to Robert Hartmann, "Proposed Executive Order," October 4, 1974; Stan [Ebner] to Jerry Jones, October 10, 1974; Tom to Frank [Zarb], handwritten note of November 1, 1974, all in GFL, WHCF: FG 999, Box 77, [FG 999 10/1/74–10/15/74] and [FG 999 10/16/74–10/17/74].

32. P.L. 95–200. "*Miller v. Robertson*," June 1, 1977; M. Rupert Cutler to Bert Lance, June 10, 1977, both in NARA, RG 51, *OMB Office of the Director: Executive Order Files 1977–80*, Box 3, [To change the boundaries of the Bull Run National Forest].

33. Barefoot Sanders to Joe Califano, October 18, 1968, and handwritten notes of November 25, 1968, in LBJL, WHCF, Box 8, [FE6 6/25/68–].

34. C. E. Wilson to Frederick Lawton, June 14, 1951, and June 19, 1951, NARA, RG 304, Entry A1–274, *Defense Production Administration: Office of Civil and Defense Mobilization: Records Relating to the Defense Production Act of 1950*, Box 4, [1951—Small Business—Misc. correspondence, Comments on Proposed Legislation & Proposed Executive Orders].

35. Morgan, *The President and Civil Rights*; Mayer, *Stroke of a Pen*, 196–200.

36. PHA Commissioner to Robert Weaver, July 31, 1963, NARA, RG 196, Entry A1–61, *Records of the Public Housing Administration: General Legal Opinions Files, 1936–1970*, Box 2, [Equal Opportunity in Housing (Executive Order 11063)—2 of 8].

37. Gardner Dickinson to Richard Ervin, December 3, 1962, NARA, RG 196, Entry A1–61, *Records of the Public Housing Administration: General Legal Opinions Files, 1936–1970*, Box 2, [Equal Opportunity in Housing (Executive Order 11063)—1 of 8].

38. Milton Semer to Bill Moyers, May 3, 1965, LBJL, WHCF: Human Rights (HU), Box 47, [HU2–2/Housing, 11/23/63–11/11/65].

39. CEA Chair to Lee White, "Economic Effects of a Broadened Anti-Discrimination Housing Order," March 27, 1965, LBJL, WHCF: EX FE 6 (11/23/63–), Box 8, [FE6, 1/26/65–10/10/65].

40. Robert Weaver to Jacob Javits, June 26, 1963, NARA, RG 196, Entry A1–61, Box 2, [Equal Opportunity in Housing (Executive Order 11063)—2 of 8].

41. "Confidential Draft: Findings," n.d. [July 1964], NARA, RG 196, Entry A1–61, Box 2, [Equal Opportunity in Housing (Executive Order 11063)—6 of 8 (7/1/64–8/1/64)].

42. Lee White to the President, "Executive Order on Housing and Governor Lawrence's Committee," December 2, 1964, LBJL, WHCF: Human Rights, Box 47, [HU2–2/Housing, 11/23/63–11/11/65].

43. White to President, "Extension of the Executive Order on Housing," May 10, 1965; Humphrey to President, June 9, 1965 (6 p.m.), both in LBJL, WHCF: Human Rights, Box 47, [HU2–2/Housing, 11/23/63–11/11/65].

44. White to Sen. Jacob Javits, September 20, 1965, LBJL, WHCF: Human Rights, Box 47, [HU2–2/Housing, 11/23/63–11/11/65].

45. Draft memo by Norman Schlei, p. 3, transmitted by Nicholas Katzenbach to Joseph Califano, Lee White, and David Lawrence, September 25, 1965, LBJL, WHCF: Human Rights, Box 47, [HU2–2/Housing, 11/23/63–11/11/65].

46. Lawrence to the President, November 10, 1965, emphasis added; Califano to the President, October 28, 1965, both in LBJL, WHCF: Human Rights, Box 47, [HU2–2/Housing, 11/23/63–11/11/65]; see too Mayer, *Stroke of a Pen*, 200–201.

47. Califano to the President, October 28, 1965, and president's notes thereon, dated October 30, LBJL, [FE6 Executive Orders 10/11/65–10/16/66].

48. Califano to the President, November 20, 1965, and attached material, LBJL, [FE6 Executive Orders 10/11/65–10/16/66].

49. White to the President, December 30, 1965, and president's notes thereon, dated December 31, LBJL, WHCF: Confidential File, Box 15, [FE6 Executive Orders].

50. BoB to Califano, "Memorandum from the Vice President on Housing Steps," September 16, 1966, LBJL, WHCF: Human Rights, Box 47, [HU2–2/Housing, 11/12/65–12/9/66].

51. P.L. 90–284, Titles VIII and IX.

52. See, e.g., Ron Kienlen to Paul Fairley, "Rehabilitation Act Interagency Coordinating Council," May 21, 1979, NARA, *OMB Office of the Director, Executive Order Files 1977–80*, Box 3, [Emergency Management Council].

53. Ron Kienlen to Rick Hutcheson, cover note of September 4, 1979, NARA, *OMB Office of the Director, Executive Order Files 1977–80*, Box 3, [Emergency Management Council].

54. The other objection came from the Post Office. See Department of Justice to BoB director, March 5, 1962, and other materials in NARA, RG 51, *Executive Orders and Proclamations, January 20, 1961–January 19, 1965 (Series 61.4)*, Box 17, [Amending Civil Service Rules III, VI, and VII (11/7/61)—EO proposed—F4–9/61.2].

55. The memorandum was issued on March 9, 1981. See John White to Stu Eizenstat, "Proposed Presidential Memorandum on Alcohol and Drug Abuse Programs for Federal Employees," June 23, 1980, NARA, RG 51, Entry UD-WW 63, *Executive Order Files FY81*, Box 3, [Alcohol and Drug Abuse Programs for Federal Employees].

56. Ron Kienlen to Eliot Cutler, "CEQ Proposal for E.O.," "Speed Message" of June 8, 1979; Kenneth Weiner to Ron Kienlen, "Executive Order on Economic Assistance Initiative," June 7, 1979, all in NARA, *OMB Office of the Director, Executive Order Files 1977–80*, Box 3, [Economic Assistance Initiatives].

57. A. Vernon Weaver to James T. McIntyre Jr., August 18, 1980; Dominic Mastrapasqua to Bill Spring, "Proposed Executive Order from the Small Business Administration," August 22, 1980, emphasis in original, both in NARA, RG 51, Entry UD-WW 63, Box 3, [Business Assistance to Veterans].

58. Memorandum for the Record—Summary of Agency Comments, October 30, 1980 (see especially those of VA, Energy, HHS, NASA); Karen Hastie Williams (OFPP) to William Nichols, "Proposed Executive Order," December 5, 1980, both in NARA, RG 51, Entry UD-WW 63, Box 3, [Business Assistance to Veterans].

59. Jeffrey Farrow to Ron Kienlen, "Veterans Business Assistance E.O.," October 24, 1980, NARA, RG 51, Entry UD-WW 63, Box 3, [Business Assistance to Veterans].

60. A. Vernon Weaver to James T. McIntyre Jr., October 22, 1980, NARA, RG 51, Entry UD-WW 63, Box 3, [Business Assistance to Veterans].

61. Ibid.

62. Ronald Kienlen to Jeffrey Farrow, "SBA Proposed E.O.," October 30, 1980, NARA, RG 51, Entry UD-WW 63, Box 3, [Business Assistance to Veterans]. Emphasis in original.

63. Readers of this book are by definition too smart to need referral to *The Tempest*, IV:1:156.

64. In an interesting 1963 letter to a House committee chairman, OLC's Norman Schlei argued that "the type of document that the President uses in exercising his powers and in carrying out his responsibilities under the Constitution and statutes of the United States in a particular situation may be determined by the conditions extant and the impact that the President wishes to have." In an earlier draft of the letter, deleted from the version finally sent, Schlei gave examples: "the President might wish to issue a formal proclamation in order to galvanize national and world opinion," referring to the Cuban Missile Crisis, "or, by contrast, he might deem it advisable to minimize orders that might accentuate the existing tension in which case he might use a letter or memorandum or might even present them orally." In any case, he went on, "the need for flexible presidential authority in this regard is evident. . . . Efforts to restrict the President's choice of documents in carrying out his powers as Chief Executive could entail significant questions involving the doctrine of constitutional separation of powers." Norman Schlei to Rep. William Dawson, draft letter of April 18, 1963, and letter of November 8, 1963, JFKL, White House Staff Files: Lee C. White File, Box 12, [Proposed New System for Numbering Executive Orders].

65. EO 13788 (April 18, 2017); EO 13879 (July 10, 2019).

66. Interview by the author, September 23, 2016.

67. Interview by the author, September 2, 2016.

68. Former OMB staffer, interview by the author, April 25, 2019.

69. Frank Hodsoll to Ron Kienlen, October 26, 1982; Bernard Martin, handwritten comments on Jan Anderson to Barry White et al., "LVE Recommendation on the Draft Order on Federal Design Excellence," November 23, 1982; Jan Anderson to Mike Horowitz, "Proposed Executive Order on Federal Design Excellence," November 23, 1982, all in WNRC, *OMB: General Counsel 1959–1993*, Box 30, [Draft: Federal Design Excellence (1982)]; Phoebe Morse to Jim Miller, "Executive Orders," May 6, 1981, RRL, WHORM Subject Files, FE (Federal Government), Box 8, [FE003 (295000–332570)], item 295725.

70. Mike Horowitz to Joe Wright, "Proposed Executive Order Entitled 'Federal Design Excellence,'" November 30, 1982, WNRC, *OMB: General Counsel 1959–1993*, Box 30, [Draft: Federal Design Excellence (1982)].

71. Harold Seidman to Director, November 22, 1966, NARA, RG 51, *Series 65.4*, Box 19, [T-3–3/67.1].

72. Rogers Morton to William Saxbe, January 8, 1975; Ron Kienlen to the file, April 25, 1975, both in WNRC, *OMB: General Counsel 1959–1993*, Box 34, [EO: Occupational Health and Safety in Mines].

73. Joe Califano to Mrs. Johnson, no title, September 30, 1968, LBJL, WHCF EX FE 6 (11/23/63–), Box 8, [FE6 Executive Orders 6/25/68–]; William Nichols to Sen. John Warner, December 4, 1979, NARA, *OMB Office of the Director, Executive Order Files 1977–80*, Box 3, [Participation in Inaugural Parades].

74. F. E. Levi, Memorandum for E.O. Records of February 23, 1968; Arthur Focke to Dean Rusk, February 13, 1967 and attached material, all in NARA, RG 51, *Series 65.4*, Box 18, [K1–9/67.1—Amending EO 10973 relating to Foreign Assistance]; F. E. Levi to Arthur Focke, "Delegability of Presidential Function," October 24, 1966, NARA, RG 51, *Series 65.4*, Box 18, [K4–3/66.2—Amending EO 10973 relating to Foreign Assistance].

75. See, among other material, Chris Aughney to Ron Kienlen, "Proposed Executive Order Entitled 'Providing for Federal Personnel Management,'" July 3, 1980; Jim Tozzi to Ronald Kienlen, "Proposed Executive Order Entitled 'Providing for Federal Personnel Management,'" July 9, 1980; Hilda Schreiber to Kienlen, "OPM Draft Order on Civil Service," July 25, 1980; Alan K. Campbell to Kienlen, November 25, 1980; Kienlen to Joseph Howe, November 28, 1980; Jule M. Sugarman to Kienlen, December 10, 1980, all in NARA, RG 51, Entry UD-WW 63, Box 3, [Federal Personnel Management (revising EO 9830)].

76. Barbara Kahlow to Mac Reed, fax cover sheets, December 20, 1991, January 8, 1992; Bob Damus to Frank Hodsoll, "Alcohol Executive Order," January 14, 1992; Kahlow to Hodsoll and Janet Hale, "Alcohol Testing," March 31, 1992, all in NARA, Entry UD-UP 66, *General Counsel Subject Files: Records of the Office of the General Counsel: Assistant Counsel Mac Reed, 1989–92*, Box 1, [Alcohol Free Workplace Executive Order].

77. EO 11799 (August 17, 1974), discussed in chapter 3.

78. See, e.g., William Nichols to Distribution, "Proposed Executive Order Entitled 'Designation of Certain Officers to Act as Secretary of State,'" June 14, 1977, WNRC, *OMB: General Counsel 1959–1993*, Box 18, [EO Draft 1976: Designation of Certain Officers to Act as Secretary of State]; David Stockman, *Memorandum to Heads of Executive Departments and Establishments: Proposed Executive Orders and Proclamations* (M-81–8), March 9, 1981, in author's possession.

79. "Executive Orders Not Issued in 1981," NARA, RG 51, Entry UD-WW 63, Box 1, [Finding Aid].

80. William Nichols to Don Crabill and Harrison Wellford, December 3, 1980, NARA, RG 51, Entry UD-WW 63, Box 3, [Authority of the Secretary of the Interior with Respect to the Territories of the United States].

81. Ronald A. Kienlen, memorandum for the record of April 2, 1981, and attached material, NARA, RG 51, Entry UD-WW 63, Box 3, [Audit of unvouchered expenditures]; Kienlen, memorandum of call, November 14, 1980, WNRC, *OMB: General Counsel 1959-1993*, Box 17, [CORR (1981) Audit of Unvouchered Expenditures].

82. See, among others, the USPS, EPA, and Justice letters to OMB in NARA, *Executive Order Files FY81*, Entry UD-WW 63, Box 3, [Providing for the Increased Representation of the Interests of Small Business Concerns].

83. Arthur Focke to Philip Hughes, February 20, 1969, NARA, RG 51, *Series 65.4*, Box 17, [F5-4/68.1 (Providing for the Consolidation of Existing Boards of Contract Appeals)].

84. Stan Ebner to Karl Bakke, September 13, 1974, NARA, RG 51, *Executive Order Files 1977-80*, Box 3, [Protection of Foreign Visitors and Dignitaries].

85. Memorandum to the file, January 29, 1969, NARA, RG 51, *Series 65.4*, Box 18, [R7-2/66.1 Federal International Education and Cultural Programs].

86. N.a., handwritten notes of May 2, 1975, NARA, RG 59, *Background and History Records Relating to EO 10422 on UN Personnel Affairs, 1946-1986* (Entry A1-1492), Box 24, [EO 10422—General and Revision, Jan./July 1975]; Rowan Wakefield to Phil [Talbot], April 5, 1962, NARA, RG 59, *State Department: Bureau of Educational and Cultural Affairs: Office of the Assistant Secretary, Subject Files 1961-62* (Entry A1-5072), Box 3, [Executive Orders]. As Schattschneider wrote in 1960's *Semi-Sovereign People*, "The most important strategy of politics is concerned with the scope of conflict.... Watch the crowd."

87. Robert B. Zoellick to John Carley, January 30, 1987, RRL, WHORM Subject Files, FE 003 (Executive Orders), Box 8, [FE003 (470302)], item #470302.

88. Civil Service Commission letters, July 16, 1963, June 25, 1964; C. Spencer Platt to Mr. Focke, "Withdrawal of CSC Proposed Order," June 25, 1964, all in NARA, RG 51, *Series 61.4*, Box 17, [Retention and restoration rights of federal employees disabled on the job, F4-36/63.2]. As a side note, this topic was the focal point of one of the least exciting executive orders in presidential history, EO 11018 (April 27, 1962): "Increasing from Three to Four the Number of Vice Chairmen of the President's Committee on Employment of the Handicapped."

89. Fred E. Levi, "Procurement of Helium," memo "for E.O. records" of April 12, 1971, and James Currie to Dwight Ink, "Procurement of Helium," December 18, 1970, both in WNRC, *OMB: General Counsel 1959-1993*, Box 34, [EO: Helium].

90. Arlene Holen to Mac Reed, "Community Service Executive Order," June 5, 1989, WNRC, *OMB: General Counsel 1959-1993*, Box 30, [Draft: Encouraging Federal Officers and Employees to Engage in Community Service (1989)].

91. OMB Executive Order Tracking Sheet, May 26, 1989, and attached material, WNRC, *OMB: General Counsel 1959-1993*, Box 30, [Draft: Encouraging Federal Officers and Employees to Engage in Community Service (1989)].

92. Nelson Lund to Mac Reed, "Proposed Executive Order Entitled 'Encouraging Federal Officers and Employees to Engage in Community Service,'" June 12, 1989; Holen to Reed, "Community Service Executive Order," June 5, 1989, both in WNRC, *OMB: General Counsel*

1959–1993, Box 30, [Draft: Encouraging Federal Officers and Employees to Engage in Community Service (1989)].

93. Robert Bergland to James T. McIntyre Jr., January 9, 1981, NARA, RG 51, Entry UD-WW 63, Box 3, [Trade Agreements Act of 1979].

94. Ibid.; John Block to David Stockman, February 25, 1981, NARA, RG 51, Entry UD-WW 63, Box 3, [Trade Agreements Act of 1979].

95. Caspar Weinberger to James C. Miller III, November 10, 1986; Malcolm Baldridge to Miller, letter of September 30, 1986; n.a., handwritten notes of December 3, 1986, all in NARA, RG 51, Entry UD-UP 65, *OMB Records of the Office of General Counsel*, Box 2, [Export Administration Act Executive Order 1986].

96. Farris Bryant to Charles Schultze, September 20, 1966, NARA, RG 51, *Series 65.4*, Box 18, [M1–10/66.1—Assigning Certain Emergency Preparedness Functions for Construction to the Secretary of Defense].

97. Material from this case, including Julius Becton Jr. to James C. Miller III, March 31, 1988; Mac Reed to Distribution, clearance letter of October 21, 1988, and attached material; and Jack Kress to Alan Raul, letter of November 18, 1988, is located in NARA, RG 51, Entry UD-UP 66, Box 3, [National Security Resources Preparedness 1989–90]. Emphasis in original.

98. See, among other materials, George Watson to Mac Reed, "Comments on Revised Executive Order 10480," February 24, 1989; James M. Brown Jr. to Mac Reed, fax of December 6, 1989, both in NARA, RG 51, Entry UD-UP 66, Box 3, [National Security Resources Preparedness 1989–90].

99. Mac Reed to Antonio Lopez, January 31, 1990, NARA, RG 51, Entry UD-UP 66, Box 3, [National Security Resources Preparedness 1989–90]. Note that in September 1991 George H. W. Bush did issue EO 12773, which amended EO 10480, but this dealt only with the Defense Department and the General Services Administration separately from the draft empowering FEMA.

100. EO 325-A (May 18, 1905).

101. Arthur Focke to William Carey, "Congressional Inquiry—Executive Order re Prison Labor," November 22, 1961, NARA, RG 51, *Series 61.4*, Box 17, [Restrictions on the use of convict labor—EO proposed—F5–13/61.1 (F3–17/53.1)].

102. Ibid.

103. Myer Feldman to Arthur Goldberg, November 15, 1961; Feldman to Clem Miller, January 8, 1962, and other material, all in JFKL, White House Central Files: Subject File, Box 100, [FE 6: Executive Orders: Executive: 10/1/61–1/30/62]. See also [FE 6: Executive Orders: Executive: 5/1/61–9/30/61] in the same box.

104. Focke, "Congressional Inquiry—Executive Order re Prison Labor"; Nicholas Katzenbach to Focke, February 6, 1962, and attached letter to members of Congress of February 2, 1962, NARA, RG 51, *Series 61.4*, Box 17, [Restrictions on the use of convict labor—EO proposed—F5–13/61.1 (F3–17/53.1)].

105. Sen. Clinton Anderson to Pres. Kennedy, April 22, 1961; Abraham Ribicoff to David Bell, May 5, 1961, both in NARA, RG 51, *Series 61.4*, Box 17, [P2–6/61.1—(EO Proposed)].

106. Carl H. Schwartz Jr. to chiefs of Bureau offices and divisions, "Draft of an Executive Order defining certain responsibilities with respect to natural resources and public works," April 3, 1961; Harold Seidman and Carl Schwartz to Elmer Staats, "Draft Executive Order on

National Resources and Public Works," April 25, 1961, both in NARA, RG 51, *Series 61.4*, Box 17, [P2–6/61.1—(EO Proposed)].

107. E.g., Lawrence O'Brien to Rep. Wayne Aspinall, April 29, 1961; see also O'Brien to Sen. Alan Bible, April 26, 1961, both in JFKL, WHCF: Subject Files, Box 100, [FE 6: Executive Orders: Executive: 1/1/61–4/30/61].

108. David Bell to Sen. Anderson, May 5, 1961, NARA, RG 51, *Series 61.4*, Box 17, [P2–6/61.1—(EO Proposed)].

109. That particular proposed EO was eventually transmuted into a press release. See the materials in NARA, RG 51, *Executive Order Files 1977–80*, Box 3, [Use of Chauffeur Driven Limousines].

110. Except as noted this case is drawn from Ellis, *Development*, 313–14; Mayer, *Stroke of a Pen*, 206–8.

111. Quoted in Nicolas Laham, *The Reagan Presidency and the Politics of Race* (New York: Praeger, 1998), 23.

112. See EO 11246 (September 24, 1965) and EO 11375 (October 13, 1967); Ellis, *Development*, 313–14; Mayer, *Stroke of a Pen*, 203–4.

113. Terry Eastland, *Energy in the Executive* (New York: Free Press, 1992), 355–56.

114. Ellis, *Development*, 317.

115. Mayer, *Stroke of a Pen*, 206.

116. Max Friedersdorf and M. B. Oglesby to Al Kingon, "Developments in Jim Miller's Confirmation," September 26, 1985, RRL, WHORM Subject Files FG006–11, Box 5, [331700–338999], #331782. See also the thick file of communications from the public and officialdom opposing rescission of EO 11246 in WHORM Subject Files FE003, Box 8, [332572–399999].

117. The coded reasons for non-issuance in this category ($n = 56$) were: bureaucratic dissent (25%), White House implicit veto (23.2%), alternate release (23.2%), OMB/legal objection (16.1%), other EO (8.9%), legislation (1.8%), end of term (1.8%).

118. Interview by the author, September 2, 2016.

Chapter 8. Incorrigibly Plural: Concluding Thoughts and Next Steps

1. All documents cited here are drawn from NARA, RG 51, *Directors, Deputy Directors and Assistant Directors Office Files, 1961–68 (Series 61.1b)*, Box 1, [BoB-OMO Division]; *Executive Orders and Proclamations, January 20, 1961–January 19, 1965 (Series 61.4)*, Box 8, [EO 11045]; JFKL, WHCF: Subject Files, Box 100, [FE 6: Executive Orders: Executive: 8/21/62–12/31/62].

2. Quoted in Laurence E. Lynn Jr., *Managing the Public's Business: The Job of the Government Executive* (New York: Basic Books, 1981), 177.

3. Derived from the calculation of weighted and unweighted frequencies of decentralized EOs in Tables 4.2a and 4.2b.

4. Morgan, *The President and Civil Rights*, 2.

5. Meena Bose, *Shaping and Signaling Presidential Policy: The National Security Decision Making of Eisenhower and Kennedy* (College Station: Texas A&M Press, 1998), 12.

6. Williamson, *Economic Institutions of Capitalism*, 35, 56, 70.

7. Jacob Lew, comments at Hofstra University conference on executive policymaking, April 11, 2019.

8. John White to Charles W. Duncan Jr., February 1, 1979, NARA, *OMB Office of the Director: Executive Order Files 1977–80*, Box 3, [Veterans' Preference Laws].

9. Recall George W. Bush White House counsel Fred Fielding's comment quoted in chapter 2.

10. Roger W. Jones, interview of July 13, 1967, Eisenhower Administration Project, Oral History Research Office, Columbia University, 52.

11. Rossiter, *American Presidency*, 40.

12. See, e.g., Cooper, *By Order of the President*, or the substantial literature on presidential signing statements.

13. Clinton interview with Charles Gibson, "Philanthropy and the Presidency," ABC News, September 26, 2007, https://abcnews.go.com/amp/WN/story?id=3656216&page=1.

14. Michael Fitzpatrick to Sally Katzen, "SBREFA Requirements re Reagan Era Executive Orders," n.d. [July 1996], WJCL, Kagan Emails Received, Box 1, Folder 6, https://clinton.presidentiallibraries.us/items/show/24798.

15. Cynthia Rice to Michael Kharfen, June 22, 1998, WHSOF: DPC: Cynthia Rice: Subject Files, Box 6, [Child Support-Executive Orders]. See https://clinton.presidentiallibraries.us/items/show/21653. See EO 13019 (September 28, 1996); the guidelines were issued in an April 26, 1999, memo of Attorney General Janet Reno to the Cabinet.

16. See Crouch, Rozell, and Sollenberger, *The Unitary Executive Theory*, chap. 2, for these and additional examples.

17. See "Larry" [Levinson] to Joe [Califano], September 29, 1965; Moyers handwritten note on John Schnittker to Moyers et al., October 15, 1965, both in LBJL, WHCF: EX FE6, Box 8, [FE6 Executive Orders 1/26/65–10/10/65] and [FE6 Executive Orders 10/11/65–10/16/66], respectively.

18. Dawes, Circular 21, issued August 16, 1921, NARA, RG 51, Entry 7A, *Records of the Bureau of the Budget: General Subject File (Series 21.1)*, Box 95, [Executive Orders—General].

19. Allison, *Essence of Decision*, 172–73.

20. Barry Clendenin, personal communication with the author, December 21, 2014. This observation is backed up by a research project along these lines from over forty years ago, which found surprisingly little agency compliance (well over half of directives were "ignored"). However, given the research design and limited data available it is hard to assess those findings. See Raymond L. Chambers, "The Executive Power: A Preliminary Study of the Concept and of the Efficacy of Presidential Directives," *Presidential Studies Quarterly* 7 (Winter 1977): 31.

21. Neustadt, *Presidential Power*, 4, 10; emphasis added. However, keep in mind that Howell, at least, clearly states that he is *not* using Neustadt's definition of power. See *Power without Persuasion*, xiv.

22. Neighbors, "Presidential Legislation by Executive Order," 107.

23. Michelle Belco, "Presidents Acting Alone in the First 100 Days: Using Command and Persuasion to Get What They Want" (paper presented at the Annual Meeting of the Southern Political Science Association, Austin, TX, 2019); "Implementing the Orders of the First 100 Days" (paper presented at the Annual Meeting of the American Political Science Association, Washington, DC, 2019).

24. Joshua B. Kennedy, "'Do This! Do That!' and Nothing Will Happen: Executive Orders and Bureaucratic Responsiveness," *American Politics Research* 43, no. 1 (2015): 59–82; Kennedy, "The Limits of Presidential Influence: Two Environmental Directives and What They Mean for Executive Power," *Journal of Policy History* 30 (January 2018): 1–24. See also Alex Acs, "Presidential Directives in a Resistant Bureaucracy," *Journal of Public Policy* 40 (2020), doi.org/10.1017 /S0143814X20000264.

25. Thrower, "To Revoke or Not Revoke?"

26. The regression used here includes some basic political and temporal controls, but the substantive impact and statistical significance of the "time to issuance" variable seem sensitive to the specification used. The relationship is tentative, then, but the potential linkage of pre-issuance bargaining to "quality" is well worth exploring.

27. Robert A. Dahl, "The Concept of Power," *Behavioral Science* 2, no. 3 (1957): 202–3.

28. Author interview with then current, now former, OMB staffer, April 25, 2019.

29. Theodore Olson to Edward Schmults, September 7, 1983, RRL, WHORM Subject Files, FE 003 (Executive Orders), Box 8, [FE003 (170000–294999)], #179187.

30. Kennedy, "The Limits of Presidential Influence," 17, 5, 8.

31. Kennedy, "'Do This!'" 77.

32. See, e.g., Andrew Rudalevige, "Government in a Box: Challenges of Policy Implementation in the American System," in *Carrots, Sticks, and the Bully Pulpit*, ed. Frederick M. Hess and Andrew P. Kelly (Cambridge, MA: Harvard Education Press, 2011).

33. R. S. Moore to Fred Levi, "Meeting between Mr. Belcher and Mr. Francis on Executive Order implementing S. 2475," July 7, 1954, and attached material, NARA, RG 51, *Executive Orders and Proclamations, 1953–1961 (Series 53.2E)*, Box 25, [EO 10560].

34. E.g., Eric Patashnik, *Reforms at Risk: What Happens after Major Policy Changes Are Enacted* (Princeton: Princeton University Press, 2008); Jeffrey Jenkins and Eric Patashnik, eds., *Living Legislation: Durability, Change, and the Politics of American Lawmaking* (Chicago: University of Chicago Press, 2012). For an important earlier take on a related topic, see Moe, "The Politics of Bureaucratic Structure."

35. See also Ian R. Turner, "Policy Durability, Agency Capacity, and Executive Unilateralism," *Presidential Studies Quarterly* 50 (March 2020): 40–62. Turner argues that since executive orders are less durable than legislation, agencies have less incentive to invest in implementing them effectively. Thus, as agency capacity rises the more attractive legislating should be vis-à-vis executive action.

36. April 27, 1971, Tape 251–17, Miller Center, University of Virginia. The snippet noted here starts 1:51:40 into the conversation, which was recorded from 2:25 to 4:40 p.m. in the Old Executive Office Building.

37. The "we" in my transcription refers to the Interior department, but the tape is unclear and the word used may be "he," with Morton referring to Interior Undersecretary William Pecora, who was also in the room. White House aides John Whitaker and John Ehrlichman were present too.

38. The EO flowed from the recommendations of an Advisory Committee on Predator Control jointly appointed by CEQ and the Interior Department. The hope was to better target the individual predators causing damage rather than indiscriminately eliminating coyote populations. For a useful summary, see "Background" in Jim Cannon, "Meeting on Coyote Predation,

Tuesday, April 29, 1975," GFL, WHCF: Subject File NR2, Box 2, [NR 2 Fish & Wildlife 4/1/75–6/30/75].

39. John Campbell to Dick Fairbanks, handwritten note of February 7, 1972, emphasis in original. See also Sec. Earl Butz to George Shultz, February 2, 1972; James Bradley to Attorney General John Mitchell, February 7, 1972, all in RNL, WHCF: Subject File NR 2, Box 3, [EX NR 2 Fish-Wildlife (3 of 7)].

40. See A. B. Gilbert to Omar Burleson, February 24, 1972, and other materials in RNL, WHCF: Subject File NR 2, Box 3, [EX NR 2 Fish-Wildlife (3 of 7)].

41. "MAA" to Michael B. Smith, handwritten note of March 28, 1972, RNL, WHCF: Subject File NR 2, Box 3, [EX NR 2 Fish-Wildlife (3 of 7)].

42. The Hansen story is quoted from Michael J. Horowitz's retelling of it to Edwin Meese III, "Revocation of Executive Order 11643," January 20, 1982, WNRC, *OMB General Counsel: Executive Orders and Proclamations: 1959–1993*, Box 2, [EO 12342—Environmental Safeguards on Activities for Animal Damage Control].

43. Donald Dworsky to Frank Zarb, "October 17 Meeting," October 16, 1974, NARA, RG 51, *Records of the Associate Directors, 1970–78*, Box 4, [Energy—General].

44. Doug Costle to Jim Cannon, "Coyote Predation," May 27, 1975, GFL, WHCF: Subject File FE 6 (Executive Orders), Box 2, [FE 6 5/1/75–12/31/75]. On the impact statement question, see also Dudley Chapman to Jim Cannon, "Coyote Paper," July 2, 1975, GFL, Domestic Council: George Humphreys Files, Box 17, [Decision Paper on Proposed Amendment to EO 11643].

45. Jim Cannon, "Meeting to Discuss Predator Control, July 11, 1975, 9:15 am"; Cannon to the President, "Coyote Paper," July 3, 1975; Dudley Chapman to Jim Cannon, "Coyote Paper: Intermediate Options," July 3, 1975, all in GFL, Domestic Council: George Humphreys Files, Box 17, [Decision Paper on Proposed Amendment to EO 11643]. Cannon told Ford that a wide range of White House staffers as well as OMB director Jim Lynn had reviewed the options paper. Interestingly, Interior took somewhat of a back seat in the 1975 debate because the new secretary, Stanley Hathaway, had served as governor of Wyoming when that state had sued the federal government over its predator control restrictions—in his confirmation hearings Hathaway promised to recuse himself from all departmental decisions on the matter. Thus Interior was represented by its solicitor's office in the discussions.

46. The proposed EO would have allowed poison whenever other coyote control methods proved "inadequate" and removed the extant requirement for interagency consultation over poison usage. Russell Train to Jim Cannon, May 14, 1975 [while the letter is actually dated "1976," it was placed in the White House Central Files on July 11, 1975, and its text clearly places "fall 1975" in the future], GFL, WHCF: Subject File NR2, Box 2, [NR 2 Fish & Wildlife 4/1/75–6/30/75].

47. Gordon Jones (office of Sen. Jeff Bingham) to Tod Hullin, July 18, 1975, GFL, Domestic Council: George Humphreys Files, Box 17, [Executive Order 11643]. For context, see the materials in GFL, Domestic Council: George Humphreys Files, Box 17, [Decision Paper on Proposed Amendment to EO 11643].

48. Bob Namovicz (budget examiner) to Mr. Mitchell, "Modifying Executive Order 11643," n.d., GFL, Domestic Council: George Humphreys Files, Box 17, [Executive Order 11643].

49. Russell Peterson to James Cannon, "Predator Control," July 9, 1975, GFL, Counsel to the President: Dudley Chapman Files, Box 10, [Coyotes (1)–(4)].

50. EO 11870 (July 18, 1975). See William Nichols to Robert Linder, "Proposed Executive Order," July 17, 1975; James Lynn to the President, "Proposed Executive Order," July 17, 1975, emphasis added, both in NARA, RG 51, *Executive Orders and Proclamations, FY 1969–1976 (Series 69.4)*, Box 27, [EO 11870]. Ford's choice is reflected in the president's handwritten notations to Jim Cannon to the President, "Executive Order on Predator Control," July 17, 1975, GFL, WHCF: Subject File NR2, Box 2, [NR 2 Fish & Wildlife 7/1/75–7/21/75]. For OMB's opinion, see the materials in GFL, Counsel to the President: Dudley Chapman Files, Box 10, [Coyotes].

51. Dick Dunham to Tod Hullin, no title, memo of July 8, 1975, GFL, Domestic Council: George Humphreys Files, Box 17, [Decision Paper on Proposed Amendment to EO 11643 (3)].

52. Russell Train to the President, September 30, 1975, GFL, Counsel to the President: Dudley Chapman Files, Box 10, [Coyotes (4)].

53. EO 11917 (May 28, 1976). OMB's first letter to the attorney general with an approved EO draft was dated November 5, 1975; see William Nichols's letter to Edward Levi of that date, GFL, Counsel to the President: Dudley Chapman Files, Box 10, [Coyotes (5)]. The quote is from Domestic Council staffer George Humphreys's handwritten notes on Humphreys to Cannon, "Predator Control," November 10, 1975, GFL, Domestic Council: George Humphreys Files, Box 19, [Miscellaneous, 1975].

54. Dudley Chapman through Phil Buchen to Jim Connor, "Proposed Amendment to Executive Order on Predator Control," December 22, 1975. See also William Nichols to Staff Secretary, "Proposed Amendment to Executive Order on Predator Control," January 13, 1976, both in GFL, Domestic Council: George Humphreys Files, Box 19, [Miscellaneous, 1975].

55. George Humphreys to Jim Cannon, "Decision Memo—Predator Control," and attached material, April 8, 1976, GFL, Domestic Council: George Humphreys Files, Box 19, [Miscellaneous, 1976].

56. Ibid.

57. See the chronology in Cannon to the President, "Predator Control," December 20, 1976; John Busterud to Ford, "Predator Control Executive Order," December 27, 1976; James Lynn and James Cannon, "Memorandum for the President," n.d., all in GFL, Domestic Council: George Humphreys Files, Box 19, [Miscellaneous, 1976]. See also Jim Cavanaugh to Cheney, "Status Report," January 8, 1977, GFL, Cheney Files, Box 12, [Transition (1977)—general].

58. George Humphreys used this phrase in a January 5, 1977, note to CEQ director John Busterud, GFL, Domestic Council: George Humphreys Files, Box 19, [Miscellaneous, 1976].

59. "Interview with the President: Remarks and a Question-and-Answer Session with Members of the National Association of Farm Broadcasting," September 29, 1978, https://www.presidency.ucsb.edu/node/243595. The EPA ultimately licensed a different mode of predator control—via carbon monoxide gas cartridges. These could be used on private property but, because of the EO, not on federal lands.

60. Lynn and Cannon, "Memorandum for the President."

61. See "Information-Gathering Hearings on Predator Control Toxicants," *Federal Register* (July 2, 1981): 34698.

62. "Federal Page: Yesterday," *Washington Post*, November 20, 1981, A29.

63. Paul Laxalt to Edwin Meese III, December 3, 1981, WNRC, *OMB General Counsel: Executive Orders and Proclamations: 1959–1993*, Box 2, [EO 12342—Environmental Safeguards on Activities for Animal Damage Control].

64. Kenneth Cribb Jr. to Craig Fuller, "Repeal of Executive Order 11643 Which Prohibits the Use of Compound 1080," December 16, 1982, WNRC, *OMB General Counsel: Executive Orders and Proclamations: 1959–1993*, Box 2, [EO 12342—Environmental Safeguards on Activities for Animal Damage Control].

65. "CF" (Craig Fuller) to "Mike" (Michael Horowitz), January 26, 1982, WNRC, *OMB General Counsel: Executive Orders and Proclamations: 1959–1993*, Box 2, [EO 12342—Environmental Safeguards on Activities for Animal Damage Control].

66. Cribb to Fuller, "Repeal of Executive Order 11643."

67. Michael J. Horowitz to Edwin Meese III, "Revocation of Executive Order 11643," January 20, 1982, WNRC, *OMB General Counsel: Executive Orders and Proclamations: 1959–1993*, Box 2, [EO 12342—Environmental Safeguards on Activities for Animal Damage Control].

68. As summarized in ibid.

69. "CF" to "Mike," January 26, 1982. Emphasis in original.

70. Stockman to the President, "Proposed Executive Order Entitled 'Environmental Safeguards on Activities for Animal Damage Control,'" January 26, 1982, WNRC, *OMB General Counsel: Executive Orders and Proclamations: 1959–1993 (#051-12-0087)*, Box 2, [EO 12342—Environmental Safeguards on Activities for Animal Damage Control]. In October 1982, the EPA ruled that "there are certain situations where there are no currently available satisfactory alternatives to Compound 1080 for the control of coyote predation." Its use was approved within collars placed around the throats of livestock or via "small drop baits" containing a single lethal dose, though not in large-scale bait stations. That decision was finalized in October 1983. See Office of the Administrator, "In the Matter of Sodium Fluoroacetate (Compound 1080) to Control Predators," FIFRA Docket 502, decided October 31, 1983, in *Decisions of the United States Environmental Protection Agency, March 1972 to March 1985*, vol. 1 (Washington, DC: GPO, 1995), 792–810. The quoted conclusion is at p. 800.

71. See especially Paul Pierson, *Politics in Time: History, Institutions, and Social Analysis* (Princeton: Princeton University Press, 2004); Andrea Louise Campbell, *How Policies Make Citizens: Senior Political Activism and the Welfare State* (Princeton: Princeton University Press, 2011).

72. Leslie Gelb, "Muskie and Brzezinski: The Struggle over Foreign Policy," *New York Times Magazine*, July 20, 1980, 26.

73. See, e.g., John H. Kessel, "The Structures of the Reagan White House," *American Journal of Political Science* 28 (May 1984): 231–58; Joseph A. Pika, "White House Boundary Roles: Marginal Men amidst the Palace Guard," *Presidential Studies Quarterly* 16 (Fall 1986): 700–715.

74. From "Snow," in *The Collected Poems of Louis MacNeice* (London: Faber, 1966), 30.

75. Bob Woodward, *Fear* (New York: Simon and Schuster, 2018), 261–62, and see also 237, 271; on the various factions, see Joseph A. Pika, John Anthony Maltese, and Andrew Rudalevige, *Understanding a New Presidency in the Age of Trump* (Thousand Oaks, CA: Sage/CQ Press, 2018), 5–7, 43–44.

76. Many thanks to George Krause, both in conversation and in publication, for his help in considering this issue. This discussion also echoes the overlapping issues of endogenous information raised by Gailmard and Patty, *Learning while Governing*, 278–81.

77. William J. Clinton, "Remarks in a Question-and-Answer Session at the Godfrey Sperling Luncheon," September 25, 1995, https://www.presidency.ucsb.edu/node/222120.

78. "2019 Democratic Debates, Night 2: Full Transcript," *New York Times*, June 28, 2019, https://www.nytimes.com/2019/06/28/us/politics/transcript-debate.html; Matt Viser, "If He

Gets a Presidential Day 1, Joe Biden Has a Nearly Endless List of Ways to Spend It," *Washington Post*, July 29, 2020, https://www.washingtonpost.com/politics/if-he-gets-a-presidential-day-1 -joe-biden-has-a-nearly-endless-list-of-ways-to-spend-it/2020/07/28/a9b9d7d8-cdcd-11ea -bc6a-6841b28d9093_story.html; and see more generally Chelsea Janes, "Democrats Hate Trump's Executive Orders: Why Are They Promising So Many of Their Own?" *Washington Post*, October 3, 2019, https://www.washingtonpost.com/politics/democrats-hate-trumps-executive -orders-why-are-they-promising-so-many-of-their-own/2019/10/03/9f065c08-d800-11e9 -a688-303693fb4b0b_story.html.

79. Quoted in Viser, "If He Gets a Presidential Day 1."

80. Quoted in Rudalevige, "Government in a Box," 38; see also Anthony M. Bertelli and Laurence E. Lynn Jr., "Public Management in the Shadow of the Constitution," *Administration and Society* 38 (March 2006): 31–57.

81. *Federalist #70*.

82. Brian J. Cook, "Restraining the Energetic Executive: Can Administrators Legitimately Check Presidential Power?" (paper presented at the Annual Conference of the American Society for Public Administration, Denver, CO, 2018).

83. As Attorney General William Barr put it, "the idea of resisting a democratically-elected president and basically throwing everything at him and, you know, really changing the norms on the grounds that we have to stop this president, that is where the shredding of our norms and institutions is occurring." Barr, CBS News interview quoted in Tim Hains, "Barr: 'Resisting a Democratically Elected President' Is Destroying Our Norms and Institutions, Not Trump," *Real Clear Politics*, May 31, 2019, https://www.realclearpolitics.com/video/2019/05/31/attorney _general_william_barr_i_dont_care_about_my_reputation_i_took_this_job_to_protect _our_institutions.html.

84. For a useful brief summary, see Donald Moynihan, "Populism and the Deep State: The Attack on Public Service under Trump," working paper (May 21, 2020), https://papers.ssrn.com /sol3/papers.cfm?abstract_id=3607309. See too Michael Lewis, *The Fifth Risk* (New York: W. W. Norton, 2018); George Packer, "How to Destroy a Government," *The Atlantic* (April 2020): 54–74; Martin Pengelly, "'Sharpiegate': Trump Insists Dorian Was Forecast to 'Hit or Graze' Alabama," *The Guardian*, September 5, 2019, https://www.theguardian.com/us-news/2019/sep /05/trump-hurricane-dorian-alabama-map-sharpiegate.

85. William Gormley Jr. and Steven J. Balla, *Bureaucracy and Democracy: Accountability and Performance* (Washington, DC: CQ Press, 2004), 81; more generally, see Charles Goodsell, *The Case for Bureaucracy*, 2nd ed. (Chatham, NJ: Chatham House, 1985).

86. Norton Long, "Bureaucracy and Constitutionalism," *American Political Science Review* 46 (September 1952): 811. See also Donald Kingsley, *Representative Bureaucracy* (Yellow Springs, OH: Antioch Press, 1944).

87. Timothy Cama, "Coal Mogul Offered Six Suggested Executive Orders to Trump," *The Hill*, June 7, 2018, https://thehill.com/policy/energy-environment/391149-coal-mogul-drafted-6 -executive-order-for-trump; Jim Edwards, "White House Considering an Antitrust Investigation into 'Online Platform Bias,'" *Business Insider*, September 22, 2018, https://www.businessinsider .com/white-house-executive-order-investigate-google-facebook-antitrust-2018-9?r=UK.

88. Katyal, "Internal Separation of Powers," 2325.

89. Paul Simon, "Train in the Distance," *Hearts and Bones* (1983).

SELECTED REFERENCES

Acs, Alex. "Presidential Directives in a Reluctant Bureaucracy." *Journal of Public Policy* 40 (2020), doi:10.1017/S0143814X20000264.

Allison, Graham T. *Essence of Decision: Explaining the Cuban Missile Crisis.* Boston: Little, Brown, 1971.

Altshuler, Alan A., ed. *The Politics of the Federal Bureaucracy.* New York: Dodd, Mead, 1968.

Arnold, Peri. *Making the Managerial Presidency: Comprehensive Reorganization Planning, 1905–1996.* 2nd rev. ed. Lawrence: University Press of Kansas, 1998.

Bardach, Eugene. *Getting Agencies to Work Together: The Practice and Theory of Managerial Craftsmanship.* Washington, DC: Brookings Institution Press, 1998.

Bawn, Kathleen. "Political Control versus Expertise: Congressional Choices about Administrative Procedures." *American Political Science Review* 89 (1995): 62–73.

Belco, Michelle. "Implementing the Orders of the First 100 Days." Paper presented at the Annual Meeting of the American Political Science Association, Washington, DC, September 2019.

Belco, Michelle, and Brandon Rottinghaus. *The Dual Executive: Unilateral Orders in a Separated and Shared Power System.* Stanford: Stanford University Press, 2017.

Bendor, Jonathan, and Thomas Hammond. "Rethinking Allison's Models." *American Political Science Review* 86 (June 1992): 301–22.

Bendor, Jonathan, Terry M. Moe, and Kenneth Shotts. "Recycling the Garbage Can: An Assessment of the Research Program." *American Political Science Review* 95 (March 2001): 169–90.

Bertelli, Anthony M., and Christian R. Grose. "The Lengthened Shadow of Another Institution? Ideal Point Estimates for the Executive Branch and Congress." *American Journal of Political Science* 55 (October 2011): 767–81.

Bertelli, Anthony M., and David E. Lewis. "Policy Influence, Agency-Specific Expertise, and Exit in the Federal Service." *Journal of Public Administration Research and Theory* 23 (April 2013): 223–45.

Bertelli, Anthony M., and Laurence E. Lynn Jr. "Public Management in the Shadow of the Constitution." *Administration and Society* 38 (March 2006): 31–57.

Bertelli, Anthony M., Dyana P. Mason, Jennifer M. Connolly, and David A. Gastwirth. "Measuring Agency Attributes with Attitudes across Time: A Method and Examples Using Large-Scale Federal Surveys." *Journal of Public Administration Research and Theory* 25 (April 2015): 513–44.

Bolton, Alexander, and Sharece Thrower. "Legislative Capacity and Executive Unilateralism." *American Journal of Political Science* 60 (July 2016): 649–63.

Bose, Meena. *Shaping and Signaling Presidential Policy: The National Security Decision Making of Eisenhower and Kennedy.* College Station: Texas A&M Press, 1998.

Brehm, John, and Scott Gates. *Working, Shirking, and Sabotage: Bureaucratic Response to a Democratic Public.* Ann Arbor: University of Michigan Press, 1999.

Bruff, Harold. *Balance of Forces: Separation of Powers Law in the Administrative State.* Durham, NC: Carolina Academic Press, 2006.

Campbell, Andrea Louise. *How Policies Make Citizens: Senior Political Activism and the Welfare State.* Princeton: Princeton University Press, 2011.

Carpenter, Daniel P. *The Forging of Bureaucratic Autonomy: Reputation, Networks, and Policy Innovation in Executive Agencies, 1862–1928.* Princeton: Princeton University Press, 2001.

———. *Reputation and Power: Organizational Image and Pharmaceutical Regulation at the FDA.* Princeton: Princeton University Press, 2010.

Carpenter, Daniel, and George A. Krause. "Transactional Authority and Bureaucratic Politics." *Journal of Public Administration Research and Theory* 25 (January 2015): 5–25.

Chambers, Raymond L. "The Executive Power: A Preliminary Study of the Concept and of the Efficacy of Presidential Directives." *Presidential Studies Quarterly* 7 (Winter 1977): 21–37.

Chiou, Fang-Yi, and Lawrence S. Rothenberg. "The Elusive Search for Presidential Power." *American Journal of Political Science* 58 (July 2014): 653–68.

———. *The Enigma of Presidential Power: Parties, Policies, and Strategic Uses of Unilateral Action.* New York: Cambridge University Press, 2017.

Christenson, Dino P., and Douglas L. Kriner. "Does Public Opinion Constrain Presidential Unilateralism?" *American Political Science Review* 113 (November 2019): 1071–77.

———. *The Myth of the Imperial Presidency: Political Checks on Unilateral Power.* Chicago: University of Chicago Press, 2020.

Clinton, Joshua D., Anthony Bertelli, Christian R. Grose, David E. Lewis, and David C. Nixon. "Separated Powers in the United States: The Ideology of Agencies, Presidents, and Congress." *American Journal of Political Science* 56 (April 2012): 341–54.

Clinton, Joshua D., and David E. Lewis. "Expert Opinion, Agency Characteristics, and Agency Preferences." *Political Analysis* 16 (Winter 2008): 3–20.

Coase, Ronald. "The Nature of the Firm." *Economica* 4 (November 1937): 386–405.

Cohen, Michael, James March, and Johan Olsen. "A Garbage Can Model of Organizational Choice." *Administrative Studies Quarterly* (March 1972): 1–25.

Cook, Brian J. "Restraining the Energetic Executive: Can Administrators Legitimately Check Presidential Power?" Paper presented at the Annual Conference of the American Society for Public Administration, Denver, CO, March 2018.

Cooper, Phillip J. "By Order of the President: Administration by Executive Order and Proclamation." *Administration and Society* 18, no. 2 (1986): 233–62.

———. *By Order of the President: The Use and Abuse of Executive Direct Action.* 2nd ed. Lawrence: University Press of Kansas, 2014.

Corwin, Edward S. *The President: Office and Powers.* 3rd ed. New York: New York University Press, 1948.

Crouch, Jeffrey P., Mark J. Rozell, and Mitchel A. Sollenberger. *The Unitary Executive Theory: A Danger to Constitutional Government.* Lawrence: University Press of Kansas, 2020.

Dahl, Robert A. "The Concept of Power." *Behavioral Science* 2, no. 3 (1957): 201–15.

Dawes, Charles G. *The First Year of the Budget of the United States*. New York: Harper & Brothers, 1923.

Dearborn, John A. "The 'Proper Organs' for Presidential Representation: A Fresh Look at the Budget and Accounting Act of 1921." *Journal of Policy History* 31 (January 2019): 1–41.

Deering, Christopher J., and Forrest Maltzman. "The Politics of Executive Orders: Legislative Constraints on Presidential Power." *Political Research Quarterly* 52 (December 1999): 767–83.

Demsetz, Harold. "The Theory of the Firm Revisited." *Journal of Law, Economics, and Organization* 4 (1988): 141–61.

Destler, I. M. *Presidents, Bureaucrats, and Foreign Policy: The Politics of Organizational Reform*. Princeton: Princeton University Press, 1972.

Dickinson, Matthew J. "We All Want a Revolution: Neustadt, New Institutionalism, and the Future of Presidency Research." *Presidential Studies Quarterly* 39 (December 2009): 736–70.

Dickinson, Matthew J., and Jesse Gubb. "The Limits to Power without Persuasion." *Presidential Studies Quarterly* 46 (March 2016): 48–72.

Dickinson, Matthew J., and Andrew Rudalevige. "'Worked Out in Fractions': Neutral Competence, FDR, and the Bureau of the Budget." *Congress and the Presidency* 34 (Spring 2007): 1–26.

Dimock, Marshall E. "The Study of Administration." *American Political Science Review* 31 (February 1937): 28–40.

Dodds, Graham G. *Take Up Your Pen: Unilateral Presidential Directives in American Politics*. Philadelphia: University of Pennsylvania Press, 2013.

Eastland, Terry. *Energy in the Executive*. New York: Free Press, 1992.

Ellis, Richard J. *The Development of the American Presidency*. 2nd ed. New York: Routledge, 2015.

Epstein, David, and Sharyn O'Halloran. *Delegating Powers: A Transaction Cost Politics Approach to Policy Making under Separate Powers*. New York: Cambridge University Press, 1999.

Fairlie, John A. "Administrative Legislation." *Michigan Law Review* 18 (January 1920): 181–200.

Farber, Daniel A., and Anne Joseph O'Connell. "Agencies as Adversaries." *California Law Review* 105 (2017): 1375–1469.

Farina, Cynthia. "The 'Chief Executive' and the Quiet Constitutional Revolution." *Administrative Law Review* 49 (Winter 1997): 179–86.

Fine, Jeffrey A., and Adam L. Warber. "Circumventing Adversity: Executive Orders and Divided Government." *Presidential Studies Quarterly* 42 (June 2012): 256–74.

Fiorina, Morris. *Congress: Keystone of the Washington Establishment*. 2nd ed. New Haven: Yale University Press, 1989.

Fisher, Louis. *The Law of the Executive Branch: Presidential Power*. New York: Oxford University Press, 2014.

Friedman, Barry D. *Regulation in the Reagan-Bush Era*. Pittsburgh: University of Pittsburgh Press, 1995.

Gailmard, Sean. "Multiple Principals and Oversight of Bureaucratic Policy-Making." *Journal of Theoretical Politics* 21, no. 2 (2009): 161–86.

Gailmard, Sean, and John W. Patty. *Learning while Governing: Expertise and Accountability in the Executive Branch*. Chicago: University of Chicago Press, 2013.

Gibson, Tobias T. "The Office of Legal Counsel and the Presidency: The Legal Strategy of Executive Orders." PhD diss., Washington University, 2006.

Gilmour, John B., and David E. Lewis. "Political Appointees and the Competence of Federal Program Management." *American Politics Research* 34, no. 1 (2006): 34–50.

Gitterman, Daniel. *Calling the Shots: The President, Executive Orders, and Public Policy*. Washington, DC: Brookings Institution, 2017.

Glennon, Michael. *National Security and Double Government*. New York: Oxford University Press, 2015.

Goodsell, Charles. *The Case for Bureaucracy*. 2nd ed. Chatham, NJ: Chatham House, 1985.

Gormley, William, Jr., and Steven J. Balla. *Bureaucracy and Democracy: Accountability and Performance*. Washington, DC: CQ Press, 2004.

Grove, Tara Leigh. "Presidential Laws and the Missing Interpretive Theory." *University of Pennsylvania Law Review* 168, no. 4 (2020): 877–930.

Halperin, Morton, with Patricia Clapp and Arnold Kanter. *Bureaucratic Politics and Foreign Policy*. Washington, DC: Brookings Institution, 1974.

Hart, James. *The Ordinance Making Powers of the President of the United States*. Baltimore: Johns Hopkins University Press, 1925.

———. *The Presidential Branch*. 2nd ed. Chatham, NJ: Chatham House, 1995.

Heclo, Hugh. *A Government of Strangers: Executive Politics in Washington*. Washington, DC: Brookings Institution, 1977.

Hilsman, Roger. *The Politics of Policy Making in Defense and Foreign Affairs*. New York: Harper & Row, 1971.

Howell, William G. *Power without Persuasion: The Politics of Direct Presidential Action*. Princeton: Princeton University Press, 2003.

———. "Unilateral Powers: A Brief Overview." *Presidential Studies Quarterly* 35 (September 2005): 417–39.

Huber, John D., and Charles R. Shipan. *Deliberate Discretion? The Institutional Foundations of Bureaucratic Autonomy*. New York: Cambridge University Press, 2002.

Hult, Karen M., and Charles Walcott. *Governing Public Organizations: Politics, Structures, and Institutional Design*. Pacific Grove, CA: Brooks/Cole, 1990.

Jenkins, Jeffrey, and Eric Patashnik, eds. *Living Legislation: Durability, Change, and the Politics of American Lawmaking*. Chicago: University of Chicago Press, 2012.

Kagan, Elena. "Presidential Administration." *Harvard Law Review* 114 (June 2001): 2245–2385.

Katyal, Neil Kumar. "Internal Separation of Powers: Checking Today's Most Dangerous Branch from Within." *Yale Law Journal* 115 (September 2006): 2314–50.

Kelley, Christopher, and Bryan Marshall. "The Last Word: Presidential Power and the Role of Signing Statements." *Presidential Studies Quarterly* 38 (June 2008): 248–67.

Kennedy, Joshua B. "'Do This! Do That!' and Nothing Will Happen: Executive Orders and Bureaucratic Responsiveness." *American Politics Research* 43, no. 1 (2015): 59–82.

———. "The Limits of Presidential Influence: Two Environmental Directives and What They Mean for Executive Power." *Journal of Policy History* 30 (January 2018): 1–24.

———. "Who Do You Trust? Presidential Delegation in Executive Orders." *Research and Politics* (January–March 2016): 1–7.

Kessel, John H. "The Structures of the Reagan White House." *American Journal of Political Science* 28 (May 1984): 231–58.

Kingdon, John. *Agendas, Alternatives, and Public Policies.* 2nd ed. New York: HarperCollins, 1995.

Kmiec, Douglas. "OLC's Opinion Writing Function: The Legal Adhesive for a Unitary Executive." *Cardozo Law Review* 15 (October 1993): 337–74.

Krasner, Stephen D. "Are Bureaucracies Important? (Or Allison Wonderland)." *Foreign Policy* 7 (Summer 1972): 159–79.

Krause, George A. "Organizational Complexity and Coordination Dilemmas in U.S. Executive Politics." *Presidential Studies Quarterly* 39 (March 2009): 74–88.

———. *A Two-Way Street: The Institutional Dynamics of the Modern Administrative State.* Pittsburgh: University of Pittsburgh Press, 1999.

Krause, George A., and David B. Cohen. "Presidential Use of Executive Orders, 1953–1994." *American Politics Quarterly* 25 (1997): 458–81.

Krause, George A., and Jeffrey E. Cohen. "Opportunity, Constraints, and the Development of the Institutional Presidency: The Issuance of Executive Orders." *Journal of Politics* 62 (2000): 88–114.

Krause, George A., and Anne Joseph O'Connell. "Experiential Learning and Presidential Management of the U.S. Federal Bureaucracy: Logic and Evidence from Agency Leadership Appointments." *American Journal of Political Science* 60 (October 2016): 914–31.

———. "Measuring Bureaucratic Leadership in the Administrative Presidency." Paper presented at the Annual Meeting of the American Political Science Association, Washington, DC, September 2014.

Lewis, David E. *The Politics of Presidential Appointments: Political Control and Bureaucratic Performance.* Princeton: Princeton University Press, 2008.

———. *Presidents and the Politics of Agency Design.* Stanford: Stanford University Press, 2003.

Lewis, David E., Mark D. Richardson, and Eric Rosenthal. "OMB in Its Management Role: Evidence from Surveys of Federal Executives." In *Executive Policymaking: The Role of the OMB in the Presidency,* ed. Meena Bose and Andrew Rudalevige, 175–206. Washington, DC: Brookings Institution Press, 2020.

Lewis, David E., and Jennifer L. Selin. *Sourcebook of United States Executive Agencies.* 2nd ed. Washington, DC: Administrative Conference of the United States, 2018.

Light, Paul C. *The Government-Industrial Complex: The True Size of Government, 1984–2017.* New York: Oxford University Press, 2019.

Lowande, Kenneth S. "After the Orders: Presidential Memoranda and Unilateral Action." *Presidential Studies Quarterly* 44 (December 2014): 724–41.

Lynn, Laurence E., Jr. *Managing the Public's Business: The Job of the Government Executive.* New York: Basic Books, 1981.

Marshall, Bryan W., and Richard Pacelle Jr. "Revisiting the Two Presidencies: The Strategic Use of Executive Orders." *American Politics Research* 33, no. 1 (2005): 81–105.

Mayer, Kenneth R. "Executive Orders and Presidential Power." *Journal of Politics* 61 (May 1999): 445–66.

———. "Going Alone: The Presidential Power of Unilateral Action." In *The Oxford Handbook of the American Presidency,* ed. George C. Edwards III and William G. Howell, 427–54. New York: Oxford University Press, 2009.

———. *With the Stroke of a Pen: Executive Orders and Presidential Power.* Princeton: Princeton University Press, 2001.

McCubbins, Mathew, and Thomas Schwartz. "Congressional Oversight Overlooked: Police Patrols versus Fire Alarms." *American Journal of Political Science* 28 (1984): 165–79.

Milgrom, Paul, and John Roberts. "Bargaining Costs, Influence Costs, and the Organization of Economic Activity." In *Perspectives on Positive Political Economy*, ed. James E. Alt and Kenneth A. Shepsle, 57–89. New York: Cambridge University Press, 1990.

Milkis, Sidney M., and Daniel J. Tichenor. *Rivalry and Reform: Presidents, Social Movements, and the Transformation of American Politics.* Chicago: University of Chicago Press, 2019.

Miller, Gary J., and Andrew B. Whitford. *Above Politics: Bureaucratic Discretion and Credible Commitment.* New York: Cambridge University Press, 2016.

Moe, Terry M. "An Assessment of the Positive Theory of 'Congressional Dominance.'" *Legislative Studies Quarterly* 12 (November 1987): 475–520.

———. "The Politicized Presidency." In *New Directions in American Politics*, ed. John E. Chubb and Paul E. Peterson, 235–72. Washington, DC: Brookings Institution, 1985.

———. "The Politics of Bureaucratic Structure." In *Can the Government Govern?*, ed. John E. Chubb and Paul E. Peterson, 267–329. Washington, DC: Brookings Institution, 1989.

———. "The Presidency and Bureaucracy: The Presidential Advantage." In *The Presidency and the Political System.* 4th ed. Ed. Michael Nelson, 408–39. Washington, DC: CQ Press, 1995.

———. "Presidents, Institutions, and Theory." In *Researching the Presidency: Vital Questions, New Approaches*, ed. George C. Edwards III, John H. Kessel, and Bert A. Rockman, 337–86. Pittsburgh: University of Pittsburgh Press, 1993.

———. "The Revolution in Presidential Studies." *Presidential Studies Quarterly* 39 (December 2009): 701–24.

Moe, Terry M., and William G. Howell. "Unilateral Action and Presidential Power: A Theory." *Presidential Studies Quarterly* 29 (1999): 850–73.

Moe, Terry M., and Scott A. Wilson. "Presidents and the Politics of Structure." *Law and Contemporary Problems* 57 (Spring 1994): 1–57.

Morgan, Ruth P. *The President and Civil Rights: Policy-making by Executive Order.* New York: St. Martin's Press, 1970.

Nathan, Richard P. *The Administrative Presidency.* New York: Macmillan, 1983.

Neighbors, William. "Presidential Legislation by Executive Order." *University of Colorado Law Review* 37 (Fall 1964): 105–18.

Neustadt, Richard E. "Presidency and Legislation: The Growth of Central Clearance." *American Political Science Review* 48 (September 1954): 641–71.

———. *Presidential Power and the Modern Presidents.* New York: Free Press, 1990.

Nickerson, Jack A., and Todd R. Zenger. "A Knowledge-Based Theory of the Firm." *Organization Science* 15 (November–December 2004): 617–32.

Nou, Jennifer. "Agency Self-Insulation under Presidential Review." *Harvard Law Review* 126 (May 2013): 1755–1837.

———. "Civil Servant Disobedience." *Chicago-Kent Law Review* 94, no. 2 (2019): 349–81.

Nou, Jennifer, and Edward H. Stiglitz, "Strategic Rulemaking Disclosure." *Southern California Law Review* 89 (May 2016): 733–92.

Patashnik, Eric. *Reforms at Risk: What Happens after Major Policy Changes Are Enacted.* Princeton: Princeton University Press, 2008.

Pierson, Paul. *Politics in Time: History, Institutions, and Social Analysis*. Princeton: Princeton University Press, 2004.

Pika, Joseph A. "White House Boundary Roles: Marginal Men amidst the Palace Guard." *Presidential Studies Quarterly* 16 (Fall 1986): 700–715.

Ponder, Daniel E. *Presidential Leverage: Presidents, Approval, and the American State*. Stanford: Stanford University Press, 2017.

Potter, Rachel Augustine. *Bending the Rules: Procedural Politicking in the Bureaucracy*. Chicago: University of Chicago Press, 2019.

Pressman, Jeffrey L., and Aaron Wildavsky. *Implementation*. 3rd ed. Berkeley: University of California Press, 1984.

Reeves, Andrew, and Jon C. Rogowski. *No Blank Check: Public Constraints on Presidential Unilateral Power*. New York: Cambridge University Press, forthcoming.

———. "The Public Cost of Unilateral Action." *American Journal of Political Science* 62 (2018): 424–40.

Resh, William G. *Rethinking the Administrative Presidency*. Baltimore: Johns Hopkins University Press, 2015.

Richardson, Mark D. "Politicization and Expertise: Exit, Effort, and Investment." *Journal of Politics* 81 (July 2019): 878–91.

Richardson, Mark D., Joshua D. Clinton, and David E. Lewis. "Elite Perceptions of Agency Ideology and Workforce Skill." *Journal of Politics* 80 (January 2018): 303–8.

Robinson, Greg. *By Order of the President: FDR and the Internment of Japanese Americans*. Cambridge, MA: Harvard University Press, 2001.

Rodrigues, Ricardo J. P. *The Preeminence of Politics: Executive Orders from Eisenhower to Clinton*. New York: LFB Scholarly Publishing, 2009.

Roisman, Shalev. "The Real Decline of OLC." *Just Security*, October 8, 2019. https://www.justsecurity.org/66495/the-real-decline-of-olc/.

Rose, Richard. "Organizing Issues In and Organizing Problems Out." In *The Managerial Presidency*, ed. James P. Pfiffner, 105–19. Pacific Grove, CA: Brooks/Cole, 1991.

Rossiter, Clinton. *The American Presidency*. London: Hamish Hamilton, 1957.

Rottinghaus, Brandon, and Jason Maier. "The Power of Decree: Presidential Use of Executive Proclamations." *Political Research Quarterly* 60, no. 2 (2007): 338–43.

Rottinghaus, Brandon, and Adam L. Warber. "Unilateral Orders as Constituency Outreach: Executive Orders, Proclamations, and the Public Presidency." *Presidential Studies Quarterly* 45 (June 2015): 289–309.

Rourke, Francis E. *Bureaucracy, Politics, and Public Policy*. 3rd ed. Boston: Little, Brown, 1984.

Rudalevige, Andrew. "Beyond Structure and Process: The Early Institutionalization of Regulatory Review." *Journal of Policy History* 30 (October 2018): 577–608.

———. "Executive Branch Management and Presidential Unilateralism: Centralization and the Issuance of Executive Orders." *Congress & the Presidency* 42, no. 3 (2015): 342–65.

———. "Executive Orders and Presidential Unilateralism." *Presidential Studies Quarterly* 42 (March 2012): 138–60.

———. "Government in a Box: Challenges of Policy Implementation in the American System." In *Carrots, Sticks, and the Bully Pulpit*, ed. Frederick M. Hess and Andrew P. Kelly, 37–60. Cambridge, MA: Harvard Education Press, 2011.

———. "Inventing the Institutional Presidency: Entrepreneurship and the Rise of the Bureau of the Budget, 1939–1949." In *Formative Acts: American Politics in the Making*, ed. Stephen Skowronek and Matthew Glassman, 316–39. Philadelphia: University of Pennsylvania Press, 2007.

———. *Managing the President's Program: Presidential Leadership and Legislative Policy Formulation*. Princeton: Princeton University Press, 2002.

———. *The New Imperial Presidency: Renewing Presidential Power after Watergate*. Ann Arbor: University of Michigan Press, 2006.

———. "The Obama Administrative Presidency: Some Late-Term Patterns." *Presidential Studies Quarterly* 46 (December 2016): 868–90.

Rudalevige, Andrew, and David E. Lewis. "Parsing the Politicized Presidency: Centralization and Politicization as Presidential Strategies for Bureaucratic Control." Paper presented at the Annual Meeting of the American Political Science Association, Washington, DC, 2005.

Schlesinger, Arthur M., Jr. *The Imperial Presidency*. Boston: Houghton, Mifflin, 1973.

Schultz-Bressman, Lisa, and Michael P. Vandebergh. "Inside the Administrative State: A Critical Look at the Practice of Presidential Control." *Michigan Law Review* 105 (October 2006): 47–99.

Seidman, Harold, and Robert Gilmour. *Politics, Position, and Power: From the Positive to the Regulatory State*. 4th ed. New York: Oxford University Press, 1986.

Selin, Jennifer L. "What Makes an Agency Independent?" *American Journal of Political Science* 59 (October 2015): 971–87.

Shull, Steven A. *Presidential-Congressional Relations: Policy and Time Approaches*. Ann Arbor: University of Michigan Press, 1997.

Sullivan, Terry, ed. *The Nerve Center: Lessons in Governing from the White House Chiefs of Staff*. College Station: Texas A&M Press, 2004.

Tadelis, Steven, and Oliver E. Williamson. "Transaction Cost Economics." In *The Handbook of Organizational Economics*, ed. Robert Gibbons and John Roberts, 159–89. Princeton: Princeton University Press, 2012.

Thrower, Sharece. "To Revoke or Not Revoke? The Political Determinants of Executive Order Longevity." *American Journal of Political Science* 61 (July 2017): 642–56.

Turner, Ian R. "Policy Durability, Agency Capacity, and Executive Unilateralism." *Presidential Studies Quarterly* 50 (March 2020): 40–62.

Vanhoonacker, Sophie, and Patrice Wangen. "Graham T. Allison, *The Essence of Decision: Explaining the Cuban Missile Crisis*," in *The Oxford Handbook of Classics in Public Policy and Administration*, ed. Martin Lodge, Edward C. Page, and Steven J. Balla, 272–86. New York: Oxford University Press, 2015.

Vaughn, Justin S., and José D. Villalobos. *Czars in the White House: The Rise of Policy Czars as Presidential Management Tools*. Ann Arbor: University of Michigan Press, 2015.

Villalobos, José D. "Agency Input as a Policy-Making Tool." *Administration and Society* 45, no. 7 (2013): 837–74.

Warber, Adam L. *Executive Orders and the Modern Presidency: Legislating from the Oval Office*. Boulder, CO: Lynne Rienner, 2006.

———. "Public Outreach, Executive Orders, and the Unilateral Presidency." *Congress & the Presidency* 41, no. 3 (2014): 269–88.

Warber, Adam L., Yu Ouyang, and Richard W. Waterman. "Landmark Executive Orders: Presidential Leadership through Unilateral Action." *Presidential Studies Quarterly* 48 (March 2018): 110–26.

Weingast, Barry R., and Mark J. Moran. "Bureaucratic Discretion or Congressional Control?" *Journal of Political Economy* 91 (1983): 765–800.

Williamson, Oliver E. *The Economic Institutions of Capitalism.* New York: Free Press, 1985.

———. *Markets and Hierarchies.* New York: Free Press, 1975.

———. *The Mechanisms of Governance.* New York: Oxford University Press, 1996.

———. "The Theory of the Firm as Governance Structure: From Choice to Contract." *Journal of Economic Perspectives* 16 (Summer 2002): 171–95.

Wilson, James Q. *Bureaucracy.* New York: Basic Books, 1989.

Wilson, Woodrow. "The Study of Administration." *Political Science Quarterly* 2 (June 1887): 197–222.

Wood, B. Dan, and Richard Waterman. "The Dynamics of Political Control of the Bureaucracy." *American Political Science Review* 85 (1991): 801–28.

Wozencraft, Frank M. "OLC: The Unfamiliar Acronym." *American Bar Association Journal* 57 (January 1971): 33–37.

Yaver, Miranda. "Inter-Agency Learning in United States Regulatory Policymaking." Working paper, September 13, 2016, https://papers.ssrn.com/sol3/papers.cfm?abstract_id=2838457.

———. "When Do Agencies Have Agency? The Limits of Compliance in the EPA." Working paper, March 19, 2015, https://dornsife.usc.edu/assets/sites/741/docs/Panel_1b_paper1 _Yaver_When_Do_Agencies_Have_Agency_EPA_Compliance_SoCLASS_USC_2015 .pdf.

INDEX

Aberbach, Joel, 42
Addington, David, 94, 95
Administrative Procedure Act (1946), 239n16
administrative state, ix, 10–11, 29, 53, 145, 203, 218
Advisory Council on Historic Preservation, 63
agencies. *See* bureaucracy
Agency for International Development (AID), 90
Agricultural Trade Development and Assistance Act of 1954, 211
Agriculture, Department of, 42, 45, 58, 62, 64, 84, 86, 88, 112, 180, 193, 195, 208; and area redevelopment EO, 140–42; as "lead agency," 151–52; and outdoor recreation EO, 65; and predator control EOs, 212–15
Air Force, U.S., 87, 105
Alabama, 147
Alaska, 95
Alexander, Lamar, 4
Allison, Graham, 18, 29, 30, 208
American Bar Association, 89
American Legion, 185
Ames, Aldrich, 89
Anderson, Clinton, 195–96, 247n122
Area Redevelopment Act (1961), 140
Area Redevelopment Administration, 140–42
Arizona, 51
Armey, Richard, 13

Army Corps of Engineers, 63
Army, U.S., 63, 87
asset specificity, 37, 53, 73, 236n72, 236n77
Atomic Energy Act Amendments (1958), 92
Atomic Energy Commission (AEC), 92–93

Baker, James A., III, 71, 178, 198
Bannon, Steve, 223n6
Bardach, Eugene, 44
Barr, William, 230n87, 279n83
Begala, Paul, 3
Belco, Michelle, 45, 209
Bell, David, 90, 196, 201
Bergland, Robert, 193
Bertelli, Anthony, 118
Biden, Joseph R., Jr., 218
Bies, John, 63
Block, John, 193
Bolton, Alexander, 258n28
bounded rationality, 30
Bowles, Erskine, 7
Brock, William, 197
Browner, Carol, 6
Brundage, Percival, 64
Buchen, Philip W., 57
Budget and Accounting Act (1921), 53–54
Budget, Bureau of the (BoB). *See* Office of Management and Budget
Bull Run National Forest, 180
Bundy, McGeorge, 201–2
Bureau of Indian Affairs, 33, 190

11, 13–14, 38, 59–60, 78, 91, 164, 187, 209,
210, 219–20; press/communications and
scheduling issues, 62, 147–48, 157, 162,
163, 173, 184, 197, 206; public standing of,
122–23, 126, 130, 260n50; relationship with
bureaucracy as "two-way street," 9, 21, 22,
27, 33, 134, 167, 203; and staff organization,
35–36, 94, 216–18; and unissued EOs,
166–67, 178–80. *See also* bureaucracy;
individual presidents
Pressman, Jeffrey, 145
principal-agent models, 9, 21, 27, 30–31, 33–34,
42, 73, 80, 205, 219; and multiple principals, 42, 111, 118, 126
procurement policy, 12, 114
Public Housing Administration, 181
Public Papers of the President, 148, 157

Randolph, A. Philip, 85
Rankin, J. Lee, 67
rational actor models, 18
Raul, Alan, 90
Reagan, Ronald, 5, 56, 66, 78, 79, 86, 92, 95,
96, 187, 191, 256n82; and mean centralization levels for, 101, 103; and predator control EO, 215–16; presidential library of, 77;
and proposed EO on affirmative action,
197–98; and regulatory review, 97–98,
208; and "troika," 197
Reed, Bruce, 7
Reed, McGavock (Mac), 70
Regas, Diane, 6, 7
regulations, 10, 31–32, 51, 184, 189, 209; and
regulatory review, 12, 32, 66, 97–98, 208,
255n74 (*see also* Office of Information
and Regulatory Affairs)
Rehnquist, William, 66
reorganization, 44–45, 54, 56, 112, 128;
Carter's use of, 103
Rethmeier, Blain, 2
Reynolds, William Bradford, 197
Rice, Condoleezza, 266n20
Richardson, Mark, 119
Rockman, Bert, 42

Roosevelt, Franklin D., 11, 13, 22, 45, 46, 52,
64, 69, 78, 85, 100, 201; and central clear-
ance, 53–56; as assistant secretary of the
Navy, 55; death of, 62
Roosevelt, Theodore, 13, 51, 195, 232n22
Rose, Richard, 50
Rosenthal, Howard, 118
Rossiter, Clinton, 29, 207
Rothenberg, Lawrence, 113, 114, 124, 126, 129,
130
Rottinghaus, Brandon, 45
Rourke, Francis, 25, 32
Rusk, Dean, 146
"Russell Rider," 60–61
Ryukyu Islands, 249n2

Safire, William, 28
Sampson, W. S., 201
Saudi Arabia, 2
Scalia, Antonin, 28
Schattschneider, E. E., 192
Schlei, Norman, 269n64
Schlesinger, Arthur, Jr., ix
Schmults, Edward C., 247n117
Schultze, Charles, 141–42, 188, 252n45
Scully, Tom, 88
Security Policy Board, 89
Seidman, Harold, 25, 29, 31; as Budget
Bureau staffer, 52, 94
Selective Service System, 83, 112
Selin, Jennifer, 117, 152
service medals, 68, 85
Sessions, Jefferson, 6
Shalala, Donna, 88
Shipan, Charles, 29
Shull, Steven, 16
Shultz, George, 92, 198
Simon, Herbert, 203, 232n29
Simon, Paul F., 220
Small Business Administration (SBA), 140,
172, 191; and proposed order regarding
Vietnam-era veterans, 185–86
Small Business Liability Relief and Brown-
fields Revitalization Act (2002), 86

A NOTE ON THE TYPE

This book has been composed in Arno, an Old-style serif typeface in the
classic Venetian tradition, designed by Robert Slimbach at Adobe.

GPSR Authorized Representative: Easy Access System Europe - Mustamäe tee
50, 10621 Tallinn, Estonia, gpsr.requests@easproject.com

www.ingramcontent.com/pod-product-compliance
Lightning Source LLC
Chambersburg PA
CBHW031356270326
41929CB00010BA/1206